GUERRILLA TACTICS For Getting The LEGAL JOB OF YOUR DREAMS

by Kimm Alayne Walton, J.D.

The BarBri Group, Inc.
111 W. Jackson Blvd., 7th Floor, Chicago, IL 60604
Phone: 1-800-787-8717

Acknowledgements

Every book I've ever read had an acknowledgement page that started with the line, "This book would not have been possible without . . . " and so on. I really didn't want to start this page that way. But there's no getting around the fact that this book *really, really, really* would not have been possible without the generous help of many talented career counselors from law schools across the country. The fact is, as you read this book, it's *their* advice you're reading, not my own. I've worked on lots of books, and I've talked with lots of people, but I've never talked with any other group of people whose members were more dedicated, open, and delightful than this bunch!

Ergo — that's a word you don't get much chance to use! — I want to express my thanks to the following career services directors who helped me with their advice, their stories, their time, articles they'd written and collected, and their general good humor, all of which made this book such a joy to write:

Sandy Mans, Albany Law School
Betsy Armour, Boston University School of Law
Lisa Kellogg, California Western School of Law
Amy Thompson Briggs, Catholic University of America School of Law
Lisa Abrams, Chicago-Kent College of Law
Ellen Wayne, Columbia University Law School
Ann Skalaski, University of Florida College of Law
Kathleen Brady, Fordham University School of Law
Sophie Sparrow, Franklin Pierce Law Center

Laura Rowe, George Washington National Law Center
Marilyn Tucker, Georgetown University Law Center
Cindy Rold, University of Illinois College of Law
Drusilla Bakert, University of Kentucky College of Law
Andrea Swanner Redding, Lewis & Clark School of Law
Tammy Willcox, University of Maine School of Law
Jose Bahamonde-Gonzalez, University of Miami School of Law
Nancy Krieger, University of Michigan Law School
Gail Cutter, New York University School of Law
Mary Obrzut, Northern Illinois University School of Law
Susan Benson, University of San Diego School of Law
Linda Laufer, St. John's University School of Law
Maureen Provost Ryan, St. John's University School of Law
Wendy Werner, St. Louis University School of Law
Annette Jones, University of Texas School of Law
Gail Peshel, Valparaiso University School of Law
Pam Malone, Vanderbilt University School of Law
Teresa DeAndrado, Washington University School of Law
Diane Reynolds, Willamette University College of Law
Robert Kaplan, William & Mary Law School

. . . and most of all, I want to thank the career services director
at my alma mater, Case Western Reserve University School of Law
— Debra Fink. It was Debra's unstinting support, encouragement
and enthusiasm that made me believe this project was possible
in the first place!

My thanks also go to those who generously allowed me to
reprint their materials as part of this book:

Case Western Reserve University School of Law, the *Student
Employment Handbook,* written by Debra Fink

Chicago Bar Association, The Chicago Bar Association Record,
"Legal Fantasies: Why Lawyers Choose Law," by Cheryl
Rich Heisler and Arlene S. Hirsch, March, 1990.

And finally, I thank those people who generously gave of their
time and advice from a perspective *outside* of law school:

J.T. Mann
Deanna Coe Kursh
Ralph Martire

. . . and other practicing attorneys who, by dint of the advice they
offered, preferred to remain nameless. You know who you are,
and thank you!

This book is dedicated to my wonderful brother, Keir,
who has always given me the greatest gift there is:
the belief that anything is possible.

Table of Contents

How to Use This Book

Boy, are you in for a treat! In this book, I'm going to teach you everything you need to get the job of your dreams. I'll show you exactly how to step out into the legal world and knock 'em dead. But I'm going to start with something a little bit more mundane than that: I'm going to tell you how to use this book, so you can achieve that goal.

The first three chapters of the book are what I'll call "prep" work. They tell you about what you'll need to do, and know, before you can make any outward steps towards getting the job of your dreams. You may be tempted to skip ahead to the meaty chapters on things like interviewing, and cover letters, and résumés, but I'd strongly encourage you *not* to do that. I don't write this stuff for my own edification, you know. I write it to help you get the job of your dreams — and the prep work you do is just as important as your résumé or your interview skills, even though you may not recognize that right now!

The next four chapters, Chapters 4 through 7, are where I'll give you the meat-and-potatoes of your job search tools. In those chapters, you'll learn how to make contacts, and you'll discover everything you need to know about correspondence, and résumés, and interviews.

In Chapters 8 through 13, I'll cover what you might think of as special situations, because I'll be giving you specific advice which may or may not apply to your situation. For instance, if you don't want to work for a large law firm, you probably won't want to read Chapter 12 on getting the large firm job you're dying for — because you aren't dying for it! And if your grades are pretty good, then Chapter 7, "Help! My Grades Stink!," probably won't interest you, unless you're into gloating (I hope you're not). And if you're interested in working for a law firm, you won't want to bother with Chapter 13 on Nontraditional Careers.

The final chapter of the book, Chapter 14, is a kind of roundup of classic mistakes law students make when they look for jobs. What I've done with this chapter is to gather up in one place the worst, most common boners you can make when you look for a legal job. The idea here, of course, is to stop you from falling into the traps other, less fortunate law students have fallen into!

So that gives you a basic idea of what to expect from this book. By the way, everything that's on the cover is true. All of the blurb material on the back cover — it's all here. And all of the advice *is* from the country's most innovative career services counselors. I haven't attached a name to every line, but where you don't see a particular expert's name connected with a piece of advice, that only means that it represented a consensus of opinion, and I didn't get a particularly ringing quote from anybody to back it up.

I could go on and on, but I won't. You're going to be spending plenty of time with me throughout this book as it is. So let's get on with it!

Kimm Alayne Walton
Wilton, Connecticut

Chapter 1

The Two Sure-Fire Keys to Getting the Job of Your Dreams

"Whether you think you can or think you can't, you're right."
Henry Ford

This book is going to change your life.

Starting right now, if you follow the step-by-step advice I'm going to give you, you *will* get a job. One that you enjoy, with people you like. I promise.

And if you go on using the techniques you'll learn in this book *after* you begin your career, your professional life will *forever* be more rewarding and far more lucrative than it would have been otherwise. You'll be more successful, wealthier, and a whole lot happier!

From where you're sitting now, you might have a hard time buying that. "Geez, Kimm," you're saying. "Come on. The job market *stinks.*" Well, you're right. It *does* stink. That's no headline. It was stinking up the joint when I graduated from law school, 10 years ago, and it hasn't improved since then. Want figures to back that up? OK. Large firms frequently get *several thousand* applications for 20 summer clerkships. Only about *12%* of law students get jobs from on-campus interviews. And more than *half* of the law students who graduate every year don't have a job at graduation.

You know what I say to that? SO WHAT. Statistics don't matter, because all you need is one job. I don't care if there are 10 jobs available or 10,000 — I'm going to show you how to *get* one of those jobs. The fact is, what you've got in your hands is a book packed with the tools you need to get the job you want, no matter how bad your grades are, no matter where you go to school, and regardless of your work experience. Use it, and you *will* get the job of your dreams. I promise.

You've probably already glanced at the Table of Contents, so you know that I'm going to lead you through every aspect of getting your dream job — from deciding what that job *is,* to making contacts, to handling correspondence, to interviews. I have special chapters for special situations — like getting a large firm job, or handling truly awful grades, or overcoming the fact that you didn't get an offer after your summer clerkship. And it's not just tidbits off the top of my head, either. It's the best advice from the country's top law school career counselors — the tips that have gotten jobs for thousands of law students, just like you.

But I want to start you off by introducing you to the two lynchpins of my approach. No matter which specific task you're undertaking in your job search, you will need to remember these two basic principles in order to succeed:

1. Take the initiative.
   Nothing comes to (s)he who waits!
   and

2. Show honest enthusiasm.
   Once you can fake that, you've got it made!

Let's take a closer look at them!

First, let's talk about taking the initiative. What does that mean? It means taking *action.* If you want the job of your dreams, you've got to take action to get it. Don't worry about what kinds of action you have to take — I'll coach you every step of the way. But the point is, you can't expect to sit back and watch the job of your dreams fall into your lap. Case Western's Debra Fink has a wonderful quote along these lines, that goes like this:

"Parties who desire milk should not seat themselves in the middle of a field in hopes that a cow will back up to them."

Now if getting a great job were simply a matter of taking action *once*, pretty much everybody would do it. But taking the initiative means more than that. It means *persistence*. I'm lying to you if I tell you that the first phone call you make will get you your dream job. (It would be great if it *did*, but it's not very likely!) You'll have to work at it for a period of time, probably a few months. Fordham's Kathleen Brady likens the job search to an annoying two-credit class: you *have* to make time for it, and stick with it. And you know what makes that tough? If you're not careful, you'll get demoralized in the process. Having to stick with it for a period of time means that not every contact you make will pan out. Not every avenue you research will bear fruit. And every time you get turned down, every time you face rejection — well, that's not pleasant. Rejection never is. *Nobody*, no matter how self-confident they are, likes to stick their neck out and get slapped. It's just that if you put these temporary setbacks in perspective, they won't defeat you. As Mets' manager Dallas Green says, "Winning is just a matter of getting up one more time than you're knocked down." And that's what persistence is. It's forcing yourself to keep on trying. Remember that every phone call you make, every person you contact, every time you casually mention that you're researching the job market — you inch one step closer to the job of your dreams.

And you know what helps make that a whole lot more bearable? The idea that once you get what you've been dreaming of, nobody — including you — will care about what you went through to get it. What you *went* through were little chunks of rejection, all in a row. That's what people overlook when they talk about the payoffs of persistence. When you look at the stories of successful people, it's very easy to overlook what persistence *means*, that path strewn with setbacks, because it's too easy to focus on the payoff. I'll give you a couple of my favorite examples. Take Dr. Seuss. You know that he sold a bazillion books, but what you might *not* have known is that he got rejected by *23 publishers* before one agreed to publish his books.

Here's another man's story: He failed in business in 1831. He was defeated when he ran for the legislature in 1832. He failed in *another* business in 1833. He *was* elected to the legislature in 1834, but that was immediately followed by his sweetheart dying in 1835. He had a nervous breakdown in 1836. He was defeated for speaker in 1838, for elector in 1840, for land officer in 1843. He was elected to Congress in 1846, but defeated when he ran for reelection in 1848. He was defeated for Vice President in 1856, and defeated for the Senate in 1858. Then what? In 1860, he was elected President of the United States. Yep. Abraham Lincoln.

Now I know what you're thinking. "Geez, Kimmbo, those are really heartwarming stories. How sweet." Well, I'm not telling you about them to give you a warm fuzzy glow. Instead what I want you to focus on is how Dr. Seuss must have felt after his first rejection, or fifth rejection, or twentieth rejection. He didn't know he was going to strike gold on number 24! And Honest Abe honestly couldn't have foreseen hitting the jackpot after a steady 27 years of failures. The reason it's so easy to overlook their rejections is that we're looking back on their stories, *knowing* the final outcome — *knowing* that they were both successful. When you're looking for a job, you don't know what the outcome will be. If you run into a handful of setbacks, you may be tempted to sit back on your haunches and wait for a job to come to you. *But it won't.* I promise you that if you do everything I tell you to do, you'll get a great job, and it won't take more than a few months. During that time, sure, you might meet with some setbacks. But you've got to be persistent. You've got to take the initiative. That's the message I heard time and time again from law school career services directors, who say that that's the most important secret to getting the job of your dreams!

In fact, I've heard a bunch of stories about how persistence works for law students. Here are a couple of them.

- One First Year at a southern school had set his sights on one particular firm. He contacted them as a First Year, and they told him, "We don't take summer clerks. Sorry." They let him talk to a couple of associates, but that was it. He cooled his heels for a year, and then applied again during his second year. Same response; no luck. He gets to third year. Now he's waited 2 *years* for this firm, with no luck. They weren't doing on-campus interviewing, and hadn't put up any job notices. But he contacted them again anyway. He didn't have a stellar record — no great job experiences, no great grades. But they made him an offer anyway. Why? They said they admired his persistence!

♦   A Third Year at a northeastern school had her heart set on a particular small firm. She went on other interviews, but nothing interested her except this firm, and they wouldn't bite. She graduated without a job. And in fact, she was unemployed for *13 months* after graduation, all the while politely — but persistently — staying in contact with this one firm. They hemmed and hawed, and she finally said: "I'm so confident this is the right match that I'm willing to volunteer for a month, for free, to prove it." She got the offer!

These are just a couple of examples, but the fact is, persistence doesn't mean you have to do anything extraordinarily creative; you don't really have to do anything except to *keep at it.* Throughout this book, I'll knock down any obstacles you think are stopping you from going after your dream job. You think your school's reputation is holding you back? Bull! As Washington's Teresa DeAndrado says, "You can go anywhere from any school, because getting hired has to do with *you* and your self-confidence. People hire *people,* not *schools.*" Or maybe you're discouraged because you don't see anybody getting jobs. Well, they *do.* As Georgetown's Marilyn Tucker says, "Don't believe that people don't get hired. They *do.* Every day!" You think your grades aren't good enough? Well, the *heck* with the top 10% of the class. I'll show you how to get a great job if you're in the *bottom* 10%! (That's in Chapter 10, by the way.) The bottom line is, no matter what you think is holding you back from going after your dream job, I *promise* that I've heard about people who faced *exactly* the same hurdles as you, and they got *great* jobs. And you can get those jobs, too — if you're willing to take the initiative!

So that's the first guiding principle you have to remember — take the initiative. The second is to show honest enthusiasm. Enthusiasm and initiative go hand-in-hand. Initiative is the action, and enthusiasm is the attitude that goes with, and propels, that action. What's enthusiasm? It's showing that you're interested, that you'd like to know more about something. And why am I so hot on it? Because when you're looking for a job as a law student, *it works.* People *respond* to it, in a big way. If you can make an employer believe that you're truly interested in *them,* that you want more than anything to work for *them,* that attitude will leapfrog you over other candidates with much better credentials, from much better schools.

Now, you may have a real problem with showing enthusiasm. Maybe you think it's not cool. Maybe your experiences in your personal life have shown you that you do better when you play hard to get. Well, do what you want personally. I don't care. All I care about is you getting a job. And to do that, you've got to bite the bullet and show an honest interest in the other person. Or maybe you think that you're going to be interviewing for some jobs that you just can't get really excited about. Well, you may want to reconsider whether you want to interview for those jobs in the first place, but assuming you do, I *still* don't care if you don't *honestly* feel any enthusiasm for those jobs. I'm not telling you you have to *feel* honest enthusiasm. I'm saying you have to *show* it. And if you can dredge up the wherewithal to do that, nobody cares that you had to *create* it and it didn't come naturally to you.

I'll tell you something else that might make you uncomfortable about showing enthusiasm. It puts you in a one-down position, because when you show an interest in someone else, that puts them in the position of being able to reject you. You've admitted you want something, and that's not terribly comfortable for a lot of people. Guess what. I *still* don't care. Employers respond so positively to enthusiasm that you're going to have to put up with the few, the *very* few, the *positively tiny minority* who are jerks and don't respond to it. You will be so far ahead of the crowd if you greet every potential opportunity with enthusiasm that it's well worth it.

At least, that's what I heard over and over and over from law school career services people. Here are a few anecdotes to prove the point:

- One law student at a law school out west was absolutely obsessed with the idea of working for Disney. He took every opportunity to meet with anybody who worked there. He even found out the CEO's birthday, and sent him a card! But when it came to getting a job there, or even an interview, he struck out. Well, he found out that Disney was holding a conference for its executives, during the spring of his second year in law school. He flew to where the conference was being held, and hung around the elevators at the hotel.

When the CEO got onto the elevator, he got in with him, and made a thirty-second pitch for a summer job. His enthusiasm cut through any objections. And he got the job!

♦ One woman at a southern school set her sights on practicing environmental law. She had one particular specialty firm that she really wanted to work for. She read everything she could about them, and found that several of the associates were from her school. When she got herself an interview there, she took paperweights with a picture of the law school on them, and presented them to the alumni.

Were they impressed with her thoughtfulness? Wouldn't you be? And wouldn't you want to work with someone like her? *They* did!

♦ Another woman, this one at a school in the southwest, went to an out-of-town interview with a firm she just loved. When she got back, she went out of her way to get photos of a new renovation to her law school, and with her thank-yous, she sent the photos to the alums she'd spoken with at the firm. You know the outcome already. She got an offer.

Now I'm not saying that initiative and enthusiasm are the *only* things you need. You need to know *what* to do; you need to know *how* to get across the idea of enthusiasm without seeming desperate or pushy. If you didn't need those things as well, this book would only have to be 10 pages long, wouldn't it? But the reason I mention them here is that as we embark on this journey of yours — from right here, right now, to your dream job — you've got to keep those two principles in mind: **Take the initiative; Show honest enthusiasm**. And, of course, apply them to the steps you'll learn in the rest of this book. If you can do that (and I'm confident you *can*), you *will* get your dream job.

I promise.

Chapter 2

Deciding What The Heck the Job of Your Dreams *Is,* Anyway

"What surprises me most about law students is that they don't have a perception of what they're in for; they don't have any idea of what a job will be before they get there. It's not a matter of not caring, it's just that they seem not to have thought about it at all."
Deanna Coe Kursh
Benesch, Friedlander, Koplan & Aronoff

"Law firms' pet peeve with students is that they don't understand what the work is all about. It's not that they're not willing to work hard enough, they just don't know what it's about."
Ellen Wayne, Career Services Director,
Columbia University School of Law

"Uh-oh," you're thinking. "I know what's coming — a lot of those touchy-feely, what do I want to do with my life kind of questions." Well, you're *partially* right. But there's no avoiding it. I was a law student myself, and I know that what you'd prefer is a list of a hundred true-false, black-and-white questions, with the results spitting out your dream job, all wrapped up in a neat little package. Anyone who tells you they can do that for you is lying to you, because deciding on your dream job *inevitably* means some self-analysis, some prioritizing of your needs and desires, and some gray areas. I *will* give you the tools you need to decide what your dream job *is*, but there's no getting around the fact that you're going to have to think, really *think*, about what you want. No matter how distasteful that seems to you now, I've got a fairly strong incentive for you to do it, and it's this:

You need to know what your dream job is
before I can help you get it.

That may seem hopelessly self-evident, but it's incredible how few students actually make that decision! What law school career counselors hear all the time is, "I'm willing to do anything, anywhere. I just want a job." You may think that that makes you a more attractive job candidate, because it widens your possibilities. Wrong! Paradoxically, it has just the opposite effect, because it doesn't convince *any* employer that you're truly interested in *them*. As St. John's' Maureen Provost Ryan says, "It's a lot easier to find something if you state a preference. For instance, it's easier to find work if you can say, 'I want to practice environmental law!' as opposed to, 'I'll take anything!'" And St. Louis' Wendy Werner adds, "When I hear a student say 'Any job would be fine,' all that shows me is that they've done *no* self-analysis."

So the bottom line is, you *have* to decide what it is that you want from a job. What we'll do for the rest of this chapter is to talk about the two elements that go into that decision:

1. Figuring out what's important to you; and
2. Finding out what's "out there."

We're going to go through these two elements in detail, and ideally, when you're done, you'll have a pretty good idea of what your goal is. If *not*, don't sweat it. Later in this chapter, on page 34, there's a section called "Help! I'm stuck!" to help you if you still can't figure out what you want. And you may want to check out Chapter 13, on nontraditional careers. But, as I said, you're likely to come out of this chapter with a much clearer picture of exactly what your dream job *is*. And that takes a load off *my* shoulders, because once you've decided what it is, I'm confident that with the advice you'll get throughout this book, you'll be able to *get* that dream job!

A. FIVE IMPORTANT OBSTACLES TO TEAR DOWN, FIRST

Before we go whole-hog on deciding what you want to do, I want to discuss just briefly the things you shouldn't allow into your decision-making process — at least, not right now.

1. DON'T BELIEVE THAT YOUR DREAM JOB WILL SATISFY *ALL* OF YOUR NEEDS

No job in the world will supply *everything* you want. As NYU's Gail Cutter points out, "Maybe being a litigator will satisfy many of your needs, but if you also need to be creative, it won't do that. But you could satisfy that creative urge by writing articles on the side." The point is, you have to *prioritize* your needs, and act accordingly. So when we discuss what your dream job is, it's the job that satisfies your needs the best — taking into account that no job will satisfy them *all*.

It's also important to be realistic about what practising law is like, and not to be deluded by fantasies . . . perhaps the kind of fantasies that lured you to law school in the first place. The *Chicago Bar Association Record* ran an excellent article about just this problem, called "Legal Fantasies: Why Lawyers Choose Law," by two career counselors, Cheryl Rich Heisler and Arlene Hirsch. I've included it at the end of this chapter as Appendix A, on page 41, because it raises some important cautions about being realistic in deciding what your dream job is. I encourage you to read it!

2. DON'T BE INFLUENCED BY YOUR GRADES OR YOUR SCHOOL

I'm going to point out something kind of ironic to you. That is, you're *more* likely to get your dream job right out of the gate if you're *below* the top 10% of your class, rather than being *in* the top 10%! Don't believe me? Well, I can tell you why that's true.

Students in the top 10% of the class don't have to *think* about what kind of job they really want, they don't have to do any research, because they've got plenty of job opportunities. They can basically go to on-campus interviews and get a job. But you know what? That doesn't mean that they'll be happy, and in fact a lot of them wind up miserable a couple of years down the road — *because they never did the kind of soul searching you're doing now!* As Gail Cutter points out, "People outside the top 10% *do* get it right the first time. They *have* to do the thinking and research that the top 10% *don't* have to do, just to get a job in the first place!" So if you're feeling at all sorry for yourself because of your grades, you can take solace in that!

Ultimately, you can get almost any legal job there is, *regardless* of how bad your grades are or where you go to school. OK, if you want to be a Supreme Court justice, it would help if you're going to Harvard or Yale or schools of that ilk — but if that's your goal, you probably know that already. So outside of being a Supreme Court justice, there really aren't any jobs that are barred to you because of your grades or your school.

All I want right now is for you to think in terms of what you want to do, regardless of what you think your credentials can get you. Because with the right attitude and the right plan, *in spite of* awful grades and an ill-regarded school, you *can* get where you want to go, even if it's by a somewhat circuitous route. But I'm getting ahead of myself; those are things we'll discuss later in the book. The point is — all we're doing right now is deciding what you want to do, and you have to do that without giving your grades a second thought.

3. DON'T BE INFLUENCED BY WHAT OTHER PEOPLE (OR YOU YOURSELF!) MAKE YOU FEEL YOU *OUGHT* TO WANT

Boy, is *this* a tough trap to avoid. Benesch Friedlander's Deanna Coe Kursh advises, "Think about what *you* want to do, not what your parents or the students next to you want." I'll bet everybody you know has told you what you ought to do when you graduate from law school. And even if they *haven't* told you, no doubt you feel the pressure of their expectations anyway.

I'll never forget the day I graduated from law school, when I told my dad that I didn't want to be a lawyer, I wanted to be a writer instead. I don't know if he's gotten over it to this day . . . and that was *10 years* ago!

It's not just families who create expectations. Friends do it, neighbors do it — heck, your law professors do it, as well. As Wendy Werner points out, "The definition of success that's played out in law school is the job with the high profile, that pays the most money." Michigan's Nancy Krieger gives a speech to First Years during their first semester. She calls it her "happy life" speech, because she tells them, "Just because your dad or neighbor says working at a particular place will make you happy, it may not." The point is — don't let other people try and decide what will give *you* a happy life!

The problem is that when other people form expectations for you, inevitably what they're looking at are money, prestige, and things that they perhaps *think* you ought to want. The implied message here is that if you don't go to the biggest, most prestigious firm you can get into, you're "wasting" your degree. Chicago-Kent's Lisa Abrams calls this the "destructive family" problem, and says, "If you enlist any help at all in deciding what you want, enlist *constructive* help. Family expectations are just wrong; they're myths." And they're particularly destructive because they can dissuade you from a job you'd truly love. One law school career counselor in the northeast told me about a law student who interviewed to be executive director of a YMCA. With a background in social services, this job was something she really wanted. However, she went to talk to the counselor because her professors and peers had told her she shouldn't want to do it, the old "you're-wasting-your-law-degree" argument. The career counselor talked her *into* accepting it, and she did. And you probably already know the moral of the story — she loved the job and is thrilled she took it.

There are a million stories like that. The fact is, *you're* the one who's got to *go* to that job every day, who's actually got to *perform* — nobody else. You don't spend your life *telling* people what you do for a living — you spend your life *doing* it. So the message is: when you're making a decision about what you want, make sure it's that and *only* that — what *you* want and not what somebody else wants!

4. THINK ABOUT WHAT YOU WANT TO *DO,* NOT WHICH FIRM YOU WANT TO WORK FOR

When you're deciding what your dream job is, focus on what you want to do, not which employer you want to work for. Later we'll spend plenty of time deciding whom you should approach for a job, but you can only do that *after* you've decided *what* it is that you want to do.

Why do you have to do it in this order? It's because of the risk of being seduced by the wrong kinds of factors. When you choose who you want to work for before deciding what you really want to do, you're making a decision based on image. You're probably being heavily swayed by things like prestige and money, without paying attention to what it is that those people *do* on a day to day basis. And when you make decisions on that basis, it's a formula for disaster.

So set aside, for the moment, any notion of any particular employer you want to work for. Trust me — if you go through all of the decision-making that I'm prescribing here in this chapter, and you find that the employer you thought you wanted *really is* the kind of place you'd like to work, I'll give you everything you need to get that job. But don't jump the gun! Make sure it *really is* what you want, and that you're not just hooked on a false image.

5. DON'T THINK ABOUT MONEY

"Ha!" I hear you saying. "It's easy for *you* to say. *You* don't have a kajillion dollars in law school loans to pay off!" Well, you've got me there. I don't. But what I'm asking you to do is to make your decision on what you want to do, *regardless* of money, for right now. I want you simply and purely to think about *what you want to do.* It's difficult enough to look in the mirror and decide exactly how you want to spend your time, without clouding the picture with issues of money. And in fact, if all you pay attention to is money, there's a strong chance you'll lead yourself straight to a job that will make you miserable. After all, to paraphrase Citizen Kane, it's not difficult to make a lot of money, if money is all you want. And if you want a job that will make you rich but miserable, you're reading the wrong book — I'm supposed to be helping you to get your *dream* job, remember?

I'm not saying money is not important; I'm just saying that it's not relevant right now. In fact, there are many options for structuring loan payoffs. They're outside the scope of this book, but your career services office can tell you everything about them. I think you'll find that there's a lot more flexibility to loan pay-backs than you think. So, for right now, cast aside issues of money, and let's find out what you really want to do!

Now that I've aired those concerns, let's get to work! Remember, there are two essential tasks we're going to accomplish in this chapter. First, you're going to do a little soul-searching and find out what you really want. And second, we're going to delve a little bit into what's "out there," to see what kinds of jobs you ought to pursue.

B. *WHEN* SHOULD YOU DECIDE ON A CAREER?

Now. That's when. In fact, you can never decide too soon. Ideally, according to William and Mary's Rob Kaplan, "You should start thinking about what kind of job you want *before* you go to law school." If you don't know what you want, take heart — most law students don't. As Boston University's Betsy Armour says, "Not many law students have their eyes open coming in. You should start thinking about careers right off the starting blocks!" And Case Western's Debra Fink says, "The kind of job you're looking for determines how early you should start your research. If you want to work at a large firm, start networking when you're ten." Of course she's joking, but the point is, you can't make career decisions too early. The earlier you decide what you want to do, the sooner you can choose the right courses, start meeting the right kinds of people, and doing all the other things that I'll recommend later in the book that will help position you for the job of your dreams.

Now is it *really* such a sin if you're already in school and you don't have any idea what you want to do? No, it's really not. As Wendy Werner says, "It's OK if you're a first year and you're saying, 'I just want to get my feet wet. I want a legal employer.' Nobody's going to look down on you for that. But if you get to your third year and you're still saying, 'Any job would be fine,' that's bad news."

So the watchword here is, *the sooner the better!*

C. FINDING OUT ABOUT WHAT YOU REALLY WANT

Wendy Werner calls this the "internal piece" of deciding on a dream job. Now as a law student, when you think about the icky part of choosing a job, it's this internal part you're probably dreading. Because it's not intellectual. It's not cut-and-dried. It's the antithesis of what you're taught in law school. In law school, you analyze elements and come to a conclusion. As Maureen Provost Ryan says, "Law students like action, results, formulas. Soul searching is *not* a strong suit for them."

But the fact is, to choose your dream job, you *have* to do some soul-searching, no matter how much you hate the prospect. To make the whole thing a lot more palatable for you, though, I'm going to give you a whole bunch of questions to think about. You can call it a checklist, if that makes the whole thing a lot more concrete for you. And I urge you, I *implore* you, to take this seriously. Or if not seriously, at least *please* go through these questions, and get to know yourself and the kind of job environment that will make you happy. And I've got a great reason for you to do that.

So you don't make the mistake I made, that's why.

When I was in law school, about 10 years ago, if you had told me to do some soul searching about what kind of a job I wanted, I would have looked at you as though you had lobsters crawling out of your ears. I wanted what everybody wanted: a job with the biggest law firm that would take me. Did I do any research? No. Did I think at all about what would make me happy? Of course not. I figured that the jobs everybody else seemed to want would be fine with me, too. So I clerked after second year for the biggest, most prestigious law firm that would take me. One of the biggest firms in the country, in fact.

Big mistake!

Even an hour with the kinds of questions I'm about to ask you would have saved me a summer of misery. You know why? Because the kinds of things that are absolutely crucial for me, for my job happiness, are *not* what that law firm was all about. I enjoy helping people. I like to be creative. I'm not very conservative. I'm very blunt, which makes me bad at office politics. And I like a lot of autonomy. We haven't discussed large firm practice yet — we'll get to that in Chapter 12 — but take my word for it, *none of those qualities are an asset at a large firm.* But you know if you had asked me at that time, I wouldn't have been able to tell you any of those things about myself. It was largely a function of going through that awful experience that *taught* me those things. And you know what? I don't want the same thing to happen to you. And nobody who cares about you would wish it on you, either. So do yourself a favor, bite the bullet, and do a bit of soul-searching before you decide what you want. It's the most valuable possible way to spend your time.

Most importantly, look at soul searching for what it is — a means of getting you to your dream job. If you're at all afraid of doing this, it might be because you're concerned that what you'll come up with is not what you pictured yourself doing. Maybe it will tell you that you shouldn't pursue a career path to being a name partner at a huge law firm. But remember: the important thing is to know what your dream job is, so you can go after it. And you can't know what that is without first getting to know yourself.

Now, there's no magic formula for this kind of self-analysis. I've included a few quizzes, but I'm warning you up front that they're *very* basic — they're just designed to get you thinking along the lines of self-analysis, and the reason I include them is that if you're anything like me, I wouldn't have any *clue* where to start if someone asked me loosy-goosy questions like, "Who *are* you? What do you *really* want?" I'd be tempted to answer, "I'm Kimm Walton, and I really want a cheeseburger, thank you." So what I'm doing with these quizzes is to get you thinking about what you're really like, what makes you tick. Your career services director can give you more elaborate tests, like the Myers-Briggs test (which gives you a lot of true-false questions to determine your basic personality type). Once you've taken the quizzes here, you may find that you really *do* want to do more of this kind of self-analysis. The goal is to come up with a basic knowledge of the kinds of things that are important to you, the kinds of things you want to spend your life doing. And whether you do that with these quizzes, with a Zen master on a mountaintop in Tibet, with 10 years of psychoanalysis, or with an astrologer . . . it just doesn't matter, as long as it works for you.

By the way, what you should wind up with is a pretty decent laundry-list of what you're like, and what you're looking for in a career. As you go through the activities outlined in the rest of this book, be sure that any job you look at satisfies the basic needs you've identified in yourself. See if the people at your potential workplace have the same values as you, if the same kinds of things that are important to you seem important to them, as well. See if the nature of the work they do comports with the factors that are important to you. If the job doesn't meet these criteria, then it's not your dream job!

1. THE THREE BASIC ELEMENTS OF KNOWING YOURSELF

Deborah Arron, in the book "What Can You Do With A Law Degree?," says that there are three essentials for job hunting:

Who am I?

What do I want?

What am I willing to give up to get what I want?

Answering these three questions gives you a *great* framework for learning, in concrete terms, more about exactly who you are and what you ought to do with your life. So let's take a look at those questions in turn.

A. WHO AM I?

No, we're not talking about any cosmic, wow-where-do-I-fit-in-the-Universe type of thing. Instead, we're looking at five basic characteristics: your interests, your skills, your values (that is, what gives meaning to your work and motivates you), the kind of people contact you like to have, and the kind of work environment that would make you happy. Some of these questions are open ended; for others, I've given you specific checklists (again, modified from "What Can You Do With A Law Degree?" and other sources). For all of these questions, make sure that you *write down your responses*, either in the margins of this book or on a separate piece of paper. Don't just think about them; your picture of yourself will be much more concrete if you get it down on paper!

So let's go through each of those five elements and get an idea of what you're like!

1. WHAT ARE MY INTERESTS?

What we're looking for here are the kinds of topics that intrigue you. Here are a few questions to get you thinking in the right direction:

♦ Go through the Sunday paper. Which articles do you read?

♦ What kinds of magazines do you read?

♦ What kinds of subjects in books draw your attention?

♦ When you talk with your friends about substantive issues, what do you like to talk about?

♦ What kinds of television programs do you watch?

♦ Also take into account — do you have many different interests that change over time? Or do you focus on one field and delve into it at great depth?

A job that's your dream job will ideally absorb you because the subject matter interests you. By identifying what intrigues you *now*, you can identify what is likely to stimulate you in your career. Of course, no one job is likely to encompass *every* subject that interests you; you'll have outside activities to round out your life. But since your job will take up the lion's share of your waking hours, it should be something that engages you.

2. WHAT ARE MY SKILLS?

Figuring out what your natural abilities are is *very* important to determining your dream job. Why? Because people enjoy most the work that uses their natural aptitudes. The things that come naturally to you are the things you do best!

So think about the things you've achieved, the abilities you have that other people have commented on, the kinds of activities that have brought you the most success. As you do this, *don't feel guilty about naming activities that come too easily to you!* I'll give you a personal example. It's always been very easy for me to write advertising copy. It's so easy, in fact, that I used to ignore it when I thought about what I was good at. Part of it was that I figured if it came so easily to me, it must be easy for everybody, and so I felt silly mentioning it. *Don't make that mistake!* What you want is to itemize *everything* that you do well.

Also don't worry about coming up with a whole range of skills, for fear that there won't be any one career that utilizes them all. As it turns out, most people have a skill set that can be satisfied by one job. And if you really have skills that aren't amenable to just one job, then you can always use your leisure time as an outlet for your other skills!

3. WHAT ARE MY VALUES? WHAT GIVES MEANING TO MY WORK? WHAT MOTIVATES ME?

What you're looking for here are the specific, nonsubstance-oriented elements that create job satisfaction for you — things like recognition, autonomy, variety, intellectual challenge, helping others.

I realize that talking about "values" is a very loosy-goosy thing, and you may not feel comfortable with it. So I've included a little quiz to make it easier for you. (This quiz is adapted from Deborah Arron's "What Can You Do With A Law Degree?")

QUIZ – WHAT ARE MY VALUES?

Directions: Scan this list. Cross off values that don't matter to you. Then, hone the ones remaining down to six. Your dream job has to have these attributes!

_____ Achievement, accomplishment

_____ Action, adventure, fast-paced environment

_____ Aesthetics, appreciation of beauty

_____ Autonomy, the freedom to make your own choices

_____ Creativity and self-expression, generating new ideas

_____ Peace of mind

__√__ Being genuinely yourself with others

__√__ Sense of humor, wit

__√__ Intellectual challenges, learning new things

_____ Treating others fairly, wanting equity for them

_____ Knowledge, seeking truth or information

__√__ Love and family, affection, intimacy

_√_ Loyalty, allegiance to a person, group, or cause

_√_ Integrity, morality, following standards of honor

_√_ Nature, appreciating the natural world

_√_ Pleasure, fun, enjoyment

_____ Influence, power to get things done

_____ Recognition

_____ Religious conviction

_____ Security

_____ Helping others, serving a cause

_____ Skill, being good at something

_____ Tangible results of effort

_____ Variety in terms of number and type of experience

_____ Wealth, ample money for things you want

_√_ Wisdom, insight, judgment

_____ Productivity at work

_____ Leisure, lots of time off

_____ Opportunities to travel

Remember — write down the results of this quiz on a separate sheet of paper, and hang onto it! What you'll do as you refine your search for a dream job is to talk with your career services director, talk with people doing work that tentatively interests you, and find out from them what kinds of values are served by the job. Later on in this book, in Chapter 4 on Making Contacts and Chapter 7 on Interviewing, I stress asking people quasipersonal questions about their work — what they like about it, why they chose it, what they wish they'd known before they started. Answers to questions like these give you insight into their values. And the more those values mesh with your own, the more likely you are to be happy doing the work they do.

4. WHAT KIND OF CONTACT WITH PEOPLE DO I LIKE TO HAVE?

This translates into contact with coworkers and clients. The kinds of questions you should ask yourself here include:

- ◆ What age group would you like to work with? The elderly? Children?
- ◆ How many people would you like to work with?
- ◆ What are the personality traits of the people you'd like to work with? Bright or learning disabled? Troubled or those with their lives under control?
- ◆ What kind of interaction do you want with your coworkers? Do you want to work in a team, which includes a willingness to subordinate your need for recognition and prestige? Or do you prefer to have others around just to brainstorm and share ideas? Or do you prefer to work alone?

As you research potential jobs by talking with people and interviewing, take note of the people contact involved with various jobs. If you're a loner and a job you're looking at involves constant contact with people, it's not your dream job!

5. WHAT KIND OF WORK ENVIRONMENT WOULD MAKE ME HAPPY?

Now what we're concerned with here isn't naming the firm you'd like to work for, or even the intellectual content of what you want to do. We'll talk more about that when we get to "Finding out what's out there," on page 26 — and in two appendices to this chapter, Appendix C on different work settings (page 67) and Appendix B on the 31 most popular specialties (page 49). Instead, what we're concerned with here are questions like:

- ◆ What kind of office atmosphere would you like? Friendly and casual, or intense and driven?
- ◆ What kind of aesthetics and physical setting do you need, or is it important to you at all?
- ◆ Do you like the idea of casual or formal attire for work?
- ◆ Would you be willing to work long hours if you love your work, or do you prefer a set schedule? Is it OK to work long hours if you get to pick the hours and the location? Would you prefer a serious time and attention commitment for a few

months, followed by a few months off?

As you look at various jobs in various kinds of settings, look around and see how the work environment meshes with what you like. See if the people seem intense, or casual. And how they dress. The question of work hours is a taboo question in an interview situation; it suggests you're not willing to work hard. So that's something you'd want to find out about a particular employer by speaking with your career services director, or from someone who's already clerked there, or perhaps an alum who's there now (although again, be careful how you ask; it's wise to preface a question about hours by saying, "I'm not afraid of hard work. What kind of hours do you normally put in?" That helps remove the "sting" from it).

B. WHAT DO I WANT?

What you're looking for here, in Deborah Arron's words, is "Your own personal definition of success." And how do you figure it out? Well, one way is to take the little quiz just a little further ahead, on page 24, called "Some Open-Ended Questions That Help You Get to Know Yourself Better." Another is to ask how you spend your time outside of law school. When you're free to do whatever you want to do, what do you do?

Another is to pay attention to your "evil secrets." For instance, you like to be the center of attention. Or you want a pot full of money. Or you don't want a career at all, you want a variety of work experiences. You may consider these an "evil secret," something you don't want to admit. But they're an important part of figuring out what you *want*.

C. WHAT AM I WILLING TO GIVE UP TO GET WHAT I WANT?

This is a difficult issue! The two basic conflicts for lawyers are money versus meaning, and work versus family.

Money vs. Meaning — Don't overvalue money! According to the *Utne Reader*, 62% of Americans say that "a lot of money" is important to a good life. But paradoxically, only 6% of those earning more than $50,000 a year say they've achieved the American Dream, compared to 5% of those who earn less than $15,000 a year.

Work vs. Family — How long are you willing to spend away from your family, including weekends? Also, is it the time away from your family that you're most concerned with, or feelings of guilt about how *they* feel?

It's impossible to get *anything* without giving something up, and analyzing *specifically* what you're willing to give up will go a long way toward guiding you to your dream job. (This is especially true if you think you want to work for a large firm, because the lure of money and prestige leads many law students to believe they're willing to give up quality-of-life elements that they aren't, in fact, willing to sacrifice. For more on this, see Chapter 12.)

2. QUIZ: SOME OPEN-ENDED QUESTIONS THAT HELP YOU KNOW YOURSELF BETTER...

Virtually every career book I've ever read included a list of questions designed to deepen your knowledge of yourself and your motivations. I've included them here to help you "flesh out" your answers to the three questions we've been discussing: Who am I? What do I want? What am I willing to sacrifice to get what I want? In fact, your answers to some of the questions we've already discussed will help you answer the questions in this quiz.

Take as long as you need to think, really *think,* about the answers to these questions. And be sure to write in the answers! When you're done, at the bottom of this quiz I'll show you what to do with your answers. (This quiz is adapted from one by Laura Rowe, at the George Washington National Law Center.)

1. When were you the happiest in your life? Why?

2. Think about any jobs you've held in the last several years. What was it in those jobs that allowed you to shine and really feel good?

3. Think about the classes you've taken in the last several years. What was it in those classes that allowed you to shine and really feel good?

4. When did you first start thinking about going to law school?

5. What did you want that made you decide to go to law school?

6. Think back over the last several years. What are the jobs, classes, and other work-related activities that you *disliked* the most?

7. Why, specifically, did you find those activities unpleasant?

8. Even though you may hate to admit it, what do you really need?

9. What kinds of things do you tend to procrastinate to avoid doing?

10. What three kinds of things have you always done well?

11. Time flies for you when you're doing what kinds of activities?

12. What do you think will be the most wonderful things about being a lawyer?

13. What kinds of activities would you most often enjoy in your legal work?

14. If money and education were no object and you could have any job you wanted, in 5 years you'd be . . .

15. What are the five qualities about that job that most attract you?

Once you're done answering these questions, go through your answers and look for themes. You'll probably find a lot of insight into exactly what kinds of activities make you happy, and, hence, the features that a dream job would have to have. Remember — the whole point of this chapter is to help you draw a bead on exactly what you *want*. So keep these answers in your hip pocket as you research possible employers. If the work you're looking at doesn't comport with your answers here, you won't be satisfied with it for very long!

D. FINDING OUT WHAT'S OUT THERE

Now that you have an idea of what *you're* all about, let's talk about how you go about matching yourself up with jobs you'll like. And that means getting a basic idea of exactly what kinds of jobs there *are* out there. If you're anything like I was as a law student, I only had the vaguest notion of what the various specialties were, and what the differences were between practicing in different kinds of settings. So what I'm going to do here is three-fold: First, I'm going to help you figure out what appeals to you intellectually; that is, what kind of a specialty might attract you. Second, I'm going to tell you how to figure out how your personality meshes with the specialties that appeal to you. And third, I'm going to talk about settings. Now for each of these, I've included a pretty sizeable appendix at the back of this chapter that goes into a little more detail. Appendix B is called "Specialties: The Nuts-and-Bolts of 31 Popular Areas of Practice." Appendix C is called "Traditional Career Settings for Law School Graduates." (Remember if you're particularly interested in a large firm, read Chapter 12; and if you think you might be interested in something nontraditional, go to Chapter 13.)

As you'll see, the touchstone of my approach is to gather as much information as you can, both about yourself and about the kinds of work lawyers do. As Nancy Krieger says, "It's a big decision. Make it with all the information you can get!"

1. FIGURING OUT WHAT APPEALS TO YOU *INTELLECTUALLY*

Law is a thinking career. People turn to you not for the amount of weight you can bench press or to clear their plates after dinner or to spackle tiles. They need you to *think*. So it's a *big* help if what you have to think about appeals to you intellectually. In fact, if it doesn't, you're going to be miserable.

How do you determine this? It's pretty easy, actually. I'll go over these steps in detail, but in a nutshell, you want to narrow your choices down to three or four. To do that, you want to:

♦ Think about classes you've enjoyed.

♦ Think back to what you wanted to do *before* you went to law school. If you can't remember, go to your admissions office and get your application, and look at the essays you wrote, to get a handle on what kind of lawyer you wanted to be.

♦ Find out about different specialties. For one thing, you can read the capsule descriptions of various specialties that I've summarized in Appendix B at the end of this chapter. You can talk to your career services director to learn about specialties, as well. And you can talk to upperclassmen and any lawyers you already know to see what it was that attracted them intellectually to any particular subject area.

Once you've established a short list of three or four potential specialties, go ahead and:

♦ Read professional publications in a specialty, either from practitioners or from your career services director, and see if those publications hold your interest.

♦ Find practitioners in those specialties (from your career services director, professors, or any personal contacts you have), and conduct information interviews with them. (You'll want to do information interviews for a number of different reasons, which are outlined in Chapter 4 on page 143; so you may want to combine finding out about specialties with information interviews for other reasons.)

♦ Go to meetings of the local bar association for specialties that spark your interest.

After you do all of this, you ought to wind up with a couple of specialties that you'd consider practicing. With those in mind, you can delve further, having narrowed your search to manageable proportions.

So let's look at those steps in detail. **Remember:** For the first three steps, your goal is to come up with a list of three or four specialties that intrigue you. Don't worry — you're not making a lifetime career decision here, and you can *always* go back and change your mind. But the idea is just to come up with a few options to research further, at this point.

1. THINK ABOUT CLASSES YOU'VE ENJOYED

A good place to start in deciding what appeals to you intellectually is to think about which classes you've enjoyed the most in law school. After all, *all* you're getting in the classroom is an exposure to the intellectual side of various specialties. Even if you truly dislike your classes in general, there are probably one or two that have attracted you. If so, put them on your list!

2. THINK BACK TO WHAT YOU WANTED TO DO *BEFORE* YOU WENT TO LAW SCHOOL

Law school has a way of messing with your mind. No matter how clear-headed you might have been before, law school undermines the confidence of almost every student. So, one way to get a handle on what you want to do is to think back to what motivated you to enter law school in the first place. You probably had a vision of what you wanted to do with your degree. If necessary, go back and look at your admissions essays for clues as to what kind of specialty appeals to you.

It's worth making a couple of points here. One is that it's possible that what lured you to law school was a fantasy, perhaps one of the ones described in the "Legal Fantasies" article in Appendix A on page 41. If so, that doesn't do you much good in terms of picking a specialty, because it helps to be realistic about what a specialty is like. For another thing, it's entirely possible that you had *no idea* of what you wanted to do with your law degree before you entered school. I sure didn't. What motivated me to go to law school was the fact that I had a college degree in a subject I hated (Accounting), I had no job, and I lucked out and scored high on the LSAT. I gave more thought to what color socks I was going to wear the next day than I did to what I was going to do with a law degree! You're probably not as clueless as I was, but my point is this: it may be that you didn't have any idea what you wanted to do before you went to law school. And if that's the case, that's OK — you'll just have to use the other resources I describe here to decide what appeals to you intellectually.

3. FIND OUT ABOUT THE TASKS INVOLVED WITH DIFFERENT SPECIALTIES, AND CHOOSE THREE OR FOUR TO RESEARCH FURTHER

When it comes right down to it, you probably don't have a very good idea of what exactly is involved in different kinds of specialties. That's OK; as a law student, why the heck *would* you? But before you can make a decision as to what you want to do, you really do have to find out what various specialties involve. There are several ways to do this. You can talk with your career services director, and brainstorm about various specialties that might appeal to you. Don't be embarrassed if you just don't know what those specialties are all about! You can also talk to upperclassmen and any lawyers you already know to see what the intellectual appeal was for them for the specialty they've chosen. And to start you thinking along these lines, I've included in Appendix B, on page 49, a capsule description of 31 of the most common specialties, just to give you a quick peek at what it's like to practice in these areas. Scan these, and see if any of them spark your interest!

4. READ PROFESSIONAL PUBLICATIONS IN THOSE SPECIALTIES, AND SEE IF THOSE PUBLICATIONS HOLD YOUR INTEREST

You may be thinking, OK, what the heck are professional publications? Well, those are the magazines, newspapers, and other periodicals that people in a certain profession read. For instance, for me, since I'm a writer, that would be things like *Writer's Digest, Publisher's Weekly,* and any publication I'm interested in writing for.

You'll find that every specialty in law has publications written especially for it. What you should do is to go to your career services director and find out what it is that lawyers in those specialties read on a regular basis, to tell them what's going on in the field. (If your career services director doesn't know — although they probably will! — they'll be able to direct you to someone who *does* know.) Get ahold of those publications through your law school library, and sit down and read them. As Gail Cutter says, "This is a good way to see if you really want to practice in that area. If you nod off, maybe it's not for you!"

If you find that you *are* interested in these publications, that's great! Make a note of what they are, and continue reading them. As I'll detail in Chapter 4, professional publications can provide a great (and sneaky) way to get in the door at your dream job!

What if none of them appeals to you? Well, back to the drawing board. Remember, every time you eliminate a possible specialty, you narrow the field, and that makes choosing the right one a little bit easier.

5. CONDUCT INFORMATION INTERVIEWS WITH PRACTITIONERS IN THE SPECIALTIES THAT PIQUE YOUR INTEREST

Now that you've got *some* ideas about what you think you might want to do after law school, it's time to go talk to people who are actually *doing* those things. What you're after is information, and that's why this process is called "information interviewing." (Pop quiz: If you were looking for a job, it would be called — you got it — a *job* interview.) I go over information interviewing in detail on page 143 in Chapter 4. But the reason I mention it here is that part of what you want to do with an information interview is to gather information about the intellectual content of the work.

How are you going to find those practitioners? Easy. Talk to your career services director, who'll put you in touch with alumni who practice in the specialties you want to check out. You can also see if your professors, family members, and friends know any practitioners in those specialties. I mentioned your career services director first because it's part of their *job* to maintain a network of contacts like this, simply for the purpose of giving you the chance to speak with them. So take advantage of it!

6. GO TO MEETINGS OF THE LOCAL BAR ASSOCIATION FOR SPECIALTIES THAT SPARK YOUR INTEREST

Very, very few law students bother to get involved with the local bar association, *and that's a big mistake.* When I talk about making contacts in Chapter 4, going to bar association meetings is one of the most important things you can do.

Finding out about the intellectual content of a specialty isn't the only reason to go to a bar association meeting, but it *is* an important one. What you'll want to do is to get the number of the local bar association from your career services director. Call and find out who chairs the committee on whatever specialty you happen to be researching. Call that chairperson, find out when the meetings are, and *go.* As I said, there are other reasons you'll want to do this — to make contact with people who may become your peers, to become known in the community and in doing so, grease the wheels when you *are* ready to look for a job, and so on. But finding out if the work itself is something that will intrigue you is *very* important, and you can do that by talking with people who already practice it.

By the way — make it clear at this early stage that what you're doing is researching possible specialties. There's no point in pretending that you're looking for a job, because you don't have the research under your belt to *get* one until you're sure about what it is that you want. Don't worry — nobody will think the worse of you because you're looking. Quite the opposite: practitioners will be impressed with the creative and diligent way you're going about your research!

2. FIGURING OUT HOW YOUR PERSONALITY MESHES WITH THE SPECIALTIES THAT APPEAL TO YOU

Ahhh — this is where all that legwork about getting to know yourself really pays off! The fact is, it doesn't much matter if a specialty appeals to you intellectually if you've got completely the wrong personality to practice it.

How do you figure this out? One is to think about what you've learned in this chapter, and piece it together for yourself. Look at the extracurriculars that have attracted you, the values you have, and think about how those might match different specialties. Florida's Ann Skalaski points out, "If you like helping people, go to legal services or the public defenders' office — not corporate law. If you're shy, and that's stopped you from doing a trial competition at school, then it probably says you'd never want to be a litigator." Lisa Abrams adds, "If you're an extrovert, and you get your energy from people, you'll be unhappy holed away doing research, away from people contact." Gail Cutter says, "If you don't like having the rug pulled out from under you, you don't like risk-taking, then you shouldn't go to the district attorney's office or a small firm." And if your family is important to you and it's a high priority for you to spend a lot of time with them, *don't* go to a large firm — quality family time and 100-hour workweeks are not compatible!

So you clearly *can* draw a few conclusions from the work you've done in this chapter. But that's not the only way to figure out where your personality would fit the best. Talk with your career services director, telling them what you've learned from thinking about yourself and what you want. They'll be able to guide you toward specialties that you'd enjoy. And you can use information interviews the same way (remember, I discuss those in detail in Chapter 4 on page 143). When you do information interviews, look at the personality of the person you're interviewing, and their colleagues in the same specialty. Are these people like you? Do you feel comfortable around them? You can even ask questions directly on point, like, "What kinds of personal traits do you think successful practitioners in this field have?" The message here is: use all the tools at your disposal to see if you've got the right personal fit with the specialty!

3. FIGURING OUT WHAT KIND OF *SETTING* APPEALS TO YOU

When I talk about setting, I'm talking about all the nonintellectual aspects of the work you'll be doing. Do you want a large organization, or a small one? Private practice, or working for the government? Working for the judiciary? Or the military? You may already have a notion of the kind of setting you'd most enjoy, and if so, that's great! If not, you can use many of the resources I've discussed elsewhere in this chapter to help make your decision, including:

+ Your career services director.

+ Any alumni your career services director steers you to.

+ Any practitioners you already know.

You can also use information interviews and bar association meetings as a vehicle for discussing not just the intellectual appeal of various specialties (as I've discussed before), but also to pick people's brains about why they chose the specific setting they chose. If you speak with enough people, I promise you you'll find someone who practices in a setting that appeals to you!

You can also scan Appendix C, on page 67, at the end of this chapter, which gives you an idea of the traditional settings for law practice. It's not an exclusive list by any means, but it *does* give you a snapshot of what the most common settings are. In a nutshell, the traditional settings are law firms, sole practice, government, administrative agencies, the judiciary, the legislature, the military, public interest organizations, and corporations.

Think you might want a nontraditional career instead? Go to Chapter 13, where I'll give you some leads to pursue in deciding if that's really what you want.

E. HELP! I'M STUCK!

So. Here we are. You've done whatever soul searching you're willing to do. You've thought about specialties, to the extent you're willing to think about them. You've considered settings you might want to work in. And you're stuck. You just don't know what the heck you want. Tsk, tsk, tsk. What am I going to do with you? I'll *tell* you what. For a start, I'm not going to make you feel guilty about it. Heck, I don't think I knew what I wanted to do until the week after graduation, and I don't think I started thinking about it until then, either. (I'm not recommending that, by the way.)

What I'm going to do is to go through a few things that might have gotten you stuck in the first place. Maybe if you read them you'll recognize yourself, and it'll help get you unstuck. If you're still stuck, I'd strongly recommend that you go and meet with your career services director, and tell them your predicament. Trust me. It won't be the first time they've heard it. In fact, it probably won't even be the *hundredth* time they've heard it. And they may be able to get you off of Square One.

If none of that works — I'm going to end this section with a rather radical suggestion for you. But first, let's take a look at what the problem might be.

1. SO . . . WHY ARE YOU STUCK?

A. YOU'RE IN DENIAL

You've probably already heard the old saw (and you have to say it out loud to get it), "Denial isn't just a river in Africa." Law school career counselors all over the country report that there's a large segment of the law school community who just don't want — simply put — to *grow up*. "Some people just don't want to deal with life, to grow up and find a job," one of them told me. Another said, "Some law students don't even recognize it on a conscious level — they just don't want to have to deal with the idea of getting a job." Lisa Abrams goes even further: "Many people go to school to *avoid* thinking about what to do with their lives!" She herself was an English major, and felt that Society pushed her into law school!

So the reason you may be stuck is that you either consciously or subconsciously don't want to think about what you're going to do when school's over. You may not want to do what Peter Pan did and go and live with the fairies, but you sure don't want to grow up. Does that sound a bit harsh? Maybe. But I know how you feel, because that's how *I* felt. Thinking about what I wanted to do with my law degree was the *last* thing I wanted to do. But you know what? No matter how distasteful it is to you, you have to choose. And if you don't choose, your choice will be made for you, and it won't be pleasant. If you don't take an active role in deciding what you want, the people who *are* willing to do that are going to snap up all of the good jobs, and you'll be left with a bow-wow because you didn't want to step up to the plate and take a swing.

Why is it so difficult to take that plunge? Geez, there are a million reasons. One is that it's finally and irrefutably waving bye-bye to your childhood. The idea of being a grownup with responsibilities is *scary*, but once you've got a graduate degree, you really can't put it off much longer. Another is that while you're still in school, you haven't had to make a choice and stand by it. Any talk about careers was always in the future, and what you might decide later on. You can't be attacked for your decision when you haven't had to make one yet. But as soon as you pick something, there's a whole contingent of people who attack you for it, because no one job is perfect to every person. That's difficult to take.

Can I make it easier for you? Sure. All I'm asking you to do right now is pick something that you're going to go for, *first*. I'm not saying that you can't be a fireman or an astronaut or King of the Gypsies, I'm just telling you to make a choice — *now* — about what you want to do as soon as you get out of school. You've hopefully got a whole bunch of time to change your mind down the road. In fact, very few people are in their first job within 8 years of graduation. It's not forever we're talking about; you're not getting married. You're just making a preliminary choice about something you may want to do. So don't horribilize it and make it worse by considering yourself trapped forever!

B. LAW SCHOOL HAS LEFT YOU AFRAID TO TAKE A RISK

Maybe you can't make up your mind because your dreams have been dashed. And the reason for *that* could be that law school has made you risk-avoidant.

I wish I could take credit for this theory, but I can't. Wendy Werner at St. Louis University came up with it, and I think it's brilliant, and that's why I'm including it here.

Her theory is that law students are afraid to take risks because their dreams are destroyed by law school. As Wendy says, when people first start law school, they've got all kinds of dreams. They want to do nontraditional things, they want to do public interest — the whole gamut. But 3 years later, all they want is a safe job. They've canned any idea of dreams and adventures. Why? Her theory is that studying law makes people risk-avoidant, because they've spent all of their time studying cases about people who've experienced the negative outcomes of risk-taking. All of the cases you read are about people who stuck their neck out somehow, and wound up paying the price. And the inherent message in that becomes don't stick your neck out in the first place.

She says that the environment in law school only exacerbates the problem. When people go to law school, they learn a new teaching style that's very hard on their sense of self-esteem. And because everybody in school is bright and successful, all of a sudden you don't stand out the way you've done before. You might get mediocre grades. That does a *terrible* number on your self-confidence! As Wendy says, "It's too easy for law students to lose sight of who they are!"

Now, I'm no psychologist, and I'm in no position to tell you how to get out from under a risk-avoidant cloud that, until now, you may not have been aware of. But if you think this might be affecting you, *go* back to your admissions essay. *Go* back to your pre-law school dreams, and see why the heck you went to school in the first place. Sure, it could be because you were trying to delay the inevitable and avoid getting a job, but you must have had *something* in mind. Talk with your family, your friends, anyone with whom you feel comfortable, and get back in touch with your dreams!

C. THE THOUGHT OF STARTING AT THE BOTTOM OF *ANYTHING* APPALLS YOU

I've read a bunch of books on careers for lawyers, and I have to tell you, some of them make me laugh. Actually, some of the things in the appendices to this chapter make me laugh, too, because some of the jobs I've listed are ones you sure aren't going to be getting when you graduate from law school — like a federal judgeship, or as in-house counsel to a large corporation. They're ones you can *work your way into*. And the reason I mention it here is that something that may be discouraging you from making a career decision is the notion that you can't get what you want *right away*, and the idea of spending a few years toadying as you climb the ladder insults your vision of yourself. One career services director told me a story about a guy who got a clerkship at a law firm for the summer, and in the first week, all of the clerks were shown the copy room and how to work the fax machines. He walked out in a huff, saying he had *no* intention of making any copies, and so he wasn't going to learn how to work the machine. Well, kids, word like that travels fast, and needless to say, he didn't have to worry about working a copy machine anymore. The deep-fry machine at a fast-food joint, yes, but not any kind of equipment in a law firm!

The point is, as a law student you may be dazzled by what you've accomplished, but in the eyes of the working world, you haven't accomplished *anything* yet. You've proven you can go to school. And if you have the attitude that you won't work your way up, virtually nobody in the working world will sympathize with you, *because everybody there has already had to work their way up, and they won't respond well to someone who considers themselves too good to do that!*

So if you aren't making a decision about what you want to do because you aren't willing to work your way to it, get off your high-horse. There's no dream job *anywhere* that will fall in your lap — you've got to be willing to work for it!

D. YOU'RE AFRAID OF ADMITTING WHAT YOU WANT, FOR FEAR THAT YOU MIGHT NOT GET IT

One of the scariest things in the world is to admit that you want something you might not be able to get — at least not right away. Because then on top of disappointment, you've got humiliation — you staked a claim to what you wanted, and you couldn't make it happen. And that leaves you open to ridicule.

I'm hoping against hope that this isn't true for you. Dreams are wonderful things. They're part of what makes life worth living. And people who *have* them are a joy to be around. So if there's a little voice inside of you telling you what you really want, I'm *begging* you — give it a hearing! If you have even a slight notion of what you want, no matter how ridiculous you think it sounds, go straight to your career services office and talk to your career services director about it. I'll bet you your dream isn't so ridiculous, after all. And I'll bet it's not as unattainable as you think it is, either. (At least it's no more unattainable than *my* secret dream. I want to win an Academy Award for Best Original Screenplay. There. I told you. And you know something? It wasn't so tough!)

2. HOW TO GET UNSTUCK: PLAN A

Maybe nothing I've said here will help you. If that's the case, then *please* go talk to your career services director. And just sit down and say, "I'm stuck. I need help. I have no idea what I want to do." Trust me, going through that door and *saying* that puts you *way* closer to deciding what you want to do. The rest is comparatively easy. Most career services directors have a background in counseling, and they live to help people like you, with the help of all kinds of tests and resources that are way beyond the scope of this book. So make them happy. Give them a chance to help you!

3. HOW TO GET UNSTUCK: PLAN B

Now, where are we? You've done all the thinking, all the soul searching, all the talking you can possibly put up with, and you aren't any closer to deciding what you want to do. I gave you the job search equivalent of an Allen charge in this little section (an Evidence joke — go look it up), and it didn't do any good. You're at the end of your rope. What should you do?

Leave law school.

That's right. Go. Leave. Scram. At least for now. You know why? Because you're in a rut, and by staying in law school right now you're either (a) wasting money or (b) piling up debt, for no good purpose.

Now, what's the downside of doing this? One is that you've got a lot of explaining to do to people you care about. You might feel as though you're letting them down. Now this is going to sound hackneyed, but if they really care about *you*, they'll understand. *Nobody* who truly cares about you would want you to be unhappy. And remember — you're not saying you're going to stay away from law school *permanently*. You're just taking a break while you decide what it is that you're going to do with this dagnabbit degree.

You may also worry how it will look to future employers if you take time off from school. Will you seem like a wimp and a quitter? No — in fact, just the opposite! They will *applaud* you. If you can take time off, decide what you want to do with your degree, come back with a renewed sense of purpose, and be able to look interviewers in the eye and say, "I didn't know what I wanted, but I took a year off, and doing so gave me the perspective to be able to say for certain that I want to do the kind of work you do," *trust* me — *you'll shine!*

Now, this isn't to say that you should take a year off and sit around watching soap operas and eating cheese doodles. As Rob Kaplan points out, "You've got to use your sabbatical in a productive way. Get a sense of what you want to accomplish." Speak with practitioners, do some information interviewing, and see more of what's out there. Do some traveling, if that helps clear your head. Whatever it takes to help you decide, do it. And if after a semester or a year you decide that you don't really want the law after all, then you've saved yourself all of the time and money you would have spent completing a degree that you really don't want!

"Legal Fantasies: Why Lawyers Choose Law."

by Cheryl Rich Heisler and Arlene S. Hirsch

Reprinted with permission from The Chicago Bar Association Record (March 1990)

A seductive mythology has grown up around the issue of what it means to be a lawyer in America. For some, it is an expedient route to professional credibility. Others perceive it as the ultimate vehicle for personal wealth and power. Then, there are those who are captivated by the democratic ideal of liberty and justice for all. The strength of these fantasies propels students to obtain their law degrees without a deeper awareness of what it means to practice law on a daily basis.

Although these fantasies may undergo transformations in law school, most new lawyers still hope that the profession can and will meet their expectations. But recent statistics suggest otherwise. In fact, the legal profession appears to be suffering from a revolving-door syndrome. While national law schools enroll some 40,000 students annually, an equal number of practitioners leave the profession each year. When questioned, many defectors cite increased hours, greater pressure, more competition, less professional courtesy, and an overall decrease in the quality of life as the key reasons for their departure.

But too many lawyers are leaving the profession to chalk it up entirely to such causes. Intelligent, articulate individuals are continuously seduced by images that the practice of law can never wholly accommodate. By surrendering to the lure of these fantasies, they unwittingly make flawed career decisions that become precursor to later career conflicts.

Based on our work with disenchanted lawyers, we have identified six widespread fantasies that can interfere with professional satisfaction. For purposes of this article, we present these fantasies as if they exist in isolation; in reality, individuals may be influenced by several fantasies simultaneously.

THE PERRY MASON SYNDROME

To those of us who grew up in the "TV" generation, Perry Mason embodied the ideal of a lawyer. Mason was always on the side of justice. He was honest, ethical, highly respected, and tirelessly devoted to his (always innocent) clients.

Today's legal professional can never live up to that image. No one wins every case. Justice does not always prevail. The question of guilt or innocence is often secondary to the principle of fair and equal representation. In real life, attorneys compromise, play games, and take unreasonable positions — all in the name of zealously representing their clients.

Attorneys who model their professional image after Perry Mason may become discouraged when they discover that litigation often requires far more effort, and yields less dramatic results, than television melodrama.

BOB

Bob grew up in a small town where lawyers were more than just legal practitioners. They were also respected, civic-minded members of the community. A new associate in an aggressive mid-sized firm, Bob longed for the recognition and professional courtesy accorded to his small-town role models. Instead, he had little client contact, limited opportunity for firsthand involvement in his cases, and no free time to pursue other civic or personal interests. After almost 5 years of trying to reconcile his image of a lawyer with his real-life career, Bob fantasized about leaving the profession all together.

THE GOOD KIDS

Children often fantasize about what they want to be when they grow up. They pretend to be movie stars, astronauts, professional baseball players, and even Presidents of the United States. Many want to be just like their parents — like 8-year-old Becky who wanted to be a human resources director (just like her mom) or 10-year-old Lisa who already had plans for Harvard Law School.

Such ambitions often reflect more fantasy than reality. Children turn naturally to their parents for guidance. When parents have personal needs that interfere with their ability to advise their offspring, children can end up trying to please parents with their choices, rather than selecting occupations that genuinely reflect their interests. In essence, these individuals end up with someone else's career choice.

MICHAEL

Michael's father was a judge, whose entire professional life revolved around the law. He strongly encouraged Michael to choose the law because it was a "good profession." Although he practiced for 7 years, Michael never really enjoyed his career. Michael was surprised to discover that his father did not particularly enjoy the law either. By "good profession," he had meant that Michael could make money and be a professional. Enjoyment was never a factor in his father's career equation, but for Michael, success and satisfaction were intertwined.

ANDREA

Andrea's mother had given up her career ambitions to marry and raise a family. In different times she might have elected to become a lawyer. By realizing her mother's abandoned ambitions, Andrea made her mother very happy. Unfortunately, Andrea's personal satisfaction suffered. With no particular interest in practicing law, Andrea's work days were tedious and stressful. Lately, she has resurrected a college dream of becoming a fashion designer.

PROFESSIONAL FEMME FATALES

Before the women's movement altered society's consciousness about women's potential and place in the world, the formula for female happiness and success followed a cookie-cutter mold: husband plus children plus beauty equals nirvana. To enforce that ideal, a strict dichotomy between men's work and women's work was established. Women who worked outside their home after marriage were concentrated almost exclusively in nurturing and caretaking positions like nursing, teaching, and secretarial jobs. The more achievement-oriented arenas of law, business, and medicine were reserved for men. Once the rules changed, liberated women began to stake out new territorial rights in the law.

Armed with new opportunities to enter the professional work force, many women were ill-prepared to make informed career decisions. Instead, they continued to choose myopically from a new handful of acceptable occupations, using traditional male definitions of success as their barometer. Law quickly replaced teaching as the new gold standard for women. The new formula for female happiness and success became: law degree plus high-powered career plus sophistication equals respect.

Having achieved these goals, many women lawyers soon realized there was no room in the formula for "husband plus children." Feeling torn between two opposing roles, these women began to reevaluate their commitment to a profession that had not proved to be the panacea they hoped for.

SHEILA

Sheila was a 6-year associate with a prestigious firm. Married for 4 years, her timetable for achieving partnership overlapped with her plans for starting a family. Past experiences indicated that a maternity leave at this point in her career would be anathema to her partnership ambitions. Short of becoming the proverbial "super-woman," she had trouble envisioning how to satisfactorily achieve both goals.

THE GOOD SAMARITANS

Another common stereotype is that of the "good samaritan." Good samaritans enter the profession with lofty ideals. They often buck peer pressure to pursue careers with the goal of doing good for mankind.

But many of the good samaritan ideals cannot be borne out in today's world. The groups most in need of help may resist their efforts. Bigger, richer adversaries make formidable foes. And even the most zealous advocates can feel stymied when confronted with masses of rule, regulations, and governmental obstacles placed in their paths.

Many chose the law in order to contribute to society, to be part of a helping profession. But as social service-oriented lawyers often attest, their contributions usually lack the impact they had hoped to achieve. They go into the law to "change the world" without considering the difficulties inherent in executing that plan.

JENNIFER

Jennifer was a 10-year practitioner in the area of consumer rights. Having devoted her entire practice to helping individuals defend their rights against large institutions, Jennifer suddenly realized that her clients' adversaries were no weaker or poorer for her efforts. She had won some major battles, but she was clearly losing the war. To make matters worse, while Jennifer was just scraping by financially, her friends were making significantly more money and enjoying fancier lifestyles. Feeling like a failure, Jennifer began to question both her abilities and her values.

LOST SOULS

There are over 26,000 occupations in the United States. But few confer the kind of instant recognition our society confers on lawyers and doctors. Its extensive and rigorous training makes medicine untenable for many individuals; law, on the other hand, has often proved the most expedient road to a professional career. A mere 3 years of law school education, makes it a popular choice for bright, educated individuals who would otherwise have no idea what career to choose.

The law appeals to many because it is a clearly identifiable profession that comes complete with a professional identity that others can recognize. There is a ring of authority to the law that makes others take notice. Because this kind of recognition is hard to find in other professions, it can be equally hard to leave behind.

JAY

Jay enrolled in law school because "everybody said it was a good degree to have," even if he didn't practice law. He disliked it from the beginning, but for lack of a better alternative, he continued. Five years into his practice, Jay was unfulfilled. However, with 8 years invested in his legal career, the stakes had grown higher. In addition to the time, energy, and money invested in his career, he had also acquired a professional identity that was difficult to shed. In essence, he had buried himself behind a professional facade that was largely unrelated to his genuine desires and interests.

THE POWER BROKERS

The power brokers view a career in the law as their ticket to fame, fortune, and power. These lawyers fancy themselves "wheeler-dealers," and often envision using their knowledge of the law to their own advantage. Power brokers erroneously assume they can achieve their goals without pain or sacrifice. They quickly learn, however, that the law requires a tremendous commitment in order to develop the kind of knowledge and/or clientele that will allow them to be recognized as a force in a particular area. While many lawyers do attain a certain amount of notoriety and power from their practices, a legal career provides no guarantee of fame and fortune. Of those who do achieve such stature, many place their commitment to the law ahead of all other aspects of their life. They often come to regret such single-minded focus.

JAMES

Having geared himself towards a career "doing deals," James maneuvered himself into a position on his firm's mergers and acquisitions team. At first, the work was exhilarating: secret meetings, late nights at the printers, early morning flights to New York and Washington. After the deal was done, James proudly displayed a lucite cube of the "tombstone" ad announcing his client's newest acquisition. Over the next 2 years, he collected a series of cubes, but his enthusiasm waned. Although the deals were getting bigger, his role stayed much the same. As a further frustration, James lost control of his personal life. He could never keep dinner plans and his vacations were often canceled at the last minute to accommodate his clients' needs. Trapped by his own ambitions, the enjoyment soon wore off.

Conclusion

Every occupational choice requires an act of self-definition. The decision to become a lawyer (or a doctor or an accountant or a teacher) carries with it an implied set of values and ideals. It harbors a dream for the future — an answer to the troubling question, "What do you want to be when you grow up?"

Perhaps it is a compliment to the range and diversity of the legal profession that it aspires to satisfy so many different needs and motivations. Given the growing levels of attorney dissatisfaction, however, it must also be recognized that many of the myths that propel ambitious careerists to choose the law are engendered more by fantasy than reality. Increasingly, the legal profession finds it difficult to satisfy what must clearly be labeled unrealistic expectations.

Lawyers who are unhappy with their career choice are really saying that the profession is not meeting enough of their needs. These attorneys must retrace their career steps in order to discover where the road veered off — why their profession diverged from what their fantasies had promised them. When the fantasy fails to be met by reality, they often decide that the law is not for them.

Specialties: The Nuts-And-Bolts of 31 Popular Areas of Practice

This is a *very* brief introduction to the 31 most common specialties. It gives you a basic idea of the kinds of tasks you'd perform in these specialties. This is just intended to whet your appetite for these specialties. For more details, I *urge* you to talk with your career services director, and any alumni and practitioners you contact either through your career services office or on your own.

(These descriptions are adapted from the *St. John's University School of Law Guide to Career Development*, written by Linda Laufer.)

1. ADMIRALTY

If you practice admiralty or maritime law you'll likely spend most of your time involved with litigation — either defense work or representing plaintiffs in cases involving collisions, cargo loss or damage, personal injury or wrongful death, charter party disputes, general salvage, marine insurance, and limitation of liability.

Aside from litigation, as an admiralty lawyer you might be involved with:

♦   Ship financing.

♦   Drafting and interpreting bills of lading.

♦   Charter parties.

♦   Stevedore contracts.

♦   Pier leases and general agency agreements.

♦   Ship construction and repair contracts.

♦   Towing contracts.

♦   Pilotage contracts.

Also, because there's a lot of international shipping, you may find yourself involved with conflict of law issues.

In terms of setting, admiralty attorneys are found in solo practice, in firms, and in administrative practice. Some firms devote themselves entirely to admiralty practice, while others have a separate admiralty department, and still others include admiralty as a specialized area within their litigation departments. Administrative law practice in admiralty involves practicing before the Federal Maritime Commission, the Interstate Commerce Commission, and the Maritime Administration. You may also find yourself involved with arbitration, because that's how most charter party disputes get resolved. And you may even represent clients before the Boards of Contract Appeals in government contracts involving "disputes" clauses.

2. AVIATION

When you practice aviation law you may be involved in litigation or in rendering advice.

As an aviation litigator, your cases may involve crashes of commercial or private airplanes, helicopters, military planes, or space shuttles; lost, damaged or destroyed baggage, or injuries incurred during flight (for instance by baggage falling on a passenger's head or a hot drink being spilled by a flight attendant). Your clients might include aircraft and component manufacturers, airlines, individual airplane owners, mechanics, and pilots. Airplane manufacturers might be sued for property damage, personal injury, or wrongful death, with those claims being based on defective design or manufacture. Many lawsuits involve the crash of small privately-owned airplanes, and these suits may be brought against not only the plane's manufacturer, but also the pilot and mechanics who were responsible for servicing the plane. Airlines face lawsuits for injuring passengers and for losing, damaging, or destroying baggage. (These kinds of suits are generally controlled by the language in the ticket and on tariff regulations, which constitute a contract between the passenger and the airline.)

Aviation attorneys also get involved in FAA enforcement proceedings. In those, the attorneys may represent a pilot or maintenance facility charged with negligence in operating or repairing an aircraft.

Outside of litigation, aviation attorneys are sometimes called on to represent and give advice to corporate clients who want to purchase or lease a plane or create rules for using corporate aircraft, or clients who want to build an airport.

3. BANKRUPTCY

As a bankruptcy attorney, you may represent the debtor, creditor, and other parties in interest like landlords, tenants, and people who contracted with someone who can't meet their obligations. On one side in bankruptcy cases you have the debtor, who wants to work out its debts to rehabilitate and reorganize its business. On the other side you have creditors of that debtor, who want to maximize how much they'll receive from the debtor. Several scenarios are possible. One is direct negotiations between the debtor and creditor, where there's only one creditor involved. A second is multiparty workouts, where the debtor and a number of creditors try to restructure the debt obligations so that creditors get full payment over an extended period of time, or so that creditors get only partial repayment and forgive the rest of the debt. A third scenario is bankruptcy proceedings under the Federal Bankruptcy Code, which include Chapter 7 (where the debtor gets a fresh start after its assets are distributed to creditors); Chapter 11 (where the debtor is "reorganized" and creditors get an interest in the reorganized entity); and Chapter 13 (where an individual debtor with regular income agrees to devote portions of future income to creditors, while still holding onto his existing property).

When you practice bankruptcy you'll also touch on other areas of the law, including corporate, litigation, commercial, real estate, and tax, and you'll also require skill in conducting negotiations.

4. CIVIL RIGHTS

As a civil rights attorney, you handle matters involving discrimination on the basis of race, color, religion, sex, national origin, handicap, ancestry, or age. Discrimination can arise in several different contexts, including employment, housing, credit matters, and access to and use of public places. You can bring cases before a city or state's civil rights or human rights commission, a federal agency, or in state or federal court. If you practice civil rights law, you may work for a city, state or federal agency, or for firms, corporations, or legal services organizations.

5. COMPUTER LAW

When you practice computer law you may represent either the high-tech companies who sell computer goods and services, or those who use those goods and services. Your practice involves negotiating and drafting agreements, including software licenses, hardware purchase agreements, software development agreements, and equipment leases. You find that a lot of attorneys who practice computer law have a background in computers and experience as systems analysts, software developers, and computer consultants.

6. CORPORATE

As a corporate lawyer you provide a wide range of legal services to publicly and privately-held businesses. Your services are likely to include rendering advice and preparing documents on many different things, including:

♦   Forming and starting-up companies.

♦   Directors' and shareholders' meetings.

♦   Annual meetings.

♦   Annual reports.

♦   Securities filings.

♦   Mergers and acquisitions.

♦   Joint ventures.

- Leveraged buyouts.
- Contracts for the sale of goods or services.
- Employee contracts.
- Restrictive covenants or covenants not to compete.
- Proxy solicitations.
- Reports to state and federal regulatory agencies.
- Dissolving companies.

As a corporate lawyer you may also negotiate transactions like mergers and acquisitions for your corporate clients. In terms of setting, you may work for a law firm or as in-house counsel for a corporation. If you work for a corporation, you'll likely wind up involved in strategic business planning.

7. CRIMINAL

When you practice criminal law, you've got one of two basic choices to make. Either you prosecute people accused of a crime, or you defend them. Attorneys who prosecute people accused of violating state or local criminal laws are called "district attorneys" or "DA's". Those who prosecute people accused of violating *federal* criminal statutes are called "U.S. Attorneys."

If you choose to defend suspects instead of prosecute them, you may find yourself representing people accused of crime ranging from the pettiest of thefts to highly publicized drug deals or securities frauds.

In terms of getting started in a criminal law practice, you'll find that District Attorneys' offices, as well as firms and Legal Aid offices, hire people who've just graduated from law school. The U.S. Attorneys' offices usually consider only attorneys with at least 2 years' experience.

8. DEFAMATION/FIRST AMENDMENT LAW

With this specialty, you'll be involved with questions of whether written or spoken statements harmed a person's reputation, as well as constitutional questions involving the rights of free speech and free press. Your clients may include:

- Media companies like newspapers, magazines, and television networks.
- People who work for media companies.

- People who are considered public figures.

- Any other people who claim their reputations were harmed or that their rights to free speech or free press were infringed.

9. ELDER LAW

In this unique area of the law, you're called upon to integrate a broad knowledge of the law with an understanding of the needs of older people. When you practice elder law you get involved with a variety of issues, including:

- Life planning and the use of directives like powers of attorney and healthcare proxies.

- Social Security and Medicare benefits.

- Medicaid planning.

- Spousal support.

- How to treat income and resources for institutionalized individuals and legally responsible relatives.

- Appointing conservators.

- Admitting people into nursing homes and nursing home residents' right.

- Estate planning and administration.

- Estate and gift taxes.

10. ERISA/EMPLOYEE BENEFITS AND EXECUTIVE COMPENSATION

When you practice in this area, you give advice on creating and administering employee benefit and retirement plans and executive compensation plans to clients like corporations, public and private employers, unions, banks, and trust departments. Benefit plans include qualified pension plans, profit-sharing plans, stock bonus plans, health benefit plans, and disability plans. Executive compensation includes incentive compensation plans, stock option plans, and capital accumulation plans.

If you practice in this area you'll probably be called an ERISA attorney, because a lot of your work will involve complying with the Employee Retirement Income Security Act of 1974 (ERISA). You also have to make sure that your client's benefit and retirement programs comply with the Internal Revenue Code. Mergers and acquisitions are another source of potential business for you, because they involve issues of what to do with benefit and retirement programs.

11. ENTERTAINMENT/SPORTS

If you are an entertainment or sports lawyer, your practice will involve representing entertainers and professional athletes in a variety of ways, including:

♦ Negotiating employment contracts.

♦ Negotiating endorsements and other marketing agreements.

♦ Interpreting contracts and other relevant rules and regulations in grievance or arbitration proceedings involving issues like salary, working conditions, discipline, equal employment compliance, drug testing, or injuries.

♦ Preparing tax and estate plans.

♦ Reviewing investments or developing investment strategies.

12. ENVIRONMENTAL

As an environmental attorney, you may work for either the public or private sector. In the public sector, you can work for either the federal, state, or local governments. In the private sector, you'll likely be representing businesses engaged in real estate development, industry, or manufacturing activities that raise environmental issues. Law firms also represent environmental and citizens' groups seeking to enforce environmental laws.

As an environmental attorney, you can get involved in a number of different activities, including:

♦ Providing advice regarding the requirements of federal, state, and local environmental laws (like the Clean Air Act, Clean Water Act, and Toxic Substances Control Act).

♦ Providing representation for actions charging violations of environmental laws (as well as in Superfund cases in which the federal government, states, or private parties can bring suit for injunctive relief from the release of hazardous substances and for the cost of cleaning up already-released hazardous substances).

◆   Engaging in negotiations with respect to permits for constructing industrial-type facilities impacting the environment.

◆   Providing representation at administrative hearings involving challenges to permits that have been granted.

◆   Interpreting the results of environmental assessments.

◆   Providing advice regarding environmental clauses in contracts involving the purchase and sale of businesses.

13. FAMILY LAW

As a family lawyer you'll need to know about domestic relations, as well as litigation, tax law, negotiating contracts, drafting, estate planning, and, sometimes, psychology and sociology. You may become involved in the most personal aspects of your clients' lives, particularly where child custody is an issue. Most of your practice will involve the dissolution of marriage and the economic partnership created by marriage. However, an emerging aspect of family law involves premarital advice and planning.

Representing someone getting a divorce may involve negotiating an agreement or litigating. Regardless of whether the marriage dissolution is contested, you'll often be concerned with matters of property distribution, alimony, child support, child custody, and visitation rights. After the marriage is dissolved, you may be involved with negotiations or proceedings to modify or enforce the divorce decree and/or separation agreement.

14. HEALTH

If you practice health law, your clients may include hospitals and doctors, as well as other healthcare entities like nursing homes, HMO's, and ambulatory care facilities.

If you represent a hospital, you may become involved in things like:

◆   Corporate, tax, and labor matters.

◆   Capital financing.

◆   Medical staff disciplinary matters.

◆   Medicare and Medicaid issues.

◆   Contracting for services and equipment.

♦   Physician recruitment and acquiring physician practices.

If you instead represent doctors, the matters you handle may include forming professional corporations, estate and tax planning, and third-party reimbursement.

15. IMMIGRATION

You'll enjoy immigration law if you enjoy lots of client contact. You need good interpersonal skills, and it helps to know a foreign language (although it's not absolutely necessary). It's also personally rewarding to practice immigration law if you went to law school with an eye toward helping others.

As an immigration lawyer, you deal with the legal and administrative problems of people who've entered the U.S. both legally and illegally, and also employers who want to hire aliens legally. You'll work not only with people trying to enter the U.S. for economic or personal reasons, but also with refugees and those who seek political asylum.

You can practice immigration law for the federal government, in enforcing immigration laws. You can also enter private practice, typically with small or medium-sized firms. A few large corporations hire experienced immigration attorneys to service their multinational clients.

16. INSURANCE

As an insurance lawyer, you're typically called on by insurance companies to defend insured parties in lawsuits where liability may be covered by an insurance policy. There are many different kinds of policies, and, as you might imagine, many more different types of lawsuits that might spring from them. For instance, people with auto insurance may find themselves as defendants in lawsuits involving property damage or personal injury caused by a car accident. As an insurance attorney you may also represent insurance companies in matters involving various types of claims, like eligibility for benefits or enforcing surety bonds.

17. INTELLECTUAL PROPERTY

The term "intellectual property" includes trademark, copyright, and patent law. You don't need any special training for trademark or copyright practice. However, to be a patent attorney, you need a technical background, and if you want to prosecute patents you have to pass a separate Patent Bar exam.

As an intellectual property lawyer, you'll prepare and file applications for registering trademarks (like company logos), copyrights (for things like novels, plays, songs), and patents (like mechanical inventions). You'll also handle any problems or objections connected with those applications, and you'll counsel clients and draft and negotiate licensing agreements.

If your client's trademark, copyright, or patent is infringed, you'll engage in settlement negotiations or resort to litigation to stop the infringement, pay damages, and, in some cases, relinquish or destroy the infringing items.

18. INTERNATIONAL

As an international lawyer you'll handle a variety of matters for U.S. and non-U.S. clients in connection with activities that extend beyond U.S. borders. You'll represent businesses in matters involving things like:

- International mergers, acquisitions, joint ventures, or other investments.
- International financing transactions, such as issuing Eurobonds.
- International development projects, like mining or other resource development.
- International licensing, sale, or enforcing of intellectual property rights.
- International trade and trade finance, like shipping disputes, sales agency, and letters of credit.
- International trade regulation.
- International tax.
- International arbitration of business disputes.
- International real estate transactions.

Apart from representing businesses, you may also represent individuals and their families for issues like immigration, residency, investments, estate administration, and taxes. You may also work for the U.S. or foreign governments and their agencies, in matters like trade and government contract.

19. LABOR AND EMPLOYMENT

As a labor lawyer you may represent a variety of clients, including employers, employees, or unions. You may work in a variety of settings, including private practice, or a government agency like the NLRB.

The kinds of issues you'll work with may involve:

+ Labor relations matters like collective bargaining negotiations, affirmative action compliance, and strike litigations.

+ Matters relating to employee health and safety.

+ Litigating employment matters like Title VII claims for discrimination under the Civil Rights Act of 1964, ERISA claims, wrongful discharge claims, and breach of employment contract claims.

+ Matters arising before administrative agencies, including the NLRB, EEOC, and OSHA.

20. LEGAL AID AND PUBLIC INTEREST

As a legal services attorney you'll represent the poor, the elderly, the disabled, or those deprived of their civil or human rights with respect to civil or criminal matters. (This obviously encompasses a broad spectrum, and to get into any detail at all, talk to your career services counselor).

21. LITIGATION

You're probably most familiar with litigation already, since courtroom drama is the kind of legal practice that appears on TV and in the movies. So you already know that litigators are simply trial attorneys. Your work can involve criminal or a wide range of civil matters, from admiralty to workers' compensation. You can specialize in one area of civil law, such as aviation, intellectual property, personal injury, or securities. Or you can "mix it up," and handle a variety of different kinds of cases.

As a litigator, you need to know how to handle a lawsuit from beginning to end. That means you need to know more than just the area of law governing the dispute, but also the rules of criminal or civil procedure. Your work includes all aspects of trial preparation, including:

+ Legal research.

+ Drafting legal memoranda, pleadings and discovery documents.

+ Conducting and defending depositions.

+ Producing documents, and examining documents the opposing side produces.

+ Preparing and arguing motions (like motions to dismiss for failure to state a cause of action, summary judgment motions, or motions for a change of venue).

+ Conducting trials.

As a litigator you also have to be a skillful negotiator, so you can successfully settle cases before or during trials.

22. MEDICAL MALPRACTICE

When you practice medical malpractice, you litigate claims brought by patients against doctors, dentists, and other health-care professionals who have allegedly been negligent. You may also represent insurance companies representing both patients and healthcare providers. So you can either do plaintiff's work (where you represent the injured patients) or defense work (representing the accused healthcare provider).

Given the nature of medical malpractice, expert medical testimony plays a significant role in determining the outcome. Each side relies on its own experts, so you work closely with your experts in analyzing the claims, gathering medical information, and preparing for depositions and trial. In doing so, you develop an understanding of complex medical information, which you simplify and put in everyday terms when you present your case.

Although it helps to have a medical background, you don't need one in this specialty. Instead, you can develop medical expertise, just as you develop litigation expertise — you learn by doing.

23. MILITARY (JAG CORPS)

Each branch of the Armed Forces — Army, Navy, Air Force, Coast Guard, and Marines — has its own JAG Corps, which stands for "Judge Advocate General's" Corps. To become a member of the JAG Corps, you must enter active duty in one of these branches. Because of the way that military courts-martial have appeared in movies like "A Few Good Men," when people think of military justice we normally think of JAG Corps attorneys as prosecuting or defending soldiers charged with violating the Uniform Code of Military Justice. However, as a member of the JAG Corps, your practice involves not only representing officers and enlisted men in matters of military justice, but it sometimes also involves representing and assisting soldiers and military dependents in other types of matters. You may also get involved with:

- Becoming a claims attorney (in which case you investigate and settle claims for damage by or to government property, or for injury to people who receive medical care from the military).

- Becoming a legal assistance attorney (where you counsel soldiers and their families with respect to all matters other than military justice, such as taxes, trusts and estates, and family law).

- Becoming an administrative law attorney (where you handle many diverse matters involving things like labor law, contract law, environmental law, the Freedom of Information Act, the Privacy Act, access to military installations, or interpreting military regulations).

If you are in the Army or Air Force JAG Corps, you may try cases before the Armed Services Board of Contract Appeals. (In the Navy, this kind of work is done by civilian civil service attorneys.)

24. PERSONAL INJURY

As a P.I. lawyer, you litigate claims brought by people who suffered physical injury against whoever allegedly caused that injury. You also litigate claims by insurance companies representing both perpetrators and victims.

You can litigate on behalf of either plaintiffs or defendants. Normally this kind of practice is handled by solo practitioners or small to medium-sized firms.

25. PRODUCTS LIABILITY

As a products liability attorney, you'll be heavily involved in litigation. People who were allegedly injured by products bring claims against manufacturers or suppliers of those products. By way of research and discovery, you have to become thoroughly familiar with the product, its manufacture, and how it is supposed to work, and you also have to ascertain the way the plaintiff used the product.

26. PUBLIC SECTOR/MUNICIPAL

Municipal law involves many substantive areas, including litigation, public finance, environmental, labor, education, elections, real estate, and intergovernmental relations. If you practice municipal law you'll probably find yourself specializing in one or two of those areas. Your clients may include state and local governments and their agencies, as well as private sector entities dealing with those governments.

You can do municipal work in a variety of settings — you can work for state or local governments, or represent private clients in law firms.

27. REAL ESTATE

When you practice real estate law, you can get involved in both commercial and residential real estate equity, as well as mortgage, investments. Your work will include things like real estate purchases, sales, project development, mortgage sale-leaseback syndication, and joint venture financing. In troubled times, your functions will often include work on defaults, workouts, foreclosures, and bankruptcy.

You can work in a variety of settings — firms, corporations, banks, or other financial institutions. And your clients may include buyers, sellers, developers, lenders, and borrowers. Residential real estate is primarily handled by solo practitioners.

28. SECURITIES

As a securities lawyer, you'll be involved in all matters related to common or preferred stock, bonds, notes, debentures, and any other form of investment in a business. Your clients may include the corporations offering securities for sale, investment firms, broker/dealers, underwriters, or the exchanges on which securities are traded. You may also work for the Securities and Exchange Commission which oversees securities registration, and which enforces the federal laws governing securities.

As a securities lawyer, you work will include things like:

♦ Determining whether securities must be registered under federal or state "blue sky" laws, or whether they fall within an exemption.

♦ Negotiating agreements with underwriters or any other parties involved in the financing.

♦ Preparing registration statements for public offerings, which disclose the history, business, and financial condition of the company making the offering.

♦ Filing registration statements with the SEC and answering any questions the SEC poses before it allows the registration statement to become effective and for the sale of securities to take place.

♦ Preparing and filing quarterly and annual reports with the SEC.

♦ Preparing proxy statements soliciting votes at a company's annual meeting.

♦ Complying with state "blue sky" registration laws.

♦ Preparing disclosure documents that must be provided to investors as part of a private placement of securities.

♦ Litigating when something goes wrong in the purchase or sale of securities.

29. TAX

As a tax attorney, you provide counsel to many different kinds of clients regarding federal and state tax laws and regulations. Your clients may include publicly- and privately-held corporations, not-for-profit organizations, partnerships, and individuals.

The kinds of issues you'll deal with include questions about income taxes, gift and estate taxes, tax-exempt status for healthcare institutions and not-for-profit organizations, public and private financings, and employee benefit plans such as pension, profit-sharing, and 401(k) plans.

Your practice may involve business planning with clients, handling audit and other matters before the IRS, and litigating tax matters brought before the court. As a tax lawyer you may work closely with attorneys in other kinds of practice. For instance, divorce lawyers consult with tax attorneys to determine the tax impact of financial arrangements between the divorcing couple. Similarly, corporate lawyers need to know the tax implications of corporate transactions. You may also find yourself working closely with accountants, financial planners, and people in other business-related fields.

30. TRUSTS AND ESTATES

In this specialty you'll typically represent wealthy clients in all the issues surrounding property ownership. You'll play a particularly specialized role in planning for effectively transferring assets at the owner's death, or some other specified time.

This kind of work requires that you analyze your client's assets, elicit and develop your client's wishes for how those assets should be distributed, and educate your client about the effective of substantive and tax laws on any actions they want to take, and make any modifications necessary as a result.

You also prepare documents like wills and trust instruments to effectuate your clients' wishes, and after that you monitor future developments, both in your client's life and in the law, to ensure that the planning remains current.

After a client dies, you are usually retained by the client's executor to render advice concerning how the estate should be administered, including probating the will and preparing the appropriate tax returns for the estate, and the executor's accounting and release. As a trust and estates attorney you are also usually retained to render advice to the trustees of trusts your client creates.

Although each stage of estate and trust administration can be routine, each can involve litigation, and almost every matter has some unique element to it. Trust and estate work has the advantage of not facing strict deadlines, but it requires a lot of attention to detail, and it involves more contact with clients and less contact with fellow attorneys than other specialties.

31. WORKERS' COMPENSATION

As a workers' comp attorney, you can represent either employees or employers with respect to claims for benefits to compensate employees for work-related injury or disease. Workers' comp matters start as administrative proceedings, and may work their way into the state court system if there's an appeal from an administrative decision.

If you represent employers, you may also become involved in matters relating to workers' comp premiums, self-insurance arrangements, and establishing safety programs.

Traditional Career Settings for Law School Graduates

The following descriptions give you a basic snapshot of the most common settings for practicing law: Law firms, sole practice, government, administrative agencies, the judiciary, the legislature, the military, public interest organizations, and corporations. This is, by necessity, just a quick glimpse; to learn more, you really should talk with your career services director, and any alumni or practitioners you contact through your career services office or on your own. For a little more detail on large firm practice, see Chapter 12. For more detail on nontraditional careers, see Chapter 13.

(The descriptions here are adapted from the *Case Western Reserve University School of Law Career Services Handbook*, written by Debra Fink.)

1. LAW FIRMS

A law firm is basically a for-profit business, with partners as co-owners and associates as employees. They generate income by cultivating and satisfying clients and maintaining and improving the quality of service they provide, while reducing their costs, which includes overhead like associate salaries!

When you work for a law firm, you typically start as an "associate," which means that you do work on a salary basis. After that, with luck, skill, and savvy, you move on to partner, where you actually go out and solicit clients (and in that way generate income) and you get a share of the partnership's profits. (The associate-to-partner track isn't the only way to operate in a law firm; especially in large firms, there are nonpartnership-track job possibilities as a staff or contract attorney. I talk a lot more about those in the chapter on large firms, Chapter 12.)

By way of size, firms go all the way from megafirms with more than 1,500 attorneys, down to simple partnerships. In fact, most lawyers practice in firms with fewer than 10 lawyers, but since they don't get as much press as the giant firms, it sometimes doesn't seem that way. If a firm has over 100 lawyers, it will typically have a lot of different practice areas, so that one client can work with many lawyers in different departments, typically in different cities, depending on what the client's needs are.

There are two different basic types of firms: client-driven or substantively-oriented. Client-driven firms handle clients' needs on demand, no matter what they are — mergers, dissolutions, acquisitions, bankruptcies, labor, estate planning, real estate, divorces, you name it. Substantively-oriented or "boutique" firms specialize in a specific field — like labor arbitration, or criminal defense, or education board representation, municipal bond work, oil and gas rights — you name the specific field, and there are boutique firms who focus on it!

Law firms also vary in terms of how rigidly structured they are. For firms with more than a hundred lawyers, there are typically structured departments — for instance, a litigation department, and a labor department, and a trusts and estates department, and a tax department. In these firms, it's typically very difficult to move between departments, once you're assigned to one. For firms with fewer than 100 lawyers, associates can typically rotate through several departments before choosing one.

Firms also vary by the types of clients they service. Very large firms typically have as clients medium to large corporations and their executive boards and managers, as well as government offices and institutions. Smaller, general-practice (as opposed to boutique) firms typically service smaller businesses, as well as individuals.

The atmosphere of any particular firm is unique, and so only the broadest generalizations are possible about the kinds of tasks new associates face, and what the atmosphere is like. (In Chapter 4 on making contacts, and Chapter 12 on large firms, I'll tell you exactly how you go about finding out what it's like to work at any firm, regardless of size.) However, in a very large firm, for the first couple of years, you'll typically handle research on a very large case, so that you'll be exposed only to a small slice of the total business of any one case. Small firms vary, although because you're a larger part of the staff in a small firm, you'll typically get more responsibility. While large firms tend to be very institutionalized and structured, small firms vary. Some are hard-driving and results-oriented, and others are more collegial. They also differ greatly in management responsibility and power of junior associates.

By the way, the purpose of summer jobs differs between large and small firms, as well.

For firms with more than 50 lawyers: They'll typically have a summer program for summer associates, whose main purpose is to lure top students in the hopes they'll accept permanent offers when they graduate. So the aim isn't primarily to get work done! This explains the wining and dining and sky-high salaries you associate with these summer programs.

For firms with fewer than 50 lawyers: They'll typically hire clerks year-round because they legitimately have work they need to have done, but the work doesn't require full-time lawyers or support staff. These clerkships typically pay on an hourly basis, and the experience you get varies on the work they need done. You typically don't get exposure to clients unless you ask for it. And when it comes to permanent job opportunities, they may or may not exist. But compared to large firms, there *are* some advantages. One is that they're easier to get. While I'll tell you in Chapter 12 how to get into a large firm if you don't have top grades, the biggest firms typically only take students who are at the top of their classes. A second benefit to clerking for a smaller firm is that since there are fewer layers of organization, you'll have more of a chance to work with senior partners, and since the work is less complex, you'll get a better overall picture of how cases and client are handled.

2. SOLE PRACTICE

Hard as it is to believe, 40% of practicing lawyers are sole practitioners!

There are a couple of ways to get into sole practice. One is to hang out your own shingle and develop your own clients and practice from scratch. That's very tough to do unless you have a prior career or some other built-in route to developing clients. For instance, one career services director told me about three students who were detectives. When they graduated, they set up a practice of their own. They continued to work nights as detectives, and spent their days a civil lawyers (so as not to create a conflict with their criminal work). As their practice picked up, they cut down their detecting hours. So you see my point: It helps to have an avenue for quick client development if you want to go into practice for yourself right away.

The other way to enter sole practice is to go into an office-sharing arrangement with another practicing attorney, who may subcontract work to you. If you want to hang out your own shingle, it certainly pays to either have a career before law school to use as a client base, or get some experience with another firm before striking out on your own.

Sole practice typically attracts experienced lawyers who are not team-oriented and are more entrepreneurial. It's more financially risky than firm practice, but it's potentially more rewarding a well.

3. GOVERNMENT

Did you know that the U.S. Department of Justice is the single largest employer of lawyers in the country? Outside of the Justice Department, lawyers are employed in every branch and at every level of government. The job opportunities are virtually endless; check with your career services director or a local law library for government publications that include explanations of department structure, number of attorneys, and contact names.

The most difficult aspect of government jobs is getting hired. The application process, even for summer clerkships, is slow and tedious, especially if the job you're applying for requires a background check. It's a crucial first step to identify specific departments and their hiring authorities. How do you do this? Go through your career services director, and from there find the names of alumni who work for the government. Contact them, and anyone else you can find who has a lawyering job for the government. Even if openings don't currently exist in the department, keep in contact with people so that when an opening comes up, you're the first person they think of! (Chapter 4 goes into detail on how to make and maintain contacts.)

4. ADMINISTRATIVE AGENCIES

Not many students think of administrative agencies as a career goal, but they're a great way to learn a specialty. You spend your time creating policy and gaining contacts that you can transfer to your own practice afterwards, or to law firm practice, or a corporation. (Incidentally, this is a great "back door" way to get into a large or boutique firm if your grades wouldn't get you in the front door!)

If you go to an administrative agency, be prepared to contend with a fair amount of bureaucracy. You won't last long if you're entrepreneurial. And also be prepared to make a time commitment to the job — sometimes there's a contractually-minimum 4-year stint. You're more likely to get hired or advanced if you're geographically flexible, since it's easier to get a job offer for a rural area. However, don't be too quick to dismiss a job in a rural area. For instance, for federal administrative agencies, where wages are fixed, your money will go a lot further out in the country than it would in a big city. (State wages vary by state.) Also, there's always the possibility of a transfer to another place further down the road.

5. THE JUDICIARY

As you might imagine, lawyers are found everywhere in the judiciary, as judges, magistrates, referees, clerks, and prosecutors.

JUDGES

Obviously you're not likely to start your legal career as a judge! The best way to learn about being a judge is to spend time as an intern (which is called an "extern" in this context). It's sometimes a nonpaying job (especially at low-level courts), but the benefits are great: you get direct contact with judges, you get to attend trials, research actual cases, draft orders and opinions, and gain insight into the workings of courts and judicial decision-making. And the icing on the cake is that you get a judge as an employment reference, and that's tough to beat.

What kinds of judges are there? In the federal system, there are district court (which are trial court) judges, appellate judges, and Supreme Court justices. There are also specialized courts, including bankruptcy, tax, claims, and international trade. Federal court judges are appointed by the President, and don't need to have prior judicial experience. (However, as a new graduate, don't plan on getting a federal court judgeship unless you have particularly compelling pictures of the President.)

The structure of state court systems vary by state. They typically have three levels: trial, appellate, and supreme courts, as well as special courts like probate, juvenile, and domestic relations. Most state judges are elected.

JUDICIAL CLERKS

A judicial clerk isn't a clerk in the way you typically think of a clerk, that is, as a summer associate for a firm. Instead, judicial clerks are law school graduates, typically straight from school. They act as a judge's right hand person for either a set term (1 to 3 years, typically), or permanently. Most clerks do a lot of research and analysis for the judge, and present it orally or in writing to the judge. At the trial level, clerks handle administrative tasks for the judge, as well.

A judicial clerkship is considered an honor, especially for federal judges, so the competition is intense. Grades are typically important, although if you make contacts effectively, as I'll teach you in Chapter 4, they can be circumvented. You generally apply for a judicial clerkship in the winter of your second year. A great way to learn more about judicial clerkships is to find out from your career services director about which of your professors had judicial clerkships, and talk with them directly. (A judicial clerkship is a common experience for law professors.)

MAGISTRATES AND REFEREES

As a magistrate or referee you reign over court proceedings and have decision-making capabilities, although not as extensively as judges. Many magistrates and referees also have externs and clerks, as judges do.

PROSECUTORS

Prosecutors work on the federal, state, county, and city level. Depending on where they work, they go by a variety of names. For instance, U.S. Attorneys are federal prosecutors, Attorneys General are state prosecutors (as well as being the title for the head of the U.S. Department of Justice), and then there are district attorneys, prosecuting attorneys, and so on.

There are a number of benefits to being a prosecutor. For one thing, it's a great place to get experience in criminal or civil trial work. Prosecutors' offices are known for offering early responsibility, and a very fast-paced environment.

Most prosecutors' offices hire students as volunteers or in paying jobs. Except for the U..S. Attorneys' office, they also hire new graduates. If you're interested in long-term job potential, politics play a big part. Prosecutors are usually either elected, or appointed by the chief elected figure in the jurisdiction.

As with administrative agencies, it's generally easier to get a job in a rural area and plan on moving to a higher court or a big city later on, because the competition is pretty strong for these jobs.

6. LEGISLATURE

Working for the legislature typically means being an aide to an elected representative, either on Capitol Hill in Washington, or for state governments.

Your duties as a legislative aide include supervisory duties, speech writing, committee and subcommittee activities. You deal with lobbyists (or you can become one), and you can influence legislative voting significantly.

If you want this kind of job, it helps to be the ultimate political mixer. It also helps to have some time networking under your belt, and so it's a tough job to get for a new graduate.

Your career path as a legislative aide is varied. Some aides ride their employers' coattails to the top. Others leave for administrative or executive office positions, or create or join lobbying firms or institutions lobbyists support.

Being a legislative aide isn't the *only* way to work for a legislature. You can also work for the Senate or Congress as a whole, where you get involved in cutting-edge issues through detailed research and high-level briefings before legislators and their aides. After all, for both federal and state levels, it's commonly lawyers who draft legislation.

7. THE MILITARY

Each branch of the armed services has a JAG (Judge Advocates General) Corps. I'm not going to go into detail on this here, since it's mentioned in the capsule summaries of career specialties in Appendix B, on page 60.

8. PUBLIC INTEREST ORGANIZATIONS

There are many public interest organizations, including the ACLU, Legal Aid offices, and Public Defenders' offices.

Naturally, the kind of work you do in a public interest organization depends on the nature of the organization. For legal aid and public defenders' offices, you directly represent indigents (the difference is that while the public defenders' office is an actual government office, legal aid is not). In other kinds of public interest organizations, you may work with special populations and/or causes, class actions, and legislative reform.

Both legal aid and the public defenders' office hire students and new graduates. You get terrific exposure to client situations. However, unless you go to a legal reform unit, your writing experience is minimal (although if you dislike writing, this is a real plus).

The process for getting into this kind of work is unique. Since it's real trench work, you'll be grilled on the depth of your commitment and your ability to relate to clients with whom you may have little or nothing in common. You may also be able to get in through a fellowship or grant — that is, where your pay is funded by someone other than the public interest organization (check with your law school for availability). You may be able to get your foot in the door by volunteering on a Pro Bono Students America project (described in detail on page 159). Your school may be a member of the National Association for Public Interest Law (NAPIL) or have a student chapter of the Student Public Interest Law Fellowship (SPILF), and there may be funding opportunities through them. Also, check with your career services office to see if any of your professors were public interest lawyers before they became professors. If so, they may still serve on the board of that organization, and that's a possible way in. The competition is pretty stiff for permanent jobs because the funding has been cut in recent years. You'll have to graduate and pass the bar before you're offered a job. Persistence pays! Show you're interested through repeated, polite contact. If you can't be this assertive, you'll have a hard time with the work itself!

For public interest organizations that are national (like the Sierra Club Legal Defense Fund), it's tough to get in as a new graduate. They typically hire experienced attorneys, whom they discover through *pro bono* projects. (If that's your dream, make contact with lawyers for the organization, as I'll teach you to do in Chapter 4, and get their advice about career paths that are most attractive to the organization.)

9. CORPORATIONS

It's comparatively easier to get a job with a corporation as an intern than it is as a new graduate.

Some corporations offer summer internships. Of these, some are in the legal department, on things like purchase/sale agreements and employee contract negotiations. Others involve work in areas specific to the corporation's products or services, like patent applications, trust and estate planning, and regulatory compliance. They may also involve work in tax, personnel, and risk management.

Permanent opportunities are limited for new graduates, since corporations typically recruit experienced attorneys from law firms. There's a good reason for that — they typically need substantive expertise and the ability to understand and control law firms' functions and costs in dealing with corporate clients, and that only comes with law firm experience.

There are real benefits to working for a corporation instead of a law firm. For one thing, you only have one client, the corporation. You may have to sell your ideas and recommendations to higher-ups, but you don't have to woo clients the way private attorneys do. Also, corporate practice tends to be more relaxed than private practice. The downside to corporate work is that it's typically not as prestigious or high-paying as private practice.

Chapter 3

Getting the Most Out of Your Career Services Office
(In Ways You've Never Dreamed Of!)

"Career services directors are possibility makers. They help you decide what job you want, and then help you figure out how to get that job."
Maureen Provost Ryan, Career Services Director
St. John's University School of Law

I've got a little fantasy for you. Imagine that I called you and said, "Guess what! For your birthday, I'm going to buy you a private career counselor. . . . I know, I know, they're expensive, but you're worth it. . . . Take as much time as you want. . . . Sure, she'll help you figure out what job you'd like. . . . Résumé, cover letter, no problem. . . . Of *course* she'll help you with your interview skills! . . . What? Contacts? Yeah, she's got a bunch of them. . . . Of *course* she'll call them for you . . . "

Now, if I gave you that, you'd be *thrilled*, right? I'm giving you something that's worth thousands of dollars! You'd never say, "Oh, ho-hum, Kimmbo, I think I'll pass. Thanks anyway." No way! You'd *kiss* me, right?

Well, then — *why the heck don't you talk with your career services director* — because that's what *they* are! A private career counselor for you, and they're *free!*

OK, OK, I know what you're thinking. "Oh, they won't help *me*. All they do is run the on-campus interview program. Swell. That does *nothing* for me, because I'm not in the top 10% of the class!"

Well, guess what. That on-campus interview program is only the tip of the career services iceberg. Most students think that's all career services offices do only because it's their most visible activity. *Every* career services director I spoke with bemoaned this misconception. "Most of the work we do isn't with the top 10%, because they don't *need* it. It's the other 90% of the class who need us," says Willamette's Diane Reynolds. Chicago-Kent's Lisa Abrams adds, "Most students don't realize it, but we identify with students who aren't in the top 10% of their class — because *we* weren't in the top 10% of *our* law school classes, either!"

So that begs the question — what should you use your career services office for? They can help you in virtually aspect of your job search, including:

1. HELPING YOU DECIDE WHAT KIND OF JOB YOU WANT

That's right. You don't have to wait until you know what you're after to go to your career services director. It's the one place where you should feel perfectly comfortable admitting, "I just don't know what the heck I want to do. I don't even know if I want to be a lawyer!"

They'll help you lock onto what kinds of jobs you'd enjoy, with all kinds of self-assessment tests. And they'll help you identify particular practice areas that you'll enjoy the most. So don't wait, and suffer, before you talk to your career services director!

2. HELPING YOU FORMULATE AND REVIEWING ALL OF YOUR WRITTEN MATERIALS, LIKE YOUR RÉSUMÉ AND COVER LETTERS

Don't send out *any* cover letter or résumé until you've given your career services director the chance to see it. Don't be coy — they've seen it all, and the more pairs of eyes you have proofing your work, the better off you are.

In this book, I'll tell you how to setup résumés and cover letters. But much as I'd like to, I can't review what you come up with to see if you got it right. Your career services director can, and would be delighted to help out. Take advantage of that!

3. Putting You in Touch with Alumni and Practitioners Who Can Help You

As I explain in Chapter 4, personal contact is by *far* the best way to get a job. If the idea of making personal contacts yourself makes you cringe, then take heart. Your career services director is a walking, talking, networking *machine*. As William and Mary's Rob Kaplan points out, "Career services directors are a kind of chamber of commerce for the law school — their primary function is to market students to employers." In the process, they meet and maintain a network of *innumerable* alumni and practitioners. So if you tell them what you want, they'll undoubtedly be able to put you on to someone who can help you!

4. Matching You up with an Alumni Mentor

Now not every school has these, but most *do*. What happens is that you're fixed up with what amounts to a "big brother" or "big sister," who gives you whatever advice you want. The beauty of this is that you've got a knowledgeable person you *know* wants to help you — that's why they offered to take part in the mentoring program in the first place! You can rely on them for all sorts of advice, and also to introduce you to anybody they know who might be helpful in your job search. And don't be shy about relying on them because you're afraid of bogging them down! As Columbia's Ellen Wayne points out, just the opposite normally happens; alumni volunteer to be mentors, and *nobody* calls them. That's a real waste of talent. If your school has a mentoring program, don't let it happen to *your* alumni!

5. Providing a Library of Resources, Both in Hard Copy and On-line

Books, directors, magazines, newsletters, law firm brochures and profiles, Lexis and Westlaw, Martindale-Hubbell . . . you'll find a virtual Aladdin's cave of research materials at your career services office. As I mention elsewhere, research is crucial at several junctures in your job search process, from finding out what's "out there" to getting the basic information about specific employers in preparation for an interview. Many career services offices go far beyond this, and keep files of *anything* they find — newspaper clippings, articles, you name it — that they think might help you. So for basic research, your career services office is a *very* useful tool!

6. GIVING YOU THE INSIDE SCOOP ON EMPLOYERS

The information you can get from directories and on-line databases only goes so far. If you *really* want the scuttlebutt on employers, go to your career services director. They keep their ear to the ground, and hear all *kinds* of gossip — and if they don't know the juicy stuff about a particular employer, they'll probably be able to put you on to someone who *does*. That kind of information can go a long way toward helping you assess if you really want to pursue a job with a particular employer. Don't overlook your career services director as a source of it!

7. MAINTAINING JOB LISTINGS

Now if you've skipped ahead at all, you know that I'm not a big fan of job listings; a lot of great jobs never show up on them, so it's a mistake to rely on them exclusively. But the fact is, some students *do* get jobs this way, and *you* might, as well! Here are a couple of tips on using job listings for maximum benefit:

♦ Make sure your career services director knows you and knows what you want. That way, when a job listing comes in, they'll call you if the job in question is something they think you might like!

♦ As San Diego's Susan Benson recommends, "Keep in mind that job ads look for *ideal* candidates. Even if you don't fit *every* requirement, apply as long as you approximate the credentials they list. That's because the ideal candidate might not apply for that job, and they *will* hire *somebody!*"

8. GIVING YOU WORKSHOPS AND SEMINARS ON EVERY ASPECT OF THE JOB SEARCH PROCESS

All the career services directors I speak with break their backs to put on all kinds of seminars and workshops, from career days to panel discussions to roundtable dinners with practitioners. And some of them even *videotape* those seminars and workshops so you can see them at your convenience!

Now these activities do more than just teach you job search skills. Your career services office puts them on to give you a chance to rub elbows with attorneys — a great way to rustle up great career advice, and maybe even a job. So don't ignore the missives you get about job search seminars and workshops. They're valuable!

9. TEACHING YOU INTERVIEWING SKILLS THROUGH MOCK INTERVIEWS

I can tell you exactly how to prepare for an interview and how to conduct yourself, but to get it right, you've got to *practice*. Every career services office offers mock interviews so you can hone your interviewing skills. Many videotape their mock interviews so you can see how you come off. Some even bring in real practitioners to do mock interviews — and some students have gotten *jobs* as a result of these mock interviews, with the interviewer saying afterwards, "You did a great job. Send me your résumé!" (Some students get even luckier than that. Maine's Tammy Willcox told me about a student who showed up for a mock interview with a local practitioner, and they wound up getting married!)

10. PROVIDING A SHOULDER TO CRY ON!

Everybody faces setbacks in law school as they search for a job. If you do, don't suffer alone! Remember, your career services director is first and foremost a *counselor*. Part of their job is providing comfort, and if you need it, reach out for it. "Don't worry," says Georgetown's Marilyn Tucker, "we're used to it!"

11. MAKING JOB LISTINGS AVAILABLE EVEN IF YOU GO TO ANOTHER SCHOOL

What if you want to use *another* career services office, for another law school in another city? You might be able to do just that! Rules on reciprocity vary from school to school, but most schools will at least let you look at their job listings and use their materials, as long as you have a letter of reciprocity from your own career services director. This is *particularly* useful if you're doing a job search in another city. And what the heck — it can't hurt to ask if they'll help you out!

Phew! Convinced? These really *are* wonderful people. I spoke with dozens of them and they *genuinely* care about you and want to help you find a job!

Now apart from using them for these specific purposes, here are a few general tips to keep in mind:

1. KEEP AN UP-TO-DATE RÉSUMÉ ON FILE WITH THE CAREER SERVICES OFFICE

It's a good idea to leave a copy of your résumé with career services, even if you aren't leaving it for a particular employer. Why? Because career services offices frequently get calls from lawyers who say, "I need résumés faxed to me *today*." Well, it doesn't matter how perfect you are for the job if your career services director can't track you down and get a résumé from you!

If you leave a copy of your résumé with career services, that's not a problem. That, along with telling your career services director the kinds of jobs that interest you, may be all you need to get you on your way to the job of your dreams!

2. MAKE SURE CAREER SERVICES KNOWS ABOUT ANY SPECIAL SKILLS YOU HAVE

If you are a whiz with computers, or you speak a foreign language, or you have any other special proficiency, let career services know! A lot of times jobs will come in that call for a special skill, and if your career services director doesn't know what you can do, she can't recommend you for that job. So don't be modest — make sure career services knows about your special skills.

3. MAKE SURE CAREER SERVICES KNOWS THAT YOU'RE LOOKING FOR A JOB — AND WHAT *KIND* OF JOB YOU'RE LOOKING FOR (IF YOU'VE MADE THAT DECISION ALREADY)

Many students mistakenly believe that if they don't say anything, everybody will *assume* they're looking for a job. Wrong! The assumption is just the opposite; if you don't tell people you're looking for a job, they'll assume you *aren't* looking. And that means that if they get any good leads for you, they won't tell you about them!

As I advise in Chapter 4, broadcasting that you're looking for a job (or researching the market, to people you don't know very well), is something you should do with everyone you know. You should *certainly* do it with career services. That way, when they hear about any positions you might like (or people who might be able to help you), they'll be able to pass those opportunities on to you. They can't do that if they don't know what you want, because you've kept it a secret!

4. REMEMBER THAT YOUR CAREER SERVICES DIRECTOR IS AN IMPORTANT RESOURCE, TO BE TREATED WITH CARE AND RESPECT

You wouldn't *believe* the whiny kinds of things students say to their career services directors. At least I'm *hoping* you wouldn't believe them, because I hope you're not one of the ones who *says* them! Remember that your career services director is the conduit to jobs, to alumni who might help you find jobs, and to the legal community in general. True, it's their job to help you with your job search. But it's human nature to go that extra mile for people you like. So when you deal with career services, make yourself likeable! Be enthusiastic, be polite, be grateful, and don't take them for granted. Think about it: You wouldn't want to help out someone who treated you like dirt. Well, neither do they. So don't do it!

5. REMEMBER THAT IT'S *YOUR* JOB SEARCH — YOUR CAREER SERVICES OFFICE IS JUST THERE TO *HELP* YOU WITH THAT JOB SEARCH

Boy, this is something that *lots* of career services directors beef about. Franklin Pierce's Sophie Sparrow told me about students who walk up to her and say, "So where's my job?" To which she responds, "I don't know. Where is it?" Tammy Willcox adds, "Some students have this misconception that I'm going to be this matronly woman who's going to feed them candy. No! I'm there to *help* students, and not just the top 10%, get jobs!" Washington's Teresa DeAndrado says, "It's a *partnership* between career services and the students."

So you shouldn't treat your career service office as executive headhunters or a placement service; they're simply not that. That may anger or upset you, but as Valparaiso's Gail Peshel points out, it's ultimately a good thing that they don't just place you in a job. "Some students think that they'll just walk in and get a list of employers who will hire them. Instead, we *teach* them how to find a job. That makes them happier in the long run, because even if someone *would* automatically hire them, that employer might make them *miserable!"*

Instead, career services gives you all the tools I've been talking about, so that *you* can find the job you want. Now throughout this book, I detail exactly how you should go about finding that job, and in many instances I encourage you to get the help and support of your career services office. But remember — no matter how much you turn to anyone else for help (and you should do that a lot!), it's ultimately *your* search.

So now you have a great idea of exactly how your career services office can help you. No matter where you are in your job search — and *especially* if you really don't know what you want to do — I *encourage* you to visit them. They're there to help you — and they've got lots of resources to do just that!

Chapter 4

Your Job Strategy: Making Your Dreams Come True by Making Contacts

(It's Easier Than You Think!)

"Law students have this misconception that their dad will be playing golf, mention them to someone in the foursome who happens to be a lawyer, and that lawyer will call them and give them a job. That's wrong! Getting a job isn't about in-place contacts — it's about meeting people who introduce you to other people."
Susan Benson, Career Services Director
University of San Diego School of Law

In this chapter I'll teach you the one absolute essential to getting your dream job. You could blow off every other chapter in this book — the cover letters, the résumés, everything — and *still* get a job if you do what I tell you to do here. (I wouldn't *advise* that, but you *could* do it.) Why? Because what I'm going to do here is teach you how to get a job by the most popular method in the history of mankind, and it boils down to one simple axiom:

It's not who you know. It's who you *get* to know.

Maybe those words strike fear in your heart. Maybe they create images of schmoozing, or glad-handing, or maybe even the dreaded "n" word — networking. In fact, you're probably saying to yourself, "Come on, Kimmbo, 'fess up. I know what you're talking about. *Networking.* And you just didn't have the guts to say it." Well, as a matter of fact, you're right. The reason I didn't call this chapter "networking" is because that word makes me want to throw up. When I think about networking, I think about standing around at a cocktail party with a bunch of people I don't know, clutching a glass of scotch in my white-knuckled hand, trying desperately to make small talk with some middle-aged lawyer-type with whom I have *absolutely nothing* in common, smiling a frozen smile and hoping against hope that there's nothing stuck between my front teeth. If you had mentioned the word "networking" to me when I was in law school, I would have run shrieking from the room, saying, "That's it — I'll work the drive-thru window, *but you're not gonna make me network!"*

But you know something? The reason I was so hotly against it, and the reason the word "networking" still makes me queasy, is that it's *grossly* misunderstood. Networking *isn't* schmoozing a bunch of strangers. It's taking advantage of people you already know to meet *more* people. You could compare it socially to meeting friends of friends — or to joining clubs and organizations because you have an interest in something, knowing that you'll meet other people with an interest in the same thing, and you'll have that common interest to discuss. That last sentence pretty much sums up what most of this chapter is about. Now, having said that, when we start talking about advanced contact techniques later in this chapter, it's true that I'll show you how to contact people with whom you have no connection, no mutual acquaintance. I'm even going to make *that* easy for you — but you could easily get a job without *ever* having to do that. So take a valium, OK? Trust Auntie Kimmbo.

I'll help you get a job, and I *promise* it won't hurt. In fact, you know something? I actually think you might *enjoy* some of this stuff! But let's say that you still have misgivings about the concept of making contacts, networking, relationship-building, making professional contacts, whatever euphemism you want to use is OK with me. Maybe you think no matter what I say, you don't want to give it a try. Well, I've got a bunch of great reasons why you should put aside any concerns you have, and at least *consider* putting into effect some of the networking strategies I'm going to give you.

A. A BUNCH OF GREAT REASONS TO GIVE N-N-N-NETWORKING A TRY, NO MATTER HOW MUCH YOU *HATE* THE IDEA OF IT

1. PERSONAL CONTACT IS THE *SINGLE MOST EFFECTIVE WAY* TO GET A JOB

There is *no question* that contacting employers in person is *far and away* the most common way of getting a job. And by that I don't mean having your father belong to the same country club as the employer, or any other kind of "built-in" contact you might imagine. No, I'm talking about simple, personal contact, by *any* means. In a recent survey by the National Association of Law Placement, *almost half* of the jobs law students got were through self-initiated contact with the employer or by referral from a friend, relative, or faculty member. (The next highest source of jobs was on-campus interviews, but that was *way* back with only 12% of the jobs found.) So if you make contacts, and you let everyone you know in on the fact that you're researching the market, you're *way* ahead of the game. As St. John's' Maureen Provost Ryan says, "Spend your time on the method that has the greatest likelihood of success! The one that definitely works the best is networking and personal contacts." Rob Kaplan, from William & Mary, points out that this is a lesson many law students refuse to believe until *after* they get out of school. "I get many calls from graduates who got jobs months after they graduated. And they'll tell me, 'When you told me to network, I rolled my eyes, internally at least. But when I actually got my job that way, I wish I'd done it while I was still in school!'"

Don't *you* make that mistake. I'll show you the specific techniques you need to make all the contacts you could possibly want, starting today. And you'll see that it is, indeed, *the* single most effective way to get a job!

2. *90% OF JOBS ARE UNADVERTISED* — AND NETWORKING IS VIRTUALLY THE *ONLY* WAY TO FIND OUT ABOUT THEM!

Boy, I heard this *everywhere*. Cal Western's Lisa Kellogg says, "Students don't realize it, but it's *rare* for jobs to be advertised. Ads in the paper just aren't the way to get a job!" Catholic's Amy Thompson echoes that: "Hardly *anything* is advertised anymore!"

Now if that figure seems unbelievable to you, look at it this way. As Albany's Sandy Mans explains: "Sixty percent of law students go into private practice. Most of *them* go to small employers; that is, law firms with between two and ten lawyers. Those kinds of firms just don't do campus interviews!" That makes personal contact the inside track for the vast majority of jobs in law — and that most likely includes your dream job, as well!

My own experience in legal publishing bears this out. Over the years, I've had to hire a number of law students as researchers, and I've *never* gone through any formal advertising process. I made a few phone calls to career services directors and professors, and asked them to put me onto students they thought might do a good job. I never wrote up a job description, I never did any interviews, and frankly I never looked at a single résumé. So you know what got *those* students their jobs? The simple act of letting their career services directors and professors know that they were interested in writing — that's it! Now, admittedly, some law firms are more formalized than that, and certainly *large* firms are. But I'll bet my experience is a lot more typical than you'd like to think. So when I tell you that networking can get you jobs and that most jobs aren't advertised — believe it!

3. YOU'LL GET THE COMPETITIVE EDGE BY BEING REFERRED *DIRECTLY* TO EMPLOYERS

If that iceberg hadn't sunk the *Titanic,* the amount of mail that law firms get from anxious law students *could* have. The number of job applications law firms receive every year is simply staggering! As Northern Illinois' Mary Obrzut points out, "Many law firms get two thousand applications for thirty summer jobs; Baker & McKenzie got *twelve thousand* résumés last year!"

Now, honestly – how are you going to distinguish yourself from *that* mob? As Maureen Provost Ryan says, "You *have* to avoid the flood of résumés." And the way to do that is through contacts that you make, starting today. You know how you can tell this is true? Let's do a little creative visualization. Let's say that you're the hiring partner at a hotshot law firm, Scrooge & Marley. And you've got a stack of résumés on your desk, all neatly typed, all on 100% rag content bond paper, and you've got to find yourself an associate. Just at that moment, you get a call from your old friend Fred McFarkle telling you that he met this law student at a CLE seminar, and he think the student would be great for your firm. Now what's going to have more of an effect on you — the fact that Student A's résumé is embossed on gold leaf in that stack on your desk, or the fact that you've got a personal recommendation for Student B? Human nature says that you're going to be far more influenced by the personal recommendation, and in fact that's exactly what happens. So instead of resenting that, why not make it work for you? I'll show you how to do it, and you'll see — it *will* give you a competitive edge!

In fact, you may find that you don't even *need* a résumé. One career services director in the southwest told me about a student who really wanted to work in Mexico for the summer. She had mediocre grades, and her only asset was that she spoke Spanish. She told her career services director what she wanted, and the career services director put her in contact with some companies near the law school that had plants in Mexico. She called them, and it was only *after* she interviewed that they asked for a résumé, as a formality. So you see, if you network well, not only will it distinguish your credentials from the rest of the pack . . . you may not need a résumé at all!

4. EFFECTIVE NETWORKING SKILLS ARE THE EQUIVALENT OF BEING IN THE TOP 10% OF THE CLASS

Everybody knows that on-campus interviews are typically only available to people in the top 10% of the class. Well, guess what. If you know how to use your networking skills effectively — and I'm going to show you *exactly* how to do that — there are *no* employers who are off-limits to you, *regardless of whether they normally recruit only through on-campus interviews.* As Willamette's Diane Reynolds says, "Students who are good about networking can propel themselves into the same category as the top 10%." And you know what that means? That means that regardless of what your grades look like, you can get the *very same* jobs as people at the top of your class. (If you really want to interview on-campus, turn to page 489 in Chapter 12 and read the topic called "Sneaky Ways to Get an On-Campus Interview," and Chapter 7 has advice for you if you're worried that your grades are really terrible.)

5. THE ANSWER TO "HOW MANY LETTERS WILL I HAVE TO SEND TO GET A JOB?" MAY WELL BE — ZERO!

The time-honored way law students think they'll get a job in law is to send out a bajillion-piece mass-mailer . . . although the use of the word "honored" in this context is really misleading, because *mass mailers just don't work.* You'll spend a lot of time doing a mail-merge on your computer, and you'll spend hundreds of dollars on postage, and you'll wind up with *el zippo.* And what's even worse is that because mass mailings bear all the visual proof that you've *really* done a lot to look for a job, you'll be all the more disappointed when they don't work.

Instead, you'd be *much* better off making even *one* contact for every 100 letters you were planning on mailing. As Florida's Ann Skalaski says, "Unless your résumé is stellar and your mailings are personalized, you *shouldn't* send out stacks of letters." And if you learn to network, as I'm going to teach you in this chapter, you won't *have* to. When your friends ask you how many letters you had to send to get *your* job, you can tell them the truth — none!

6. THE NETWORKING SKILLS YOU'LL USE TO *GET* TO BE A LAWYER ARE THE SAME ONES YOU'LL USE TO *ACTUALLY BE* A LAWYER

Think about it. The way you enlarge a legal practice is to make new contacts through existing ones. And the way you deal with existing clients is to make them feel comfortable confiding in you. As Miami's Jose Bahamonde-Gonzalez says, that means that "The same interviewing and networking skills you use to *get* a job are what you'll use to *perform* that job." St. Louis' Wendy Werner adds, "If you intend to go into private practice, your success depends on your ability to generate business. That means meeting people and talking with them. And that *is* networking." Boston University's

Betsy Armour continues, "It's crucial to be good at talking with people, at gaining their confidences. That's what networking does."

So when you master the art of networking, you're doing something that'll do more than get you a job; it's a dress rehearsal, as well, for what you'll be doing *after* you get your dream job. One career services director in the northeast told me about a student who volunteered at a lot of local bar association functions. When she interviewed with a firm, the senior partner was particularly impressed that she knew *tons* of people; it was much of the reason the firm made her an offer. So, if you have any qualms at all about networking, think of the long-term benefit you'll derive from it!

7. NETWORKING IS VIRTUALLY THE *ONLY* WAY YOU'LL GET OTHER JOBS DOWN THE ROAD

The heck with the job you're looking for now. Over the space of your career you'll probably have several jobs. And how will you get those? Through contacts you make. In other words – exactly the way I'm advising you to get your *first* job. As Rob Kaplan points out, "I'm always telling students that the reality is, once people graduate and change jobs, networking is the way you *get* those jobs. It's all based on your reputation and the contacts you have."

And that has some interesting ramifications for you, right now. That means that if you don't have the credentials to get a bunch of on-campus interviews — if you're not in the top 10% of your class — you may actually have an *advantage* over your credentially-gifted classmates. Why? As NYU's Gail Cutter says, "On-campus interviewing actually does a lot of students a *disservice*. Because they can throw their résumés anywhere and get a job, they don't develop the skills they need to get jobs. They use it as a lottery, instead of thinking about how well a job will be suited to their needs." In fact, studies have shown that students who graduate in the *middle* third from the Harvard Business School wind up being much more successful than students who graduate in the *top* third, largely because of their skill, born of necessity, in making contacts.

So it's true, you've got to muster the courage by forming a network now, and a few of your classmates with stellar credentials don't, because they can rely on on-campus interviews for a job. But you'll be *much* better off than them in the long run, because you'll already have the skills you need when it's time to find a second, even *better*, job!

What does all of that add up to? The simple fact that *networking works*. It'll work for you now, and it'll work for you forever!

But to get the maximum benefit from networking, you've got to enter it with the right mindset, and you've got to get over any mental roadblocks you have that will prevent you from networking. The next two sections address those two issues.

B. "REWIRING" YOUR THINKING TO PREPARE YOURSELF FOR NETWORKING

One of the things that makes networking difficult is that the subtext of it is that you want a job. And when we talk about jobs, we talk about someone *giving* you a job. The problem with wording it that way, or even thinking of it that way, is that it puts you in a one-down position; it makes it seem as though you're getting something without giving anything in return. Of course that's going to make you anxious! So what I want you to do here, starting right now, is to focus on the fact that networking is *not* a one-way street. You're not primarily *asking* for something, you're *offering* something wonderful in return — your services. You may not be used to looking at it that way, because you may not believe you really have very much to offer. Or you may feel like there are tons of other qualified law students who have just the same things to offer as you do. That's b.s., and if you think in those terms, it'll show in the way you comport yourself. You'll behave with less confidence, and that'll make you a less attractive job candidate. So instead of talking to yourself in negative terms, I want you to think this way, and talk to yourself in these terms: "What I'm doing is offering an employer the lion's share of my time, and my energy, and my drive, and my talents. And that's a great gift." Instead of thinking about how lucky you'll be to get a job, think about how lucky *they'll* be to have you. This may sound corny to you, but the words you use to talk to yourself have a *huge* impact on how you feel. After all, you think in words, and if you're going to make the most of your job search, make those words *positive*, not *negative*.

I'll give you an example. When I started my first legal publishing company, I was fresh out of law school, and I had to find investors. And if you think looking for a job is tough, try begging for *money* sometime. It's brutal! But if I had taken the attitude that there were tons of other investments people could make, that I had no background to suggest I could do *anything*, much less run a successful publishing company, and they were doing me a favor by giving me money — well, I'd have gotten nowhere. Instead, I *acted*, I *talked*, and I started to genuinely *believe* that I was giving them a great opportunity to invest in something that stood to make them a lot of money. They weren't *giving* me anything! Now, talking to myself that way, and manifesting that belief, didn't change the essence of what I was doing. I was still looking for money. But recasting it as a two-way street was the more fruitful way to look at it!

So don't think of your job search as a matter of anybody *giving* you anything. Along the way, sure, people who help you out with advice *are* giving you something, but people enjoy helping out that way. I'm talking about your ultimate employer. They're giving you an opportunity, but you're giving them the opportunity of getting something equally wonderful — you!

C. OVERCOMING ROADBLOCKS TO NETWORKING

Maybe you're starting to think that networking isn't so bad. Maybe you *can* convince yourself that you have something valuable to offer. But you may have roadblocks in your mind that stop you from networking effectively. Let's look at some of those misconceptions, and see how you should overcome them.

1. "I DON'T KNOW ANYBODY . . ."

For one thing, this isn't true. As Franklin Pierce's Sophie Sparrow says, "You've always been by yourself? You were raised by wolves?" You have family, friends, a social network. Teachers. Classmates. Barbers or hairdressers. When I talk about networking, I talk about *every adult* you know, *not just* those you think may have professional connections. It doesn't matter if you don't know any *lawyers*. As Ann Skalaski points out, "You may not know any lawyers, but you definitely know people who *do* know lawyers." Amy Thompson adds, "You don't need to *know* people, you need to *meet* them." And that's what I'm going to teach you how to do in this chapter. All you're going to do is what you've done for years without being aware of it — that is, you've expanded your social network by meeting friends of friends and taking part in activities. Now it may not seem to you as though *any* of the people you've met that way will be useful to you professionally, but the fact is that you don't know who your contacts are — who the friends of your friends are

— until you start advertising that you're researching the market. (By the way, I'll never say "looking for a job" here; it scares people off. You're just exploring your options.)

I can give you a concrete example from my own experience. Maybe you'll remember from the last chapter that my secret ambition — at least, as secret as it can be, appearing here — is to win an Academy Award for Best Original Screenplay. Well, to get the chance to clutch an Oscar and thank the members of the Academy, it generally helps to get a studio to actually make a movie out of a movie script that you've written. I've been writing scripts as a hobby for about 9 years, and I have a drawer full of them. Now, it's almost impossible to get a script directly into the hands of anyone at a studio; you have to get an agent. And they aren't exactly easy to come by, either. So when I started thinking about actually getting a script produced, my first thought was — OK, Kimmbo, who do you know? And you know how many people I know in the movie business? *None.* And I don't know anybody who might know anybody in the movie business, either . . . or so I thought. And here's where the lesson is, kids. I started telling everyone I know that I'm trying to sell a movie script. One person I told was my little sister, who's the assistant branch manager at a bank in Westchester County, New York. Now, I don't know if you know Westchester County, but trust me — you wouldn't exactly call it a direct conduit to Hollywood. Well, it turns out that my sister has a nice old gentleman as one of her customers. And she's chatting with him one day, and they're trading social niceties. She asks him about his family, and he proudly talks about his children, mentioning at one point that he has a daughter-in-law who reads scripts for a big Hollywood movie studio. My sister mentions my interest in selling a script, and he tells her, "Get me a copy of it, and I'll be sure to get it to my daughter-in-law." Lo and behold, she got it, read it, and liked it, and I've taken my first step closer to my secret ambition.

Now the point of this little story is pretty obvious. The assistant branch manager at a suburban New York bank is the *last* person you'd expect to have connections to Hollywood. Her elderly customer wasn't a whole lot closer. But it just goes to show what I've been trying to tell you — It's not who *you* know, it's who the people you know, know. So what you'll be doing is telling *everybody* about what you're doing, regardless of how unlikely you think it is that they'll be able to help you. I'm *sure* you'll be pleasantly surprised!

2. "I Don't Like the Idea of Using People..."

You may think of networking as using people to get a job. As George Washington's Laura Rowe points out, "Students think of networking as cheesy! It's taking advantage of people. It hurts your pride." Well, let's assume *arguendo* for a moment that networking *is* using people. Is that so unique in your life? When you ask a friend for a recommendation for a car mechanic, you don't have a problem with that, even though you're using your friend, in a sense. You're not manipulating your friend, and I think that's the important distinction to make. So it's only characterizing "using" people as a sort of evil manipulation that gives you qualms about networking.

There are a couple of other things to keep in mind. One is that networking is *not* using people to get a job. As Laura Rowe says, "You aren't putting people on the spot! You're flattering them by asking what they do, for their perceptions." You *aren't* asking for a job. What you're doing is laying the groundwork for people to *offer* you jobs. There's a world of difference there. So don't get all riled up over the concept of using people to get jobs, because you aren't doing that.

What you *are* doing is asking for help, and people *like* to help. So if you consider letting people help you as using them, then in this particular way you could say that people *like* to be used. People sometimes call me for advice about legal publishing, and I'm always delighted to help. In fact, it's something of a compliment to be considered expert enough to be asked for advice in the first place!

Being afraid of using people is a particularly insidious trap if it stops you from contacting connections you have. One career services director told me about a law student who desperately wanted to work for the EPA. She tried the conventional route of a cover letter and résumé, and didn't get anywhere. She wracked her brain for any connections, and told the director she didn't have any . . . all she had was a guy she'd worked for as a mother's helper on the Cape when she was 12, and she remembered he was a big shot lawyer in Washington. However, she was reluctant to contact him because she hadn't spoken to him in over 10 years and felt uncomfortable calling for a favor. The director convinced her to contact him anyway. She wrote a letter that started out by saying, "As you may remember, . . . " and recounted how they knew each other. She then expressed her interest in working for the EPA and welcomed any advice from him. As it turns out, he was *delighted* to help. He introduced her to his connections, and you've already guessed the outcome — she's working for the EPA!

So — don't let any misgivings about using people hold you back from making contacts!

3. "THE IDEA OF TALKING TO A BUNCH OF STRANGERS TURNS MY STOMACH..."

There's no question about it. As Wendy Werner points out, "Some people find it *very* hard to talk to people they don't know." And you don't have to be particularly shy for that to be true; meeting strangers can be intimidating.

How do you get around this? Don't talk to strangers! I don't mean to be flip, but what you're doing when you network is to use whatever connection you have, be it a person or an activity, to meet someone who will be valuable to your job search. Whether it's the mutual acquaintance or the activity you have in common, you've got a basis for conversation — so you're not really talking to a "stranger" in the technical sense. A little later on in this chapter, I'm going to give you a whole litany of ways to meet new people. Easy, straightforward ways that won't leave you at a loss for words. Once you meet them, it's just a matter of being outgoing enough to say, "I'd like to hear about what you do." If you think you can do *that,* you can easily master networking.

4. "I CAN'T STAND REJECTION"

Join the club. *Nobody* likes being rejected. And any time you have an activity which involves meeting people, as networking does, it will carry with it an aura of rejection. Whenever you're asking for help, advice, or information, there's the inherent risk the answer might be *no.* That's what leads students to far less effective, paper-oriented job searches. As Wendy Werner points out, "Students would like the job hunt to be paper-oriented. It's less personal if 'my paper meets your paper.' So I'll send a paper, and get a paper, and even if it's a rejection, it's a lot less painful than it would be in person." Amy Thompson adds, "Students are worried that people won't want to help them. It's like being rejected when you ask for a dance!"

You know why you shouldn't worry about rejection? Because it's very unlikely you'll get rejected if you make the right kinds of approaches, and of course I'm going to teach you what those are.

The key thing to remember is that what you're asking for is advice — *not a job*. And you're doing it through mutual contacts. As Amy Thompson says, "Put yourself in their shoes. If a friend of a friend asked you for advice about law school, you'd be happy to give it!" And Washington's Teresa DeAndrado adds, "You're not looking for a job. You're saying, 'I'm interested in doing what you do. How should I go about it?,' or 'What advice do you have?,' or 'I'm trying to find out what classes I should take,' or 'I'd love to hear what you think of your job.' Then it's *flattering* for people to talk about themselves. Even their spouse's eyes will glaze over if they try to talk about work, so you're flattering them when you ask them about their work!"

So your odds of getting rejected in the first place are pretty slim. But that's not to say that you'll *never* get rejected. The idea is to do enough networking so that it puts your relatively few rejections in perspective. Remember, networking is far and away the most successful means of getting a job, so you simply can't let an occasional rejection demoralize you. As Ann Skalaski says, "Don't get discouraged! It'll lead you to *nothing.*"

In fact, if you let what few rejections you get stop you from trying, you're giving those people a lot more power than they deserve. You're giving them the power to make you a failure, and they can't do that without your help. Instead, view occasional rejections as an inherent part of the process. Take a deep breath, and move on. I speak from experience on this one, because even in the act of writing this book, I networked my way to a few rejections. You've been seeing names of all of the career services directors I spoke with pop up throughout this book. There were dozens of them, and they gave me the great advice that I'm passing along to you. Well, how do you think I found them? I networked. Every time I spoke with a career services director, I wound up with the question, "Who else do you think I should talk to?" And in that way I spoke with great people all over the country. But along the way, there were a couple who just wouldn't speak to me. Sure, I wish they *had,* but they didn't. Now if I'd given up because of those rejections, you wouldn't be reading this book right now. Instead, I focused on the dozens of career services directors who *did* speak to me. And when you do your networking to find your dream job, you've got to do the same thing! As Teresa DeAndrado points out, when you network, "The worst that'll happen is they'll blow you off. They can't take your birthday away!"

5. "I'M AFRAID OF LOOKING STUPID"

Let's face it — law school is inherently designed to make you look stupid. There's a clinical diagnosis for people who go through First Year unscathed, without feeling inadequate *somehow*. As Sophie Sparrow points out, "Law school makes people question the way they think. They go to law school, and they just don't get it. They don't understand the cases. They start to not trust their instincts." Vanderbilt's Pam Malone adds, "Most students have been successful *before* law school. But then in law school they're graded against a much higher caliber of students." That leaves law students, as Maureen Provost Ryan points out, "With no faith in themselves!" So you've been humiliated and demoralized and put down in school. Why *wouldn't* you be wary of looking stupid when you have to make professional contacts?

Well, you can take the "sting" out of making contacts by wording your approach correctly, so as to minimize the possibility of feeling stupid. As Sophie Sparrow points out, you probably *would* feel stupid if you approached people saying, "I'm out of work; I can't get a job." That's like wearing a "kick me" sign. Don't do it! Instead, say "I'm exploring a lot of options," because that's exactly what you *are* doing.

Now one of the sources of networking I'm going to be recommending to you is your professors. I realize that there's probably no one you figure will make you feel more stupid than them! But you can minimize that risk, as well. If you network with professors, only go to ones for whom you've gotten good grades, or ones whose classes you haven't taken. If you're a First Year and you don't have any grades yet, go to professors in whose classes you feel comfortable. There's no point in going to a fire-breathing dragon for advice. Or maybe you'll decide you don't want to use your professors at all; you'd rather rely on alumni or some other source I'll recommend. That's fine, too.

The point is, the mere fact that you're researching the job market doesn't make you stupid; every single employed person in the country did that at one time or another. Don't let it hold you back from making the valuable connections you need to get a dream job!

6. "I DON'T HAVE TIME TO WASTE TALKING TO PEOPLE. I'VE GOT TOO MUCH ELSE TO DO, AND I WANT TO GET A JOB *FAST*"

There's no question that networking *does* take longer than mail-merging 200 letters to law firms. As Maureen Provost Ryan says, "Networking is a career-building activity that doesn't necessarily have immediate results." Fordham's Kathleen Brady goes further, adding, "You have to think about the whole job search as an annoying two-credit course."

So if it's such a time-consumer, why do it? Because it *works,* ultimately better and faster than any other job search method — and *certainly* better than mass mailers. But networking *will* take time. Making phone calls, meeting people, taking part in the extracurriculars I'll recommend to you — they all take time. And the fact that the task is ongoing means that there may be times when you just want to give up. Ann Skalaski says one of the main problems with networking is that students give up too easily. Well, you just *can't*. It's work finding work, but look at the pot of gold at the end of the rainbow! In Alcoholics Anonymous, they advise people who are tempted to have "just one" to "look past the drink" — that is, ignore immediate gratification in favor of long-term goals. As Maine's Tammy Willcox says, "No one has sympathy for people who don't try hard!" So if you want the job, you simply *have* to set aside the time to find it. You won't get your dream job *tomorrow.* But it won't take very long, and I'll tell you *everything* you need to do along the way. And when you're looking back from that dream job, you'll realize it was all worth it!

7. "I'M EMBARRASSED ABOUT MY GRADES . . ."

You may be worried about talking to people because your grades aren't too good. Well, grades aren't everything, contrary to what the on-campus interviewing process would suggest. Remember, only 12% of people get their jobs from on-campus interviews. As Ann Skalaski points out, "Grades will never get you hired. People hire based on who they *like.*" (If you want specific advice on how to handle really bad grades, turn to Chapter 7, entitled "Help! My Grades Stink!")

In terms of networking, what you *have* to do is to come up with a bit of patter about your grades that you feel comfortable rattling off. Rehearse it until you can say it freely. Run it past your career services director. It could be something a simple as, "I've got a 2.5 GPA. Boy, am I glad I didn't have to show my mom my report card! But my interest in environmental law stems from my work on a Law Review article for Professor Phlebitz. If you talk to him, you'll see. . . . " Or, "I've got a B-minus average. It would be a lot better if I hadn't crashed and burned first semester! Since then, I've done a lot better, and I've taken a real interest in Tax Law because of. . . , " and so on. You know your own circumstances, so you can come up with the appropriate statement. The idea is, have a couple of lines to say, don't apologize, don't be defensive, but then immediately take the conversation back to where you want it to go — your career interests. If you do that smoothly, you'll *doubly* impress anyone you meet. Why? Because you'll display self-confidence, a very important trait for a lawyer. The fact is, nobody can make you feel bad about *anything* without your help — you have to be an active participant in that conspiracy for anyone to make you feel bad. And you'll also be impressive because the clients you'll have as a lawyer will *never* have an airtight case. You have to know how to handle their flaws. So if you can do it with your own flaws with finesse, that augers well for you when you actually practice law. The bottom line is — don't let bad grades hold you back from networking your way to your dream job!

8. "I RESENT THE IDEA THAT I'VE GOT TO GO THROUGH THIS KIND OF HASSLE TO FIND A JOB . . . "

Maybe you feel the way I did when I was in law school. I thought, *Boy, I've done enough already. I'm more educated than most of the people in the country. Heck, whenever they ask for "Last degree completed" on those surveys, I'm gonna be able to fill in the very last box: "Graduate degree." I shouldn't have to do anything else!*

Well, I was wrong. And if you feel that way, *you're* wrong, too. As Chicago-Kent's Lisa Abrams points out, "As a law student, you just can't have the attitude, 'I've paid my dues.'" Because the unfortunate fact is — you haven't. All that going to classes and doing your homework get you is a law degree. If you want to get the job of your dreams *with* that degree, you'll have to work for it, just as if you were taking an extra class called "Job Search 101." The bottom line is, as Illinois' Cindy Rold says, "Nobody *owes* you anything."

Having said that, it's true that if you were the editor-in-chief of the *Harvard Law Review*, you wouldn't have to work to find a job. But you aren't. And between you and me, I wasn't either. Whatever it took to get into that position, I didn't do, and neither did you. Now what? You've got to do a little more work to get what you want, that's all. The work you *didn't* do to get into Harvard is work you'll have to do now. If you resent the fact that you have to do that and you don't make any contacts as a result, that's OK. You just won't get the job you want, that's all.

The fact is, resentment can torpedo *everything* you want, if you let it. I know that from personal experience. I was a fat pig for a long time because I was so resentful of the fact that my slender sisters could eat anything they wanted and not gain weight. I couldn't do that; if I ate anything I wanted, I blew up like a rubber raft, and stayed that way. But I didn't realize that it was the resentment holding me back until I read a diet book that focused exclusively on that issue. It basically said, "OK, thin people can eat what they want, and you can't. So that's not fair. Now what?" It was only then that I realized that I could let resentment keep me fat forever, or I could take matters into my hands, eat less, and lose weight. The job search is the same thing for you. Yes, a very few fortunate souls with great credentials don't have to work to get jobs. But you do. Now what?

Cold drink of water, isn't it? Well, the truth hurts. But I'll tell you a few things to make it more bearable. One is that networking really *does* get you closer to your goal with every step you take, even if you don't realize it. You never know when the next phone call, the next meeting, will open the door to the job of your dreams. Every time you make a new connection, your odds of nailing your dream job increase exponentially. Contrast this with the hapless student who doesn't read this book, and spends all of their time sending mass mailers, getting angrier and angrier, and gobbles up hours feeling resentful over not getting a job. As Georgetown's Marilyn Tucker says, "These students say, 'I've done *everything* and I can't get a job.' Well, 'everything' doesn't mean going over in your mind that you don't have a job. *Ruminating* isn't doing something!" So if you diligently follow the plan I'll lay out for you, you'll avoid that resentment trap.

Another way to avoid resenting networking is to look at it as an opportunity to widen your circle of acquaintances, and make new friends. You may be lukewarm on some of the people you meet, and may actively dislike a few of them, but you'll undoubtedly meet some that you like very much. On top of that, you'll be forging valuable professional connections. *That* makes networking a very valuable exercise indeed!

You can also get over your resentment by keeping your eye on the prize — your dream job. Yes, you *do* have to make contacts to get it. But once you're there, anything you had to do to get there will quickly fade. In fact, you may actually be proud of the diligent way you pursued your dream — as well you should be!

And finally, if your resentment leaves you truly discouraged and I can't say anything to make you feel better, then don't suffer alone. You can *always* cry on your career services director's shoulder — "Every day, if you want to," says Marilyn Tucker. Don't worry. They're used to it.

9. "NETWORKING GOES AGAINST EVERYTHING I LEARNED AS A KID, LIKE 'BE MODEST,' 'DON'T TALK ABOUT YOURSELF,' 'DON'T BRAG'"

When you were little, your parents told you not to brag. And they were right, socially — people who display an ego the size of Montana are typically shunned by polite society. But your job search ain't polite society; what you're implicitly doing is selling yourself, and so you better be high on your product, and *show* it. What you'll be doing is to walk the fine line between self-confidence and arrogance.

You've probably heard the axioms that convey this thought. Fordham's Kathleen Brady cites the Irish proverb, "If you don't toot your own horn, no music gets played." And Teresa DeAndrado points out, "For networking you *have* to brag. You *have* to talk about yourself. You *have* to bother grownups and busy people." In other words — you've got to ignore a lot of what you learned as a kid! Is that tough? Sure it is. But it's necessary. By way of personal example I'll use my experience with this book. When Harcourt Brace, my publisher, asked me if I could write a book like this for them, how do you suppose I responded? "Oh, gee, I don't know, it's not for me to say, I guess I can kinda sorta put a couple of sentences together. . . . " Well, if I *had* responded that way, you wouldn't be reading this now! I don't remember the exact words I used, but they were something like, "Are you kidding? I'll write you a *killer* book. I'll contact all of the best people in the field, and get all their best advice . . . " and so on.

Now if you're like most people, this kind of brazen self-promotion doesn't come naturally to you. It doesn't come naturally to me, either, but if I want to be able to keep my nifty "Kimm Alayne Walton — author" business cards, I *have* to do it. I learned to do it, and so can you. Don't worry. As you practice saying good things about yourself, they'll start coming naturally to you. And trust me on this one — it makes a huge difference if you speak with confidence about your abilities. After all — people won't appreciate what you can do unless you *tell* them!

10. "I WANT TO DO *CONCRETE* THINGS TO FIND A JOB, NOT JUST SCHMOOZE PEOPLE ... "

Let's take a look at this one. For one thing, remember, networking isn't schmoozing. It's just talking with people who know people *you* know, and asking them for advice. There's nothing cheesy about that.

But what the whole statement suggests is the underlying notion that there's something half-baked about networking. That comes from the sense that networking doesn't have the feel of doing something *tangible* about finding a job. As Rob Kaplan points out, "Networking just doesn't have the quantifiable quality that other elements of the job search have. If you bang out 200 letters, you can feel them, you can touch them, you feel like you've *done* something. Whereas setting up an interview with an '82 grad to talk about the job market in St. Louis doesn't give you that same feeling of accomplishment." And that's really the heart of the problem, isn't it? Telling people (and yourself) that you've sent 500 letters sounds so much more impressive than saying you've talked with 10 practitioners, regardless of whether those two activities took the same amount of time. But remember — those 10 conversations will get you *leagues* closer to your goal than the 500 letters *ever* will!

So it's important to get past images and think about what really works, regardless of how it feels. If you don't believe that now, you will by the time you finish this chapter!

D. STEP-BY-STEP STRATEGIES FOR MAKING CONTACTS

1. THE "P.A." SYSTEM

When you think of a P.A. system, you think of the public address system at your high school, right? Where they made announcements during home room every morning? As you know, the goal of any P.A. system is to *broadcast* something to a lot of people. Well, that's what making contacts is like; that's what networking *is*. You're making *yourself* known to people who can help you. But there's another reason to call your networking strategy the P.A. system — P and A happen to stand for the two avenues you'll use to get your dream job: People and Activities. In short, you'll go through people you know to meet *other* people. And you'll take part in activities that will create common ground between you and potential job contacts.

Now I'm going to be recommending a lot of specific strategies in this section. Of course you won't do them all — but if you take the initiative and make all of the contacts you can, and take part in all of the activities that interest you, I *promise* you'll get the job you want!

A. PREPARATION

Before you make any contacts, there's a little bit of preparing that you have to do. Let's see what you have to have in place.

1. HAVE YOUR "PITCH" DOWN PAT

You have to be armed with a few readily-available pieces of information when you start contacting people. Remember, these are professionals, and they'll be judging you as a professional. So every minute of prep time is valuable!

First of all, know what it is that you want. We spent all of Chapter 2 talking about *that*. (And we also talked about how networking was one way you could *decide* what your dream job is, by meeting people and asking what they like about *their* jobs. For more on this, flip ahead to page 143 where we'll talk about information interviewing.) So, in this chapter, I'm assuming that you have no more than three or four specific areas in which you're interested. Now if you find something else that interests you more in the process of networking, by all means pursue that instead! You're not married to whatever you chose first; you're perfectly entitled to change your mind. But it is important to have some kind of goal in mind as you network.

You should have a brief introduction to yourself ready and rehearsed: "I'm Kimm Walton. I'm a Second Year student at Case Western. I took a great seminar on Family Law, and I want to learn more about the field." Something like that, tailored to your situation. It's just important for you to be able to get the basics out of the way quickly, without stumbling. (In a minute, I'm going to talk about why it is you can't say you're looking for a job, in case you're wondering why I didn't mention that in this little mock introduction.)

You should also have your patter on any credential deficiencies down pat. For instance, if you've got bad grades, Betsy Armour advises, "You should defuse it by saying, 'Here's what I *can* do.'" I've discussed before the importance of being able to speak with confidence, regardless of your credentials. Get comfortable with them before you let yourself into situations where you might be put on the spot to defend yourself. As Kathleen Brady points out, "Remember that networking isn't a confessional! Don't ever say, 'Although I'm at the bottom of the class. . . . '" Keep your strengths at the front of your mind!

If you're worried that you won't be able to think quickly on your feet when you talk with lawyers, read the section in Chapter 7 on Interviewing that's called "Killer Answers to the Toughest Interview Questions They'll Ever Ask You." It's on page 356. That way, you'll be confident that you can handle *any* question a new contact throws at you!

2. ESTABLISH A CARD FILE AND A CALENDAR

When you're looking for a job, it's crucial that you keep good records. You need to know when to contact and recontact people, and you need to keep track of every scrap of information you learn about the people you meet.

How do you do that? Simple. You use a card file and a calendar. Let's go over what goes into the card file first. You'll need the large cards, the 5"x8" cards, and a box to put them in, with alphabetical dividers. For every single professional contact you make, you'll want to record everything you know about them on that card. Information to record:

♦ Name, address, phone (typically from a business card).

♦ When and how you met them.

♦ Who referred you to them.

♦ Who they in turn referred you to.

♦ Any correspondence back and forth.

♦ Anything personal they mentioned (e.g., interests, spouse's name, children's names, birthdays, anniversaries, anything that comes up).

♦ Salient points of your conversation(s) with them (e.g., what their specialty is, what they like or dislike about it).

Why keep track of all of this? Because you are establishing contacts you may have for a very long time, and you want to know everything about them that you can. Remember that the contacts you make may wind up being your key to a great job, even if they aren't in that position now; so you can't just think of contacts as being people you pick up and discard. As Mary Obrzut says, "Keep up with your contacts forever — you don't know who they know! Periodically let them know what you're doing." But months may pass when you don't speak with them, and you don't want to forget anything about them in the meantime. There's no way to do that other than to write everything down! And that includes offhand stuff like birthdays and family names and interests. It may sound corny, but people are really impressed when you mention their children's names, or make reference to something that they may have told you about months ago. (I know from personal experience how handy a file like this is. I *wish* I had the memory people think I have — I do it all with index cards!)

So that's the card file. You'll also want to maintain a calendar, so that you can mark on it when you should contact people. For instance, if you send a letter today saying that you're going to follow-up with a phone call in 2 weeks, mark a date about 2½ weeks hence (leaving time for the letter to be delivered) so that you're sure to remember to follow up.

The point here is — don't pretend that you'll be able to remember everything in your head. Take great notes, and keep a calendar.

3. REMEMBER THAT NETWORKING IS A TWO-WAY STREET: YOU SHOULD *GIVE* INFORMATION, TOO

This goes along with the point I just made, that what you're developing are long-term contacts. When you're networking, it's possible to become too focused on what people can do for *you* — who they know, what advice they can give you. But always remember that the contacts you make have interests and needs of their own, as well. (That's part of the reason you want to keep a card file on them!) As Valparaiso's Gail Peshel says, "Always remember that networking is a two-way street. If you see something of benefit to the other person, send it!"

So, let's say you meet a lawyer, Gisela Werbezirk, who happens to mention that she's very interested in Thomas Jefferson. Well, when you get home, you note on her card her interest in Jefferson. And the following month, lo and behold, you notice that *Civilizations* magazine has an article about how Jefferson's original draft of the Declaration of Independence was modified by others. Well, make a photocopy and send it to Gisela, with a note mentioning that she might find it interesting in light of her interest in Jefferson.

The same goes for contacts. It may be that in your networking experiences you meet two people who really ought to know each other. Here's your chance to help *them* out!

What does this do? It reinforces the fact that what you're doing is becoming part of a professional community; you're not just taking handouts from others. When you have the chance to return the favor — do it!

4. ACCEPT THAT IT'S GOING TO TAKE *TIME* TO FIND YOUR DREAM JOB

There's no point in being anxious about finding a job. I promise you that you *will* find one, but I won't pretend that the first call you make will get you a job. It will take effort, it will involve some inevitable setbacks, and it will take time.

Remember that networking is a process of making contact, and that *inherently* takes time. You have to contact people, set up meetings with them, take part in activities, do a whole host of things that don't happen overnight. As San Diego's Susan Benson says, "It may seem like an eternity, but within a year, you'll be sending out a business card. Time is a leveling factor. It doesn't matter how old you were when you learned to read, as long as you do now."

So don't be anxious about whether you'll find a job or not. If you do everything I tell you to, you will. In the meantime — be patient!

5. BE *PROACTIVE* THROUGHOUT YOUR SEARCH

I'm going to encourage you to rely on all kinds of people during your job search. But don't forget — This job search is *your own.* *You're* the one who's going to wind up with the dream job. And *you've* got to take responsibility for it. One career services director told me about a survey she did of graduates who didn't have jobs yet. She got a note back from one of them saying, "I've been looking for a job for 6 months and have gotten nothing. What are you people getting paid for?" That's exactly the kind of attitude you *can't* have. If your job search takes you past graduation, so be it — over half of law students don't have jobs at graduation. But you have to remain active, you've got to keep making contacts, taking part in activities, staying upbeat. Sitting at home moping about the fact that you're unemployed doesn't get you any closer to *being* employed. Take on a part time volunteer job, if need be; or do a Pro Bono America project (I outline those later in this chapter). That will give you not only experience, but also some great job contacts. As Sandy Mans says, "If you don't get your dream job right now, do *something*. Get *some* job. Don't sit at home waiting for your dream, because that only shows you're lazy." The point is, don't ever feel you can sit back and do *nothing*. You won't get your dream job that way!

6. START MAKING CONTACTS *TODAY*

All right. Enough prep work. You have an idea of what you want, and it's flexible enough to incorporate new possibilities you might find as you meet new people. You're comfortable with what you have to say about yourself and your credentials. You can't put it off any longer. As Ann Skalaski says, "The most difficult thing about networking is picking up that first phone!"

So let's hurry and get started, and get you over that first hurdle!

B. THE "P" IN THE "P.A." SYSTEM: NETWORKING THROUGH PEOPLE YOU KNOW

Remember, I'm going to show you how to get a job by making contacts via two routes: through people you know, and through activities. What I'm going to do first is to outline the people you should contact, and then I'll tell you the kinds of things you should say, and then I'll talk about the activities you should take part in.

In this first part, talking about people you should use, there are two very important things to remember:

♦ Don't leave *anybody* out. That's right; you've got to think of everybody, and when I talk about chance meetings, you've got to be aware of finding appropriate ways to work your interest in the legal market into the conversation. The thing that will hold you back from making a complete list is to tell yourself, "Oh, Fred (or Mom, or Dad, or Grandma, or whoever) doesn't know anybody." Well, you don't know that! As I've said before, you don't know who the people you know, know. So I want you to make a *complete* list, and I'll give you all the tools you need to jog your memory. And I'll also give you anecdotes about students' experiences, highlighting how important it is to be thorough!

♦ Don't assume that *anybody* knows you're looking for a job! As Gail Peshel point out, "In fact, the perception is just the opposite; people *don't* think you're looking if you don't say so." Laura Rowe goes even further, and says, "Definitely let your career services office know that you're looking for a job. You can't assume that they know you're looking; in fact, you can't assume they even know who you *are!*" So, no matter how obvious you think it is that you're in the market, say it anyway. When you're trying to meet people who can help you, it doesn't pay to leave *anybody* with the wrong impression!

With those two points in mind, let's go through everybody you should consider contacting. Some are obvious, some aren't so obvious — but don't leave anybody out!

What I want you to do is to get out a pad of paper, write each of these possible contacts on a separate sheet, and fill in as many names as you can. Think, really *think*, of all of the people you could possibly contact. Then put the list down, and go back to it over the next couple of days as more names come back to you. The point is to make the list as full as possible.

1. YOUR CAREER SERVICES DIRECTOR

I list your career services director first as a means of starting with the most important person for you to contact. Why? Because your career services director is a networking *machine*. That's most of their job, whether you realize it or not; they're constantly in contact with all kinds of people, in the hopes of scaring up jobs for you and your classmates. And contrary to popular belief, they do it for *everyone* — not just the top 10% of the class! Not only that, they're frequently the *first* person to hear about new job openings. As Lisa Kellogg says, "I get casual job requests from alums all the time. They'll want someone who's looking for environmental law, or someone who speaks a language like Mandarin Chinese. If a student lets me know they're looking, lets me know what their skills are, I'll know to call them when these jobs come in." And don't assume that your career services director will necessarily have time to come and track you down first. Lisa Kellogg points out, "A lot of times lawyers decide they need a clerk *today*, so they want résumés faxed *right away*." Diane Reynolds echoes this. "Make yourself *known* to your career services director. People who are known get jobs! I get a dozen casual calls a week from alums who are looking for students to hire. I'll post those jobs, sure, but if a student has let me know they're interested in something, I'll be sure that they hear about that job opportunity right away." It boils down to this: If your career services director doesn't know who you are, and doesn't know you're looking for a job, they won't be able to put you in contact with employers who might be looking for someone just like you!

In Chapter 3, I talked about your career services office in detail, so I'm not going to beat it to death again here. But you should never overlook the fact that your career services director can put you in touch with people in virtually any specialty, in any city in the country. They can put you in touch with law school alums who can help you out. In short, they're plugged in. They're a *great* way to get to other people who can help you. Don't overlook them as a resource!

2. ALUMNI OF YOUR LAW SCHOOL

You're probably thinking, "Gee, I don't *know* any law school alums. Why *would* I?" Good point. I realize that I'm cheating a little bit here, because I don't actually expect you to know any. But your career services director sure does, and alumni are one of the best routes for networking, which is why I've included them in this list of people you know.

One of the first things you should do when you speak with your career services director is to find out which alums practice in the city and/or specialty you're interested in. Then, you can either call them (if you're bold) or write to them or fax them (if you're a little less bold), telling them that your career services director recommended that you contact them, and that you're looking for advice, and you'd appreciate any they could offer. I'll get a lot more into the kinds of things you should find out in a few minutes, but that's your basic approach.

You may find that your school has a mentoring program; that is, a list of alums who have expressly stated their will'ngness to give advice to students. If your school has a program like this, by all means take advantage of it. And don't be worried that you'll be overloading these mentors with questions. As one career services director told me, the complaint is normally the other way around; the mentors call and say, "Why isn't anybody calling me for advice?" My answer would be, *because they haven't read this book, that's why!* When someone reaches out to be a professional contact for you, take advantage of that!

3. ALUMNI OF YOUR UNDERGRADUATE SCHOOL WHO NOW PRACTICE LAW

How do you find this out? Easy. On either Lexis or Westlaw, you can do a search that tells you the undergraduate school of practicing lawyers. Either that, or you can do a manual search with the Martindale-Hubbell directories (although that'll take a lot longer).

You may feel uncomfortable about contacting people you don't know, with your only connection being that you happened to go to the same school. But trust me on this one, people are almost always open to helping out someone who went to their own undergrad school. As Teresa DeAndrado says, "Go ahead and contact 10 or 20 undergrad alums who practice law in an area where you want to practice. Most people are happy to help. It's flattering!" And Maureen Provost Ryan adds, "Having the same undergrad school as someone else is a point of commonality. The more you have, the better off you are."

So when you're making a list of contacts, don't forget to do a search for *undergrad* alums who are now lawyers, as well.

4. PROFESSORS

"Eeeeuuuwwww!!" you're probably thinking. "I don't want to talk to my *professors* about looking for a job!" Well, nobody's twisting your arm, and I certainly wouldn't talk with professors you don't like — I can personally think of a couple *I* had in law school who I wouldn't have touched with a twenty-foot barge pole. But it's a different story for the ones you *can* stand, and who teach subjects you enjoy. You should certainly approach them, because they can be useful to you in several different ways. Sandy Mans explains one way: "Alumni sometimes call their old profs looking for talent." So, if you make it known to professors who teach subjects that you like that you're looking for a job, yours will be a name they remember when alumni come calling. This is *particularly* useful if you don't have a good overall

GPA, but you've got one or two stellar grades. The professor(s) for whom you excelled are sources you should *definitely* tap.

Another way to use professors you like is to get a list of alumni who practice in an area that interests you, and then take that list to one or more profs to see who they remember, and who you should contact. As Case Western's Debra Fink explains, "Then you can call those alumni and say something like, 'Professor Ignatz told me you might be particularly helpful,' or, 'Your old law school prof, Professor Bungle, told me to give you a call. . . . '" That way you turn what might otherwise have been a cold call, or a blah cover letter, into something that will definitely create interest in you.

You *may* also want to use professors to clinch a job you really want. One career services director down south told me about a law student who had so-so grades, who really wanted to do a judicial clerkship. By using her family and alums for contacts, she got an interview at the county prosecutor's office. After the interview, she asked a couple of her professors to call the county prosecutor's office with unsolicited recommendations for her. These calls pushed her over the top and she got the job. And it's *also* the way she got her next job — a federal district court clerkship, which, in case you don't know it, is a real plum that normally requires excellent grades. Now I wouldn't lean on your professors too much as unsolicited references like this, but it's a definite possibility if you feel you're close to getting a job you really want.

5. TEACHING ASSISTANTS (LIKE LEGAL WRITING INSTRUCTORS WHO ARE UPPERCLASSMEN)

Teaching assistants can be particularly useful to you because you know them pretty well, and they're likely to be close to your own age, which makes them easier to approach. As Sophie Sparrow recommends, "Just go to them and ask them how they figured out what they wanted to do, and how they're going about getting there." It may turn out that they've got contacts they can put you on to, and since they're familiar with your work, their recommendation will carry some real weight.

6. CLASSMATES

As Teresa DeAndrado points out, "Don't forget that your classmates are going to be your professional colleagues. Look at them that way! You can use them for networking, too." That's a good point because it's very easy to overlook your classmates as being sources of contacts. I know I always thought of my classmates as drinking buddies, and that's about it. But everything that could be said for any other kind of contact, be it a family member or friend, could be said for your classmates as well. Let them know you're looking for a job, and what kind of thing interests you.

What may make this difficult for you at first is that you may feel competitive with your classmates, as though you're all looking for the same jobs. It's worth getting over that, because what you're likely to find is that if you've thought about what you want to do, your interests are sufficiently different from your colleagues' so that you don't have to worry about competition. And remember to reciprocate! If colleagues tell you about what *they're* looking for, put them onto any contacts you find who may be able to help *them!*

7. PARENTS

If your father is a partner at Shearman & Sterling, my guess is that you've already thought of this one. But the fact is, most of us *don't* have parents who are attorneys. And it may strike you that your parents don't know any attorneys, so it's pointless to shake them down for their contacts. But there are two good reasons to try no matter how futile you think it is. One is that your parents, more than anyone else on Earth, have a vested interested in seeing that you do well — after all, you're a reflection on them. So you know that they're likely to wrack their brains to help you if you let them know what you're looking for. Furthermore, you don't know who *they* know. It's very likely that even if your parents themselves don't know any lawyers you can contact, their friends would be happy to help out and pass along names of people *they* know. So the watchword here is: turn to your parents for networking, even if you don't believe it'll help you! The same goes for the next three categories.

8. FRIENDS

9. FAMILY FRIENDS

10. NEIGHBORHOOD FRIENDS

11. EX-EMPLOYERS — NONLEGAL

Don't overlook old nonlegal employers of yours as a networking source. They may not *be* lawyers, but they probably *know* lawyers. The most likely contact they'll have for you is the firm who represents them. Ann Skalaski points out that this form of networking, getting to a firm through its clients, can be particularly effective.

So pick up the phone and call past employers, and see which law firms they have relationships with. Do some research on Lexis, Westlaw, or through your career services director, and see if those lawyers do something that interests you. If so — pursue it. If *not,* consider setting up an information interview with them anyway — because after all, you never know who *they* know!

12. EX-EMPLOYERS — LEGAL

This is a bit of a no-brainer, eh? Assuming that you left the employer on good terms, that employer can be a great resource — because you *know* they know other lawyers! But don't confine yourself that way; it may be that past legal employers went to law school with people who'd be good contacts for you, so be sure to ask them about their classmates, as well.

What if your past employer wants you back, and you don't want to practice law with them? Well, it may make you uncomfortable to ask them for contacts, but it makes a lot of sense if you can muster the wherewithal to do it. If you're honest with them, and explain that you've decided that you'd be better suited to practicing some other kind of law, they might make an excellent contact, and here's why: They're likely to say good things about you, because, after all, they made you an offer! You can't get a reference that's much better than that. So even if you don't want to return to a former employer, don't overlook them as a source of contacts!

13. COWORKERS AND CUSTOMERS FROM OLD JOBS

When you're thinking about old employers, don't confine yourself to thinking just of your bosses as contacts — think of your former coworkers and customers, as well. Even if they're not lawyers, I harken back to the point I've made over and over again — you don't know who *they* know.

14. HIGH SCHOOL FRIENDS

There are really two categories of friends to think about: one is friends to contact even though you don't know if they can be helpful. The other category is high school acquaintances who may not be close enough to consider friends, but are worth contacting because they're in a position to help you. Remember — when you ask people for help, you don't want to ignore any points of commonality, and attending the same high school is fertile common ground. After all, let's say you got a call from someone who went to high school with you. You didn't know them particularly well, but they heard you were going to law school, and since they were thinking of going, they wanted your opinion about it. Would you give it? Sure, you'd be happy to help. And that's the way you ought to look at contacting your own high school colleagues, even if you weren't particularly close to them.

Teresa DeAndrado told me a great story about a student who got a job in exactly this way. He went home for Christmas, and ran into an old high school buddy. They got to chatting because the buddy was thinking of going to law school. Shortly after that, the buddy visited Los Angeles, and went to a gym there to work out. He got on a StairMaster, and on the StairMaster right next to his was a partner from a large Los Angeles law firm. They started chatting, and hit it off, and the buddy mentioned that he had a friend in law school who was looking for a job. The partner said, "Well, have him send me his résumé." The buddy passed along that request, and as you've probably already guessed, the guy wound up with a job there. As Teresa DeAndrado points out, "Tell *everyone* that you're looking. You just never know!"

15. HIGH SCHOOL TEACHERS

16. UNDERGRAD FRIENDS AND ROOMMATES

17. UNDERGRAD TEACHERS

18. EVERY SERVICE PERSON YOU USE OR KNOW: DOCTOR, DENTIST, HAIRDRESSER/BARBER, INSURANCE AGENT, REAL ESTATE PERSON, GARBAGEMAN, POSTMAN, AND THE LIKE

Very few law students use this avenue of making contacts, even though it's one of the most fertile hunting grounds there could possibly be. Why? Because service people come in contact with more people than almost anybody else. So they're more likely to know lawyers, no matter how far removed their own profession is from practicing law! As Lisa Abrams points out, "My *hairdresser* knows more lawyers and judges than anyone!" Kentucky's Drusilla Bakert agrees: "Definitely call your family doctor, your barber. I had a student who got on the phone and started calling these kinds of contacts, and he had a job in 2 days."

One of the best anecdotes about using service people for contacts comes from author Cynthia Chin Lee. She tells of a law school graduate who was unemployed. He's taking his trash out at 11 in the morning, and the garbageman stops by and asks what he's doing there during the day. The guy says that he's an unemployed law school graduate, and the garbageman says, "Oh, there's a partner at a law firm three doors down." The guy goes and introduces himself, and the long and the short of it is that he winds up with a job . . . and all because he stated his desires to his *garbage man!*

So think of all of the people you know, whether you use their services or not, who are in a position to talk with all kinds of people. Odds are they'll know someone *you* should contact!

19. PEOPLE YOU KNOW FROM CHURCH OR TEMPLE

People you know through religious affiliations can be a great resource. As Lisa Abrams says, "My mother-in-law is a church secretary. If I had a student call her, she'd have a list of 30 names to give them for information on *any* job."

20. COMMUTING FRIENDS: PEOPLE YOU KNOW FROM BUSSES, TRAINS OR SUBWAYS

If you commute, you probably see the same people over and over again. And you may spend more time talking with them than with people you'd consider a lot closer to you. So casually work into the conversation the fact that you're researching the legal market, and ask them if they'd think of anyone you ought to talk to. Remember: most people are happy to help, once you tell them what you want!

21. ANYBODY ON YOUR CHRISTMAS CARD LIST

22. "REGULARS" YOU SEE AT YOUR DELI, GYM, OR WATERING HOLE

23. INTERVIEWERS FROM EMPLOYERS WHO REJECTED YOU

"Geez, Kimmbo," you're thinking. "Why the heck would I want to talk with somebody who *rejected* me? Good move!" Calm down, calm down — that's not what I'm recommending. What I'm talking about are situations where the employer in general rejected you, but you got along great with a particular interviewer. For instance, let's say that you interviewed with four lawyers at the law firm Lower & Boome. And let's say that you got rejected by the firm, but you really hit it off with Bambam Winneboso, one of the lawyers there. Well, as Teresa DeAndrado recommends, call Bambam "and ask for advice. Say something like, 'I enjoyed our conversation. Can you give me advice? Or refer me to others?'" Since they liked you, they'll probably be happy to help you, if they can.

If you do use this route to network, remember not to say anything negative about the employer. This is not the place to say, "Boy, I really liked you. Too bad you work with such a bunch of clowns." You can state your disappointment over not getting an offer from the firm, but do it nonoffensively, and immediately move on to how much you appreciated talking with that interviewer and how you'd like any advice they can offer.

24. CASUAL CONTACTS AT WEDDINGS, PICNICS, PARTIES . . . *EVERYWHERE!*

As Laura Rowe points out, "Every stranger is a potential contact." And Cindy Rold adds, "Casual contact just can't be beat as a means of networking." She tells the story of a student who found his dream job through someone on an airplane! It turns out this student launched a conversation with the person sitting next to him on a plane trip. That person wasn't a lawyer, but *knew* some lawyers — and those lawyers gave the student a job!

Another career services director told me about a student who graduated from law school without a job, and out of desperation he took a job at Wal-Mart. He'd wanted to get into politics, but kept hitting his head against a wall trying to get into it. Well, there was a customer who frequented this Wal-Mart, and he was running for public office. Through seeing him at the Wal-Mart, the student figured he was a promising candidate. So he volunteered to work for him. What happened? The guy was elected attorney general and hired the student as a special assistant!

Another career services director told me about a student who was vacationing at a beach and decided to go for a jog. He caught up to an older guy who was also jogging, and they started to chat. It turns out that the guy was a partner from a prestigious firm in Oregon. And you know what happened . . . this student wound up with a job there — and all because he made his desires known to a *very* casual contact!

C. HOW TO TALK TO THE CONTACTS YOU MAKE

At this point, you may be wondering: All right, I've mustered the courage to make all of these connections. Now what the heck am I supposed to say to these people? Well, I'll tell you what to say — and perhaps even more importantly, what *not* to say — but I'm not going to do it right here. I'm just teasing you with it, because I thought that at this point, you'd be curious about it.

What I've done instead is lumped all of the information about dealing with contacts into one section called "How to Talk to the Contacts You Make: Informational Interviewing."

And you'll find it just a few pages ahead, on page 143.

D. The "A" in the "P.A." System: Networking Through Activities

OK, let's say that the idea of making contacts through people you already know makes your skin crawl. Well, that doesn't mean you can't network — it just means you may prefer a different route. That is, you may prefer to take part in *activities* that will bring you into contact with lawyers. I'd recommend that you do both — use people *and* activities to network — but you can do whatever you want.

Now, a lot of what I'm going to recommend to you will involve you sacrificing some of your time — and you have to resign yourself to that if you want to network through activities.

What I've done here is to group these activities under three general headings: Writing, Volunteering, and Attending. Choose what makes you feel most comfortable, and remember — the more you do, the more people you'll meet, and the easier it will be to get the job you want!

1. Writing Activities

Writing is a *very* important skill for you to demonstrate to employers. So anytime you write *anything* you're putting a feather in your job search cap. But if you're smart about it, the way you go about writing can also create excellent networking opportunities. Here's how . . .

A. Publish an Article on the Area of Law That Interests You

This is one of the best, and most overlooked, things you can do to boost your career opportunities. Marilyn Tucker says, "It not only gives you a great résumé item, but it proves to employers that you really are interested in what you say you're interested in — and of course it proves you can write!"

This doesn't mean Law Review, necessarily. There are tons of legal publications, like bar magazines and specialty newsletters, and they *all* need articles. (Check your law school library or your career services office to get an idea of what's out there.) As Marilyn Tucker points out, "Writing articles makes a *tremendous* difference for you."

But remember — the key here is to *pick your topic carefully*. There's no point in doing an article on securities law if you want to practice domestic relations. So, for instance, if health law interests you, consider doing an article for a health law newsletter.

How do you find a cutting-edge topic? Easy. Ask a professor who teaches that subject — he'll be well-versed on what needs to be covered, and alternatively what's overworked and ought to be avoided. Or, you can ask at career services for a practitioner in a specialty that interests you, and call them with the same request — a topic for an article. You may find that that call in and of itself makes you a valuable contact, because at the very least the practitioner will want to read what you write!

B. TAKE ADVANTAGE OF YOUR SCHOOL'S WRITING REQUIREMENT (IF IT HAS ONE) TO NETWORK WITH PRACTITIONERS

Many law schools have a writing requirement, and if *yours* does, it gives you a perfect opportunity to approach prospective employers in a nonthreatening way. Tammy Willcox advises that you call lawyers who practice in an area that interests you, explain that you have a school writing requirement to fulfill, and ask what they'd like to read about. They're likely to come up with topics for you, and they'll be not only flattered that you asked, but also impressed with your initiative. *And* it gives you a perfect opportunity to keep in touch with them — when you finish your writing project, you can send it to them, or, better yet, ask if you can hand-deliver it and take the opportunity to talk about their practice.

So, if your school has a writing requirement, don't waste its networking potential!

C. APPROACH LAW FIRMS YOU WANT AND VOLUNTEER TO DO A RESEARCH PROJECT

Here's the idea, courtesy of Tammy Willcox. Go to a partner at a law firm who practices in an area that interests you. Say that you'd like to do a research project for them as a volunteer, and ask for a topic that they'd find useful. And tell them that you'll publish the article when it's done. If the partner's contribution merits it, you could share a byline for the article.

You can see that this is a great way to get to know a particular partner, but it also has the collateral benefit of getting you a writing credit that demonstrates your concrete interest in a particular area.

D. DO ARTICLES ON PRACTITIONERS FOR YOUR LAW SCHOOL NEWSPAPER — AND IF YOUR SCHOOL DOESN'T HAVE A NEWSPAPER, START ONE!

There's no better and more flattering way to talk with people than to tell them that you want to write an article about them. So, write for your law school newspaper! As Gail Cutter suggests, use your career services office to see which alums (or other prominent area lawyers) practice in an area that interests you. Then, contact them and tell them that you'd like to write about them for the law school newspaper. Have a list of questions ready. You'll want to ask many of the same kinds of things that you'd ask in a job interview, ironically enough — things about how they chose their specialty, what they like about their job, what a typical day is like for them, what they wish they'd known before they started the practice, what kinds of traits it takes to be successful in their specialty, and things like that. But you also have the benefit of being able to ask very valuable questions that you couldn't ask on an interview — things like what kinds of advice they would offer to people who want to break into their field, and what the downsides are. Of course, when the article is published, be sure you follow up with the person you interviewed. And if you find that you really would like to pursue a job with them or in their specialty, you've got the perfect calling card! You can say, "Having interviewed you, I'm really excited about what you do, and I'd like to break into it myself. How should I go about it?" Be sure that you also ask them who *else* you should talk to about breaking into the market. The more contacts you make, the better!

What if your school doesn't have a newspaper? Consider *starting* one. Newsletters are very inexpensive to publish, and so it's not a hard sell for a Student Bar Association to support one. You'll, of course, still be able to interview people — that, after all, is the point of this exercise — but you'll *also* have the feather in your cap of *starting* something, and that's great. Initiative is a trait highly prized by employers!

E. WORK AS A RESEARCH ASSISTANT FOR A PROFESSOR

As Gail Cutter points out, "Professors have great connections! Students think professors are in an ivory tower, but they're not. Even if they don't practice law, they've got great contacts. And you'll get a great recommendation!"

If there are professors you feel comfortable enough to approach yourself, then get ahead and do that. Otherwise, ask your career services director for guidance as to who's doing what. Either way, you'll get excellent research and writing experience, as well as a very useful means of networking.

F. START A BRIEF WRITING SERVICE!

That's right. Try offering to write briefs for lawyers who don't need full-time help, but need some help with briefs anyway. Now this might be a bit too much of a time commitment for you if you're still in school, but if you're a new graduate and you're looking for work, "It's a great way to make, and impress, new contacts," says Case Western's Debra Fink. For one thing, it shows great initiative. For another, it demonstrates your writing ability. And for a third, it helps you expand your network. If you want to pursue this, talk with your career services director for names of local alums and sole practitioners who might be able to use your services.

2. VOLUNTEERING ACTIVITIES

There are *lots* of ways to volunteer, and if you choose wisely, you can turn these activities into valuable career contacts. Some of them involve volunteering at school, and others involve volunteering locally. But, in every case, they'll bring you into contact with practitioners, and they'll do so in a nonthreatening way — that is, you'll be meeting people because of what you're *doing*. Even if you're shy, this makes it very easy to talk with new people!

A. VOLUNTEER AT YOUR CAREER SERVICES OFFICE!

Think about it. Your career services office sets up dozens of on-campus activities, and *somebody's* got to do all that work. Most offices set up panels and seminars, and find on-campus speakers, and all of them run on-campus interviews. Those all generate *incredible* opportunities to meet employers if you help out at career services. For example:

- You could help set up panels and receptions by being a liaison with alumni and local practitioners. You're the one who contacts them to see if they can come and speak, or take part in a panel, or attend a reception. This gives you an *excellent* opportunity to introduce yourself to potential employers. And, because you'll be working at career services, you'll have input on exactly who those speakers and reception guests will *be* — and, of course, you'll choose ones who practice what you'd like to practice!

- Offer to be a student escort for the on-campus interview process. You escort interviewers to the interview rooms, show them where coffee, restrooms, and phones are, and generally make yourself helpful. As Kathleen Brady points out, "There are students who've gotten jobs by being escorts!" It gives you a few minutes alone with the interviewer, and you're implicitly being shown in a positive light, because you're being helpful. And you're not under pressure, because you needn't say anything about wanting to meet with them while you escort them — it just gives you a chance to break the ice and chat with them casually. You can always follow up with a phone call or letter, which you'll open by stating that you met them at school. Assuming you made a good impression, it'll be much easier to ask for their help in either meeting with you or suggesting other people for you to talk with.

B. DO A PRO BONO PROJECT WITH PRO BONO STUDENTS AMERICA (PBSA)

If you haven't heard about PBSA, you're in for a treat. PBSA is a national program, with chapters at 50 schools (with more signing on all the time), that matches up law students with volunteer positions at almost 1,000 organizations nationwide. The experience you get is invaluable, because you can do everything from representing clients, to taking part in administrative hearings, to research and writing. It's great not only in terms of the experience you get, but also the contacts you make. Furthermore, if you ever feel disenchanted with the idea of law, a PBSA project goes a long way toward getting you excited about it again, because you're really doing hands-on, practical, and, in many cases, exciting stuff. Career services directors simply *rave* about PBSA — and bemoan the fact that more law students don't give it a try!

For instance, one career services director I spoke with had a student who spent her Christmas vacation doing a PBSA project with the Illinois Attorney General! The student did research, made great contacts, and obviously had a very influential reference when she went to find a paying job!

There are other benefits to PBSA, as well:

♦ For one thing, as Sandy Mans points out, "There's no credentials problem with PBSA. There's no screening. You can *always* get a project with them."

♦ It doesn't take much of a commitment — 50 hours is the minimum, and you can do that in about a week if you want to. As Sandy Mans says, "You can do a couple of PBSA projects in the summer, and one over winter break."

Now you may be thinking, "Swell, Kimmbo. I don't

have any money as it is, and now you're telling me to take prime moneymaking time and use it volunteering!" Well, yes I am. As Mary Obrzut points out, "While you're doing PBSA, flip burgers at night. Bartend. Whatever!" The experience is that important!

By the way — if you do a PBSA project, or *any* volunteer project for that matter, "Don't put on your résumé that it was unpaid," according to Mary Obrzut. No one cares if it was volunteer or not — the only thing that counts is that you got the experience (great for your résumé), and you made the contacts (great for networking).

If you're interested, talk to your career services office to see if your school offers PBSA, or call PBSA's national headquarters at 212–998–6222. (I've reproduced the PBSA brochure at the end of this chapter, as Appendix A, if you'd like some more basics about the program.)

c. HELP OUT WITH YOUR SCHOOL'S SPEAKER'S BUREAU, AND IF YOUR SCHOOL DOESN'T HAVE ONE, START ONE

Most schools have an organization that brings in off-campus speakers. If yours does that, consider joining it. Why? Well, if you've been awake until now, you probably already know what I'm going to say. What you can do as a member of a speaker's bureau is contact employers for whom you'd like to work, and get them to come and give a lecture on campus. This inevitably involves spending some time with the speaker, and perhaps even taking them to dinner. In any case, you've got a great opportunity to meet someone you'd like to work for.

What if your school doesn't have a bureau like that? Start one! With a small budget from the Student Bar Association, you can set up all kinds of interesting lectures. You'll help your classmates, and you'll make contacts galore. And, of course, you'll have a résumé item that shows a great deal of initiative — and that's always a plus.

Now clearly you don't want to hit the speakers over the head with the fact that you're interested in working for them. Instead, what you'll do is meet them as a result of the speaker's bureau, and *subsequently* call and ask for an information interview. I talked with more than one career services director about this networking avenue, and there are many students who've gotten their dream job just this way!

D. START A MENTORING PROGRAM AT YOUR SCHOOL, IF IT DOESN'T HAVE ONE ALREADY

Some law schools have mentoring programs; that is, programs where alumni offer to act as mentors for students, giving them advice about careers. As I mention in the next section, it's a good idea to take advantage of these programs if your school has one, but the focus here is that if your school *doesn't* have one, offer to help start one! What you'd do is to work with your career services office to contact alumni and determine their interest in being a mentor. This is obviously a great way to make contacts, and because you're helping to start the program yourself, it shows that you can take the initiative — a great asset in the eyes of prospective employers.

E. VOLUNTEER FOR THE LOCAL BAR ASSOCIATION

Very few students get involved with their local bar association. Virtually every career services director I spoke with said that's a cryin' shame, because it's an *awesome* networking opportunity.

What should you volunteer to do? *Anything* that gets you in contact with lawyers. Man tables at bar committee functions. Make phone calls. As Gail Cutter suggests, join a committee of the bar association, and ask the chairman of that committee if you can research something and report back on it. Whatever. Your career services office will tell you how to get in contact with the local bar association, and they'll be happy to have your help.

The benefits? I'm starting to sound like a broken record, but it shows initiative, enthusiasm, and dedication, and you'll get to meet practitioners doing all kinds of things. If you plan to stay in the area after you graduate from school, this is an opportunity tailor-made for getting a jump-start as a member of the local legal community. As Mary Obrzut says, "The local bar association is the single best way to network."

F. VOLUNTEER TO HELP RUN CLE's (CONTINUING LEGAL EDUCATION CLASSES)

You may already know that licensed attorneys have a continuing education requirement. So, no matter where you go to law school, the local attorneys will have to take some kind of classes to maintain their licenses. And those CLEs, as they're called, are happy hunting grounds for job-hungry students. I'm going to talk in a few minutes about simply attending CLEs, but right now I'm talking about the step beyond that — helping to run them.

What can you do? Everything from manning the reception desk to contacting people. It'll give you a great opportunity to meet practitioners. In fact, one career services director told me about a student who had poor grades, but he had an ace in the hole — his father ran CLEs, and he helped out. He got to speak with all kinds of attorneys, and he would subsequently contact them with personalized letters, talking about where they'd met. He'd say he was impressed with what they had to say, and he'd like to learn more. If you think that sounds like brown-nosing, so be it — the guy got interviews with all of the high-powered law firms in town this way, *despite* his grades.

How do you find out about where and when CLE's are offered? For one thing, a lot of them are probably offered at your school — law schools are where most CLE's are conducted. Check with your career services office, or the local bar association, to find out.

G. BARTEND AT LAW SCHOOL RECEPTIONS FOR ALUMNI

Working as a bartender adds a whole new meaning to the term "break the ice"! If you hate the thought of *attending* receptions because you feel uncomfortable at them, here's the way to do an end-round around your discomfort — *work* the reception! And if you're worried about knowing how to mix drinks, don't be. As a former law school social director, I promise you, you don't have to know much beyond "scotch and water."

Kathleen Brady points out that this is an excellent way to chat with people. You can ask where they work, how they like it, and take it from there. (And be sure to ask for business cards from people who interest you, and follow up with phone or mail requests for information interviews afterwards!)

So bartending is a great way to make the most of law school receptions for alumni and practitioners. We've all been to happy hours, and everybody knows the most popular place at a happy hour is the bar — so if you're the one standing behind that bar you're way ahead of the game!

H. VOLUNTEER AS AN EXTERN FOR A LOCAL JUDGE

Students who intern for judges are called "externs." Now while federal court clerkships are the ones most students know about, *every* judge needs helpers — and when it comes to local judges, you'll probably find that they're happy to take you on as a volunteer. You'll do research, you'll see how courts work — and, as Jose Bahamonde-Gonzalez points out, "It gives you something very solid to put on your résumé — so it's a lot more than just making contacts."

How do you know who the local judges *are,* and how do you know if they take on externs? Easy. Just ask at career services. *Especially* if you like research or would like to be a litigator, this is a volunteer opportunity you should pursue!

I. TAKE PART IN YOUR LAW SCHOOL'S FUNDRAISING ACTIVITIES

Almost every law school has phone-a-thons, where they contact alumni looking for contributions. In fact, judging from the number of calls and letters I get, approximately five bazillion people from my law school take part in this activity!

But the fact is, as Lisa Kellogg points out, it's a great way to network with alumni. That's especially true if you give "great phone."

Now if the idea of begging for money turns you off, you can make things a lot easier on yourself by considering such phone calls as an opportunity to update alumni on what's going on at school. That is, make it more of a conversation than a simple request for money.

If you *do* take part in phone-a-thons for your school, it'll do even more than get you in contact with potential employers among your alumni. It's also a great opportunity to show your rainmaking skills on your résumé. As I discuss in Chapter 11, rainmaking — that is, the ability to get and keep clients — is the golden skill for a lawyer; if you've got it, you've got it *made*. And it's pretty tough to find law school activities that *show* rainmaking ability. Fundraising is one of them, and that's just one more reason why you should consider doing it!

J. TAKE A NONPAYING JOB DOING *WHATEVER* YOUR DREAM JOB IS

If you're going to consider volunteering at all, you may want to simply go for the jugular, and try for a volunteer position doing whatever it is that you want to do. As Jose Bahamonde-Gonzalez points out, "It shows your dedication and commitment if you take a *non*paying job."

One career services director told me about a student in Washington who was gung-ho on a certain federal agency. She tried to get a paying position there, to no avail. So she offered to do an unpaid internship, and that generated paying job prospects with the agency later on. And when you think about it, that makes perfect sense. If you *volunteer* someplace, and you impress them with your skills and dedication, when there *is* a job available your name will be at the top of the list!

3. ACTIVITIES THAT INVOLVE ATTENDANCE

Your third major form of networking through activities is to *attend* different kinds of things. I use the term "attend" in the broadest possible sense, because what I'm talking about here are basically activities that don't require volunteering or writing; it's kind of a catch-all.

One thing I *don't* want you to do is to believe that "attending" means you can be passive. You can't. Whenever you take part in any activity I list here, it's *crucial* for you to reach out and introduce yourself. You can't just go to a lecture, listen, and then slink out and say, "Geez, Kimmbo, I did what you said and it didn't get me *any* contacts." Instead, what I'm talking about is attending things and then using them as a forum for meeting people. What you'll want to do is have memorized a brief introduction for yourself, and then immediately launch into questions for the other person. "Hi. I'm Kimm Walton. I'm a second year at Case Western. I loved your speech. . . . " Or, "I thought that seminar was fascinating. Have you been to others here?" Or whatever! The point is to get the conversational ball rolling and then follow it where it leads.

Now I personally think it's easier to volunteer and help set up or run an activity, rather than just attending something and trying to meet people afterwards. That's why I listed the volunteering activities *before* these attendance ones. But everybody's different, and you may be more drawn to this approach. Many people are, and the bottom line is, it works, too.

A. WATCH OUT FOR SEMINARS AT SCHOOL, AND ATTEND THE ONES THAT INTEREST YOU

Your career services office doesn't have speakers come to campus just for fun, you know. They bring in speakers as a means of giving *you* an opportunity to not only learn about new topics, but also to network with the speakers! If a practitioner in an area that interests you comes to speak at school, go to the talk, then hang around and talk with the speaker afterwards. As Marilyn Tucker points out, "Just go up and say, 'I loved your talk — I'm interested in your practice area. Can I call you and talk to you about your practice?'" It's that simple!

B. GO TO ALUMNI RECEPTIONS AT SCHOOL — ALONE!

Columbia's Ellen Wayne highly recommends attending receptions at school. But if you go, don't hang around the bar nursing a cocktail. You've got to get up the nerve to say hello to people, and initiate conversations with them. And that's also why it's a good idea to go *alone*. If you go with friends, you'll be tempted to just hang around and joke with them. That's what *I'd* do — stand huddled with a buddy making fun of what people are wearing. And if you're going to do that, then you're not networking, and that's the whole point of the exercise!

There are all kinds of books and tapes on topics like "How to Work a Room," "How to Start a Conversation," and all the basics of socializing. Basically, what you do is ask questions and make comments about whatever it is that brought you and the other person together — in the case of an alumni reception, you've got *a lot* in common, in the form of your law school. You can ask what they practice, how they chose it, what if anything they wish they'd done differently in law school.

The lynchpin of Dale Carnegie's book, "How to Win Friends and Influence People," is that if you get the other person to talk about themselves, they'll like you — because *everybody* likes to talk about themselves. If you happen to talk with someone who's a dud — smile, say "Excuse me," and move on. No harm done. And don't attach yourself like a barnacle to one person all night; the idea is to meet *people,* not *person.* You can always say, "I'm hogging your company, but I'd love to talk more about what you do. Do you have a business card with you? Can I call to setup an appointment so we can talk some more?" If you leave with even one or two business cards, then the event was a success!

Also make sure that *you've* got stuff to bring to the table. It's every person's obligation to be interesting in a social setting! So bone up on what's in the news. Have a few funny stories you can recount. Be prepared to give as well as receive information!

And by the way — don't dress too casually just because an event is at school, and you normally wear your cut-offs and barf-stained bowling shirts to class. Remember, you're in the company of professionals, and it's in these kinds of settings that you begin to be viewed as a professional, not a student. I'm not saying to wear a suit, but dress in something neat and clean.

C. TAKE PART IN YOUR SCHOOL'S MENTORING PROGRAM, IF IT HAS ONE

Some career services offices offer their students alumni mentors; that is, alumni who are willing to take the time to talk with students, and give them advice about, well, *anything*. Check with your career services office, and if they have a mentoring program, *definitely* take advantage of it. Tell your career services director what interests you, and they'll match you up with an alum who does what you want to do. This is just a phenomenal opportunity to network, because the groundwork has already been done for you; you *know* that the mentor wants to help you, because that's why they agreed to be a mentor in the *first* place!

And by the way, don't shy away from contacting alumni mentors because you're afraid they're deluged with student requests, and you'll wear them out. Most of the time, just the opposite is true. As Columbia's Ellen Wayne points out, "Many alumni who volunteer to be mentors never get a single call! You *should* call them. Lawyers like to impart information — that's what they do!"

D. READ LOCAL BAR NEWSLETTERS AND JOURNALS, AND FOLLOW UP ON THEM!

There are really two separate things I'm recommending here.

♦ Look at profiles of attorneys who are written up in local bar newsletters. Amy Thompson recommends that if you read about lawyers who practice something of interest to you, call them and tell them that you read about them, that you're very interested in what they do, and ask for a meeting so you can find out more information about their practice. (For what to ask in the information interview, flip ahead in this chapter to page 143 on information interviewing.)

♦ Scan the bar journal for your city or state, read any articles on an area of practice that interests you, and then follow up with the author. The authors of bar journal articles are usually practitioners, and if they practice what interests you, that makes them valuable contacts! Just call or write and say that you read their article, you loved it, and you'd love to hear more about what they do. From personal experience I *promise* you that *every* author is delighted when someone compliments their work. I've written books about a bunch of different things, and when people have called me with questions, on occasion I've chatted with them for hours. So, if you read something that interests you, follow up with the author! Remember, even if they themselves don't have job prospects for you, they'll be able to refer you to people who might!

E. TAKE CLE CLASSES EVEN THOUGH YOU'RE STILL IN SCHOOL

I've mentioned CLE classes before; they're "continuing legal education" classes, and lawyers have to take them periodically to maintain their licenses to practice law. Something most students don't know is that law students can *also* take CLE classes. They're given on virtually every topic under the sun, and so you'll undoubtedly find something that interests you — and since most of these CLE classes are given at law schools, they're very convenient! Furthermore, they're typically free to students or involve a very nominal charge.

By the way — as Gail Peshel suggests, it's a good idea to go to these classes alone. "It's just too easy to talk to the people you came with otherwise!"

There are several excellent benefits to taking CLE classes, including:

♦ You meet practitioners in an area you're interested in. As Gail Peshel points out, at coffee breaks or over lunch, you've got an excellent opportunity to talk with people doing exactly what you want to do — and better yet, you've got a built-in topic of conversation . . . the CLE class you're both attending! Ask what they thought of the seminar, what other ones they'd recommend — and say that you're interested in the area of practice and you want to get more practical experience in it. As Debra Fink points out, "This really shows initiative!"

♦ You learn what's going on in the practice area, and that kind of education is valuable in and of itself. It may generate article ideas for you (if you're interested in writing), and it'll key you in on what's on the minds of practitioners. You may even find that you *don't* enjoy hearing about the issues in an area of practice, and that's valuable as well. After all, if the intellectual content of a practice area doesn't interest you, maybe you should reconsider that practice area and look for another one instead.

♦ You get a *great* résumé item. Debra Fink tells students who attend CLEs to add a section to their résumé called "Additional Legal Education," and list the specific classes and CLE hours they took. For instance, let's say you want to be a litigator, and you take some CLE classes on taking depositions and cross-examination. Think about how that will separate you from the pack in the eyes of an employer! It shows dedication and enthusiasm, and those are *great* assets for you to have.

F. DON'T OVERLOOK MOCK INTERVIEWS AS A NETWORKING OPPORTUNITY

Virtually every law school's career services office offers mock interviews; that is, an opportunity for you to hone your interview skills without the pressure of a real job riding on the interview. However, you *may* be interested to know that some schools bring in local practitioners to do the mock interviewing — and you know what that means? It means you've got a terrific, and really sneaky, way to impress a potential employer!

As Gail Peshel points out, "Don't overlook these as a job possibility! Find out from the career services office if they use local attorneys for mock interviews, and if they do, research those interviewers as you would any other interview." Gail Cutter adds, "Interviewers in mock interviews have been known to say, 'Great job! Send me your résumé!'"

Now, no matter *who* does mock interviews, it's a good idea to get all the practice interviewing that you possibly can. But if your mock interviewer happens to be a real, live practicing attorney — don't miss out on a networking opportunity!

G. GO TO LOCAL BAR ASSOCIATION ACTIVITIES AND JOIN THE LOCAL BAR ASSOCIATION AS A STUDENT MEMBER

Boy, this is one that *every* career services director recommended — and they all added that students very rarely take advantage of this opportunity.

You can join the local bar association as a student. It'll either be free or at a *very* nominal fee. If you don't want to go that far, you can go to meetings anyway. Bar associations run seminars on all kinds of topics, as well as special events and social gatherings. Committees in different practice areas meet regularly, and put on programs on all sorts of topics, things like "Bridging the gap from law school to practice."

As I recommended earlier, if you want to volunteer for the local bar, that's even better. All of these programs and events need bodies to help set them up and run them, and that kind of volunteering is a great way to network in and of itself.

As Debra Fink points out, "Local bar associations *welcome* students!" If you're going to be a member of the legal community, it pays to get as early a start as possible. Not only will you meet people who might have jobs available (or will know people who do), but you're displaying the kind of honest enthusiasm that will make you shine!

H. CONSIDER TAKING PART IN "INNS OF COURT"

Here's a program you may not be familiar with, but if you're interested in litigation or government work, it's an organization you should definitely get to know. As Mary Obrzut describes it, Inns of Court is a national program with branches in various cities that brings together practitioners and judges who meet monthly, where they hear presentations on topics like conflicts of interest, discovery rules, evidence changes — all kinds of litigation issues. Not only do you get a chance to learn some interesting things, but you get a great opportunity to meet litigators, judges, and legislators.

For more information about Inns of Court, check with your career services director, or contact the American Inns of Court Foundation, 127 S. Peyton St., Suite 201, Alexandria, VA 22314; phone (703) 684–3590, and fax (703) 684–3607.

I. IF YOU'RE ATHLETIC, JOIN LAWYERS' SPORTS TEAMS (LIKE SOFTBALL AND BASKETBALL TEAMS)

If you're a semidecent athlete, you've got a *golden* networking opportunity in the form of lawyers' sports teams. Ask your career services office for advice about tracking down where such teams play, and give them a call — or just show up — and ask to be included.

Now if you're like *me*, someone who can't hit a basketball net with a bazooka, this isn't going to be a very fruitful route for networking. But if you *are* good, then you already know that taking part in sports is a great way to form a bond with people. And if those people happen to do something *you* want to do, you've created great contacts for yourself!

J. SPEND A SCHOOL BREAK WATCHING TRIALS

If you're interested in being a litigator or working for a judge, this is something you ought to try.

Here's the idea: You go to the courthouse in a community where you want to practice, ask the bailiffs and clerks what's going on and what's worth watching, and watch the trials. When you see judges who impress you, go up to them afterwards and introduce yourself. Say that you were interested in the trial, and ask them questions about it, and about being a judge, and take it from there. As Debra Fink points out, this is a particularly good opportunity for First Years and for new graduates. And apart from that – it's interesting and fun!

4. SPECIAL ADVICE FOR SHY PEOPLE

All but the most stouthearted among us are intimidated, at least at first, by the thought of networking. If you're shy on top of that, it must make you cringe; the thought of initiating conversations with *anybody* is something you want to avoid no matter *what* the payoff is. And the worst part of all is, you're exactly the kind of person a lot of legal employers need. People who are introverted are frequently able to focus better and concentrate more effectively than their more extroverted brethren.

So — what should you do? Take heart! *Many* of the career services directors I spoke with addressed the problem of shy law students, and they all regaled me with stories about shy students who did learn to network effectively, and got great jobs as a result. In a nutshell, it's just going to take you a little more preparation, a little more rehearsing, and more measured steps than a more extroverted person. But you'll get to the same place — that is, your dream job.

What I'm going to do is go back over a lot of the things I've discussed so far in this chapter, and talk about how you ought to modify them if you're shy.

A. PRACTICE WHAT YOU'LL SAY UNTIL YOU'RE COMFORTABLE WITH IT

If you're shy, the prospect of being caught off-guard can be frightening. So to minimize that, rehearse as much as possible *beforehand* the things you'll say in the situations you're likely to confront.

I advise *everybody* to have a little introduction to themselves memorized. "Hi. I'm Kimm Walton. I'm a second year at Case Western . . . " and a few more tidbits about yourself, so that you can comfortably respond to questions like, "Which classes do you like so far?" Or "What are you interested in practicing?" In the chapter on interviewing, I go over answers to questions like these, and also offer interviewing tips for shy people. I'd encourage you to read that chapter in preparation for networking, as well, so that you're as comfortable as you can be *before* you contact people.

B. START BY CONTACTING THE LEAST RISK-ORIENTED PEOPLE YOU KNOW

Start by contacting people with whom you already feel comfortable — family friends, perhaps an attorney your parents know. The people who are most closely connected with you are the ones who will most put you at your ease. Also, mention to your career services director that you're introverted, and, with that in mind, ask if there are any alums who would be helpful. Your career services director will certainly be sensitive to your shyness, and put you in touch with just the right kinds of people — heck, you may find yourself talking with an alum who is *also* shy, and can give you some advice from personal experience on how to deal with it when you practice law! Then, as Wendy Werner puts it, move down the food chain of risk to people you don't know — that is, people who your contacts refer you to. You'll find that the more you contact people, the more comfortable you'll get, no matter how unlikely that seems right now.

C. CONTACT PEOPLE BY MAIL INSTEAD OF BY PHONE

In Chapter 5, I discuss correspondence, so you'll want to read that chapter before you actually send out any letters. But the point is, if you're shy, don't put additional pressure on yourself by contacting people by phone. It's easier to do it by mail. And you'll just open that letter by saying, "So-and-so recommended that I contact you . . . " and take it from there, asking for a chance to meet with the person, and saying you'll call to follow up. That way, when you call, they'll know who you are, and that will put you much more at your ease.

D. MEET PEOPLE THROUGH ACTIVITIES, RATHER THAN THROUGH CONTACTS

As Gail Cutter points out, small talk is something that sends shivers down the spines of shy people. So if you're shy, it makes much more sense for you to meet people by taking part in activities where you'll meet them. Just go through the activities I list, starting on page 120, and see what appeals to you most. And focus on activities that involve substantive issues, rather than just meeting and greeting people; for instance, local bar association activities involving researching issues are ones you should try for, because they'll give you issues to talk about.

E. WHATEVER IT TAKES — MAKE THAT FIRST CONTACT!

Whether you start with a close friend or your career services director, and with a phone call or a letter to a contact, if you want your dream job, networking is something you've *got* to try — the payoff is just to great to ignore. As George Washington's Laura Rowe says, "It can be hard to get started, but it's not car salesmanship!"

5. NETWORKING LONG DISTANCE — WHAT TO DO IF YOU DON'T GO TO SCHOOL IN THE CITY WHERE YOU WANT TO PRACTICE

There's no question about it — it's tough to network if you're not where you ultimately want to be. As Sandy Mans says, "Geography *counts*. It determines your future." So what should you do? Take these steps . . .

A. GO TO CAREER SERVICES AND DIG UP ALUMS WHO PRACTICE LAW IN THE CITY WHERE YOU WANT TO BE

Look for both law school alums *and* alums of your undergrad school who went on to law school. You want names, addresses, and phone numbers of every alum in that city (obviously, if you're talking about a really big city like New York City, you'll just do a selection; ask your career services director which alums are likely to be the most helpful).

B. SAVE UP THE MONEY FOR A TRIP TO THAT CITY AND PLAN ONE OVER A BREAK. ONCE YOU'VE GOT YOUR DATES SET, CONTACT ALL OF THE ALUMS YOU FOUND IN STEP (A) AND SET UP INFORMATIONAL INTERVIEWS

Whether you call them or write to them, tell them who you are, and what you're doing — and, of course, if they're an alum of your undergrad school, explain that that's the connection between you. Tell them that you're interested in moving to that city and practicing there, and you'd appreciate any advice they can give you, and you'd like to setup a convenient time for a meeting — and then give them the dates you'll be available.

When you get there, ask them the kinds of questions I suggest in "Information Interviewing," just ahead on page 143, along with anything else you want to know. *Always*remember to ask if they know anyone else they think might be able to help you — and remember to thank them!

Also — return as often as possible, to network and establish yourself there. As Sandy Mans points out, "The best way to get a job in the city where you want to be is to *go there.*"

C. CONSIDER DOING A VISITING SEMESTER IN (OR NEAR) THE CITY WHERE YOU WANT TO BE

If you're still fairly new to law school, this is a possibility you should consider. As Tammy Willcox points out, "Doing a visiting semester at a school shows your commitment to the city." And she goes on to point out that it gives you other benefits, as well:

- ◆ It's easier to do a visiting semester than it is to transfer; your grades don't have to be nearly as good.

- ◆ You'll get another career services director on your side, and all of the networking opportunities that go along with that!

But the main benefit is certainly that it shows you really are interested in working in that particular city. As I mention in the chapter on interviewing, one of the toughest questions you can face is, "Why did you go to school *there* if you want to practice *here?*" No employer likes the idea that you aren't committed to their community, and if you've got a semester in law school there under your belt, you don't have to worry about it!

D. BE PATIENT! YOU'RE NOT LIKELY TO GET AN OFFER UNTIL YOU *GO* TO THAT CITY

As Marilyn Tucker points out, "You're not likely to get a job in another city until you go there and pound the pavement!" This is definitely *not* something you can accomplish through the mail. So resign yourself to saving up for a trip, setting up meetings with alums and any other contacts you have, and then going there and meeting as many people as you can.

E. REMEMBER THAT GEOGRAPHY *ISN'T* IMPORTANT FOR SOME GOVERNMENT-TYPE JOBS (LIKE THE DISTRICT ATTORNEY'S OFFICE)

I led this little section by talking about the importance of geography, because for the vast majority of employers, it *is* very important. But there's a special subset of employers for whom geography doesn't matter, and it's employers like the U.S. Attorney's office and the District Attorney's office. For those kinds of employers, as Sandy Mans points out, you're better off getting your feet wet in a rural area (where the job competition isn't so fierce), and then using that as leverage to get to the city where you want to be. Before you make a move like this, however, check with your career services director to see if the specific type of job you want fits this description. There's no point doing time out in the boonies when it's your dream to be in Chicago, if it's not going to benefit your career!

F. DON'T GIVE UP!

If I've made a long-distance job search sound gruesome, I didn't mean it to be; it's just that it's a lot harder than networking your way to a job in the city where your law school is located. But it's certainly not impossible; it just takes more planning, and as many visits as you can muster. Having said that, let me tell you a couple of anecdotes about students who were successful in their long-distance job searches.

♦ One student in the south wanted to work in Oregon. She had no contacts there, and had mediocre grades. She made a list of all of the law school alums in Oregon, contacted them all by letter saying when she'd be in town, and that she wanted to call and visit with them. She wound up visiting all of them. Some of them didn't pan out, but others were very helpful. In fact, one of them referred her to another attorney, who referred her to *another* attorney — and that attorney offered her a great job!

♦ Another student, this one from the northeast, wanted to work in Arizona. He visited during Spring Break of Third Year, and decided on which specific city he wanted. Immediately after he got back to school, he contacted all of his law school and undergrad alums who were practicing law there. After he graduated, he signed up for BAR/BRI, and got a bartending job at night to pay his bills. While he studied for the bar, he joined the local bar association (aha! Where have you heard this before?). He worked on bar association projects on a volunteer basis, setting up CLE classes, choosing speakers, and contacting them. Through these contacts he got temporary projects from three lawyers, and by September — only 4 months after graduation, and 2 months after the bar exam — he had two job offers!

D. HOW TO TALK TO THE CONTACTS YOU MAKE:
INFORMATIONAL INTERVIEWING

Informational interviewing is just a specialized kind of networking. It's basically what you do once you make contacts by networking. I've mentioned this idea of informational interviewing several times in this chapter. And earlier on, in Chapter 2, when we talked about deciding what the heck your dream job *is*, I talked about how you can use information interviews to *decide* what it is that you want to do; it's not confined to learning more about a career you've already chosen.

1. REMEMBER THAT YOU *CAN'T* SAY YOU'RE LOOKING FOR A JOB (EVEN THOUGH, OF COURSE, THAT'S ULTIMATELY WHAT YOU *ARE* LOOKING FOR)

Boy, you're probably going to hate me for this one, because I'm going to ask you to take part in a bit of a charade. I'm going to ask you *not* to tell the professional contacts you make that you're looking for a job. It's OK with your family and friends — that is, your social network — but not anybody else. "Wait a minute, Kimmbo!" you're saying. "You mean you want me to *lie?*" Well, I acknowledge that you don't pick up a book called "Guerrilla Tactics for Getting the Legal Job of Your Dreams" because you're interested in learning more about the legal market in a purely theoretical way. You got it because you *want a job*, dagnabbit! And you might be a little put off by my saying that you shouldn't admit it. But *every* career services director I spoke with offered dire warnings on this.

And when you think about it, it makes sense. I've mentioned to you before that people like to help. That's why when you call people for information, or to ask for advice, they're typically flattered. That's because they can *give* you that. They probably are not in a position, right at the moment you contact them, to give you a job. So, as Gail Cutter points out, "If you ask them a question they can't answer, like 'Can you get me a job?' it makes you *both* feel bad." I'll give you all kinds of things you *can* ask in just a minute. But avoid at all costs asking things like, "Is your firm doing any hiring?" or "Do you know of any job openings?" As Gail Cutter says, "You'll likely get, 'No' — click." Maureen Provost Ryan adds, "It's important to keep people's defenses down when you network. You don't build rapport by asking for a job!"

Rob Kaplan says that by avoiding asking for a job, you're keeping the stakes *low*, so you're more likely to succeed. You have to make clear that you're looking for information, you're looking for help. So if you do send a résumé, make clear that it's to show your background, not as part of a job application.

"But, Kimm, how'm I supposed to *get* a job if I'm not allowed to tell anyone that's what I want?" I hear your plaintive cry. Well, what you're doing when you network is putting yourself into a position where your contact will feel motivated to mention jobs to you. You're creating an environment where, when job opportunities come up, you'll be the first person they think of. Obviously, once you get to know someone better, it's fine to mention that you really want to work in the field, and you'd appreciate their help. But that's not something you're going to lead with.

When we talk, in just a minute, about networking via contacts, I'll go through exactly the kinds of things that you *should* ask. Basically, you'll be looking for advice, information, and referrals. But for right now, I just want you to remember that you *can't* tell your professional contacts that you're looking for a job!

2. OK, OK, OK — HERE'S WHAT YOU *CAN* SAY

A. START OUT WITH THE NAME OF YOUR MUTUAL ACQUAINTANCE TO FORM A BRIDGE WITH YOUR CONTACT

Always, always, *always* lead with the mutual acquaintance that got you your contact. For our purposes here, let's say it's a guy named Ethelbald Gribbetz who led me to you. So I'd call you and say, "Hi. I'm Kimm Walton. Ethelbald Gribbetz recommended that I call you." That way, you give your contact a frame of reference and set them at their ease at the same time, so that they don't have to worry that you might be trying to sell them something.

Also, as Debra Fink points out, "Always say that Gribbetz *recommended* that you call, not *suggested* that you call." That word "recommended" is a stronger, more positive word.

And by the way, I'm talking in terms of making a phone call here, but if you feel more comfortable writing a letter to introduce yourself, that's fine, too. You'd just start out the same way, saying that Ethelbald Gribbetz recommended that you contact whoever you're writing to.

B. GIVE A *VERY* BRIEF DESCRIPTION OF WHO YOU ARE

At this point, you've still got your listener hooked because you've mentioned the name of a mutual acquaintance. All you want to do is to add something to "place" you. "I'm a Second

Year at Case Western, and I met Ethelbald when we went to a CLE Seminar on the new discovery rules 2 weeks ago." The key here is — don't wear it out. I know that you've got a little description of yourself memorized, because I told you to have a pitch ready about yourself. But in this very opening part of a conversation, don't pull that out; it's really more appropriate to talk a little more about yourself if the other person asks anything along the lines of "Tell me about yourself."

So, now you've stated who your mutual acquaintance is, and you've given a very brief description of who you are. That means it's time to . . .

C. STATE WHAT YOU'RE LOOKING FOR

Ideally what you want is a face-to-face meeting, where you can get advice. As a means of *getting* to that meeting, you want to say that you're interested in X type of practice, or practicing law in X city, and that's why Ethelbald Gribbetz recommended that you make the contact. You can say, "I'm interested in the work you do. I'd like to take you to lunch (or for a cup of coffee, or whatever) and hear more about it."

Rob Kaplan describes this as looking for "AIR." That is, you're looking for advice, information, and referrals. As he says, *nobody* minds giving someone AIR!

So what you're looking for is help, for advice, *but don't mention that you're looking for a job!* By the same token, however, don't come out and say you're *not* looking for a job. "Wait a second, Kimmbo," you're thinking. "You just said I'm not supposed to mention I'm *looking* for a job! What gives?" Well, those aren't mutually inconsistent. As Debra Fink points out, "Don't say 'I'm not looking for a job, I'm only looking for advice . . . ' if you really *are* ultimately looking for a job. Because if you *say* that, you're shutting the door to a potential employer!" So — don't say *anything* about looking for a job. Then, if the opportunity arises, you can take it without seeming dishonest!

So what you want to do is just state that you're looking for advice, or information, or help, and ask for a convenient time to meet. Once you get a meeting, follow what I tell you to do on page 147. And remember — most people genuinely enjoy giving advice, so the odds are overwhelmingly in your favor that the person you're contacting will be happy to talk to you. If for some reason they're *not*, you've lost nothing. If they say they won't be able to help you, you can say, "That's all right. Can you refer me to anybody else who might be able to help?" And if that's still a zero, so be it. Maybe they're having a bad day. Or a personal crisis. Or maybe they're just a jerk. Whatever it is, it doesn't reflect on you. Be gracious — say, "Thank you, anyway" — go to the next person on your list, take a deep breath, and forge ahead!

D. IF YOU WRITE — DON'T SEND A RÉSUMÉ!

This is really a corollary of the idea that you're not looking for a job, you're looking for advice and information. You don't have a lot of credibility if you say you're just looking for information, and then you include your résumé with your letter. If your contact asks you for your résumé, then say that you'd be happy to bring it with you when you meet. If they insist on seeing it first — well, you don't have a lot of choice. The point is, what you want to do right now is to focus on gathering information and making personal contacts, without the distraction of your résumé. So avoid it, if you can!

You *should*, however, take your résumé with you when you meet; keep it discreetly in a briefcase or purse. That way, if the contact asks you for it, you've got one handy. After all, if they're that impressed with you when you meet, that's the perfect time to turn over your résumé!

E. WHAT TO SAY WHEN YOU MEET

OK — it's show time! I shouldn't say that, because in the chapter on interviewing, I call job interviews "show time." So let's call this "preview time." But since it could easily lead to job prospects for you, it's just as important, and you should treat it that way!

Now, what you've done before your interview is all of the prep work I recommend in the chapter on interviewing. That is, you want to find out everything you can about the person you're interviewing, from every source you can get your hands on. (You'll find all of this stuff starting on page 298.) Then, on the day of the information interview, dress professionally, as if you really were going on a job interview. Take a copy of your résumé, but tuck it into a purse or briefcase. Show up no more than 5 minutes early, but don't be late! If there's a receptionist or secretary at your interviewee's office, be *very* nice to them.

Support staff are very effective gatekeepers, and if you snub them, you wouldn't be the first person to be shown the door as a result!

When you meet your interviewee, they'll probably extend their hand to shake hands and say hello. If they don't, initiate the handshake, at the same time saying something like, "Thanks for taking the time to talk with me. I really appreciate it." (Remember — from the very beginning of the book — honest enthusiasm! It's irresistible.)

When you actually sit down to talk, remember that, unlike a job interview, this is an interview *you're* conducting, so you're the one asking the questions (although if the interviewee asks you anything, you should, of course, answer it!) What kinds of things should you ask? Well, all of the questions I talk about in the Interviewing chapter, on page 342, would be terrific. I would go into great detail about their own professional and school background, asking things that focus on what got them to where they are now. How did they decide on a practice area? Did they do clerkships or internships during school, and do they think you should do them? What classes did they find most useful? Which were a waste of time? Are there any CLE classes they think you'd find useful? What professional publications do they read? What do they wish they'd known about before they started working here? If they had to do anything else, what would their second choice be?

And of course, you can ask them all about what they do. What's a typical day like for them? What's the most interesting project they've worked on recently? What do they like best about their work? What do they wish they could change?

You can also bring in the fruits of your research. "I read in the bar journal that your firm just merged with Flibber, Tigibbet. How has that changed what you do?" Anytime you can bring up something you know about the interviewee and ask an intelligent question about it, is a real feather in your cap. (You may have noticed the built-in disclaimer in that last sentence " . . . *if* you can ask an intelligent question. . . . " I only mention that because there's no point in bringing up some highly technical point of law that you read in relation to the interviewee if you can't talk about it from there. 'So, I saw that in the patent application you filed for the ossification gene, you stated that the liposomes of the site are subject to the exclusive licensing rights of your client. Can you tell me more about that?' A question like that doesn't help you much unless you're a technical whiz, in which case you know that I made all that stuff up.)

The answers your interviewee gives will also point you to other questions; don't have such a set list of things to ask that you can't pursue the conversation. After all, you're not just here for advice and information. You want to impress the interviewee so that if they have a job opening or they know of someone who has one, you're the person they'll think of first. If and when they ask you questions about yourself, be prepared with answers; it would be a good idea to read the section on "Killer Answers to the Toughest Interview Questions" in the Interviewing chapter, on page 356, before you go on any information interviews, for just that reason.

F. THE LAST QUESTION YOU SHOULD *ALWAYS* ASK . . .

"Who else do you think I should talk to?" Remember, when you're networking, you're making contacts — and you're making more contacts from those contacts — and so on, and so on, and so on. If the interview went even reasonably well, the interviewee will be happy to give you other names. And even if they didn't come up with good stuff for you, that fact alone may guilt them into giving you other names!

Be sure that you write down the names of the referrals, as well as their phone numbers. Ask the interviewee if you can say they referred you to these new contacts (inevitably the answer will be "yes"). And then. . . .

G. THANK THE INTERVIEWEE FOR THEIR TIME

Remember — nobody owes you anything, and anyone who gives you their time is doing you a favor. Tell them how much you appreciate the information they gave you, and that you'll keep them posted.

H. "DEBRIEF" YOURSELF

As soon as possible after the interview, jot down everything you want to remember from what the interviewee said. If they didn't say anything you found particularly useful, make a few cursory notes anyway, in case you ever have to refer back to the meeting for any reason. Keep a file of these notes, listing the name of the interviewee, their position, address, and phone number, when you met, what was discussed, any people they referred you to, and any subsequent action you took, like sending them a thank you note or contacting the people they referred you to.

I. SEND THANK YOUS

For every informational interview you do, send a thank you note. It can be handwritten, if your handwriting is good. You want to mention any piece of advice you found particularly helpful, you want to thank them for any referrals they gave you (and state whether or not you've contacted them, and, if you haven't, when you *will* do so), and state that you'll be in touch again.

J. PURSUE THE NEW LEADS THE WAY YOU PURSUED THE FIRST ONES!

Just go back to square one, do your research, make your calls, and set up your interviews.

K. WHEN YOU SETTLE ON A JOB, LET YOUR CONTACTS KNOW!

Remember, when you make contacts, you're setting up a professional network that you should *maintain.* And that means letting people know what's going on with you. Just a quick note to get your name back in front of them, stating what you've decided to do, and thanking them for their help, is pretty much all that's needed.

L. WHEN YOU HAVE ANYTHING OF INTEREST FOR YOUR CONTACTS, REMEMBER TO SEND IT ALONG!

I stated earlier in this chapter that networking is a two-way street. When you first start, almost all of the useful information is coming *to* you. But as you meet more people, you may be the one with the information and the contacts — and when that's the case, don't forget to return the favor to people who helped *you* when you needed it!

E. INCREDIBLE NETWORKING OPPORTUNITIES FOR PEOPLE WITH BRASS *COJONES*

Not familiar with the term *cojones?* Let's just say that if you've got brass cojones, you're the antithesis of shy — or you can fake a great deal of self-confidence. Whether you're born with it or you've networked your way to great self-confidence, it doesn't matter. Either way, the world is your oyster. You'll leapfrog past the stack of résumés on any employer's desk. And even if your credentials are awful, the persistence and desire you show can get you virtually anywhere!

What I'm going to do in this section is to channel that self-confidence for maximum effect. All of the strategies I'm going to tell you about here are high-risk, high return — that is, there's a substantial risk you'll get rejected, but if you're the type who easily gets back up and dusts yourself off, or even *relishes* a challenge, you'll get job opportunities your classmates only dream of!

1. COLD CALLING

Well, if you're reading this section after reading a headline like "cold calling," then you've got what it takes to make this technique work for you. If the phone doesn't intimidate you, then you'll get a job faster than any of your classmates. Virtually every career services director I spoke with told me stories about students who got on the phone and had a job within a day or two. *That's* how effective this technique is. As Debra Fink says, "Job search for *all* the top people is done by phone. People *never* walk in after their résumés. The higher up you are, the less likely you are to send out a résumé!" So phone calling is *definitely* the way to go, if you've got the nerve for it. The downside? There are people who will reject you. They'll cut you off. They may even hang up on you. But put it in perspective; you only need one job. So it doesn't matter if 10 people in a row turn you down, or 20, or 50 — if the next one is your dream employer!

Here's what you do . . .

A. RESEARCH YOUR TARGETS

Do all the preparation I suggest in Chapter 7 on "Interviewing," starting on page 298. Learn everything you can about the employers you intend to contact. No matter how ballsy you are, nothing impresses an employer as much as someone who's taken the time to learn about them beforehand.

B. PRACTICE YOUR SPIEL

The only challenge you ought to face when you call (or meet) a potential employer is to get that person to talk with you. It *shouldn't* be stumbling over your introduction. You ought to develop an introduction that suits your personality, but remember, make it brief, and make it confident, yet humble — you don't want to seem cocky. For instance, you might try something like, "Hello, Ms. Amullmahay. This is Kimm Walton. I appreciate you talking with me. I know you must be busy, so I'll make it short. I read an article about you in the Wisconsin Bar Journal. I found it very interesting and I'd love to learn more about what you do, because I'm interested in a career in environmental law. I'm a Second Year at Case Western Reserve Law School, and I'd appreciate the opportunity to talk with you. I promise I won't take up more than 15 minutes of your time." That's no more than a minute. It's complimentary, it shows you've done some research, and it states what you want. Now, as I said, it's important for you to come up with something that's tailored to *you*; don't just memorize that little spiel. Make something up that accomplishes the same thing, in your own words!

C. MAKE THE CALL — AND GET PAST THE SECRETARY!

1. HANDLING THE SECRETARY

Secretaries are wonderful gatekeepers; if you can't get past them to the people you want to talk to, it doesn't matter *how* great your spiel is. Here's what you ought to do when you call:

◆ Avoid the secretary in the first place! As Debra Fink points out, if you call between 7:30 and 8:00 a.m., or between 5:30 and 6:00 p.m., you're likely to catch the person you want, and avoid his or her secretary altogether.

◆ If you *do* get the secretary, in a very businesslike but polite voice, say, "This is Kimm Walton calling for Sarah Amullmahay." You want to sound confident, and you want to use both your first and last names and the first and last names of the person you're calling. The idea here is that if you speak with enough authority, the secretary may not question you, and just put your call through for you.

♦ OK, let's say the secretary *doesn't* just roll over with your forceful approach, but instead comes back and says, "And which company are you with?" Say, "I'm representing myself." They'll probably ask you what you're calling in reference to. Say that you're calling in reference to correspondence, and then follow up with the question, "Is Ms. Amullmahay available?" As Debra Fink advises, "Don't ever say it's a personal matter! For all you know, the attorney is having a personal crisis, and will be *very* angry with you for lying!" And don't say you're looking for a job, either — another kiss of death! So if you say it regards correspondence, you can always tell the attorney that you're considering sending your résumé, but you wanted to speak with them first.

If mentioning correspondence to the secretary doesn't work, the secretary is likely to say that the person is busy, and will have to call you back. The problem with this is that you want to keep the ball in *your* court, and the only way to do that is if *you're* the one doing the calling. So you'll want to respond, "I'm afraid I'm going to be in and out, and I wouldn't want to miss Ms. Amullmahay's call. What's a good time to call back?" If they won't give you one, then just say you'll call back tomorrow.

Now it's important as you go through this to maintain a pleasant tone of voice, because you're bordering on being pretty pushy. In fact, even though you're just talking on the phone, be sure to smile; it shows in your voice!

♦ *Always* ask the secretary's name, so that when you call again, you can refer to the secretary by name. *Everybody* appreciates that — and befriending a person's secretary can be the very best way to get through to them!

♦ If you're calling on the basis of someone else's referral, *be sure* to mention that to the secretary. You can say, "Jingle Bellknocker told me to give Ms. Amullmahay a call." Even if the secretary doesn't know who the heck Jingle Bellknocker is, if you say it with enough authority, that, by itself, will likely be enough to get you through to the person you want to speak with.

2. GETTING PAST VOICE MAIL

I personally *hate* voice mail, and if you're cold calling, it's your worst enemy. What you want is to be in control of the phone calling, and you can't do that when you leave a voice mail message for them to call you back. So what you want to do is talk to a live person, no matter what. That normally means pressing "zero" at the earliest opportunity, because in most voice-mail systems that gets you to a live operator. Then what you want to do is go through much the same conversation I mention above for secretaries. And if you're asked if you'd like to leave a voice-mail message, the answer is, "I'm afraid I'm in and out a lot, and I don't want to waste Mr. Zapnitz's time. When would be a more convenient time for me to call back?" If they hedge and say there isn't one, then just pick an arbitrary time in the next couple of days and say you'll call back then. Find out the person's name, thank them by name, and get off the phone — then call back, as many times as it takes to get to the person you want to reach!

3. WHAT TO SAY WHEN YOU REACH THE DECISION-MAKER

Here's where your spiel kicks in — the one I told you to memorize in preparation for your calls. After you've gone through your little spiel, if your contact agrees to a meeting, terrific! Set it up, and you're on your way. But what if they're hesitant? For instance, what if they come back with "We're not hiring right now"? *Most* students would shrug, say "Thanks anyway," and leave it at that. *Don't! Be persistent!* You say, "That's fine — I'd still appreciate talking to you, so I can be successful in the future. I can schedule it in at any time that's convenient for you." If they seem hesitant because of the time involved, reiterate that you appreciate how busy they are, but you'd be grateful if they could spare 15 minutes for you at any time that's convenient for them. If they insist that there aren't any opportunities with them in the foreseeable future, say that you appreciate that, and ask if you can take them to an early breakfast at a place on the way to their office, only so you can get their advice about opportunities they see *outside* their firm.

If the contact is *still* hesitant, then ask if there is anyone else in the office with whom you might be able to speak, instead. If that's a dead end, ask what advice they have for someone in your situation. If you're still striking out, guess what? This one's a dead end. Just smile, say "Thank you anyway," and get off the phone.

Now, what have you noticed throughout this exchange? You persisted, past the first objection. A recent *Wall Street Journal* article quoted a corporate recruiter as saying, "Successful candidates don't take 'no' for an answer." And if *you're* going to be a successful candidate, you can't either!

D. COLD-CALLING IN PERSON

Maybe you don't want to mess around with the phone. Maybe you want to cut right to the chase and visit in person. Great! There's probably no faster way to get a job than to get out there and pound the pavement! Most law students don't do it, frankly, because they can't work up the nerve for it. But boy, my advice is, bite the bullet and get out there! I didn't talk with any career services director or any attorney who could find a negative with cold-calling in person. In fact, I spoke with lawyers who rued the fact that more students *didn't* show up in person looking for jobs, because that's what a lot of middle-aged attorneys had to do when *they* graduated from law school! If you plan it right, you can probably hit 20 law firms in a couple of days, and if you're interested in practicing in some other city, that's a great way to make the most of your time. As Wendy Werner told me, "I had a law student who went to a city that had a high concentration of law firms in just a few high-rises. He researched the firms before he visited, and then he just cold-called. He walked from building to building, and he knocked off eight or ten law firms in each building. He asked to see the hiring partners, and if they didn't have time, he befriended the secretaries and asked when a good time to come back might be. Using this cold calling technique he got a job in 3 days!"

If you're going to cold call in person, here's what you do . . .

1. RESEARCH FIRST!

Am I beginning to sound like a broken record again? Even if you've got the guts to cold-call in person, you *still* need to know who you're talking to. And for that, turn to the research section of Chapter 7 on "Interviewing," starting on page 298. At the very least, you need to know what the firm specializes in, how large it is, who handles the hiring, and any other tidbits you can drum up. The more you know before you walk in, the better!

2. HAVE YOUR "PAPERS" READY AND WAITING

I don't mean to make you sound like an AKC puppy, but the fact that you're calling in person doesn't mean you're off the hook when it comes to having your papers. That is, take with you a copy of your résumé, your transcript, and your writing sample. (For information on handling writing samples, look at Chapter 5 on correspondence, and for résumés, go to Chapter 6.) Have them stacked neatly in a briefcase or portfolio, ready to be handed over on request. And don't worry about whether you think your credentials are up to snuff; the fact that you've got the chutzpah to be there meeting with a decision-maker is what'll make you memorable!

3. LOOK PROFESSIONAL!

Wear a good suit, and have a portfolio or briefcase in which you carry your "paperwork" — résumé, transcript, and writing sample. Walk into the office, and introduce yourself, with a smile, to the receptionist. "Hello. I'm Kimm Walton, and I'm here to see Tojo Johosevitz." If the receptionist asks whether Johosevitz is expecting you, you have to be honest — no — but you were hoping you could speak with him for a few minutes. You can even launch into a bit of your spiel, about researching the practice of environmental law, and you'd just like a few minutes of his time, if he can spare them. And remember — say all of this with a smile! Because you've taken the trouble to show up in person, it's likely that the person you're asking for will at least come out and *meet* you, at which time you can ask for a more convenient time to come and talk with them, if this isn't convenient. If they won't speak with you, ask if there's someone else in the firm with whom you might speak. If you run into a dead end, smile graciously, and leave. I didn't promise you that every law firm was going to welcome you with open arms, but, the fact is, so few law students have the guts to show up in person like this that it makes a *huge* impact on most lawyers. It shows the kind of drive, initiative, and confidence that's really prized in job applicants, and that's why, even though you run the risk of face-to-face rejections — the kind that are the hardest to take! — you also face the greatest possibility of a reward, in the form of a job interview.

4. ONCE YOU GET YOUR FOOT THROUGH THE DOOR . . .

Flip back a few pages to "Information Interviewing," on page 143, and take it from there.

E. REMEMBER TO KEEP DEAD ENDS IN PERSPECTIVE!

Even though cold-calling is a great technique, it's not for the faint-hearted. You will face dead ends. But as Debra Fink says, "Look yourself in the mirror afterwards — you may feel awful, but you won't be bleeding." And think how proud you'll be when you *get* that dream job!

2. SNEAKY WAYS TO GET ON-CAMPUS INTERVIEWS WITHOUT GETTING AN ON-CAMPUS INTERVIEW

Normally, the only employers who do on-campus interviews are large law firms and governmental employers; it's just not cost-effective for small organizations to go through the on-campus process. For one thing, they can't afford their attorneys' time. So if it's an on-campus interview you want, I'm assuming you want a large firm job. And if you're reading a section called "Sneaky Ways to Get On-Campus Interviews," I'll take a *real* flyer and assume that you don't have the grades to go the traditional route and just drop your résumé off with career services and be chosen for an on-campus interviewing slot. Who cares! With enough guts, you can do *anything*.

In fact, there are a *bunch* of ways to get an on-campus interview without going the traditional route. I outline the whole procedure, in detail, in Chapter 12, "Getting the Large Law Firm Job You're

Dying For . . . No Matter *What* Your Credentials Are." Specifically, you'll want to read "Sneaky Ways to Get an On-Campus Interview," which starts on page 489. It takes courage, but it *can* be done — heck, it's worked for *lots* of people, just like you!

Information About Pro Bono Students America

In this chapter, I raved about a volunteer program called Pro Bono Students America. Here's more information about it, taken from PBSA's brochure. If you're interested in signing up, talk to your career services director to see if it's offered at your school. If it *isn't* offered, call PBSA directly at 212–998–6222 to see how to get the program to your law school!

What is Pro Bono Students America?

PBSA helps law students across the country find volunteer public interest positions with public interest organizations, government agencies, judges, and private firms with public interest or significant *pro bono* practices. A *pro bono* placement allows students to use their skills to make a contribution to society while also helping to develop valuable and marketable legal experience.

How is Public Interest Work Defined?

PBSA defines public interest work or public service as work in public interest or nonprofit organizations, the courts, government agencies, or private law firms with public interest or *pro bono* practices, or with law school professors on nonscholastic legal issues.

What Kind of Legal Work is Available?

Students participate in a wide variety of legal work, including research and writing, case preparation, client intake, and client representation in administrative hearings. PBSA placements are available in the areas of civil rights, criminal law, health law, environmental law, family law, nonprofit law, housing law, and alternative dispute resolution, among numerous other areas of the law. Nearly 1000 organizations nationwide list volunteer opportunities on the PBSA database.

How do Students Find a Placement?

Interested students should contact the PBSA coordinator at their law school. The PBSA coordinator meets with the student and generates a list of possible placements based on the student's areas of interest. The student can narrow his or her choices by reading through binders containing supplemental information and student evaluations of past placements. The coordinator then contacts the organization of the student's choice and arranges for the student to meet with the designated supervisor at the organization. The PBSA coordinator remains available to provide further assistance, if necessary.

What Commitment does a Student Make by Accepting a Placement?

PBSA encourages students to commit a minimum of 50 hours per placement. Some organizations may request a greater time commitment, or a student could be assigned to a special project requiring less time. The actual time commitment results from an agreement between the member organization and the student. Upon completion of a PBSA placement, a student must complete an evaluation of the experience.

What do Students Gain from PBSA?

Students acquire valuable and marketable legal experience while working on issues they care about. Work done by students aids vastly underserved communities and organizations. Students help their community while enhancing their careers.

How do Organizations Become Members of PBSA?

Membership in the PBSA program is available at no cost to organizations. Organizations simply complete the PBSA membership form and return it to the local PBSA regional director along with detailed information about the organization and the work that would be done by students.

What is Required of PBSA Member Organizations?

Organizations must agree to provide attorney supervision for students performing legal work and must provide students with substantive projects. Twice a year organizations are required to complete and return a short form to the PBSA regional director to assist in maintaining a current database. The PBSA regional director is always available to assist organizations.

What do Organizations Gain from PBSA?

Member organizations benefit from the volunteer services of highly qualified and committed law students. They can increase their caseload, take on new cases, or attack old ones with renewed vigor. By matching student interests with organization needs and educating students about organizations prior to placement, PBSA is able to make hundreds of successful placements each year.

The 16 Best Networking Tips from a Law Student Who Networked His Way to the Top

A chapter about networking wouldn't be complete if I didn't introduce you to J.T. Mann. If you look at his basic credentials, J.T. is about as average as you can get — a poli sci major with mediocre undergrad grades, 4 years after undergrad rattling around as a school teacher and working for a real estate company, and then OK grades at the University of Maine School of Law, from which he graduated last year. But if that's all you know about J.T. Mann, you don't know anything about him at all — because of all of the law students I heard about from career services directors all over the country, J.T. is the living embodiment of the fact that networking *works*. He proves that it pays to let *everyone* know what you can do, and that you're looking for opportunities. And perhaps more importantly, he shows that being a great networker isn't being a glad-handing oleaginous schmoozer — it's just making the most of people you know, and opportunities you get.

Here's his story. As you read it, pay special attention to the fact that here's a guy who *never* lets an opportunity get away!

While J.T. was a student at Maine, he stayed in close contact with the career services director, Tammy Willcox. He also got to know everyone he could, from all of his classmates all the way up to the Dean. One thing he let everybody know is that he could speak Spanish. It turns out that a large insurance company in Maine wanted to do a joint venture with a Spanish company. They weren't happy with any of the chauffeuring services in Portland, so they called the dean at the Maine law school and said they needed Spanish-speaking chauffeurs for the visiting bigwigs for a couple of days the following week. Well, since the dean knew that J.T. spoke Spanish, he told J.T. about the opportunity. J.T. signed up, and was assigned to chauffeur for a day.

During the week before his chauffeuring day, J.T. brushed up on his Spanish. He dug up some Spanish music tapes he had. And he found out who he would chauffeuring — it was going to be the president of the Spanish insurance company, his daughter, his chief financial officer, and his British banker. He did some research on the president of the company, learning about his background and his American holdings.

When J.T. picked up his "fares," he just listened — at first. For the morning, he drove them from appointment to appointment. Then, after lunch, he asked them, in Spanish, if they'd like a tour of Portland. They said yes. He put in the Spanish music tapes, and drove them around, showing them the points of interest. They were delighted he spoke Spanish and loved the tapes. They talked to him, and the conversation strayed from business. He told the chief financial officer where he could get a good deal on golf clubs. He told the president's daughter about great places to shop. He dropped them off in the afternoon, knowing he'd be back to pick them up to drive them to dinner.

After he dropped them off, he went and bought a wide-angle photo of Portland. You see, it was a rainy day, and although he had said Portland was a lovely city, it wasn't shown to its best advantage that day. When he picked them up for dinner, he presented them with the photograph. By the time they got to the restaurant, the president of the company insisted that he join them for dinner. So he did. And during dinner, where J.T. was seated next to the president, they talked about all kinds of things. The president mentioned a city in Spain where his daughter was working, and J.T. mentioned that all he knew about it was that it was where Christopher Columbus had died. The president asked him how he could possibly know that, and J.T. said it was because he had seen a wonderful painting of Columbus on his death bed, and it was in that city. The president was very surprised, and said, "I know that painting. I *love* that painting." Then he looked at J.T. and said, "You should work for me."

So that summer, he did. He went to Madrid, and lived in a company apartment with maid service. He did bits of everything for the insurance company, including some work in the legal department. He made himself as useful as he could be, and he wound up writing an article for a Spanish insurance industry magazine about his internship.

In the meantime, he stayed in touch with the Spanish company's British banker — the other guy he'd chauffeured in Portland. The banker offered him a job in London doing corporate finance. It was a tiny company and the position was a volunteer position, but J.T. jumped at the chance. He worked there for a little while, again making himself as useful as possible. In his free time, he used his computer and the library to research articles that might help them. While they were still too small to hire him full-time, when he got back to the States he kept in touch with them every month, by phone or by fax. Just friendly things — they talked about their kids, about the news. He went to the library once a month and researched U.S. banks and insurance companies for the British company, on a volunteer basis, and sent them anything he thought they might find useful (by the way, he maintains this contact today).

Skip ahead a little bit to his Third Year in law school. He still had hopes of going back to London, but in the meantime, he kept his ear to the ground for other opportunities. He visited the career services office every other day or so to see what was new. In May, a federal district court judge was elevated to the Circuit court, and his budget allowed for another law clerk. The judge called the Maine career services office, and Tammy Willcox called J.T. He sent a letter that day; just a very short, straightforward letter, explaining that he had done a lot of computer-based research and had worked in the law school library for four semesters, so he'd be a great researcher. He wound up saying he thought he could do a good job, and he hoped the judge would consider him for the position. He got an interview, and came in second out of seven applicants, behind a Harvard student.

But the story doesn't end there. After graduation, he hung out his own shingle, but kept in touch with his colleagues from law school. In November, a large firm in Portland called the Maine Law Review office, looking for someone to work a few hours a week. Since most Law Review people have jobs by November, there were none of them available — but the student who answered the phone knew J.T., and knew he might be interested in the job. So the student called J.T., and J.T. called the firm, saying he was already licensed and he could work as many hours as they needed. They were excited. He worked a few hours a week for them, and went out of his way to use his computer to find useful research for them. After 3 weeks, they offered him a position as a contract associate. But then, *after* that, the person who'd beaten J.T. out for the appeals court clerkship couldn't do it, and the judge called J.T. back. And that's why he's now got a real plum of a job. After the clerkship? He really wants to go back to London.

Do you think he'll make it? With his networking skills, if he wanted a job on the *moon*, he'd get it!

I asked J.T. to share his best networking tips with you, and he graciously agreed. Here they are:

J.T. MANN'S 16 BEST NETWORKING TIPS

1. LET EVERYBODY *KNOW YOUR INTERESTS*

"I had three basic things that I communicated to everyone. I was interested in international work, I was interested in business, and I wanted to use my ability to speak Spanish. I told *everybody* that, even the Dean. That way when the chauffeuring job came up that required a Spanish-speaker, he thought of me."

2. REMEMBER THAT EVERYBODY IS IMPORTANT!

"When I started my own private practice out of law school, I was introduced to the shoeshine guy in a high rise office building downtown. He was a Cuban immigrant, and he turned out to be my best contact, because he knew *everybody* in the Spanish-speaking community. I got all kinds of work, from immigration cases to representing a Spanish-speaking church, because of this guy. So remember that *everybody* is important."

3. IGNORE PEOPLE WHO ARE PESSIMISTS!

"If you want to do something out of the ordinary, ignore people who are downers. *Everyone* can go to a law firm, and everybody will applaud you if you want to do that. But if you want to try something different, it's hard to stand your ground. People don't understand why you'd want to do something that pays less than a law firm. Don't listen to anyone who's going to pull you down!"

4. HELP OTHER PEOPLE WITH WHAT THEY *WANT*

"It's an old saying, but it's true — what goes around, comes around. When I talk to people and they tell me what *they* want, I try to help them. Sometimes I'll come across job opportunities that I'm not interested in, and I'll pass them on to people I think might want them. That way, when they run into something they don't want that's right up my alley — like something international, or something involving Spanish — then they'll think of me."

5. REMEMBER THAT YOU ONLY NEED ONE JOB!

"The idea of getting multiple offers is exciting, but remember that you only need one job. Whenever I've had trouble finding a job, I've told myself that, and I've always found it very motivating."

6. EVERY SUCCESS MASKS A STRING OF FAILURES

"Whenever anybody hears about my internship in Spain or my clerkship for the judge, they think, wow, he was really lucky. But that's not true. I've gotten a bunch of rejections, a lot of unreturned letters, a lot of different failures. That's true for anybody with any successes; there's always a history behind them. So whenever you see someone you consider a success, pay attention to everything that went into that success. And remember: you have to try as many times as it takes to get what you want!"

7. GO THE EXTRA MILE — PUSH TO GET WHERE YOU WANT TO GO

"If you want something, no matter whether you think you can get it and whether anyone's ever tried and failed before, *try* for it. When I was chauffeuring the people from the Spanish insurance company, I spent some time beforehand trying to think of what

I could offer, what extra things I could do. And I realized that the one thing that I had was that I was the local. They didn't know Portland, and I did. So I made the most of that, taking them on a tour, and finding them things I thought would interest them. *Always* be on the lookout for extra things you can do to distinguish yourself."

8. KNOW YOUR PROFESSORS!

"It's too easy to show up at class and then leave. When you're in law school, you need to line up references. When you get out, most of your experience in law will be law school, and those professor references are good ones to have. Get to know your profs, even if at first they seem like stinkers, or they seem crotchety. Maybe they're that way because what they're really interested in is research. Find out what they like, and take an interest in *that* as a means of getting to know them. It's worth it."

9. REQUEST SPECIAL OPPORTUNITIES

"If there's something special that you want, ask for it! At Maine, I wanted to take an international tax class, but there weren't any offered. I'm interested in international business, so I pushed for a seminar or a special research project on it. A lot of times, students go through their law school's catalog, and they'll see opportunities like that, but when they get there they don't pursue it. That's a shame because those are a great way to pursue a special interest."

10. TAKE ADVANTAGE OF UNPAID INTERNSHIPS AND VOLUNTEER OPPORTUNITIES

"It doesn't take much to make the most of internships and volunteering opportunities. I volunteered for a congressional campaign. The guy got knocked out in the primaries, but I met a friend of his during the campaign who was a senior partner at a law firm, and I wound up with an offer from them. When you volunteer, it doesn't matter what you do. Nobody cares if you lick envelopes. The important thing is, they get a chance to *see* you. A lot of times that's all it takes."

11. LEARN LEXIS AND WESTLAW!

"Get good at using Lexis and Westlaw. They're a terrific research tool, and a lot of research in the future is going to be on-line. Also, you'll have a skill that senior partners don't feel comfortable with, so they'll rely on you for it. When I was clerking at a firm, a big litigation case came in. There was a nationally-known case that was something like it, so I went on-line to get the briefs from that other case, figuring that there might be some issues that we could use in *our* case. I got the briefs, and took them to the partner in charge of the case. It turns out the briefs were really useful, because there were a lot of issues on point, and having those briefs condensed many hours worth of research to about an hour. He thought it was great!"

12. FOREIGN LANGUAGES ARE A GREAT RESOURCE

"If you ever took a language, keep your fluency or tune it up. Almost every community can use a lawyer who speaks another language — it's a very marketable skill."

13. ALWAYS SAY THANK YOU!

"When people help me out or give me tips to get in the door somewhere, I send them a bottle of sparkling cider as a 'thank you.' For some situations that would be overbearing, but in other situations, it's just right — and people really appreciate the special 'thank you.'"

14. DON'T OVERLOOK THE OPPORTUNITY TO CREATE YOUR OWN JOB

"If you listen carefully in interviews, you'll sometimes learn very valuable things even if you don't get an offer. For instance, if the interviewer says that the firm's paralegals are overworked or they're not happy with their research, there's an opportunity between the lines. What does that tell you? Especially for firms away from big communities, it's tough for them to get good research. You could offer a service for $15 or $20 an hour to do basic research. So even if you don't get the offer, you may find ways to create your own job."

15. DON'T OVERLOOK YOUR CAREER SERVICES OFFICE!

"Your career services office can be your best friend. A *lot* goes through there. You can read books, newsletters, and find something on anything you want. I found lots of things about international issues and tax, which are two of my interests. You get all this information and you can mold it and craft it to your needs. It's a gold mine!"

16. ALWAYS HAVE A WRITING SAMPLE READY!

"Always have your paperwork together — your résumé, your writing sample, a transcript. You can even have the basic paragraphs of a cover letter ready, although you'll want to customize that for every situation. The point is that every time you apply shouldn't be a struggle. Also, make sure your writing sample shows your style. I use the first 10 pages of an independent study I did on international law. It shows them how I write and also shows what my interests are."

Chapter 5

Correspondence – Making Your Letters to Potential Employers *Sing!*

I'm going to start this chapter with something that's a little bit unfair. That's because although I'm going to spend this chapter teaching you exactly how to write letters to potential legal employers, I'm going to start you off with something that has nothing to do with law at all. But stay with me for a minute, because I'm doing it to prove a point.

Here's the setup. Since you're reading something that I wrote, it doesn't take Einstein to figure out that I'm a writer. When writers send letters to publishers to see if they'd be interested in publishing something, those letters are called "query letters." (Perhaps you're beginning to see the analogy here, since the letters you send will also be designed to pique someone's interest in something — namely, meeting with you. Although the interest you'll be piquing is different, the principles are exactly the same. Trust me on this one.) Anyway, back to query letters. Now, publishers get a kajillion query letters, and so the sole purpose of query letters is to try and get them to nibble, and take a look at a manuscript.

Just by way of an example, let's say that I've got a book that I want to get published. (That happens to be true.) Let's say that the book is a funny book about dating. (It is.) And let's say that I do some research and find out exactly who would be the perfect publisher for this book, based on other books they publish. (Also true.) So I find out the name of the acquisitions editor at that publisher (which I did) — that is, the person who decides which books to publish. Let's say that person's name is Muggo Doodleberry. (It's not.) So I sit down at my trusty word processor, and I start to bang out a letter:

> Dear Mr. Doodleberry,
>
> *I have been a writer for 10 years, since I graduated from law school at the Case Western Reserve University School of Law. I have an extensive list of writing credits, starting with a book I wrote about investing in biotechnology, followed by a series of legal study aids called "Law In A Flash," as well as some articles about travel writing and some screenplays. My most recent project is a new book from Harcourt Brace called "Guerrilla Tactics for Getting the Legal Job of Your Dreams."*
>
> *I am writing to you because I have manuscript I am interested in submitting to you for your perusal. . . .*

Gee, what do you think so far? Z-z-z-z-z-z-z? That's my reaction, and that would be Muggo Doodleberry's reaction, too. This letter commits the cardinal sin of letter-writing, and the sin applies equally to letters to legal employers as it does to publishing houses. It's this: *It's boring. Nobody* I write to gives a damn about me. They don't care what I've done. That doesn't matter to anyone except me and maybe my family. All they want to know is *what's in it for them?* I'm telling you this at the beginning of this chapter, because there's nothing more important I can tell you about letter writing than this:

> *The entire focus of every letter you write to any prospective employer is this: What's in it for them? What can you bring to the table for them? Why should they want to meet you?* **That's the only thing that matters.**

I'm sorry if that's a cold drink of water for you, but that's why I used myself as an example. That letter I wrote to Muggo Doodleberry? It didn't capture his interest. If anything, it belied the whole purpose of my letter, which was to convince him that I'd written a *funny* book. That letter makes me sound like a *stiff,* not a comedy writer.

Now as you've probably already guessed, that's not *really* the letter I sent to Muggo Doodleberry. The real letter started like this:

Dear Mr. Doodleberry:

If Henry the Eighth wrote himself a singles ad, how would it start? "Male, divorced, widowed, widowed, divorced, widowed . . . "

How could a guy blow it at the very beginning of a blind date? How about exclaiming, "My mom has that very same dress"?

How would you define a dating service? Perhaps as "Paying someone else to introduce you to the kind of person they couldn't pay you to date"?

These are some of the bits from a book you may be interested in publishing under your Peacock imprint. I've tentatively titled it "Dating 101," and I'd like to submit it to you because I think it would fit well with the humor books you already publish, like "The Worst Ideas of the Best Thinkers" and "My Car And Welcome To It." It's about the same length as those books, it's targeted at the same audience, and I like to think it's just as funny!

"Dating 101" features. . . .

. . . and so on. Now, put yourself in Muggo Doodleberry's shoes. If you got that letter, would you be enticed into seeing the manuscript? I already know the answer to that, because old Muggo had his secretary call me within an hour of when he received the letter, asking to see the book itself. I'm not telling you that as a means of patting myself on the back, but instead to drive home a very simple point — the *only* thing I had in mind when I wrote that letter was this: *What's going to make him want to see my book?* And I thought, well, it would make sense to start the letter with some of the stuff from the book, because it's funny, and because it will intrigue him enough to make him keep reading. It was clear very quickly what was in it for him — the opportunity to get his hands on a very funny book.

Now, it just so happens that the kind of stuff I included in the first, boring example I showed you *is* somewhat relevant. Publishers *do* want to know what else you've published, so they have some assurance that you're not going to send them something fit to line a bird cage. But that's icing on the cake, and that's why I included that kind of information (worded more interestingly than it was here) in the last paragraph of my letter. But I'm getting away from my central thesis, which is: never forget who your audience is. And never forget their entire motivation as they read anything you send them, which is: *What's in it for me?*

If you stopped reading this chapter right now and went away with that one simple message, your letters to legal employers would be a thousand percent better than the ones your uninformed classmates will send. But you know me better than that; I'm not going to leave you hanging out to dry. I'll show you everything you need to know to write killer cover letters — ones that will make legal employers *want* to interview you. And that's all that counts, right?

So, in this chapter, I'm going to show you how to write letters that *guarantee* you'll get a response. I'll show you exactly what your letters ought to do, and what they *shouldn't* do. The long and the short of it is — I'll show you how to make the most of every letter you write!

How am I going to do that? Well, we're going to go in this order:

♦   First, I'll show you the prep work you have to do before you send any letter. *Mark my words — you can't send a great letter without doing research first, any more than you can cook a great dish without having the ingredients.*

♦   Then, we'll go over the different kinds of letters you may be tempted to send. And in this section, I'll show you the seven magic words that *guarantee* you'll get a response to your letter.

♦   After that, we'll go through exactly what ought to go into your letters. We'll talk about format, and elements, and overall concerns.

♦   As a coda to talking about letters, I'll take you through the biggest mistakes students make when they write letters to prospective employers. And I'll include some truly hilarious boners that career services directors told me about.

♦   I'll talk about the pros and cons of including résumés with your letters.

♦   Then, we'll talk about writing samples, and what they ought to look like.

♦ I'll give you some special advice about how to contact small firms.

♦ Finally, we'll deal with what you do *after* you send your letters; that is, follow-ups and thank yous.

With that little introduction in mind — let's get started!

A. *RESEARCH* YOUR QUARRY BEFORE YOU SEND *ANY* LETTER!

I said it in the introduction, and I'll repeat it again here: you simply *must* research anyone to whom you send a letter, and I'm talking about more than making sure you've got their name spelled correctly (although that's really important, too). What you have to do is gather all the information you possibly can before you write a letter to any prospective employer. Why? Because you're going to use that information in your cover letter to make the employer feel as though you're particularly interested in them, that you're really enthusiastic about working for that specific employer. Albany's Sandy Mans puts it succinctly: "Do your homework!"

If that bothers you, it could be for one of two reasons. One is that you don't want to be bothered to make the effort when it would be so much easier to just come up with a generic letter and send it to everyone you might want to work for. Well, too bad. You've got to do more work than that — at least, if you actually expect to get responses to the letters you write. And I'm not talking about a lot of effort, anyway; no more than 15 minutes per employer. As NYU's Gail Cutter points out, "All you really need is one little nugget of information, and 15 minutes on Nexis will give you that!" If *that* time commitment bothers you, it's time to put things in perspective. What you expect the employer to do is to take the time to interview you (which is time they could spend billing their clients), and to make you an offer, and to invest tens of thousands of dollars in paying you and training you. All *I'm* asking you to do in return is to spend 15 measly minutes learning about them before you write to them, OK?

The other reason you may be bothered is that you're not sure *how* to go about researching potential employers. That's no big deal. I'll show you *exactly* how to do that. In fact, I think that what you'll find is that there's a smooth continuum from making contacts, to sending correspondence, to interviewing. In every one of those instances, I'm telling you to get as much information as you can about the people you're meeting, or writing to, or interviewing with. The sources you use and the kinds of information you're looking for are largely the same (and this is also a roundabout way of saying that if this advice looks familiar to you, there's a good reason for it — you've seen it before in Chapter 4 on making contacts, and you'll see it *again* in Chapter 7 on Interviewing). So the beauty of doing this kind of research is that if you do it in preparation for meeting people, or for sending letters, you don't have to do it again — you can take care of it all in one fell swoop!

With that in mind, let's talk about the research that you have to do before you write to any prospective employer. You're really looking for three things: a mutual acquaintance, and two kinds of information: hard information and "soft," or inside, information. Let's take a look at each of these.

1. A MUTUAL ACQUAINTANCE WITH SOMEONE AT THE EMPLOYER YOU'RE CONTACTING

This is the golden goose of correspondence. The thing you want to find more than anything else in the world is a flesh-and-blood link between you and the employer in question. When you think about it, all of Chapter 4, on making contacts, was about that — getting to employers by making personal contacts. Now the most likely way you're going to find a mutual contact is by doing all the kinds of networking that I suggested in Chapter 4. But it may be that you really want to work in a particular city or for a particular employer, and you strike out in your networking activities in digging up a mutual acquaintance. Then what? Well, use your career services director. Tell them what area of practice you want and what city you want to work in. I'll guarantee you that they'll be able to put you in contact with *someone* who'll be able to help you, and maybe that someone will know someone at the firm you want to contact . . . and so on. That's how contacts work; you always have to be willing to say, "Who else do you think I should contact?"

2. HARD INFORMATION

This is concrete stuff like cities where the firm has offices, practice areas, biographies of lawyers in the firm, that kind of thing. Here's a checklist for you:

♦ On-line Information from Lexis and/or Westlaw

Most schools have computer access to help you with your job search. The two major on-line services are Lexis and Westlaw. These services provide a whole treasure trove of basic information about many employers, especially the larger ones. There isn't room to detail everything you can find on them here, but here are the kinds of things you should find out:

- Size of firm.
- Areas of practice.
- Biographies of lawyers who work there — including where they went to college and law school.
- Cases the employer has been involved in.
- Clients the employer has represented.
- Any current mention of the employer in the news.

There are bunches of other things to find out, but those are the *kinds* of things you should research. What if your school *doesn't* give you computer access? You can use the NALP forms and Martindale-Hubbell, as outlined below, to get you the same information — it'll just take longer.

♦ The Employer's NALP Form

The NALP form (which stands for National Association of Law Placement) provides all kinds of basic information about the firm. Every career services office carries up-to-date NALP forms.

Now this won't be terribly useful if the employer is a small firm, because only larger employers bother with NALP forms. But you should always check to see if the employer has filled one out.

What does this kind of information help you do? It stops you from making big bad boners, for one thing. For instance, it will tell you which areas of practice the firm's involved with. By way of example, let's say the NALP form tells you that the firm in question focuses on litigation only. Well, that'll stop you from stating in your letter that you're interested in the firm's "litigation department," when that's all they do!

♦ Martindale-Hubbell

... or "Mar-Hub" as it's sometimes called, is a huge directory with biographical information on every practicing attorney in the country. It's available on-line from Lexis, but every law library in the country stocks it. (Westlaw has a similar service on-line; it's called the Directory of Legal Employers.)

You want to use Martindale-Hubbell to check the background of not just the person you're writing to, but everybody else in the firm, as well. You're looking for any possible connections between you and that person; e.g., a similar undergraduate school, or some common experience or interest. This will be very useful to you in bringing up elements about yourself in your letter that will interest that person.

3. INSIDE SCOOP

This is where you find out what it's *really* like to work at the firm. It's the kind of thing you won't find published *anywhere*, but it's the kind of stuff that's really useful to you. Remember, in the context of correspondence, what you're looking for are tidbits about the firm that you can mention in your letter. In particular, you'll want to find out if there are any particular skills or traits the employer prizes in law students, because you'll want to key your cover letter to focus on any match between what they're looking for and what you've got. And you're also looking for tidbits on anything the firm is particularly proud of, which translates into something that would earn you lots of brownie points if you mention it in your letter.

Now if you skip ahead to Chapter 7 on Interviewing, you'll see that this is very much the kind of information I implore you to dig up before you go on an interview. So if you do it in preparation for sending a cover letter, you only have to do it once — you'll have everything you need for your interview, as well!

Here's a checklist of places to look for the inside scoop:

♦ **Your Career Services Director**

An *excellent* and frequently overlooked source of gossip. Remember, a large fraction of your career services director's time is spent networking, so they normally hear the most excellent stuff. Pick their brains for it!

Also, they will be able to put you onto three other sources of good inside dirt (although, as I mentioned just above, be a little more circumspect about the questions you ask, since the people you'll talk with may be useful for putting you onto other job leads and so you want to appear professional).

- ♦ **Alumni Who've Worked at the Firm**
- ♦ **Upperclassmen Who've Clerked at the Firm**
- ♦ **Other Students Who Have Interviewed at the Firm**

And you may want to ask the opinion of:

- ♦ **Any Local Attorneys You've Contacted**

So, now you've got your research firmly in hand. Ideally, you've got a mutual acquaintance with someone at the firm (it's not fatal if you don't, but it's *vastly* helpful if you do, as I'll go into in more detail in Topic B in just a minute). You know about what the firm does, and you've got anything written about them recently in the news. You've got a flavor for what they look for in employees and what they're proud of, as well as any other interesting tidbits about them, on the basis of talking with people like your career services director and alumni who are familiar with the firm. With that in mind, let's talk about the kinds of letters you might send.

B. THE THREE BASIC TYPES OF LETTERS TO POTENTIAL LEGAL EMPLOYERS . . . INCLUDING THE SEVEN MAGIC WORDS THAT *ENSURE* A RESPONSE!

Now, it may be unfair to make this assumption, but here it is. There's a possibility that you were standing in a bookstore, and you were perusing the back cover of this book, and you saw the line about the seven magic words that ensure a response to letters you send. And you opened it to the Table of Contents, and found this section, and you figure that what you'll do is just memorize the seven words, and bag buying the book. Why do I think this? Because I'd be tempted to do the same thing, if I wasn't personally aware of how wonderful the rest of this book is.

Anyway, if this is the very first thing you're seeing in this book — hello! Welcome! As promised, in this section I'm going to go over the three basic kinds of letters you can send. Here they are:

- ♦ A personal letter, in the sense that you've either met the person you're writing to, or — as is more likely the case — you know somebody *they* know, and that somebody told you to write to them.

- ♦ A so-called "targeted" mailer, where you heavily research no more than a couple of dozen legal employers at a time, and send them distinctive letters.

♦ The old law school chestnut, the mass mailer — where you send hundreds of the same letter to legal employers, using a mail merge to change the name and address on each letter.

Let's go over each of them separately.

1. "PERSONAL" LETTERS THAT YOU SEND EITHER TO PEOPLE YOU'VE MET OR TO PEOPLE WITH WHOM YOU HAVE A MUTUAL ACQUAINTANCE. P.S.: THIS IS WHERE THE SEVEN MAGIC WORDS ARE

The very best, the very strongest, the most powerful letter you can send to any prospective legal employer starts with these seven words:

[Mutual acquaintance] recommended that I contact you.

If you can start every letter you write with the name of someone your addressee knows, I *promise* you will always get a response to your letters. *Every time.* In fact, for some attorneys, it's the *only* way they'll bother reading your letter. As Washington's Teresa DeAndrado says, "Alums tell me the only time they'll look at a letter is when it starts, 'So-and-so told me to call you.'" *That's* how powerful that opening is!

Now, especially if this is the first section you turned to in this book, you may be thinking to yourself, "Well, that's all well and good, Kimmbo. But how the heck am I supposed to find a mutual acquaintance for every job I want?" That's the whole point of Chapter 4, on making contacts! If you do the things I suggest there — like taking part in local bar association activities, and using your career services director and alumni, you should be able to find a mutual acquaintance for virtually any job you want. Or at least, you'll find a mutual acquaintance for an information interview, and through a series of referrals, you'll find *somebody* who knows someone you want to contact. So the simple fact is, yes, it *does* take a bit of work to be able to say, "[Mutual acquaintance] recommended that I contact you." But the fact that making contacts is the best way to get a job, and using this opening to a letter ensures you'll get a response, ought to be enough to convince you that it's worth it!

You may be wondering what ought to go in the letter *after* that first, magical sentence. You'll find exactly that in the section that talks about the content of letters, Topic C, below.

But first, let's talk about the other two basic types of letters.

2. "TARGETED" MAILERS – DISTINCTIVE LETTERS SENT TO A COUPLE OF DOZEN CAREFULLY CHOSEN POTENTIAL EMPLOYERS AT A TIME

Now it may well be that despite your most diligent efforts, you just can't come up with a mutual acquaintance whose name can open your letter to a potential employer. What do you do in that situation? The next best thing — a targeted mailer. It's not nearly as desirable as a "mutual acquaintance" letter, but it'll do in a pinch.

What you do with a targeted mailer first, is to do all of the research that I recommended in Topic A, above. You dig up every possible fact on the employers you intend to contact. And then you send them a letter redolent with that research. You show them how, based on what you've learned about them, you have skills they'll be able to put to use.

Now I'll go into much more detail as to what to put in the guts of your letter in Topic C, below. My only intent here is to introduce you to targeted mailings as a type of letter you can send to employers — and to tell you that they're worth sending!

3. MASS MAILERS

Boy, there was no topic that brought more colorful curses to the lips of career services directors than the topic of mass mailers. You know what I'm talking about: the time-honored law student tradition of coming up with a generic letter, getting hundreds of names from Martindale-Hubbell (or some other directory of employers), doing a mail merge, and spitting out hundreds of identical letters, typically starting out with a line like, "I am currently a second year student at. . . . " You've probably seen the kind of letter I'm talking about. I'm hoping for your sake that you haven't wasted your time sending them, and I promise you I'm going to beg you not to do so in the future! Why? There are a bunch of good reasons not to waste your time on mass mailers, including these:

♦   They don't work. Fordham's Kathleen Brady says, "Five hundred pieces addressed to 'hiring partner' simply *will not work.*" And San Diego's Susan Benson adds, "On mass mailings, a 2–3% return is considered a fantastic success!

The statistics for mass mailers are just *awful.*" The fact is, no employer wants to feel like another name on a list, and that's what mass mailers make them feel like. And *that's* why they don't work!

♦ They mislead you into feeling as though you've done something concrete to find a job. There's no question that there's a heft to a box of 500 letters, and the busywork associated with putting such a mailer together makes you feel like you've really accomplished something worthwhile. But the fact is — you haven't. As NYU's Gail Cutter points out, "You're much better off with 10 really targeted letters instead of a hundred nontargeted ones." And that's true even though the hundred will make you feel like you've done more. Don't mislead yourself!

♦ They lead to humiliation, and while rejection is a natural and unavoidable part of looking for a job, it's a good idea to minimize it. When you send out hundreds of unfocused letters, you're begging for rejection, and that'll just make you feel worse about the entire job search process — and worst of all, *your misery will be unnecessary!*

Having said all this, it *is* true that if you're the editor-in-chief of the Harvard Law Review, you can scrawl your résumé on a brown paper bag with a crayon, send it to whomever you want, and get an offer. But if you don't have screaming credentials like that, don't bother with mass mailers!

C. CONTENT: DECIDING WHAT GOES IN THE LETTERS YOU SEND

Now that you're clear on the two types of letters you'll be sending — ideally, personal letters, or, as an alternative, targeted mailings — it's time to talk about what ought to go into those letters. What I'll do here is discuss two principal issues:

♦ The *format* of your letters, including the *elements to include* in your letters; and

♦ The *style* of your letters.

Now if you've flipped ahead a few pages, you may notice that there's something distinctive about this section; namely, I'm not giving you any sample letters. Before you feel gypped, let me explain why I'm not doing that. It's because I'd be doing you a huge disservice if I did. No matter how much I begged you, I know what you'd be tempted to do; you'd be tempted to copy any sample letters word-for-word, and send them out chock-a-block to legal employers. I don't want you to do that, for two very good reasons. One is that the whole basis of my approach is that you've got to personalize your letters to the greatest extent possible. *Any* letter I'd give you here by its very nature couldn't be personalized to your needs. Instead, I'll be showing you, sentence by sentence, how to do that! The other reason is that canned letters make a horrible impression on legal employers. I promise you, if you copy a letter out of a popular cover letter book, any employer you send it to will recognize it as being identical to a bunch of other ones they've received. Suffice it to say that will not reflect positively on you!

So what I'm going to do here instead is to go through your entire letter, explaining everything it ought to contain. With my guidance and a bit of thought, you'll be able to come up with letters much better than anything you'll find in *any* book!

With that in mind — let's get started!

1. THE FORMAT FOR YOUR LETTERS

What I'm going to give you here is a basic, three-paragraph format for your letters. It gives you a good, solid framework for setting up your letters. In a nutshell, here is what each of the three paragraphs accomplishes:

- ♦ Why should the reader bother reading the rest of your letter?
- ♦ Why should they meet you?
- ♦ What do you want to happen next?

That's it. Now, we're going to go through these in a lot more detail, but don't ever take your eye off the ball: those three basic goals are all you need to accomplish in your cover letter.

Let's take a look at them individually.

A. THE FIRST PARAGRAPH OF YOUR LETTER: WHY SHOULD THE READER BOTHER READING THE REST OF YOUR LETTER?

What you're going to accomplish in this first paragraph is giving your reader some hook, some reason for going on. And what that's going to boil down to is the *why* of your letter; that is, why did you write?

This segues nicely to the two types of letters I've suggested that you focus on: namely, personal letters and targeted mailers. The opening of your personal letter is the seven magic words I discussed a few minute ago, namely:

[Mutual acquaintance] recommended that I contact you.

Well, you can see how that fits my criteria here. What that does is to make your reader say, "Hmm. I know mutual acquaintance, and if (s)he thinks I ought to pay attention to this person, I will."

Now, what about if you don't have a mutual acquaintance, and you're just sending a targeted mailing? What you're basically going to do is to state why you're writing. *Ideally*, you'll be able to draw on something you learned in your research as a means of leading off your letter. For instance:

I was fascinated to read your profile in the September issue of the Northern Moose County Bar Journal. In it, you described your firm as being on the cutting edge of biotech patent law. As a second year law student at Case Western Reserve, I have a strong, demonstrated interest in patent law, and would welcome the opportunity to work with you as a part-time or summer associate, as your needs require.

Or this one:

Susan Amullmahay, a former summer clerk at your firm, described your firm to me as a dynamic environment for learning about criminal defense work — and I found upon further research that she's not the only one who thinks so! As a first year law student at Case Western Reserve with a strong interest in criminal law, I would be very interested in pursuing possible job opportunities with you.

Clearly, it takes some work and some research to be able to come up with openings like that. And that's just the point! What you're doing with a personal letter or targeted mailing is to make the employer feel unique, and in doing so, you'll distance yourself from the competition.

Now, I've already told you that the focus of the first paragraph is to get your reader to want to read on; to explain why you're writing. So it should include:

♦ What the catalyst was for your letter, be it a recommendation from a mutual acquaintance (the best), something about the employer that struck you in particular (still very good), or a straightforward reason for your letter, like your interest in working for them (pretty good).

♦ Who you are, if you don't include it in the first sentence.

♦ What you want (e.g., an interview, a summer associate-ship, a permanent position).

That's it. With three sentences or so, you should be done. Let's take a look at how a first paragraph in a personal letter might look, with these elements in mind:

Booboo Meerschaum of Pype, Cleaner, and Toadstool recommended that I contact you. As a temporary legal clerk, I recently completed some tax work for Mr. Meerschaum. Since he was pleased with my work and familiar with your needs, he indicated that you might be interested in meeting with me to review my background and how it might fit with your plans for either this summer or next year.

Here's another one:

Babaloo Beestung, director of the Career Services Office of Case Western Reserve University School of Law, recommended that I contact you, as I have a technical and regulatory background in which you may be particularly interested. I would like very much to have the opportunity to work for you as a summer clerk, and thereafter on a part-time basis if possible, after my first year of law school.

And here's one without a personal connection:

I was very interested to read a recent article in the La Jolla Examiner about your representation of the Humpty Dumpty Diner. Upon further research, I learned that your firm gears its civil practice toward small businesses. I am particularly interested in this kind of practice, and would like to pursue an associate position with your firm should one arise. I will be relocating to La Jolla in September to rejoin close family who have moved to the area. I realize that under normal circumstances you cannot predict your hiring needs this far in advance. Thus, I would appreciate the opportunity to meet with you personally when I am next in the area to discuss the nature of your practice in more detail, and share with you those elements of my background that would be relevant to your needs, should an opening arise in the future.

OK, I realize that last one is six sentences long, and I said you could get away with no more than three. But I included it to make a point: if you're on a roll, it's more important to pursue a good concept than it is to stick with a strict sentence count.

Now, what if you're responding to a job listing in the placement office, or an ad in the newspaper? I've told you before that these aren't nearly as fertile grounds for jobs as personal contacts, but the fact is, people *do* get jobs through them. And if you respond to a job listing or ad, the same principal I've been hammering home throughout this section applies: Namely, *make it interesting!* That's not so easy to do when you're responding to an ad, but you can *always* inject enthusiasm into your response. Here's an example:

> *I was very excited to see your advertisement for a summer legal clerkship. I am extremely interested in environmental law, and so I would love to work for the Environmental Protection Agency.*

What it lacks in personalization, it makes up for in enthusiasm!

I could go on and on about the opening paragraph alone, but I think you get the point. Explain why you're writing, who you are, and what you want. Make sure you keep the focus on what *your reader's* interests are, not your own, and keep it interesting. That's it!

B. THE SECOND PARAGRAPH OF YOUR LETTER: WHY SHOULD YOUR READER MEET YOU?

The second paragraph of your letter is where you wheel in your big guns. Specifically, you bring in the specific things about yourself and your background which will make the reader think, "Gee, I really ought to give this person a chance!"

What you'll want to do here is to go through your background — exactly the same kind of background check you do in writing a résumé, as I advise in Chapter 6 — and choose the two or three things about you that will be of most use to the employer. How do you know what they need? That's part of what you learned in your research, remember? So you'll know if they need someone who's a self-starter, or someone who has taken particular classes, or exactly *what* elements of your background can be tailored to address that employer's needs. Now there are a couple of things to keep in mind here.

1. DON'T PARROT YOUR RÉSUMÉ!

The second paragraph of your letter shouldn't be a mere rehash of your résumé. As William & Mary's Rob Kaplan points out, "When you put in letter form what's on your résumé, you're showing the recipient the same information twice. They don't need that." What your résumé really represents is the bare bones, the mere facts of your background. The second paragraph of your letter has to build on that, by showing *how* your specific experiences translate into transferable skills which will be of use to this particular employer. You'll show why what you learned from what you've done can be useful to the employer. As Rob Kaplan says, "You have to first sit down and decide what two or three points you want to make about yourself in the letter. If you have strong client relation skills, that's a topic sentence. And then as support for that, pull different things from your background that support that proposition. Maybe something from law school, like success in a client counseling competition, and then something from a summer job, like being a counselor at a camp. It's *very* important to do some self-assessment first, and find what supports the contentions you make. You can't just say, 'I did this job, and here's what I did there, and I did this job, and here's what I did there.'"

You may also find that your strengths come from unusual sources, which will make for a very interesting cover letter. One career services director told me about a student who was very interested in working for Legal Aid. His problem was that as a white, middle-class kid, there was nothing to suggest that he'd have any rapport whatsoever with the clients he'd have at Legal Aid. But as it turns out, he worked as a trash collector during the summer after First Year, and his "beat" was a low-income neighborhood. He developed a rapport with people in the neighborhood, and learned a lot about a way of life he'd had no exposure to previously. When he applied for a summer clerkship with Legal Aid for the summer after

Second Year, that experience was a real plus — and made for a fascinating cover letter!

So the key here is — don't just have your cover letter mirror your résumé. Show *why* what you've learned will be useful to this particular employer!

2. DON'T LIST WHAT YOU'RE GOOD AT WITHOUT PROOF!

As Albany's Sandy Mans points out, "If you're going to say, 'I'm a great writer, a good researcher, and a hard worker,' you have to back it up! *Show* that you're a hard worker by pointing out that you've juggled several jobs, or worked without supervision, or whatever."

Rob Kaplan also offers a simple trick for determining if you've written your second paragraph correctly. That is, check for the word "because." If you're going to say that you've got strong research skills, you have to provide the "because;" for instance, because you worked for a semester as a research assistant to Professor Werbezerk.

As a final example, let's say that you're applying for a government job. You want to stress your long-standing commitment to the area of law practiced by the department or agency, as evidenced by certain undergrad and law school courses you've taken, internships, research projects, bar association activities, conferences you've attended, and the like.

Now, you may be tempted to bring in every single example you can think of to back up any contention you make. Don't fall into that trap! Two or three features, and an experience or two to support each of them, is all you need.

So the key here is: be sure to back up everything you say with *evidence*.

3. MAKE SURE YOUR LETTER SHOWS THAT YOU'VE RESEARCHED THE EMPLOYER

Remember, the thing that distinguishes a personal or targeted letter from a mass mailer is the fact that you put information about the employer in your cover letter. It's not enough that you've gone to the trouble of researching the employer — you have to show *evidence* of that in your cover letter. As Boston University's Betsy Armour says, *"Communicate* what you know about what they do!" Benesch Friedlander's Deanna Coe Kursh echoes this, saying, "At the very least, show that you've read the firm's NALP form, if they have one." (That's a form that all large employers keep on file with career services offices. So if you're applying to a large, established employer, be sure to check out their NALP form before you contact them.)

Now, what happens if you try to research an employer and come up empty? Acknowledge that in your letter! As Debra Fink says, "If you admit that you've tried to research the employer and haven't come up with anything, you've shown initiative!" That's a very positive trait, and it will put you in a good light with the employer.

4. SHOW, AND SUPPORT, YOUR INTEREST IN THE CITY WHERE THE EMPLOYER IS LOCATED!

If it's not obvious from your résumé (or you haven't included a résumé with your letter), you'll want to explain why it is that you're interested in moving to wherever the employer is located. I've stressed elsewhere in this book the importance of geography, and it applies equally to cover letters. So if you don't go to school in the city where the employer is located, and your résumé doesn't indicate why you might be interested in it, you have to provide a reason in your cover letter. For instance, you may say you want to join close friends who live there, or your parents recently moved there, or you're particularly interested in a practice area and, having researched it, you found that the city with the most growth potential in that practice area is the one where the employer is located, or something like that. A number of career services directors I spoke with were wary of saying that you're following a spouse who has been transferred there. That raises the inference that your spouse may be transferred *again,* in which case you'll leave, and the employer will lose their investment in training you. So if you're following a spouse, you may just want to say that you have family who have recently moved to the city or are about to do so, without being more specific than that.

In any case, the point here is that you have to tie yourself geographically to the city. A sentence or so should suffice, but make sure it's there!

5. IF YOU'RE STUCK IN TERMS OF GETTING YOUR PERSONALITY ACROSS — GO BACK AND REREAD THE PERSONAL ESSAYS ON YOUR LAW SCHOOL APPLICATIONS

Illinois' Cindy Rold recommends reading the personal essays that got you into law school in the first place. "As you read them, ask yourself: What from this essay, about who I truly am, can be captured in a letter to get my personality across?" It's *very* important to communicate that you're a "living, breathing person!" You're not just a collection of experiences. So, if you find your letter being boring, dig out your old entrance essays, and use them to add some sparkle to your letters!

6. IF YOU'RE WRITING TO A GRADES-CONSCIOUS EMPLOYER (LIKE A HUGE LAW FIRM) AND YOUR GRADES AREN'T GOOD, EXPLAIN YOUR GRADES IN YOUR COVER LETTER — *BUT ONLY IF YOU'RE POSITIVE THE EMPLOYER IS A GRADES FANATIC!*

Boy, am I nervous about telling you this. The reason is that because a cover letter is a marketing piece, you should only be highlighting positives about yourself — and making excuses for bad grades is *not* a positive.

However, there may be employers for whom it makes sense to violate this rule, just because you *know* that they're credential hounds. Essentially I'm talking about large, prestigious law firms, and virtually nobody else. Now I spend all of Chapter 12 telling you how to get your foot in the door at a large firm, and frankly writing a letter to them isn't the way to do it. But if for some reason that's the approach you take, and your grades aren't up to snuff because you're not at the top of your class, then you *should* say something about your grades in your cover letter. As Deanna Coe Kursh says, "Don't assume the employer won't notice that your grades aren't on your résumé. You need to volunteer information, to show that you recognize the problem." For instance, there's the old chestnut of a strong upward trend in grades. So if you bombed in your first semester of law school but you've had a four-oh ever since, definitely mention that in your cover letter. Or if you've got great job experience that compensates for your grades, mention that.

As you may be able to tell, I'm cringing as I advise you on this, because I'm really not in favor of you taking a letter-writing approach to employers for whom you don't have the right "paper" credentials. You've got to be more creative than that to get your foot in the door, and in Chapter 4 on making contacts, and Chapter 12 on getting large firm jobs, I explain exactly how to do that. So my only advice here is, if you ignore all of that and insist on writing letters, don't pretend that they won't notice your grades. They will — so you've got to acknowledge your grades and explain them away!

7. A FEW EXAMPLES OF SECOND PARAGRAPHS, TAKING INTO ACCOUNT ALL OF THESE CONSIDERATIONS . . .

Here's an example of a second paragraph, in a letter seeking a judicial clerkship:

> *I understand from speaking with two law professors who have clerked, that important criteria in the choice of judicial clerks are abilities in legal research, analysis, and writing. Through the 3 years of law school, I have assisted various professors in their legal research, most notably Professor Peter Aurbach, whose written recommendation will be forwarded under separate cover. Please feel free to contact him or the other professors whose names I have listed.*

Here's another one, looking for a permanent associate position with a medium-sized firm:

> *In the course of researching your firm, I learned that you look for associates with strong legal and analytical skills, and a strong work ethic. I believe my background exhibits all three. For example, while attending college I was simultaneously employed full-time for Ford Motor Company between the hours of 11:30 p.m. and 7:30 a.m., and yet graduated in 4 years with honors. And my legal and analytical skills were sharpened in a recent externship with the Honorable George Lowrey, United States Magi-*

strate, Central District of Ohio, where I gained extensive hands-on experience with many kinds of cases, and analyzed a wide variety of legal issues.

Here's another one, for a summer clerkship with a small firm:

I understand that you seek out summer clerks who are self-starters. That describes my legal background perfectly. My last summer was spent with Lawson Wills, a sole practitioner in Covington. As he was running for state office, I was given unusual independence in structuring and completing the tasks that were assigned to me. I produced work that was praised and used almost without revision. I was able to prove to him and myself, my self-reliance and organizational, research, analytical, and writing abilities. I would bring these same qualities to work for you.

Now, at this point, if you don't have much (if any) legal experience to date, you may be getting depressed. Don't! Remember, what you're doing is bringing skills to the table that will be useful to your employer, and if you look closely at the examples I've just given you, they mention things that aren't law-related. You may even want to address your lack of experience straight out in a sentence or so; that's what I did when I was a law student. I used to have a section in the middle paragraph of my letters that read:

I wish I could tell you I'd clerked for a U.S. Supreme Court Justice, or competed in the Olympics, or started a Fortune 500 Company. I can't do that, because I haven't. But what I lack in experience, I make up for in enthusiasm. I would love to work for you, and I promise your confidence in me would be rewarded with loyalty, dedication, and hard work.

Frankly, they ate up that kind of stuff, and if you don't have a lot of experience yourself, it could work for you, too. (But do me a favor — if you use it, reword it so that it suits you, OK? Nothing is more off-putting than plagiarized enthusiasm!)

So — the middle paragraph of your letter is the one that answers the question: Why should they meet you? That only leaves one more paragraph. . . .

C. THE THIRD AND FINAL PARAGRAPH OF YOUR LETTER: WHAT DO YOU WANT TO HAPPEN NEXT?

Here it is — the call to action. It's where you state what you're going to do, and what you want them to do. This is really pretty simple stuff; a few examples will get across exactly what I'm talking about.

For instance, here's one for an out-of-town interview possibility:

I would appreciate the opportunity to meet with you and discuss the possibility of a summer position. I will be returning to Cincinnati just before Columbus Day weekend. I will contact you when I arrive, if I have not heard from you before that time and, if appropriate, arrange a time that will be convenient. Thank you for your consideration.

Or:

If my experience and background meet your requirements for a new associate, please contact me at the address or telephone number listed above. I will be available to interview in Detroit throughout the winter/spring semester.

Or:

I look forward to hearing from you to arrange a personal meeting. You can reach me at the phone number and address listed above.

Or:

I would appreciate the opportunity to discuss how my background may fit your needs. I look forward to hearing from you.

Or:

I would welcome the opportunity to meet with you at your convenience, either at your office or before the workday. You may reach me at the above address and phone number to arrange a meeting, if appropriate. Thank you for your consideration.

Or:

I would very much welcome the opportunity to meet with you personally should you have an appropriate opening. I can be reached at the telephone number or address above, and can arrange an appointment at most any time that is convenient for you. Thank you for your consideration.

You can see what I'm saying, since it's not exactly rocket science, is it? Just say what you'll do, what you want them to do, and get out gracefully.

Having said that, there's a great deal of controversy over whether or not you should *expressly* tell the recipient that you'll be following up on your letter. I'm not talking here about whether you should actually follow up on your letter or not; I cover that in Topic H, on page 207. I'm just talking about whether you should have a line at the end of your letter saying, "I will call to follow up within 2 weeks," or something like that. Some people agree with George Washington's Laura Rowe, who says, "Be proactive! In this job climate, organizations don't feel compelled to respond. So, say that you'll call by X date." On the other hand, some people agree with Miami's Jose Bahamonde-Gonzalez, who says, "Don't say 'I'll follow up within a week,' because that translates into, 'I'll be a pain.'" And Rob Kaplan says, "Ending a letter with something like, 'I will call you sometime within the next 10 days' strikes some people as though it's taking the initiative, but I disagree. It's punitive finger-waving — it's telling the reader, 'You better be waiting by the phone!'"

So those are the basic arguments "for" and "against" saying that you'll follow up. While saying you'll follow up leaves you in the driver's seat, there's a definite element of pushiness to saying you'll follow up. I hate to say that this is your own call, but do what you feel most comfortable with. If you feel comfortable saying you'll follow up, do it; as Fordham's Kathleen Brady says, "Some people think it shows moxie!" If not — there are a lot of people who agree with you.

One thing *everybody* agrees on is that if you *do* say you're going to follow up, *do it!* Why? As Valparaiso's Gail Peshel says, "If you say you'll call, some firms, especially smaller ones, will set aside your letter and not respond, assuming you're going to call." When you do call, don't be pushy. Gail Peshel recommends that you call only to check and see if they received your material. If they did, you can ask what their timeline for making a decision is. And if there's an opening in the conversation, you may be able to press further, and ask about scheduling an interview. But if they aren't terribly forthcoming when you ask about whether your information was received, politely thank them and get off the phone.

(Remember, for more about handling follow ups, turn to page 207.)

2. THE STYLE OF YOUR LETTERS

In this section, I'll talk about some general issues affecting your entire letter, including your tone, grammar, and factors like that.

A. MAKE YOUR TONE ALIVE AND ENTHUSIASTIC!

As Franklin Pierce's Sophie Sparrow says, "If you really want to work at a place, make your letter sound *alive*. That way, your recipient will *believe* that you really want to be there. Avoid letters that are bland!" So, for instance, if you're interested in Family Law, why not say something like, "I loved Family Law. I want to help people navigate through a tough time." If you talk about what you've enjoyed, what gets you excited, that will create a positive tone that will shine in your letters. As Deanna Coe Kursh points out, "Using a positive, confident, enthusiastic tone has a psychological impact on the person reading the letter."

If you remember, way back in Chapter 1 I talked about the importance of enthusiasm. Cover letters are one of the many places where it can make the difference between a positive response and no response at all. So make it work for you!

B. HAVE YOUR LETTER PROOFREAD FOR TYPOS, GRAMMAR, SPELLING, AND PUNCTUATION

As Florida's Ann Skalaski points out, "Remember that employers assume that the quality of the cover letter you write is the quality of the work you'll produce. So make sure you proofread it!" Deanna Coe Kursh adds, "You *have* to be careful with your letters, because your reader's clients have to have confidence in you, and they won't if you can't even present yourself perfectly in a cover letter."

This may seem like common sense to you, but every single career services director I spoke with highlighted typos, grammar, and spelling mistakes as the number one mistake students make with their cover letters. And that's a shame, because I assure you, if you make an obvious mistake in your cover letter, it doesn't matter how wonderful it is otherwise — your letter will be thrown out. *Guaranteed.* And don't assume that a quick glance over it by yourself or running it through the spell checker on your computer will do the trick. For one thing, you can't proofread your own work because you won't read it as carefully as someone who's not familiar with it. (I know this from experience. As a writer, I am frequently convinced that my work is typo-free, only to have another set of eyes find *some* silly mistake I overlooked.) And when it comes to spell checking, spell checkers don't pick up words that are misspelled as other words (like "there" when you meant "their"), or grammar mistakes. So they won't work either. If you don't have a friend who will help you out, then take your letters to your career services office; they'll be happy to go over them for you. And as a bonus, you may get some helpful pointers!

C. MAKE SURE THAT YOU HAVE YOUR RECIPIENT INFORMATION CORRECT: THE SPELLING OF THEIR NAME, THEIR ADDRESS, THEIR GENDER. MAKE SURE THAT YOU MAIL MERGE YOUR LETTERS CORRECTLY, AND MAKE SURE THAT YOU PUT THE RIGHT LETTER IN THE RIGHT ENVELOPE!

Get the information about your recipient wrong, even slightly, and to borrow a baseball analogy — you're out! If need be, call the employer, and ask to have the recipient's name and the employer's name spelled for you over the phone; you don't have to give your name or any other reason for your call. Or check it in Martindale-Hubbell or some other directory. Similarly, make sure you've got the person's gender straight. I can't tell you how many letters I receive addressed to "Mr. Walton," even though I'm not a "Mr."

Beyond that, make sure that you have the right name and address on the top of each letter, and that the right letter goes in each envelope. I know what you're probably saying at this point. "Geez, Kimmbo," you're saying. "Who do you think you're talking with here? A *complete idiot?*" Well, no, but on the other hand, I should point out to you that fully *a third* of the application letters I've ever received *were addressed to the wrong person*. By that I mean that the name and address on the envelope were mine, but the letter inside was addressed to someone else. Or the name and address at the top of the letter didn't match the salutation (Dear so-and-so) line. The worst thing about a letter like that is that it means you've alienated *two* possible employers — because you can't mess up one letter like this, you've got to mess up two at a time. So no matter how much time you spend making contacts, or researching, or putting together a boffo résumé, it just doesn't matter if you screw up and send the wrong letter to the wrong person, or misspell their name or address.

How do you avoid this? Glance over your letters *as* you're putting them in the envelopes. Check the name and address and salutation line, and make sure the name on the letter matches the one on the envelope. That's all it takes. If you can't be that careful, you won't get a job from that recipient, that's for sure! And don't believe that it can't happen to you. As Ann Skalaski says, "It's amazing how careless people are, especially when you consider that you're going to be writing for a living as a lawyer!"

D. THE 13 BIGGEST MISTAKES LAW STUDENTS MAKE WHEN THEY SEND COVER LETTERS

In this section, I'm going to go through a laundry list of the mistakes that drive employers crazy — the ones career services directors hear about over and over again. To some extent, these points will overlap with what I've already told you. But I think they're sufficiently important to gather together in one place — so here goes!

1. TYPOS AND OTHER OBVIOUS MISTAKES

Since I just went over this one, I won't beat it to death here. Just remember: *Proofread!* As Catholic's Amy Thompson points out, "Employers are looking for reasons why they shouldn't hire you — they're looking for just one red flag." Don't give them that red flag in the form of an easily avoidable administrative error!

2. OVERKILL!

As Texas' Annette Jones points out, "Some students think 'the more, the merrier,' when it comes to correspondence, when they *should* be thinking, 'more is less.'" She goes on to point out the kinds of things that students have actually included in their correspondence: "Recommendation letters, fitness reports from the military, copies of award certificates, published articles, published stories, entire books and magazines with their byline buried on page 27, poetry, short stories, and copies of personal statements from grad school applications." Suffice it to say that *none* of this has a place with a cover letter! Instead, make your letters short and dynamic, and at the most include a résumé with them (I discuss the possibility of not even including a résumé, on page 204.) So the watchword here is: Don't deluge prospective employers with too much stuff. You're supposed to be enticing them, not suffocating them!

3. ADDRESSING LETTERS TO "HIRING PARTNER"

Always find a name to send a letter to. Don't use the generic "hiring partner." Why? That's the dead giveaway of mass mailers. Remember, mass mailers don't get results, and so the last thing you want is to make your letters look like part of a mass mailer! Think of it this way: "Hiring Partner" is the law firm equivalent of "Resident" on letters *you* get!

Instead, do a little digging to find out who ought to receive your letter. And here's a tip: Don't send the letter to the recruiting director at an employer. Instead, as Maureen Provost Ryan suggests, send letters to lawyers with the power to hire you, who will see the possibilities in you. As she points out, "recruiting people get résumés all the time," so they're going to be less likely to pay as much attention to each one they receive. So, if you want to practice in the environmental law division of a law firm, find out who runs that division, and write directly to *them.*

Do a little research and find out who ought to get your letter; it may mean a phone call to the employer, or just looking in Martindale-Hubbell, or checking with your career services director. No matter how you find a name, it's worth it!

4. SEEMING CLUELESS AS TO WHAT THE EMPLOYER DOES

What I'm referring indirectly to are mass mailers. Employers *hate* to get letters that fail to acknowledge even the slightest bit of research about them. Remember, if you try to research an employer and don't come up with anything, it's perfectly fine to say that. But what you have to do is make some effort to learn about the employer, and exhibit that knowledge in your cover letter. It's flattering and gratifying, and it makes the employer feel unique — and that's exactly how you want them to feel. And it's not asking much of you. After all, you're expecting them to give you a job. The least you can do is show that you've done some research on them, first!

5. BEING CONCLUSORY

This refers to the importance of backing up every statement you make. Don't ever say "I'm a hard worker" or "I'm an excellent writer," without pulling experiences from your background to back those up. And if you don't have any experiences to back up a claim you want to make, don't make it. For instance, "I'm a hard worker" is probably not the best claim for someone whose mommy and daddy are funding law school, and who spends every moment outside of class at the local watering hole downing draft beers and Buffalo chicken wings. So don't be conclusory! As Sophie Sparrow points out, "Lawyers like to analyze and draw their own conclusions — they don't like to be told what to do! So *show* them that you're a certain way, don't just *tell* them that you are!"

6. AVOIDING OBVIOUS HOOKS

This refers to some students' unwillingness to use obvious "ins" at an employer, like the fact that they know someone who works there, or, for instance, your aunt knows the hiring partner. It's a big mistake to let your pride get in the way of being able to say, "[Mutual acquaintance] recommended that I contact you"! As Sophie Sparrow says, "Always mention obvious hooks *first*. The job search process is tough, and it can be demoralizing. Don't let that over-shadow what you naturally *know* — which is that it helps to mention an obvious connection!"

7. BEING TOO COCKY

This is a major problem, and a common one, because it's easy to mistake confidence for cockiness. There's a difference between saying, "I have strong research skills, as evidenced by my work for Professor Engeweng," and saying, "Don't read another cover letter — I'm your man!" As Maine's Tammy Willcox says, "The tone you want to approximate is humble, yet secure." Gail Cutter points out, "Use wording like, 'I was fortunate enough to work for a federal judge,' or 'I was lucky to have the opportunity to take charge of client matters.' It sounds less pushy."

So — what kinds of lines will you want to avoid? Anything that sounds like these (taken from actual cover letters, horrifyingly enough):

♦ *"I'm confident that I will be an incredible asset to your firm."* (You can't *possibly* know that! Tell them the things that *suggest* you will be, but don't *say* it!)

♦ *"I'm going to bust my ass for you."*

♦ *"I'd be perfect for you because. . . . "* (Too strong; you're better off saying, "I have strong skills because . . . " and then explaining the source of your skills, letting the reader draw the conclusion you'd be perfect for them!)

As Betsy Armour points out, "Any statement like 'I'd be perfect because . . . ' rings hollow if it's so bluntly said. Support it instead!"

8. LYING

When you're trying to come up with a boffo cover letter, it may be tempting to *create* something that makes you more attractive, like a certain job experience. Don't be tempted to lie, because if you're caught, the results are *devastating.* I've pointed out elsewhere that whenever you try to be deceptive, you'll find that what previously seemed like a huge legal community is in fact very small.

And this is true even for lies that strike you as being fairly harmless. The hiring partner at one large firm out west told me about a student who wrote a letter saying, "My husband has accepted employment in your area so I'm interested in pursuing a job there." As it turns out, this student sent this *very same letter* to law firms in several different cities, not realizing that they were all part of the same law firm going under separate names, and that every application letter was logged on to a computer. When they called the student on this lie, she stumbled and said her husband was *thinking* about accepting a job in each on one of the cities — but that didn't erase the fact that her credibility was ruined with that employer.

So — don't lie! With all of the advice I've given you about how to deal with the truth (and develop solid experiences for yourself even if you don't have them already), you don't *have* to!

9. BEING BORING

Since this is the theme of this chapter and I've been hammering away at it repeatedly, you may be sick of hearing it, but I mention it again because it's so important. Remember, any employer you write to will get many letters from other students, so it's important to sound enthusiastic, and interested, and upbeat. As Chicago-Kent's Lisa Abrams says, "Cover letters are more important than résumés, so make sure they're not boring!" Make *your* letters lively! But by the same token, it's important to avoid . . .

10. BEING CUTE OR AVANT-GARDE

The importance of making your letters unique may tempt you to voyage into the cute or the avant-garde. I warn you not to, not because I have a problem with things that are cute or avant-garde — I don't. But the problem is, the profession you're looking at, law, is a conservative one. Cutesyness or things that are from way out in left field are just inappropriate, sad as that may seem. As Rob Kaplan says, "Some people just try too hard to stand out!"

I heard a bunch of incredible anecdotes along these lines, and, frankly, I applaud the creativity and imagination that went into them — although you'll immediately see why they're not appropriate. No fairly traditional lawyer would want to trust his clients to students who take approaches like this. To preserve the privacy of the perpetrators, I'm not going to match these stories to any schools, but here are some classics:

♦ One student sent her letter encased in a basketball shoe, and started the letter by saying, "At least now I know I got my foot through the door!"

♦ Another student had pencils printed to read, "I'm on Law Review," followed by his name and phone number.

♦ Another student had his cover letter and résumé disguised as a subpoena, and delivered to the hiring partner at a law firm where he wanted to work.

♦ Another student had a four-color résumé and cover letter, with artwork and testimonials on the back.

♦ One student sent a cover letter and résumé to a law firm, filling the envelope with confetti in order to stand out. The

day it got to the firm, the firm had just had the office professionally cleaned in preparation for an important presentation. When the lawyer opened this particular envelope, the
confetti sprayed everywhere. It *infuriated* everyone at the
firm.

♦ Students have been known to shrink their résumés and cover
letters and affix them to wine bottles, like wine labels.

♦ One student had a five paragraph letter, and each paragraph
strategically started with a letter of the word "READY."
The first paragraph started with an "R," the second with
an "E," and so on. The letter wound up with the statement,
"Yes, Mr. So-and-So, I am R = reliable, E = enthusiastic . . . "
and all the way to "Y = yearning to learn! In short — I'm
READY."

♦ One student sent a brochure with her name on the diagonal,
and a screaming headline reading, "Why you should hire
ROWENA BLOTZ."

I could go on, but you get the point. As Betsy Armour points
out, "Remember that you're not writing to Turner Broadcasting.
Legal employers are *conservative*." And that means that what might
work in advertising or marketing just isn't going to work with law
firms. So, while you should use every legitimate means to make
yourself stand out, don't be gimmicky!

11. FOCUSING ON WHY *YOU* WANT THE JOB

This is a big mistake, and, ironically enough, you see examples
of it in all *kinds* of books about writing cover letters — which means
it's an easy trap to fall into. The kind of thing I'm talking about here
is saying, "Working for you would give me a great opportunity
to use my history degree," or "Being associated with your firm
would give me the chance to get familiar with San Francisco, which
is something I've always wanted to do." St. Louis's Wendy Werner
advises, "You have to appeal to what the *employer* needs." Drusilla
Bakert agrees, saying, "The employer doesn't want to know why
you want the job! They *assume* you want to work for them!" San
Diego's Susan Benson says, "Don't mention 'I.' As in, 'I want to
work for you because it'll give *me* this opportunity, blah, blah,
blah. . . . " Nobody cares!

Instead, as Susan Benson says, "You should be very specific
about what you're bringing to the table, not what the employer

will give you. So if you say, 'Your firm does this kind of work, and my background includes drafting documents related to it,'" it's clear that you will be pursuing something you want because you're using talents you've developed. But you haven't framed it in terms of, "Working for you will do X for me." And *that's* what you want to avoid!

12. STRUCTURING LETTERS CHRONOLOGICALLY

As Rob Kaplan points out, it's a huge temptation to just go through your résumé , pick out things you've done, and list them in your cover letter in chronological order. But that's not helpful to the employer. You want to take what reporters call an "inverted pyramid" approach, starting with the strength that will be most important to the employer, and proceeding in order of lessening importance after that. So if your writing skill is the asset of most interest to the employer, in the second paragraph of your letter that will be the first asset you mention, followed by support for it —and it doesn't matter whether your writing skill is proven by your most recent job, because you're not listing your experience chronologically!

So make sure that your letter is structured with your "best foot forward" — not "first things first!"

13. BEING APOLOGETIC

As Rob Kaplan points out, "A cover letter is a *marketing* piece. Firms want to see how you market yourself. What are your instincts?" And that's why it's so important *not* to be apologetic! Kathleen Brady adds, "Don't focus on what you *don't* have, and what's *not* useful. Mentioning your art history major isn't a plus unless you're writing to a firm that represents clients like museums."

Rob Kaplan goes on to say, "Students have a tendency to say things like, 'Although I've never worked in a firm,' or 'Although I've never taken Criminal Law . . . ' and that's wrong. You're selling a product! When you go to buy a car, the salesman won't say, 'I should tell you up front that this car only gets 18 miles to the gallon.' Instead, they'll sell *positives,* and they only offer *negatives* if asked about them. Don't worry, you'll have opportunities to explain away your negatives. But don't do it in a cover letter — even though you'll find that with your law school training, you'll be tempted to find leaks, holes, and gaps in argument, and address those."

Remember that your cover letter is designed to give the employer reasons *to* interview you, not excuses to *avoid* interviewing you. Stick with your positives!

E. CONSIDER SENDING LETTERS *WITHOUT* RÉSUMÉS!

When you read a lot of job search books, you get the impression that a cover letter is just the icing on the cake — something to take up envelope space that's not used up by a résumé. As you can tell from this chapter, I take cover letters a lot more seriously than that. In fact, there's something to be said for the stance that some career services directors take when they suggest that you consider sending letters to employers *without* sending résumés. Why? As Debra Fink points out, a lot of times if you send a résumé along with your letter in a targeted mailing, the person you write to will just take your résumé and send it through to the recruiting coordinator, and your letter will be ignored. So if you send a letter *without* sending a résumé, that *can't* happen. You get to present everything I've told you to include — your best qualities in terms of how they will be useful to the employer, and evidence of your research, all presented in an interesting way — without worrying whether you'll just be judged by your résumé. If you do this, you'll want to state in the letter that you'll be happy to provide a résumé and writing sample, or bring them along to an interview. The point is, especially if you're not thrilled with your credentials, you may be better off not sending résumés with letters at all.

I should tell you that this isn't something every career services director agrees with. Jose Bahamonde-Gonzalez, for instance, says that every letter should include a résumé, and maybe even a transcript as well (if you've got good grades or a strong upward trend in grades).

So there are some naysayers, but sending letters without résumés is something to consider. And remember, you should *not* send a résumé if you're simply making contact for the purpose of looking for advice (e.g., a letter to an alum recommended by your career services director), or if you're seeking an information interview, as I discussed in Chapter 4. When you send a résumé in situations like these, it smacks too much of "I want you to give me a job," and that's not the purpose of communiqués like that. But even if you *are* legitimately looking for a job, it might be worth sending a few letters without résumés. Students have been successful with it, and you might be, too!

F. HANDLING WRITING SAMPLES

Inevitably, at some point in your job search process you're going to need a writing sample. It's not something that you send with your cover letter, unless you're responding to a job listing that requests one or you've already spoken with the employer and they've requested a writing sample.

Since it's going to be part of your correspondence, it's worth spending a few moments here to talk about what your writing sample ought to look like. As you'll see, a lot of what I'm going to tell you mirrors what I told you about cover letters!

1. DON'T SUBMIT WRITING SAMPLES WITH TYPOS!

I've already told you that cover letters with typos are the kiss of death; they look careless, and no employer wants careless employees. So, as Debra Fink recommends, always have another set of eyes look over your writing sample before you send it.

Having someone else read your writing sample may save you from situations more embarrassing than typos. One career services director told me about a student who was getting slammed by every employer to whom he sent a writing sample, and he couldn't figure out why. The career services director asked for his writing sample, and found, to her horror, that one of the footnotes featured a particularly rude penis joke. Well, what's a big hit at the local watering hole is somehow not quite as funny in the "In" box on a hiring partner's desk! Now, I'm not suggesting that you're likely to have a footnote problem like this in *your* writing sample — but it nonetheless makes sense to let someone else take a look at it before you send it out!

2. DON'T SUBMIT AN ENCYCLOPEDIA

You may be very fond of your hundred-page thesis, but it's much too much to foist on a prospective employer. Instead, pick 10 to 15 pages of *anything* you've written as an upper limit. If that means you're excerpting something you've written, so be it; you can include a paragraph introducing the material if it needs to be placed in context. But the point here is: Don't wear out your welcome by expecting a prospective employer to read your version of *War and Peace*.

3. MAKE SURE YOUR TOPIC IS APPROPRIATE TO THE EMPLOYER, TO THE EXTENT YOU HAVE A NUMBER OF POSSIBILITIES FOR YOUR WRITING SAMPLE — AND THAT MAY MEAN HAVING *MORE THAN ONE* WRITING SAMPLE!

J.T. Mann, my networking poster boy from Chapter 4, always makes sure that his writing sample addresses a topic of interest to the person who's reading it. This has the added benefit of proving his interest in the recipient's practice area. So, if you have a number of equally good potential writing samples on different topics, tailor your sample to the interests of your reader!

I'll give you a personal example. As I've mentioned to you before, I created a bunch of study aids called *Law In A Flash*. You're probably familiar with *Law In A Flash*, but in case you're not, it's flash cards with funny hypotheticals on them (or what I like to think are funny, anyway). When I ran *Law In A Flash*, I used to get job applications periodically, and students would inevitably include writing samples with their letters. Now the letters would talk about how the student had a great sense of humor, and could write in a very light-hearted way — all the kinds of things that would be important for anyone who writes *Law In A Flash*. However, often the writing samples they'd include would be bone-dry briefs from their First Year writing course — the *antithesis* of *Law In A Flash!* They'd have been better off not including a writing sample at all, or including a script for open-mike night at the local comedy club — at the very least showing that they could write something *other* than technical legal writing. All that their writing samples told me was that they either weren't familiar with *Law In A Flash,* or they really couldn't write funny stuff at all, or that they hadn't given any thought to what kind of writing sample would be appropriate for an employer like me.

Obviously, you're unlikely to be applying for jobs as unusual as being a writer for *Law In A Flash*, but that anecdote makes my point — be sensitive to the interests of your recipient when you choose the writing sample you're going to submit!

4. ALWAYS HAVE COPIES OF YOUR WRITING SAMPLE(S) AVAILABLE, ESPECIALLY WHEN YOU GO FOR AN INTERVIEW

In Chapter 6 on Interviewing, I talk about the importance of having your paper packet together, including copies of your résumé, transcript, references, and writing sample. You never know when someone's going to ask for your writing sample, so it makes sense to always have a few copies on hand!

G. SPECIAL APPROACHES FOR SMALL FIRMS

Don't get me wrong — I'm not including this section to suggest that you ignore everything else in this chapter. Instead, the reason I'm including it is to accentuate the importance of a personal approach when you're targeting small firms. As Columbia's Ellen Wayne explains, "For small firms, unsolicited letters just don't work! That makes sense when you think about it. If you've got a couple of partners and maybe a couple of associates, nobody has time to deal with inquiries; they're busy doing their work. That means that for small employers, you've got to make personal contact *first*, through a part-time job, or alumni, or bar association functions." In other words — the idea of making contacts to get your dream job may be not just the best, but the *only*, way to get to small employers. That highlights the importance of finding some mutual acquaintance with small firm employers you'd like to work for!

Even if you do take a targeted mailing approach, with small firms you've got to take particular care to send your letter to a *name*, not just "recruiting coordinator." Why? As Teresa DeAndrado points out, "Small firms don't have recruiting coordinators!" Instead, you'll want to do some research and find an attorney at the firm with whom you have something in common and write to them. Using the salutation "Recruiting coordinator" is bad for employers large enough to *have* such a person; it's even worse for an employer that's too small to have a person in charge of personnel!

H. FOLLOW-UP CALLS

OK. You've dropped your personalized, interesting, well-researched letters in the mailbox. Now what? Eat Cheetos and watch soap operas, waiting for responses? You know Auntie Kimm better than that. No, if you don't hear anything within 2 weeks, you've got to follow up. And that means making phone calls.

Now before the cold hand of fear clutches your heart, I'm not talking about calling the people you wrote to and saying, "Well, you gonna hire me or not? Huh? What gives?" Instead, all you're going to do — at least at the outset — is to check and see if they received your letter. And remember, you want to give them at least 2 weeks before you call — that way, they'll have had a chance to get your letter, but it won't be a distant memory. When you call, as Laura Rowe points out, you just want to be proactive and say something like, "I wanted to make sure you got my letter." You'll be able to tell by the response whether it makes sense to press the conversation any further. For instance, if they respond with an enthusiastic "yes," and say something like, "Yes, your letter was very interesting," that's an opening for asking if you might be able to schedule an interview. If there isn't a follow-up comment that gives you an opening like that, but they *did* receive your letter, then you can ask, politely, what the timeline for making a decision is. My point here is this: You start with a nonoffensive opening, about whether they got your letter or not, and then gauge the tone and content of their response to see if you should press further. Remember, even if they don't tell you anything definitive over the phone, that doesn't mean you *won't* be called for an interview; it may legitimately mean that they got your letter but haven't read it yet, or just haven't sat down to decide who they're going to interview.

By the way, follow-up phone calls can pan out in unexpected ways. Kathleen Brady has a favorite story about a student who did a targeted mailing, and then made follow-up calls to schedule interviews. One of the firms she called hadn't received her résumé, and they thought they'd lost it. They went ahead and scheduled an interview with her anyway. Afterwards, the student realized she hadn't actually written to them in the first place — and to top it off, she got the job!

So follow-up calls can *really* pay off. Regardless of whether you actually send the letters you think you're sending, the bottom line here is — just because your letter's in the mail doesn't mean your work is done. Always call within 2 weeks to follow up!

I. THANK YOUS

Thank you notes are a kind of Catch-22. As Laura Rowe points out, "A good one can't help you, but a bad one can hurt you!"

Nonetheless, any time you've interviewed with someone, whether it's an information interview or a job interview or even a particularly helpful phone call, follow up with a thank you. As Laura Rowe says, a handwritten note with a personal message is great. You thank them for their time, refer to something that you talked about (e.g., "Thanks for the tips on using WordPerfect"), and if it was an information interview, thank them for the information they provided and any contacts they recommended to you, along with any action you've taken with those contacts, or action that you plan to take (e.g., "I will be calling Winken Blinken early next week to set up an appointment."). If you are hopeful of a particular outcome — like a job offer — you will want to say something like, "Having met with you, I am even more excited about the idea of working for Snap, Crackle, and Popp," and then perhaps include a line about why you think you'd be a boffo employee (e.g., "Our conversation about the issues your clients are faced with reminded me very much of the research I did for Judge Glocken-spiel.").

Suppose you interviewed with a number of people in the same office? You don't have to send a thank you to *all* of them. Instead, as Laura Rowe advises, you can send one handwritten note to one of them (the senior person or hiring partner) that says, "It was a pleasure to meet you and the other five attorneys I met with . . . " and take it from there.

In terms of timing, the sooner the better when it comes to thank yous. Getting a note out within 24 hours is ideal; the interview is still fresh in your mind, and so it'll be the easiest time of all to bang out a personal note.

And by the way — make sure you have the recipient's name spelled right. A quick look at Martindale-Hubbell or a phone call to the employer will take care of that.

J. KEEP YOUR CORRESPONDENCE IN PERSPECTIVE!

Letter writing for law students is like a 600 pound gorilla — it's very easy to let it dominate your entire job search process. Don't let that happen! While there are sometimes situations where you won't be able to make personal contact with an employer you want to work for, the advice I gave you in Chapter 4, about making contacts to get your dream job, should be the centerpiece of your job search process. It should take much more of your time to meet with people than to formulate great letters, because you're much more likely to *get* a job by meeting people rather than writing to them. So, no matter how tempting it may be to hide behind your word processor and confine your entire job search process to the written word — *don't do it!*

Chapter 6

Résumés: The Best Résumé Is The Résumé You Don't Need

(Well, eventually you'll need one. And here's what it has to look like...)

From the title of this chapter, you may get the idea that I don't like résumés. Well, you're no dummy. I don't. For one thing, you probably won't need one, at least at first; if you follow my advice on making contacts in Chapter 4, you won't need a résumé to get you through the door. For another thing, résumés absorb *way* too many of most law students' job search brain cells. To hear a lot of students talk, you'd think that if only they found the perfect type font, or weight of bond paper, or format, or wording, the employer of their dreams would welcome them with open arms.

If you visit any bookstore, you can see what fuels this misconception about the importance of résumés. There are probably more books written about résumés than any other element of the job-search process. "The Perfect Résumé," "Five Hundred Great

Résumés," "The Résumé Handbook," "Résumés That Work" – and then on the flip side you have, "Burn Your Résumé!" and "Résumés Don't Get Jobs," and titles like that.

Why the obsession with résumés? There's probably something comforting in thinking it's not what you've done, but how you word it that makes the difference. It's kind of the feeling I get when I go to the cosmetics section of a large department store. It doesn't matter that I've already got about a million eye shadows at home; I'm always convinced that there's an eye shadow that will change my life, if only I can find it. It's the same thing with résumés. If only I worded this differently, or put this on different paper, everything would be easy.... It's a pipe dream, but it's a cozy little pipe dream, at that.

If you've been reading this book in order, you know that what I'm doing here is preparing you for a reality check. And as is true for most reality checks, it's both better and worse than misconceptions you might have had. For one thing — a résumé is *not* your key to getting a dream job. A résumé should ideally never precede you to an interview, and that means you have to do everything else I advise you to do, like making contacts and setting up interviews, *before* you need to bother with a résumé. If that sounds bad to you, look at the flip side. It means that it really doesn't matter what type font you use, or how thick your bond paper is. I'll save you from making any big mistakes, but we're not going to get anal about résumés in this chapter. And for another thing, I'll save you pots of money on résumé-writing services. I heard nothing but hilarious anecdotes from career services directors about résumés that résumé-writing services prepared for law students. They're hopelessly inappropriate for legal employers. Instead, I'll show you how to spend an hour or two on a résumé, come up with something perfect for you, and leave it at that.

With that little introduction in mind — let's get started!

A. WHAT THE HECK IS A RÉSUMÉ SUPPOSED TO *DO* FOR YOU, ANYWAY?

I get the feeling that a lot of people look at a résumé as a variation on an obituary: that is, a mere written record of what they've done, with no eye toward the future. That's an *enormous* mistake! Why? Because, as Fordham's Kathleen Brady says, "It's a *marketing* piece. It's supposed to give employers a reason to want to meet you." Case Western's Debra Fink echoes that, saying, "A résumé is a promotional piece. It should present the most attractive, albeit true, picture of you. It's supposed to pique someone's interest enough to get you through the door, where you sell yourself for the position." She goes on to say that "Your résumé answers one simple question for an employer: *What can you do for me?*" Now, it's true that a résumé is like an obituary in that it focuses on what you've done until now. But you *have* to remember that from an employer's perspective, the only thing that matters about what you've already done is how it translates into what you'll be able to do for them *in future.*

I mention this at the outset, because, although I'm going to be giving you a lot of very specific advice about what to put on your résumé, if you keep your focus on this one simple point, you're 95% of the way to a perfect résumé. So don't forget: The function of a résumé is to get an employer interested in meeting you, and the reason they'll want to do that is because they think you can do something for them.

B. DON'T THINK OF IT AS A RÉSUMÉ: THINK OF IT AS A *WARDROBE* OF RÉSUMÉS

I've already analogized résumés to obituaries. Staying with the death theme, another big mistake students make is to view a résumé as an epitaph, in that you come up with one, and it's engraved in stone. That's not the way to look at a résumé! For one thing, you should be prepared to change your résumé every semester (or if you're out of school, every 3 to 6 months). As Chicago-Kent's Lisa Abrams says, "A résumé should be fluid, and constantly changing." That's because your life changes, your accomplishments change, and your résumé should reflect that.

For another thing, as San Diego's Susan Benson points out, you should have different résumés for different types of employers. That's what I mean when I refer to a wardrobe of résumés. I'll give you a personal example of what I mean.

Let's say that I need to send out résumés for three purposes. One is that my alma mater is thinking of putting me on the Board of Trustees, and they want to see my résumé for that. Another is that I'm getting a line of credit for a publishing company of my own, and the bank wants a copy of my résumé. And another is that an established publisher wants me to act as an independent contractor and put together some books for them, and they want to see a copy of my résumé, as well. So what am I going to do — send them each a copy of the same résumé? No! That's because their interests are completely different. For the board of trustees position, I'm going to need a résumé focusing on scholarly, academic things that I've done (not that I *have* a bunch of those, but for that résumé, I'll want to display what I *do* have). For the bank, I'll want to focus on things like my undergrad Accounting degree and anything else I've done that shows business acumen. And for the publisher, they'll be most interested in whatever publishing successes I've had.

Now I'm not going to be *lying* on any of these résumés, but I'm going to be careful to *slant* them to address the interests of my audience. And you should do the same thing. The experiences, the accomplishments, the details that you include on your résumé should change if you're looking at radically different kinds of employers; it's particularly true if you're looking for a nontraditional career of the kind I discuss in Chapter 13. If, on the other hand, you're looking at a fairly homogenous set of employers — say, small to medium-sized firms practicing commercial law — then one résumé will do for all of them. But the watchword here is — *always* take into account the interests of your recipients when you send them a résumé, and if the situation calls for it, draft a *new* résumé for a specific employer!

C. HOW TO FORMULATE YOUR PERFECT RÉSUMÉ(S)

OK! Now that you know what your résumé is supposed to do for you, let's talk about how you fashion from the clay of your experience the masterpiece that best conveys to any potential employer that you're their ideal employee. And you *are* going to be able to do that, even if you don't have any work experience, or if all of your jobs have been minimum-wagers. How are you going to do that? Well, I've got a two-step process for you. First, we're going to go through a couple of exercises that help you focus on exactly what it is that you bring to the table, based on what you've done up until now. What these exercises will do is to put you in the mindset of thinking about *transferable skills* — that is, the attributes that will make an employer interested in you. Then, with that information in hand, I'll show you how to craft a résumé that best conveys a snapshot of you. And I'll provide a couple of worksheets so you can see *exactly* the kind of information you'll want to include.

1. GETTING STARTED: HOW EXACTLY DO YOU GO ABOUT MARKETING YOURSELF ON A RÉSUMÉ?

What I want you to do first is to clear your mind of any preconceived notions you may have about résumés. Maybe you've never had a résumé before; if so, that's great. You're putty in my hands! At the other end of the spectrum, maybe you've been out of law school for 20 years and you have a whole separate career behind you. If that's the case, please ignore whatever you've done before for a résumé; what legal employers will be interested in is likely very different than what your prior career involved, and so you'll have to make an *effort* to be putty in my hands.

What I want to start out with is a list of attributes that a legal employer is likely to look for. I want you to get a pencil, and go through this list a couple of times, and choose five of the adjectives that you apply to you the best. Here they are:

__ accommodating	__ achieving	__ aggressive
__ ambitious	__ analytical	__ attentive
__ bright	__ competent	__ conscientious
__ consistent	__ creative	__ decisive
__ determined	__ efficient	__ energetic
__ exacting	__ explicit	__ goal-oriented
__ imaginative	__ industrious	__ inquisitive
__ insightful	__ instinctive	__ inventive
__ logical	__ mature	__ meticulous
__ methodical	__ observant	__ perceptive
__ persistent	__ persuasive	__ probing
__ purposeful	__ resourceful	__ self-confident
__ self-reliant	__ serious	__ sophisticated
__ systematic	__ thorough	

Got your five adjectives checked off yet? Good. Now, what I want you to do, using the spaces on page 217, is to write down each of those five adjectives, and list underneath *specific experiences* that *prove* that those adjectives apply to you. For instance, if I chose "determined" as one of my adjectives, the thing I'd pull from my background to prove that would be losing 50 pounds, and keeping it off. If I chose "energetic," I'd talk about volunteering at a camp for children with life-threatening illnesses, where I had to work 20-hour days. If I chose "imaginative," I'd talk about creating the *Law In A Flash* series of study aids. Your experiences may be very different from mine, but you'll want to go through the same exact process. Let's say that you waited on tables to pay your college bills. Like most waitstaff, you probably learned on your own how to organize your trips to the kitchen and to your tables to make those trips as efficient as possible. Well, that's a very useful skill for legal employers who try to control their costs while increasing their billings. And if you worked at a very busy restaurant, that says you were also very energetic. There again, that's an important trait for law clerks and associates, since it means you'll be able to pitch in wherever needed, and manage the stress and long hours you might encounter.

As you think of your experiences, it's important not to overlook any volunteering experience you've had. For instance, are you naturally shy, but managed to be a persuasive fundraiser in raising money for a worthy cause, like finding sponsors for a 5K race for charity? Have you ever helped to organize a successful event on behalf of a political party or other organization? These kinds of things mean *tons* to an employer, not just because they say something about your transferable skills — but they *also* show that you're self-motivated, in that you've — put forth an effort for something that you didn't get paid for.

If you've got a technical undergrad major or a substantial prior career, going through this exercise with adjectives also helps you refocus your experience through the lens of a legal employer. You've got to keep your audience in mind! For instance, let's say that you were a social worker or a nurse before you entered law school. That means you've had close contact with people in times of great distress. What's the transferable skill you're bringing to a legal employer? Well, let's say the employer in question is a small law firm with a domestic relations practice. Your background will give you the ability to handle client contact, with minimal supervision, almost from the beginning — since you're used to dealing with people going through emotionally stressful times. That's a *huge* asset, but only if you think about it in terms of *what it means to a potential employer*. The mere fact that you were a "nurse" or "social worker" by itself doesn't mean that much, but the transferable skills you offer as a result of that experience are wildly valuable. I'll give you another example that a career services director told me about.

There was a student who used his computer skills during a summer job to help a company computerize its inventory control and billing and that kind of thing. The student had to analyze the existing system the company used, identify its problems, research computer programs, and present and sell his solutions to the firm owners. Then he had to set up the systems once they were bought, customize the computer applications, and train all the staff. He beat the schedule the owners had set up for him, and trained all the staff with no significant problems. Now, all of these functions he performed would be useful in a law firm, above and beyond his considerable computer skills. But instead of focusing on these transferable skills, he had simply written on his résumé that he helped in a computerization! If all you list on your résumé are job titles and a brief list of duties, you can't assume that a potential employer will be able to make the leap and figure out what your transferable skills are. It's up to *you* to show what you bring to the table based on what you've already done.

So you can see that what I want you to do is to take experiences that you've had, *whether or not they had anything to do with law or law school,* and use them as evidence of why your five adjectives apply to you. With that in mind, fill out these five little worksheets:

Adjective #1: _____

Experience(s) I've had which prove this adjective applies to me:

Adjective #2: _____

Experience(s) I've had which prove this adjective applies to me:

Adjective #3: _____
Experience(s) I've had which prove this adjective applies
to me:

Adjective #4: _____
Experience(s) I've had which prove this adjective applies
to me:

Adjective #5: _____
Experience(s) I've had which prove this adjective applies
to me:

2. CONTENT: DECIDING WHAT GOES ON YOUR RÉSUMÉ (AND SAVING HUNDREDS OF DOLLARS ON A RÉSUMÉ-WRITING SERVICE, AT THE SAME TIME!)

Now that you're in the mind-set of how employers perceive résumés — by looking at how things you've done translate into things you can do for them in future — it's time to get down to brass tacks, and look at *everything* you've done. This is a two-pronged process. First, I'm going to take you through your background, and we'll figure out the "universe" of things to choose from when you actually write your résumé. Then, we'll actually take that information and put it into résumé form.

Let's get started!

A. GETTING DOWN ON PAPER ALL OF YOUR ACCOMPLISHMENTS

What we're going to do here is to go through everything you've done, and pull from those experiences everything you've accomplished. I want to stress right now that what you've got to focus on is *accomplishments* and *transferable skills*. Accomplishments are those things that distinguish you from other people with the same job. For instance, if you were promoted in a job that normally has a high turnover rate, that's an accomplishment. Transferable skills, your second focus, were what we talked about when we talked about adjectives that apply to you. As Valparaiso's Gail Peshel notes, these transferable skills fall into four main categories: organizational skills, leadership skills, practical skills, and communication skills.

Now, why this focus? Because these are what will make you stand out to employers. All too often, people screw up résumés by focusing on their duties in various jobs. What it is that you were supposed to do on any given job doesn't say very much about what you'll bring to your next employer, and that's why it's important instead to look at accomplishments and transferable skills.

With that in mind, Let's get started.

1. LAW SCHOOL — YOUR MOST IMPORTANT RÉSUMÉ FEATURE

For any legal employer, your most important résumé item will be your law school career. (If you're looking at a nontraditional job, that may not be true; but for that situation, look at Chapter 13.) Even if you've got an extensive prior career, it's going to be your law school information that will draw a legal employer's attention first. Normally, it'll be the first thing on your résumé, under your name and address.

Here's how you ought to decide what goes in the law school section of your résumé. Using the form on page 222, entitled "Law School Résumé Worksheet," fill in the information about your school name, the city and state where it's located, the date you expect to graduate, and the names of any cocurricular or extracurricular activities you take part in, like Moot Court, journals, and student organizations. (I'm not talking work experience here, so if you hold down a part-time job or you've held summer clerkships, set them aside for now.) You'll also want to write down any CLE classes you've taken — what each class was about (e.g., taking depositions, new Evidence rules), and how many hours it was.

In the right-hand column, record your GPA and class rank. And don't round up either one! Also write down any scholarships you've received, academic awards or honors, and your Moot Court or Mock Trial ranking, especially if your results were particularly good. Include short descriptions of awards, as necessary, to make them meaningful to an employer. Also, write down the titles of any journal or association memberships or offices. As you write down any cocurriculars or extracurriculars you've participated in, make sure to include information about anything that you started or improved.

By way of example, here's how your sheet might look:

School name:	GPA: 2.95
Case Western Reserve	
School of Law	Class rank: 75/205
Location: Cleveland, Ohio	
Expected graduation date:	Scholarships, awards,
May, 1999	honors: Full tuition scholarship (awarded to 5 class members each year)

Co- and extracurriculars:	What I did, started, improved, or anything else that distinguishes me from anyone else doing the same activity:
Appellate Advocacy Program	Ranked 17/75 overall; 10th in oral moot court competition
Black Law Students Association	Secretary: designed University handout for prospective minority law students.
Continuing Legal Education Seminar: Taking Depositions. 4 hours.	Learned how to take depositions in medical malpractice cases.

Note that the left side of the sheet displays what you've done. That is, where you go to school, and the names of your activities. It's the *right* side of the page that shows what you've accomplished and how you've distinguished yourself from the crowd. Which side do you think will be of most interest to employers? That's right — it's the *right* side, your accomplishments, that will make an employer interested in you — so be sure to toot your own horn to the greatest extent possible!

Now, to the résumé worksheet —

LAW SCHOOL RÉSUMÉ WORKSHEET

Nuts & Bolts:

School Name:

_____

Location of School (City & State)

_____

Expected Graduation Date: _____

Co- and Extracurricular Activities
(e.g., Moot Court, journals, student
organizations, CLE classes):

What Makes Me Stand Out:

GPA: _____

Class Rank: _____ of _____

Scholarships, academic
awards, honors (with brief
explanation of each):

What I did, started, improved,
or anything else that distinguishes me from anyone else
doing the same activity:

2. UNDERGRADUATE SCHOOL

Now that you've done a worksheet for law school, go back and do the same for your undergraduate school, with this worksheet:

UNDERGRADUATE SCHOOL RÉSUMÉ WORKSHEET

Nuts & Bolts:

School Name:

_____

Location of School (City & State)

_____

Graduation Date: _____

What Makes Me Stand Out:

GPA: _____

Class Rank: _____ of _____

Scholarships, academic awards, honors (with brief explanation of each):

Co- and Extracurricular Activities (e.g., sports, fraternities/sororities, student government, journals, student organizations):

What I did, started, improved, or anything else that distinguishes me from anyone else doing the same activity:

So now you've got a completed law school résumé worksheet, and one for your undergraduate school, as well. Those are the only two that I know for sure that you need. If you've got another graduate degree, like an MBA or a Ph.D., then you'll want to make up a similar worksheet for that degree, as well.

3. EXPERIENCE: WHAT HAVE YOU DONE, AND HOW WELL HAVE YOU DONE IT?

Once you've completed your academic worksheets, it's time to turn your attention to your nonacademic experience. That's going to include all of your employment history, as well as any volunteering that you've done. You'll want one worksheet for every employer, whether it was a full-time position, part-time, or a summer job. I've provided one worksheet each for legal employers and nonlegal employers on pages 227–228; if you've got more than one of either or both of these, just photocopy off as many as you need.

As you can see, the format for these experience worksheets is analogous to the academic worksheets you've already filled in. That's because the left-hand side of the page will focus on nuts and bolts, like jobs and duties. The right-hand side will focus on accomplishments — the kinds of things that will entice an employer to want to meet you. Let's go over what those columns ought to include, in detail. And remember — you want one sheet for every employer, whether full-time, part-time, or summer.

On the left side of each page, you enter your job title(s), the name of the organization, the city and state where it's located, and the dates of your employment. Also on the left side, list your tasks and duties. Try to be as detailed as possible. For instance, instead of writing "wrote memoranda" for a legal employer, jot down the topics you covered. Count the number of trials you attended, briefs you wrote — everything you can think of. As William & Mary's Rob Kaplan advises, "It's important to *quantify*." If you just say you "attended trials," that could be anywhere from 2 to 200. Be specific! Don't worry about including too much detail here, because this is just a worksheet for your résumé — you're just gathering facts right now, and so you need as many of them at your disposal as you can possibly remember.

For any nonlegal work you've done, you want to be just as detailed. Let's say, for instance, that you were an accountant before you went to law school. In your left-hand column, you'd write down the number of clients you handled, as well as the range of their activity and their size. You'd jot down whether you contributed to firm publications or presented seminars. Or, let's say you were a nurse before you started law school. You'd include in that left column what area you specialized in. You'd write down if you were ever a supervisor, or if you did any work under minimal supervision, or any timely decisions you were forced to make. And you'd mention whether you counseled families as part of your responsibilities. Remember — you're trying to get down on paper as much as possible!

When it comes to summer jobs, you'll still want to divide your tasks as much as possible for the left-hand column of your worksheets. For instance, let's say you were a clerk in a retail store. Were you responsible for sales and cash registers? Did you supervise other people, and if so, how many? Did you open and close the store? Did you handle customer complaints? Did you have a lot of supervision or did you work independently? As with every other kind of work experience worksheet, you've got to be as specific as you can possibly be.

At this point you're probably thinking, "OK, Kimmbo, you've beaten that left-hand column to death. What the heck goes on the *right*-hand side?" Well, you'll put things that show you were better than average. What you've got in your left-hand column are your duties; what you want in your right-hand column are the accomplishments that spring from those duties. Ask yourself: How *well* did you do those things in the left-hand column? This is *crucial*, because, remember, employers, both legal and nonlegal, aren't looking for employees with the exact background for the job. Rather, they're looking for people with the *potential* to learn and excel. How well you've done the things you've done is what tells them that. And if you *don't* tell them that, *there's no way for them to find it out!*

So, what kinds of things go in this right-hand column? Let's go back to the accounting example. Did you handle a particularly heavy portfolio of clients? Was your ratio of billable to nonbillable hours higher than the norm? Were your newsletter submissions published ahead of others at your level? Did you receive favorable comments from your clients, or from people who managed you?

If you were a nurse, you might find it harder to quantify the work you did into accomplishments for that right-hand column. But still, you'll want to think about new procedures you might have instituted in response to problems or situations. Or maybe you shortened training time, or did things to ease confusion, or reduce errors, or create a better atmosphere for patients and families. Those are certainly accomplishments that you should put on your worksheets!

Now let's turn to summer jobs, and talk about what kinds of things go in the right-hand column. Let's say you worked in temporary office positions during your breaks. Well, you learned a lot about basic office procedures, which will save an employer time in training you just so you can begin simple tasks. Many campus jobs, like library shelf-stocking, or working at the bookstore, or cataloging a professor's collection, will have taught you valuable things, whether you realize it or not. For instance, they will have taught you how to juggle competing demands of school and work, and how to organize and prioritize your study time. Also, jobs like these show that you are methodical and meticulous (remember our list of adjectives!) and that you can tolerate repetitive tasks, if you have to, without compromising accuracy.

Or let's say that your only job ever was in manual labor. If you held that job down for a while, it shows you were reliable, punctual (hopefully!), and that you understand what's involved in a perform-for-pay situation.

It might be that your only job experience is a project for a professor. Well, this shows a lot of good things about you. For one thing, it proves your academic ability, and that's especially good if you don't have stellar grades. You probably also improved your research and writing skills, and you learned more about your professor's area of research. You can see that that could easily be of interest to a legal employer!

Now, let's do the worksheets!

LEGAL EMPLOYER RÉSUMÉ WORKSHEET

Nuts & Bolts:

What Made Me Stand Out (Accomplishments and Transferable Skills Learned or Sharpened):

Organization:

_____

Job Title(s):

_____

Location of Organization
(City & State):

_____

Dates of Employment:

_____

Tasks and Duties
(in as much detail as you
can muster):

NONLEGAL EMPLOYER RÉSUMÉ WORKSHEET

Nuts & Bolts:

What Made Me Stand Out (Accomplishments and Transferable Skills Learned or Sharpened):

Organization:

_____

Job Title(s):

_____

Location of Organization
(City & State):

_____

Dates of Employment:

_____

Tasks and Duties
(in as much detail as you
can muster):

OK. Now you've got experience worksheets for your legal and non-legal employers. We've only got a couple more left to do: volunteer, and hobbies and personal interests. Let's do the volunteer sheets first. It may be that you volunteered during undergraduate school to get course credits. Maybe you still volunteer for personal reasons. Or maybe you've taken my advice in the chapter on making contacts, and you've volunteered with the local bar association or as an extern for a local judge or you've done Pro Bono America projects. Regardless of why or when you did it, write down all the volunteering you've done. Perhaps you worked on a hotline 4 hours each week for a semester or two. Maybe you taught adults to read. Maybe you did what I've done and volunteered at a summer camp, or volunteered on political campaigns. Whatever it is, write it down! You may well find that you don't have any particular achievements to include in the right-hand column, but employers will be impressed by the fact that you've volunteered *at all*. That's because it shows that you're willing to reach beyond your peer group and communicate effectively with others, and you'll tend to be more aware of others, as well. The maturity and perspective you gain by volunteering are *very* marketable achievements. In fact, if you're interested in public interest law, a record of public service can be *critically* important! And if you've done law-related volunteering, you've got legal skills to transfer as well — icing on the cake!

VOLUNTEERING RÉSUMÉ WORKSHEET

What I've done:

How well I did (e.g., dollars raised, or anything else that distinguished you — and don't worry if there's nothing that distinguished you, because the experience of volunteering in and of itself is very impressive!)

4. HOBBIES & INTERESTS: WHAT MAKES YOU A LIVING, BREATHING PERSON!

Phew! You're *almost* done with your fact-collecting. The last things I want you to focus on are your hobbies and personal interests. When we get to the next section, on actually formulating your résumé, I'll go into more detail about exactly what you want to put down. But for right now, list any hobbies or abilities that you have that don't show up in any worksheet you've completed until now. What kinds of things should you include? Well, do you scuba dive? Do you play classical piano? Do you golf or play tennis? Do you have a pilot's license? Are you a white water rafter, or windsurfer, or expert roller-blader? Are you a wine connoisseur? Do you take part in some kind of dance, like hip-hop, or swing, or ballroom? Are you fluent in a foreign language? Are you an opera or musical comedy buff? Do you take part in community theater productions? Are you a world-traveler? Did you have an unusual childhood — for instance, did you spend time abroad? Do you have a special skill, like Lexis or Westlaw, or general computer proficiency? I could go on and on because the variety of possible activities and skills is endless. The important thing here is: think about how you spend your time outside of school, and *write it down!*

HOBBIES & PERSONAL INTERESTS WORKSHEET

Activities, abilities, interests, childhood:

Now, what have you got? Probably an hour or two's worth of solid thinking about everything you've done, and how well you've done it. With these worksheets in hand, formulating your résumé is going to be a breeze!

B. FORMULATING YOUR RÉSUMÉ WITH THE INFORMATION FROM YOUR WORKSHEETS

With all the worksheets you've filled out, you've got your Universe. What I'm going to do here is show you how to pick and choose from your worksheets what should go on your résumé. And we're going to be judicious about it, because there's unlikely to be any good reason for your résumé to ooze onto two pages — it's not a biography, for heaven's sake!

So what I'm going to do here is to take you through every section of your résumé, and talk about what you ought to put there. Now, I'm not going to give you a particular style or format that's engraved in stone. At the end of this chapter, in Appendix A, I've given you a few résumés in different styles, and any one of them would be appropriate for your résumé. Just pick the one you like the best, and go with it!

With that in mind, let's talk about what should appear on your résumé.

1. NAME, ADDRESS, AND PHONE NUMBER

Hey — I didn't say every word I wrote would be a revelation to you, did I? I *know* that anyone who's ever written a résumé has put their name and address and phone number at the top. But if I *didn't* mention it, I promise you I'd get letters pointing out that I overlooked it. So, I'm just telling you — put your name, address, and phone number at the top. If your permanent address is different than your campus address, include them both.

'Nuff said.

2. ACADEMIC STUFF

This is where you pull out your law school, undergrad school, and any other grad school worksheets — because your academic record is what should go first on your résumé. And this is true, by the way, even if you've got an extensive prelaw school career in some other field. Why?

Because you're looking at legal employers, and what they'll be most interested in is your legal education. (The only time this may not be true is if you're looking at nonlegal employers; in that case, take a look at Chapter 13 on nontraditional careers.)

So — what goes in this academic section? Let's see . . .

A. LAW SCHOOL GEOGRAPHICAL INFORMATION

Put down the name, city, and state of your law school. It's best not to use abbreviations on your résumé, so write out the name of your school. For instance: University of Southern California School of Law, Los Angeles, California.

B. GRADUATION INFORMATION

Put down the year and either the month or season of your expected graduation. There are a few ways to put down your graduation date, for example: J.D. expected Year X; Candidate for J.D. year X; Expected graduation date Year X. Don't lose any sleep over this one, OK? They're all fine. The only important thing to get across is that you haven't yet graduated (if, in fact, that's the case).

C. GPA AND CLASS RANK

It's been so simple until now, and here we are — our first speed bump. Why? Because the issue of whether to put your GPA and class rank on your résumé if they aren't stellar is an issue many law students grapple with, and there's no consistency among career services counselors as to where the cut-off is. Employers will try to tell you that they want to see your grades no matter how bad they are, but as San Diego's Susan Benson points out, "If employers are going to ding you if your grades are low, then you shouldn't mention low grades, *regardless* of what they say they want!"

And you've probably heard the familiar chestnut that you should put your grades down, because if you don't, the employer will assume your grades are much worse than they really are. But the fact is, there *is* a cut-off where putting your grades down will hurt you more than help you, and I asked every career services director I talked with about exactly what that cut-off is. I heard anywhere between the top third and the top half of the class, although I'd say that most of the experts I spoke with encouraged students to include their grades if they were in the top 40–50% of the class. If you're close to that cut-off point, it's worth visiting your career services office to find out what their advice for your particular school is. After all, if you go to a top law school, you'll be able to get away with much worse grades than if you go to a marginal school.

What if you don't include your GPA and class rank? In that case, you *are* going to have to include *something* about your academic performance, and the watchword here is: put your best foot forward!

You may, for instance, have a strong upward trend in your grades. In that case, you'll want to segregate your GPA's for your different years in law school. For instance, you can put something like:

2nd year GPA: 3.5/4.0, 20th out of 250
1st year GPA: 2.5/4.0, 170th out of 250
Cumulative GPA: 3.1/4.0, 90th out of 250

That certainly highlights your upward trend, and notice what I've done: I've put the best result *first* by listing the years in reverse chronological order. There's no point in drawing attention to a strong upward trend if you're going to kick it off with your *worst* grades!

Regardless of whether you've got a strong upward trend or not, there are other things you can do if your overall GPA isn't stellar. For instance, as Cal Western's Lisa Kellogg recommends, you can put down the grades for the classes you've excelled in as long as they're relevant to the employer. NYU's Gail Cutter suggests adding a line that says, "Relevant Course Work," and putting down any stellar grades that are relevant to the employer. For instance, if you apply to medical malpractice firms, and you got an A– in medical malpractice even though you're in the bottom half of the class, definitely put that single grade down. (In fact, even if you're in the top half of the class, it would be worth highlighting a performance like that!) Or let's say that you're applying to the D.A.'s office, and you got an A in Crim Pro. Put it on your résumé! Or, suppose you're applying to a litigation firm. That A– you got in Trial Tactics is a definite plus! Or perhaps you've done particularly well in paper courses versus exam courses. You can highlight *that*, and point out in your cover letter how well you do in those kinds of classes.

You'll probably find if you "spotlight" grades like this that you'll need more than one résumé. But as I told you at the beginning of this chapter, there's no crime in having more than one résumé. The point of a résumé is to get an employer interested in you, and if that means having to come up with a new résumé for every single employer you contact, so be it!

What if *all* of your law school grades stink? Well, St. John's' Maureen Provost Ryan suggests just putting down your undergrad grades (assuming *they're* good) under the college section of your résumé. As she points out, "One semester of law school won't capture someone as accurately as 4 years of undergrad will!"

If this whole subject of grades depresses you, don't let it. As I've pointed out time and again in this book, bad grades will *not* stop you from getting the job of your dreams. As Gail Peshel points out, "Smaller employers are more concerned with whether you'll stay or leave — geographic ties and rainmaking skills are much more important to them than grades are!" And Sophie Sparrow adds, "Sell what you've got. If it's great experience — sell that. If you've got a great personality — make contacts to get your foot in the door. Consider the whole picture of you. People who don't do well in school can be stellar!" Keep this whole discussion of grades on your résumé in perspective. All we're talking about now is how to show you off to your best advantage on a résumé, and you *know* that I don't consider résumés the lynchpin of your job search by any *stretch* of the imagination. If you don't have grades, make up for it some other way — with great experience or by making contacts to skirt the whole credentials problem from the get go. All you're doing *here* is thinking of how best to present your academics. Get that out of the way, and then forge ahead!

D. OTHER GRADUATE DEGREES

You probably don't *have* any other graduate degrees, but if you do — like an MBA, or a Ph.D., or a Masters — handle it exactly the same way as for your legal education.

What about if you have *part* of a graduate degree? A common mistake students make with unfinished graduate work is to give the impression that they have a degree, when actually they only completed some of the coursework. The way to handle a situation like this is to choose a format from Appendix A that doesn't highlight degrees in the left margin. A good format to use is:

University of Transylvania, Slogolz, Transylvania
Completed 15 credits toward MBA, including courses in. . . .

If you just have a couple of graduate classes under your belt and the courses aren't relevant to any employer you're interested in, I'd leave them off your résumé altogether.

E. UNDERGRADUATE SCHOOL

Again — you'll handle your undergrad experience just like you handled your law school experience. Furthermore, if you had any undergraduate law courses in which you shined — a legal history course, or a Constitutional Law course, for instance — you may want to highlight that performance on your résumé.

F. HIGH SCHOOL

There are almost never any circumstances where you'll want to mention the high school you attended. But if you've read Chapter 11 on Rainmaking, then you know that "almost" is the operative word here. That's because if you attended a particularly prestigious private or Catholic school, that may indicate to an employer that you've got client development potential. In that specific instance, it's worth mentioning. Otherwise, leave it off!

3. AWARDS, HONORS, AND ACTIVITIES

Now, it's possible that you'll choose a format for your résumé, of those in Appendix A, that matches your awards, honors and activities, with the particular school where you received them. In that case, modify the advice I'll give you here accordingly. The point is, I'm going to tell you the kind of information about awards, honors, and activities that you'll want to include on your résumé. Precisely where you *put* it is a matter of the format you choose.

First of all, you're going to want to go through your worksheets and pull out exactly which awards, honors, and activities you want to include. Anything with an academic bent, and any activity you've taken part in in law school, is something you'll want to include. And don't forget athletic achievements! They speak very well of you, since they reflect on your competitiveness, self-motivation and self-discipline, ability to perform under pressure and, perhaps, in front of others, and your leadership skills. On the other hand, purely social activities, particularly those where you didn't hold office, may be best left off your résumé, unless they are very unusual and attention-getting (e.g., a skydiver's club). As a rule of thumb, unless the social activity will attract an employer's attention because it's unique, it's best to leave it off.

In terms of wording, you want to offer just enough description of any award, honor, or activity so that an employer will understand it. The fact that you held office, or whatever you accomplished, especially if it had never been done before, should be listed. (This is that information from the right-hand side of your worksheets that I told you was *vital* to your résumé!) Keep in mind as you work on this section that you are highlighting your achievements in order to stand out. Here are a few examples to give you an idea of how to write up your *own* awards, honors and activities:

> "James Fordham Scholar: three-time honoree for outstanding academic achievement."
>
> "Intercollegiate Golf Scholarship, full tuition and fees paid through 4 years."
>
> "Chairperson, Student Activities Committee — oversaw committee of 12 and $50,000 budget."

To help you figure out how to word other similar résumé information, here's advice on the most common types of law school activities.

A. SCHOLARSHIPS

Scholarships reflect *wonderfully* well on you, and you should *always* include them on your résumé if you're lucky enough to have them.

For full tuition scholarships, you'll want to highlight for the employer the value of the scholarship. That means that a short phrase of description will help. Try including information like this:

> "Full Tuition Scholarship: Awarded and renewable on the basis of grades; one of X distributed to incoming class."

For partial scholarships awarded on the basis of grades, you'll want to include the same kind of language. If additional factors like residential or ethnic background are involved, mention that. And you may find out during the year that your scholarship has a donor name. If so, include it. If not, such a scholarship is known simply as an "Academic Scholarship," and that's what you should call it on your résumé. If you don't know the donor name of your scholarship, or it doesn't have one, list it on your résumé something like this:

> "Academic Scholarship, partial tuition paid."
>
> "Partial Academic Scholarship: renewable for 3 years."

B. JOURNALS

Since excellent writing ability is crucial to any student editorial position and also to any subsequent legal position you will hold, you should *always* include journal experience on your résumé. But you should also take into account that journal experience will have different meanings to different employers, based on their own experience. Some employers may not realize that there are many other skills, both in editorial and managerial positions, that can be *very* highly developed on student journals! For instance, most editors select, supervise, and advise other student contributors, which adds to their leadership, management, and critical analysis skills in a legal setting. They learn how to delegate and oversee work, another valuable skill. Solicitations editors have significant managerial duties as well, including developing topics and soliciting prospective authors from the legal community. These skills involve creative and organizational thinking from the viewpoint of marketing. And that's *very* similar to client development in a private law practice, perhaps the most prized skill of all! So if you present the skills you've learned on the basis of journal experience just right, these skills can make you *very* marketable!

If your journal experience includes a writing contribution, you should give the topic of your contribution. However, keep in mind that if you write down your topic and the employer knows something about it, you may find yourself spending your entire interview discussing the topic you wrote about — so make sure you bone up on what you wrote before you go on such an interview!

1. LAW REVIEW

Here it is — the goose that lays the golden eggs of law school activities. I remember an ad a few years ago that read something like, "He's on Law Review — and he drinks Chivas." As this ad implies, *everybody* knows what Law Review is. If you're on it, you can list it on your résumé without having to describe it at all. Furthermore, you don't have to state how you were chosen (that is, whether you got on on the basis of grades or a writing competition). When it comes to law review duties, if what you've done isn't obvious from your job title, you can describe it briefly. Here's an example:

"Case Western Reserve Law Review; Articles Editor. Assumed full editorial and verification responsibility for three articles to be published in Spring, Year X. Supervised six associates."

As an aside — Law Review is really the only credential with any lasting power. Even now, 10 years out of law school, people will sometimes ask me if I was on Law Review, believe it or not. While I found Law Review the most pompous, boring, long-winded exercise in redundancy that I've ever taken part in in my entire life, if you have the opportunity to do it, do it. Even if you find that it's the experiential equivalent of a root canal, it's such an important and widely-recognized credential that it's worth having, no matter *how* painful an experience it is.

So much for my aside. Let's look at how you handle other journals on your résumé.

2. OTHER JOURNALS

Since journals other than Law Review vary from school to school, you'll want to explain any other journal experience. For instance, explain whether the journal is student-run, a scholarly publication, or exactly what the heck it is. As with Law Review, you'll want to refer to your own specific contribution(s):

"Case Western Reserve Journal of Phlegm Reclamation Law; Business Editor. Full responsibility for $18,000 annual budget of student-run scholarly publication. Negotiate contracts with publishers and reprinters; arrange copyrighting; sell subscriptions."

3. FOR JOURNAL ACTIVITY YOU HAVEN'T DONE YET . . .

Here's the set-up: It's summer, you're sending out résumés, and you're not going to take part in a journal until the Fall. For instance, let's say that you graded onto Law Review, or you wrote on in the writing competition, but you haven't done anything yet. What do you do? Well, you should definitely put it on your résumé, because journal experience is very important to legal employers. Just be careful to word it so that it's obvious you haven't started yet. Try something like this:

> "Case Western Reserve Law Review, Year X – Year Y."

If you state it like this, you'll make it plain that this is something you're definitely going to do, it's just that you haven't done it yet. Remember, you can only do this is you're *definitely* going to be on a particular journal — if you haven't received a definite invitation to take part, don't include it!

c. Moot Court Competitions

Moot Court is really important to legal employers, because it shows that you've developed your ability to research and analyze points of law, and it also shows your ability to express yourself persuasively, both orally and in writing. Beyond *that*, it's the best indicator of how you match up against your classmates in a nonexam setting. This example will give you an idea of how to describe your moot court activities and results:

> "National Moot Court Team. Selected for team after ranking among top six oral and written advocates out of 75 participants in intramural competition."

What about if you've been invited to take part in moot court, but you haven't done so yet? How does it go on your résumé? Try a wording something like this:

> "Appellate Advocacy Program, Year X – Year Y: includes intramural moot court competition during spring semester."

When is this useful? Well, let's say you're writing your résumé in the summer and interviews are in the fall. You can't wait to send out your résumé, and you definitely want to include this activity. But remember

— only use it if you're *definitely* going to be taking part in the activity.

D. MOCK TRIAL COMPETITION

Legal employers like to see mock trial experience on your résumé, because it helps develop your advocacy skills, and, in particular, your spontaneous courtroom skills, in a start-to-finish trial situation. As a result, it will likely pique an employer's interest, especially if you can also point out what you did well in the competition. Here's an example:

"National Mock Trial Competition: Ranked 12th out of top 22 teams in the United States, after winning regional competition against 25 teams. Preparation and participation involved over 100 hours per semester, without course credit."

E. CLIENT COUNSELING COMPETITION

If you do well in the client counseling competition, this will draw an employer's interest because it's a harbinger of your effectiveness in working with clients. Since this is one activity in which First Years tend to excel, it often stands alone on a First Year student's résumé. If that's the case with you, try to compose a sentence or two that will really attract a potential employer, like this:

"Client Counseling Competition: Ranked third of 48 teams in intramural competition. Judged by visiting attorneys and psychologists on the basis of ability to advise, counsel, and elicit information from clients in a mock counseling situation."

F. LAW SCHOOL CLINICS

Employers are *very* interested in students who take part in law school clinics. Why? There are a bunch of reasons. For one thing, it gives students a chance to apply theory to real life situations, and to handle clients, and to budget their time — and it also gives students a chance to get basic mistakes out of their system in a uniquely structured environment designed as much to educate them as it is to provide client care. Especially if your grades aren't outstanding, a law school clinic can give you the ammunition to show potential employers that you can be a star!

As a result, you should definitely let employers know the scope of your activities and responsibilities in any clinics you take part in, like this:

> "Law School Clinic, Intern: Served as legal counsel in seven civil cases over full academic year. Conducted client interviews, witness identification and preparation; researched and wrote memoranda, briefs, and motions; represented three clients at trials under supervision of Clinic lawyers. Gained direct experience in client contact, case development, pretrial and trial procedures, and law practice management."

G. STUDENT ASSOCIATIONS AND FRATERNITIES

I could probably give you a whole book on how to describe student associations, because there are so many of them! Instead, all I'm going to do is give you an idea of how to handle them, showing you how to focus on your *accomplishments* in every case.

1. STUDENT BAR ASSOCIATION

Whether you were elected or appointed to the Student Bar Association, you'll probably be called upon to represent and "sell" the school at various functions. What does this mean to legal employers, particularly private firms, keeping in mind that they're always looking to attract new clients and keep their current ones? *Rainmaking ability* — that's what it says. On top of that, many SBA officers also become involved in counseling and mediation, which provide direct evidence of an ability to do the same with clients. So when you present your SBA experience on your résumé, be sure to focus on the *marketability* of what you've done. Here are a couple of examples:

"Student Bar Association: Chairperson, Curriculum Committee: Targeted and recommended new international law course and clinical program to faculty, which will commence in the Year X school year, in response to student/faculty survey to identify curriculum gap."

"Student Bar Association, Cuyahoga County Bar Association Liaison: Regularly attended bar association meetings and expressed student concerns on various issues. Attracted over 50 new members through first on-campus recruitment in over 10 years."

2. OTHER STUDENT ASSOCIATIONS

Your commitment to any student association is a plus to legal employers. Again, like the Student Bar Association, you should be specific as to what you accomplished. If you have trouble with this, focus on the fact that many student associations sponsor activities, and this is a good chance to show your organizational, leadership, and oral skills. Here are a couple of examples:

"Black Law Students Association, Midwest Recruitment Conference Volunteer: Manned student and employer check-in booths. Recruited and supervised 10 students in preparing résumé binders."

"Environmental Law Students Association; Chairperson, Speaker Committee: Solicited several national speakers, generating press coverage. Events attracted greatest per-event attendance of all student groups."

While it's obvious that public interest employers will be interested in your associational activities, those aren't the only employers who will find them attractive. However, for employers outside of public interest, be very sure that your description of your activities focuses on the transferable skills you learned from them. Here is an example:

"Student Public Interest Law Fellowship, Board Member: Helped to raise awareness among law students and lawyers of employment opportunities. With fellow students, raised $13,000 during one year and $19,000 during the next year for student internships."

3. LAW FRATERNITIES

Whether you mention a law fraternity on your résumé depends on what your involvement was like. If all you did was attend social events, nix it. However, if you did more than that — for instance, you held any kind of leadership position or fundraising role — then definitely include that on your résumé. And if your title in the fraternity doesn't make plain what your role was, then explain it (for instance, if the liaison officer with your national fraternity is called a "tribune," you'll want to explain that in the description of your role). Here's an example:

"Delta Theta Phi Legal Fraternity: Active in tenants' rights issue which involved representing tenants through the media, letters, and a court appearance."

3. EXPERIENCE STUFF

This is probably the section of your résumé that will take you the most time — especially if you've held down full-time jobs before law school.

Here's how we'll tackle this section. First of all, I'll show you how to take the information from your worksheets about jobs you've had, and pull out the specific information you'll want to use on your résumé. Then I'll talk about how to organize the experience section of your résumé, and there I'll talk about legal employment, and nonlegal employment, and volunteer activities.

Let's start by talking about how you ought to present *any* job you've had.

A. USING YOUR WORKSHEET INFORMATION TO DRAW OUT SPECIFICALLY WHAT YOU'LL INCLUDE ABOUT EVERY JOB YOU'VE HAD

When it comes to describing your jobs on your résumé, all you have to do is take your worksheets and pull out the information I'm about to describe to you. But first of all, I'm going to address a couple of style issues that you should keep in mind: namely, starting your sentences with verbs, and focusing on results first.

1. STYLE ISSUES: START WITH VERBS AND RESULTS!

Let's talk about starting your sentences with verbs. Whatever kind of activity you're describing, start your descriptions with a verb; don't ever say "I did this" or "I do this." Here are a few examples:

"Wrote memoranda, researched cases. . . . "
"Process estates, assist at trials. . . . "
"Drafting briefs, preparing testimony. . . . "

And to accentuate your accomplishments, it helps to start sentences with the *results* of your efforts. Here's an example:

"Reduced overtime 23% while increasing productivity, by cross-training all staff. Virtually eliminated downtime through equitable task distribution."

2. THE PECKING ORDER OF INFORMATION ABOUT EACH JOB: KNOWING WHAT TO SAY ABOUT WHAT YOU'VE DONE

For every job on your worksheets, you're going to go through a pecking order, stopping as soon as you've got something to say about that particular job. The first rung on the pecking order is accomplishments. The second is a range to help show an accomplishment. The third is any skills you gained or abilities you sharpened on the job. And the fourth, and a very distant last place, involves listing duties and responsibilities. But remember — you only go down this pecking order until you've got something to say. In the context of your worksheets, you want to stay on the right side of your worksheet — where you wrote down what distinguished you — unless there's just nothing there.

Let's take a look at that pecking order to see how it works.

♦ Accomplishments: This is the highest level of description that you can relate to an employer. It's the one that truly highlights your successes. Here are a couple of examples:

"Began as volunteer; hired and subsequently promoted on basis of performance."

"Developed new chemical process which received patent."

"Undertook 5-year mission to explore new worlds and new galaxies. Boldly went where no one has gone before." (This is particularly useful if you happen to be Captain James T. Kirk.)

♦ Ranges: Numbers and percentages jump out on résumés, and they're particularly helpful in terms of providing evidence of accomplishments. So use them if you have them! Here are a couple of examples:

"Employed up to 30 hours per week on third shift while attending school full-time. On Dean's List six of eight semesters."

"Founded company with two fellow engineers. Built $5,000 investment into $2.5 million annual gross revenues within 5 years."

"Upon withdrawal from college, founded software company. Within 10 years, created multibillion dollar fortune."

♦ Still don't have anything to put down? It's time to drop down to talking about any skills you gained from the job, or any abilities you sharpened because of it. Those are *still* very valuable to employers. Here are a few examples:

> "As shop foreman in a union environment, developed ability to vary communication style to suit audience, from Ph.D. chemists to assembly workers. Received formal training in grievance procedures, negotiation techniques and anger defusion."

> "Journalist; developed quick, concise writing style under strict time constraints. Approach emphasized fact-gathering and distillation, and multiple angles in stories ranging from local public health crisis to international stock market trends."

> "Admissions Office Assistant: Required to work, at times, with little direct supervision; noted for accuracy, even in repetitive tasks, speed, and attention to detail. Received two merit raises in 6 months."

♦ If you can't find any accomplishments or skills or abilities, it's time to scrape the bottom of the barrel and talk about duties and responsibilities. In other words, it's time to jump back over to the left-hand column of your worksheets. That doesn't mean your résumé has to be boring, though; you can talk about your responsibilities and still make things interesting, as this example shows:

> "General Litigation Paralegal: In addition to customary duties, performed legal research and drafted briefs, which were largely accepted with little revi-

sion. Assessed computerized documentation systems and recommended package which was purchased."

If you have to focus on your responsibilities in any given job, use the opportunity to highlight any activity that put you in close contact with lawyers, or had you performing duties that reflect on what you'd do as a lawyer — like negotiating contracts or disputes, or being an expert witness, or participating in judicial boards for undergrad fraternities or student governments.

For more insight into how to word your job descriptions, look at the sample résumés in Appendix A at the end of this chapter.

B. HOW TO ORGANIZE THE EXPERIENCE SECTION OF YOUR RÉSUMÉ

Most of the résumés you see reflect a standard approach to organization experience, and it's this: you use a simple reverse chronological format, starting with your most recent experience, and working backwards. Under each specific job, the details for that job are presented.

But you know something? Depending on what your background is, that approach may not work for you. For instance, let's say you've got a lot of work experience under your belt, or several different career paths. In those instances, you may want to consider a functional format to your résumé to handle your prior career(s) (for your legal experience, you should stick with a reverse chronological format). What the functional format does is to focus on your transferable skills, rather than your job titles and employers. If you've got lots of experience, or your job titles didn't match the scope of your duties, or if you've changed jobs frequently, this format will work like a charm for you! (By the way, this format is illustrated in Résumé #6 in Appendix A.)

Here's how you go about putting together a functional résumé for your prior career(s). What you do is take out your job worksheets for your nonlegal jobs, and focus on the right-hand side of them. Rearrange your accomplishments into areas of experience, like marketing, accounting, purchasing, advertising, finance, production control, and the like. Also try grouping them under more personal attributes or skills, with headings like written and oral communication, analysis and problem-solving, organization and management, leadership and motivation, technical knowledge, and so on.

Then, on your résumé, you group your experiences by function rather than by employer. It's a very different approach, but it's highly readable, and it *definitely* focuses the employer's attention on your transferable skills!

If you want to use this functional approach, remember to confine it to your nonlegal experience, and use the traditional reverse-chronological format for your legal experience. It's really up to you to choose which format highlights your skills the best.

c. How to Describe Legal, Nonlegal, and Volunteer Activities

Now let's take a quick look at how you describe your different types of experience, starting with the most important experience first!

1. Legal Employment

This is, hands down, the most important experience on your résumé. Why? Because it says so much about your ability to handle the practical aspects of lawyering — and ideally it conveys your enthusiasm about what you've done!

What you'll want to do is take the employer's name and location, your job title, and dates from your worksheets. Unless your legal employer is very likely to be known to your target audience (e.g., it's the Environmental Protection Agency, or an enormous law firm in or near your target city), include a line briefly describing the employer to help potential employers put your experience in context with their own needs. For instance, you can describe a firm this way:

"Alias, Smith, and Jones: Springfield, Ohio. Seven-attorney firm with general civil practice."

Any work that you have performed for professors should also be included in the legal section of your résumé. Structure your descriptions the same way you've done all of your other employment experience. If you're not sure of how to title or describe your work, check with the professor! However, a typical entry would look something like this:

"Professor Shemp Stooge, Nyuck-Nyuck School of Law. Legal Research Assistant, Summer, Year X. Researched 'Negligence Cases Based On Pie Fights in Pennsylvania, 1976–1994.' Utilized Lexis and Westlaw databases daily; taught database research methods to three research assistants. Drafted two sections of article for publication."

In your legal employment section, be sure to include any legal work you've done as a volunteer — e.g., for the local bar association, or for a judge as a volunteer extern, or for Pro Bono Students America. As Northern Illinois' Mary Obrzut says, "It doesn't matter to employers if the work was volunteer or paid. Include it!" In fact, you needn't even *mention* on your résumé if you were paid for it or not!

While you want to focus on accomplishments to the greatest extent possible, it may be that you have to fall back onto the left-hand side of your worksheets and talk about your duties. If so, remember that you're trying to pique an employer's interest, so be sure to include the full range of your activities.

2. NONLEGAL EMPLOYMENT

As with your legal employment, focus on the accomplishments of what you've done by looking at the right-hand side of your worksheets. Remember: when you're talking about nonlegal jobs you've had, they're only relevant to legal employers to the extent you've drawn transferable skills from them. Make sure that your descriptions reflect that!

3. VOLUNTEER ACTIVITIES

Be sure that you give your volunteer activities the attention they deserve! As I've mentioned before, your volunteering activities may have given you a level of responsibility or results that tell prospective employers a lot more about your potential than any paid job you've had. After all, just because you didn't work for pay doesn't mean the work was any easier or the results were any less indicative of your abilities. In fact, letting employers know that you worked for no pay can highlight your commitment and drive!

As I pointed out just a minute ago, any legal work you've done on a volunteer basis should be included under "legal experience." You can include nonlegal volunteering under nonlegal experience, or under a separate activities section, or in a separate volunteering section all by itself.

Use the same approach to describing your nonpaid work as you've done for your paid work — focus on accomplishments and results to the greatest extent possible, and fall back on stating your responsibilities and duties only as a last resort. Here are a couple of examples:

"Amigos de las Americas: Community volunteer in Ecuadorian village for international volunteer health organization; summer, Year X. Introduced modern sanitation methods to village of 220 people in successful effort to stem further typhoid outbreaks. Spoke exclusively in Spanish."

"Big Brothers/Big Sisters of Fairfield County: Helped one little sister through family transition over 2-year period. Raised $450 and coordinated weekend camping trips involving 24 big and little sisters, which was reported in national newsletter."

4. PERSONAL INTERESTS AND HOBBIES

You may be tempted to leave a section like this off of your résumé, but I *implore* you to include it. Why? Because it's the one section of your résumé that will make you into a living, breathing person. It makes you *interesting*. As Fordham's Kathleen Brady says, "A personal section on a résumé makes you less one-dimensional!" Lisa Kellogg echoes that, saying, "Employers *want* to see personal interests. They make the applicant into a *person!*" Beyond that, it may make it harder for the employer to reject you.

What you'll want to do is to go through your hobbies and interests worksheet, and pull out three or four headliners. What you're looking for are the hobbies or interests that do one of three things: either they suggest rainmaking potential (like being a golf or tennis player), or they suggest a worthy trait like self-discipline (like being an AAU swimmer or a black belt in karate), or they provide conversation fodder (like being a champion clog dancer or skydiver). As Florida's Ann Skalaski points out, "Any connection you can make with the employer is a plus. It's not a science; it's just about people and how they relate to you. Personal stuff about you helps them *do* that." And Michigan's Nancy Krieger adds, "When you have an interviewer who's talked to 20 students, their only salvation is the hobby column on your résumé."

I'd be unfair to you if I didn't give you a few *serious* words of warning about this section of your résumé, because it's very easy to foul it up. For one thing, don't write mundane things. It may well be that you enjoy spending time with your wife and kids, but as Willamette's Diane Reynolds points out, it doesn't belong on your résumé. Also, don't make yourself look lazy. If you spend all of your off-time playing computer games, that's not something you want to bring up. And most importantly, don't mention *anything* that you're not willing to discuss in an interview. A brief anecdote will get this point across! One career services director told me about a student who put on his résumé, "Fluent in Swedish." It turns out that the wife of a partner at a law firm he was visiting had traced her family tree to a village near Stockholm. She had written to this village, and gotten a return letter — in Swedish, which she couldn't read. Her husband brought the letter with him to work, knowing that this guy was coming in for an interview. Without trying to put the guy on the spot, the partner pointed out what a coincidence it was that he spoke Swedish, because his wife had received this letter in Swedish and they couldn't read it. The partner handed the guy the letter, and the guy looked at it blankly for a moment. Then he looked up at the partner, and said, "It's a lie. I made it up. I can't speak Swedish." I don't think I have to tell you how the interview wound up!

Finally, when it comes to personal interests and hobbies, it may be that you take part in some controversial activities. If so, I've got some advice for you on how to handle them. But because this is such an important issue, I've given it its own topic. With that lead-in, let's move on to . . .

D. WHAT TO DO IF YOU'RE A GAY, TRANSSEXUAL, RIFLE-TOTING BEAUTY-PAGEANT WINNER: HANDLING HIGHLY-CHARGED RÉSUMÉ ITEMS

The heading to this section gives away what "highly-charged" résumé items are. They're items that are controversial; things like politics, and gay and lesbian issues, and religion. It would be wonderful if we lived in a society where none of these made any difference to any employer, but we don't. I want to spend a few minutes talking about them, because if you include them on your résumé, you should be aware that you're living dangerously — some legal employers will reject you out of hand simply because of a highly-charged résumé item. As Willamette's Diane Reynolds says, "As a rule of thumb, employers think, if it's on the résumé, it's in the office. If you're involved in a charged activity, employers figure you will bring it to the office." And if they feel uncomfortable with that, they may not even be willing to interview you.

At the outset, I should tell you that I know I'm stepping into murky waters here, because if you have so-called "highly-charged" activities in your background, they may be *very* important to you — and even the *hint* of leaving them off of your résumé may offend you. I hope you'll be able to look past that, because all I intend to do here is to explain how different kinds of highly-charged items might be perceived by employers. I'll give you several alternatives for handling them on your résumé. The decision on whether to leave such items on your résumé is entirely up to you, but if you *do* leave them on, I want you to do so knowing what you're up against.

On the other hand, it may be that you have highly-charged items on your résumé and you don't even realize that they're highly-charged! That was the case with me for two items I had on my résumé. Until I researched this book, I had no idea they were controversial. I wonder, looking back, how many interviews I lost because of them! One of the items was that I did advance work for the Jimmy Carter presidential campaign when I was in high school. And the other was my Law Review note topic, of all things; I wrote about legal liability for sexually-transmitted diseases. *I* thought it was a really interesting topic, but looking back, it may have made some employers look at me askance! So this section may also serve to put you on notice that things that seem perfectly reasonable to you may in fact be controversial to potential employers.

With that in mind, let's talk about highly-charged résumé items. First of all, let's talk about exactly what they *are*. I've separated them into eight broad categories, and highlighted potential problems with each:

1. CATEGORIES OF "CHARGED" RÉSUMÉ ITEMS AND POTENTIAL PROBLEMS THEY CREATE

♦ Religion

What's the problem here? Well, if you're heavily involved in one church, say, the Catholic church, and the partners at a firm you're applying to are all staunch Protestants, they may feel as though you won't fit in.

◆   Politics

The problem here is the same as for religion. You may be a big supporter of the Democratic party, and you probably already know that many lawyers are Republicans.

◆   Gay and Lesbian Issues

If you are involved in gay and lesbian issues, you already know how conservatives view these issues! You should also be aware that sexual orientation may be suggested on your résumé in insidious ways, even if you don't bring it up explicitly. One career services director told me about a male student who had been heavily involved in the theater before he went to law school. He was reluctant to put that experience on his résumé, since in the past people had assumed that his theater involvement meant he was gay. (As it turns out, he *did* include it on his résumé, and his résumé caught the attention of an employer who was also interested in theater.) The point is — law is by and large a conservative profession, and I'm probably not telling you anything you don't already know by telling you the impact of sexual orientation issues on it.

◆   Beauty Pageants (Like Being a Beauty Pageant Winner)

The problem here is "lookism." That is, if you're a woman, putting on your résumé that you have taken part in, and perhaps won, beauty pageants will undoubtedly get you some attention, but perhaps not in the way you intended.

◆   Fraternities

As Fordham's Kathleen Brady points out, the perception of fraternities is changing. It used to be that fraternities were viewed as a kind of "Animal House." Today, however, the message is more mixed, since fraternities are viewed more positively for their civic involvement.

◆   Gun Issues (Like Belonging to the NRA or Being an Avid Hunter)

If you include NRA membership or hunting on your résumé, be aware of the specter of militant militias that it may suggest to employers — and also be aware that hunting is a controversial activity, especially among younger and female employers.

♦   Women's Issues (Like Abortion or Battered Women's Shelters)

When it comes to abortion, if you mention either pro-choice or pro-life activities on your résumé, be aware that you'll likely alienate any employer whose beliefs differ from yours. And involvement in women's issues like battered women's shelters suggests a kind of feminism that may make conservative employers uncomfortable.

♦   Physical Handicaps

I hesitated including physical handicaps in a section on "charged" résumé items, but frankly I couldn't think of any better place to put them. The only reason I include them here is that if you have a physical handicap, it is something that may have an impact on employers who may be concerned about their ability to accommodate you — and its inclusion on your résumé is worth discussing.

2. FOUR ALTERNATIVES FOR HANDLING HIGHLY-CHARGED ITEMS

What I'm going to do is to go through the four different ways you can handle highly-charged résumé items, and, as you'll see, different kinds of charged items merit different kinds of treatment. Let's take a look at the four alternatives.

A. INCLUDE THE HIGHLY-CHARGED ITEM ON EVERY RÉSUMÉ YOU SEND

You may simply want to say "damn the torpedoes" and include charged items on your résumé. What happens if you do that? Well, as Maine's Tammy Willcox says, "Don't expect everyone to be thrilled by it." And Franklin Pierce's Sophie Sparrow points out that "Although you'll be screened out of some interviews, maybe you don't *want* to work for an employer who'd screen you out on that basis." In fact, if you do your homework and research employers up front, there's no reason why you should *ever* apply to an employer who will screen you out on the basis of something highly-charged, if it means that much to you.

The one item that you may want to include on your résumé is any obvious physical handicap. As Diane Reynolds points out, "It's probably a good idea to prepare an employer before your interview, because employers don't like surprises. For instance, what if you use a wheelchair? If you are making contact with an employer by phone, you can prepare them by saying something like, 'Is your building wheelchair accessible?' And on your résumé, you can put, 'Use wheelchair for mobility,' and leave it at that."

B. INCLUDE THE HIGHLY-CHARGED ITEM ON EVERY RÉSUMÉ YOU SEND, BUT *ONLY* IF THE ITEM PROVIDES YOU WITH TRANSFERABLE SKILLS

William & Mary's Rob Kaplan suggests that you only include highly-charged items on your résumé if they give you something an employer will find useful. By way of example, let's say that you spent a year working for a presidential campaign, as I did. I did what's called "advance" work. That is, I researched sites for rallies and speeches, I negotiated with hotel managers concerning accommodations for the press corps, and I dealt with the news media. Well, I took a lot of skills from that that an employer would be interested in, *regardless* of who my candidate was. I had to be organized, and I had to learn to negotiate, and I had to learn to deal with all kinds of problems on the spot, as well as handling all kinds of prickly personalities. Those transferable skills would be worth mentioning on a résumé. But let's say instead that all I did was to canvass neighborhoods or stuff pamphlets in mail slots. Well, there's not a lot that's transferable there. I've told you before that volunteering in and of itself is a positive attribute in the eyes of employers, but when you counter that with the highly-charged nature of politics, you may decide that it's not worth mentioning. As NYU's Gail Cutter says, "The litmus test I always use for highly-charged items is this: Was the value of the experience more important than the potential downside of a controversial name?"

This also applies to fraternities. As Kathleen Brady advises, if you mention your involvement in a fraternity, mention your involvement with civic work. For instance, did your fraternity raise money for charity? Fundraising is an activity that employers view very favorably, and so you should definitely include it. But if your fraternity involvement consisted of hearty and enthusiastic participation in the ice-shot slalom course at frat parties, then that's not a transferable skill worth mentioning!

In fact, even *with* transferable skills, you still have to be aware that you'll turn off some employers. With my own experience, working for Jimmy Carter, I found that employers were evenly split. Some responded, "Wow! That's really interesting!" and put aside any partisan politics. Others responded with a sneer, "You worked for *Jimmy Carter?*" So if you do consider including your transferable skills from a highly-charged activity on your résumé, be aware that it's a balance: there are *still* some employers who will get stuck on the item, and ignore the skills!

C. HAVE DIFFERENT RÉSUMÉS FOR DIFFERENT EMPLOYERS

One of the happier aspects of highly-charged résumés is that they cut both ways. Whereas there will be some employers who will screen you *out* because of those items, there are other employers who will take a definite interest in you *because* of them. For instance, involvement in liberal politics, volunteering at a battered women's shelter, and marching in Washington on behalf of abortion rights would all be *huge* pluses for liberal employers like the ACLU, whereas for a conservative, old-line, white-shoe law firm, these kinds of activities would likely make you about as welcome as radiation sickness.

So — why not tailor your résumés to your audience, and have different résumés for different kinds of employers? That's what Gail Cutter suggests, and I think it's a *wonderful* idea. As she points out, "Remember who it is that you're sending your résumé to, and send them an appropriate résumé."

The activities which will appeal to any particular employer will be obvious to you if you research employers up-front, as I *implore* you to do throughout this book. If you're heavily involved in any highly-charged activity, be sure that one of the things you dig up as you research the employer is how they will react to that activity. If they'll react positively, then it's something you don't just want to mention on your résumé, you want to *highlight* it. For instance, let's say that you're a member of the Tappa Kegga Brew fraternity. Well, as you do your research, your fraternity membership may provide a connection between you and someone who works at a place where you'd like a job, and those connections are valuable.

In fact, if a highly-charged activity is very dear to you, then you may find through making contacts and researching employers that you're *only* interested in applying for jobs with those employers who share your interest in the activity. I'd strongly encourage you to do that, because with shared interests you're likely to be much happier with an employer than if you feel as though you're "hiding" something.

If you have difficulty deciding if a particular employer will respond positively to a charged item, talk with your career services director about it. For instance, involvement in beauty pageants is something that's viewed positively in some parts of the country, and negatively in other parts — and that's something that your career services director will be able to give you guidance on.

So — consider sending different résumés to different employers. It's worth the few extra minutes it will take you to make up a new résumé!

D. LEAVE THE HIGHLY-CHARGED ITEM OFF OF YOUR RÉSUMÉ ENTIRELY

You may want to bite the bullet and just leave highly-charged items off of your résumé altogether. As Maureen Provost Ryan says, "You have to be conscious of the fact that a charged item may be the *only* thing an employer remembers from your résumé!"

If you think this sounds hypocritical, you should remember that all we're talking about here is whether you put something *on your résumé*. If you leave a highly-charged item *off* of your résumé, what that may do is help you get your foot in the door and get an interview with an employer who may otherwise have rejected you out of hand. You can *always* bring up the issue in an interview and deal with it there, where you can handle an employer's objections more effectively in person. As Kathleen Brady says, "On your résumé, for general interest employers, try to cut preconceived notions where you can." The only real way to do that is to leave off highly-charged items, and deal with them later on.

E. HOW TO HANDLE REFERENCES

There are a couple of ways to handle references on your résumé, and without further ado, here they are:

1. Include them;
or
2. Don't include them.

I wish I could tell you I'm being facetious, but I'm not. There *are* a few more details to consider, and what I'll do here is to go through the pluses and minuses of each alternative. But first, I want to talk about how you go about *choosing* references in the first place.

1. CHOOSING REFERENCES: WHO SHOULD THEY BE?

There are really only two things that references will do for you. They will either (a) comment on your work, or (b) impress the potential employer into thinking you're well-connected, politically or socially. That's obviously useful for rainmaking purposes.

Having said that, the far more important use of references, from an employer's standpoint, is to verify what you'll bring to the table for them. That's it. So, you ideally want former employers or professors, since they're the ones who are in a position to judge your work.

When it comes to prominent people, you have to pick and choose carefully, because if they don't truly have enough familiarity with you to say something positive about you in a professional sense, they're not worth mentioning. For instance, let's say that your parents happen to be buddies with someone with a famous name. Well, the fact that the celebrity is willing to allow their name to be used on your résumé doesn't really *say* anything about you. By way of example, one career services director told me about a student who insisted on putting Jerry Lewis's name down as a reference on her résumé. It turns out that Jerry Lewis was a family friend. But you can see the problem here; sure, it's something that will stand out on a résumé, but what does it *say* about the student? Nothing!

Of course, it would be perfect if you actually worked for a prominent politician or judge, such that you have the best of both worlds — someone whose name is instantly recognizable and who *also* happens to be familiar with your work. But if you err in favor of one or the other, err in favor of choosing someone who doesn't have a big name but is very familiar with your work.

By the same token, as Diane Reynolds suggests, don't use your clergyman or a family member as a reference. They're not familiar with your work, and, beyond that, people in your family are hardly going to be objective about you. Heck, when they talk to the mothers of Death Row inmates, the moms inevitably say, "But my little Johnny is such a *good* boy!" So having a family member say something good about you isn't really illuminating. Focus on people who will have the benefit of familiarity with your work *as well as* credibility when you're choosing your references!

2. SHOULD YOU INCLUDE YOUR REFERENCES ON YOUR RÉSUMÉ?

As I stated above, there are really only two alternatives with references: include them, or don't include them. Let's talk about each alternative.

A. ALTERNATIVE A: INCLUDE REFERENCES ON YOUR RÉSUMÉ

If you've got the room to fit the names, addresses, and phone numbers of your references on your résumé, then most of the career services directors I spoke with suggested that you go ahead and *do* that. (As San Diego's Susan Benson advises, also include a line about how the reference knows you, e.g., "supervised my summer clerkship with Jekyll & Hyde"). This is particularly useful, as Diane Reynolds points out, if you're applying to out-of-town law firms, and the reference in question is from the town where you're applying for jobs.

What's the benefit of including the names of references on your résumé? As Kentucky's Drusilla Bakert notes, "You'll find that a lot of people will *know* your references. They may pick your résumé simply because of that!"

If you *do* include your references on your résumé, warn them first — and be *sure* they're going to say very positive things about you. Why? Because a potential employer is likely to call them to find out about you, *before* they decide whether to interview you. If the reference is unprepared, the reference will feel silly, and that doesn't help you. And if they're not going to say very strong positives about you — for instance, they're going to damn you with faint praise — they're useless as references in the first place. But the fact remains: If your references are strong, noncontroversial, and you warn them up front — *definitely* include them on your résumé!

B. ALTERNATIVE B: DON'T INCLUDE REFERENCES ON YOUR RÉSUMÉ

This is something you may want to consider if either:

(1) Your résumé is too long for one page if you put them on; or

(2) There is a downside to the references you have (e.g., they're controversial, like a far-left or far-right wing politician).

It's pretty important to keep your résumé down to one page in length, unless you've got a truly extensive career before law school. So, if you find yourself toward the bottom of the page and you haven't got room for your references, leave them off.

If you *do* leave your references off of your résumé, be sure that you have a separate page with their names, addresses, and phone numbers on it. And remember to include a statement for each reference as to what your connection is; for instance, "This professor supervised me in a pro bono project."

C. STATING "REFERENCES AVAILABLE ON REQUEST" — *NOT!*

I know, I know, I know — every standard résumé book you get has résumés that have a line like this at the bottom. But the fact is, they're not résumés for legal employers; maybe what works in the mass market doesn't work in law, but the fact is, no career services director I spoke with was in favor of putting a "references available on request" line on the résumé.

And when you think about it, there's a good reason for leaving it out. *It doesn't do you any good.* If you don't mention references at all, any potential employer will *assume* that you have them — *everybody* can dig up somebody to say something good about them. And if your references are good and you want employers to know about them, then you should put their names and addresses and phone numbers on your résumé, so that they'll have the most impact. "References available on request" is a middle ground that does you no good. So don't put it down!

F. TRADITIONAL RÉSUMÉ ITEMS THAT YOU SHOULD *NOT* INCLUDE IN YOUR RÉSUMÉ

What I'm going to do here is to knock out some things that you might be tempted to include in your résumé, largely because traditional résumés *do* include them. Remember, I spoke with tons of experts, people who deal with law students and legal employers every day. They *know* whereof they speak with this kind of stuff, so if they tell you to leave something out of your résumé, *believe* them!

1. AN "OBJECTIVE" LINE

Maybe you've seen these. Some résumés include a line at the top, saying something like, "Objective: A permanent associate position with a forward-looking law firm focusing on environmental law." Don't include something like this on your résumé for legal employers. Why? Because it can't help you, and can only hurt you. If you're sending a résumé to a particular employer, they'll *assume* that it's your objective to work for them. There's no need to include it, and it's frankly something that's just not done in law. It looks out of place, so leave it out!

2. A "PERSONAL" SECTION

In the Interviewing chapter, I talk about how it's illegal for interviewers to ask about things like marital status. So why in the heck would you want to have a section on your résumé that says something like, "Married, two children, excellent health"? I realize that some traditional résumé books tell you to include a section like this, but it's not information any potential employer is entitled to. Furthermore, you just don't see it on résumés in law. So, like an "objective" line, leave it out!

I would also be very wary of stating your age or date of birth if you're approaching, or in, middle-age. In an age where we can expect to live into our eighties, it's tragic to think that some employers view applicants as "over the hill" when they've got almost half a century left to live! As Franklin Pierce's Sophie Sparrow points out, "If you're in your 40's or 50's, you may want to leave off the date when you graduated from college. That's because your age alone may screen you out of some jobs. It's not the age per se, but it's the *attitude* about new employees that age. The real problem legal employers have is the thought that if you've had an extensive career before law school, you may not be willing to take direction from a supervisor who may be 20 years younger than you." So age is touchy, and seeing as it can't help you to include it on your résumé, I'd leave it out.

3. A "Summary of Qualities" Section

On some résumés, you see a section that's called "Summary of Qualities," and it will include things like, "Talented, spirited, independent thinker." *Don't* put something like this on a résumé for legal employers. As Sophie Sparrow states, "That's a subjective evaluation, and that's the kind of thing that lawyers like to do for themselves!"

4. A Line That Says, "References Available Upon Request"

As I explained in the last section, either include full information about your references, or leave them off of your résumé entirely. Employers will *assume* that you have references they can contact without you having to mention it on your résumé. It doesn't do you any good, and it takes up space. So leave it off!

G. Administrative B.S.:
Paper, Type Fonts, and Other Issues Like Those

I'm going to knock this out in a hurry, because there's no bigger waste of time than obsessing on details that will have *no* impact on your getting hired. Remember, you're selling what's *in* your résumé, not your graphic design skills. In fact, ideally, it's the contacts you make who will get you interviews, and your résumé won't enter into the picture *at all*.

With that in mind, here's all you really need to know about the visuals associated with your résumé:

♦ Use white bond paper. Since you'll probably have to photo-copy or fax your résumé at some point, there's no reason to use anything else; any color other than white doesn't reproduce as well, and it's more expensive. It's important to distinguish yourself, but trust me on this one — colored paper is a waste of time and money, and no employer is ever going to say, "Gee, I really liked that shell pink paper. Let's interview that student!"

♦ Use paper that's 8½" x 11" — that is, standard letter-sized paper.

♦ Use a traditional type font. Anything that's not funky will be fine.

- ♦ Only use black ink.
- ♦ Use a type font between 10-point and 14-point, no smaller or larger. (Most type fonts you see are between these sizes anyway; this text you are reading is printed in 11-point type, to give you an idea of how large that is. You don't want your résumé to be printed in type so small that it's hard to read, or so large that it's cartoonish.)
- ♦ You can have your résumé printed or photocopied; as long as it's clearly readable, any means of reproduction will be fine. The only kind of printer I would avoid is a dot matrix printer, since their results can be hard to read. Any ink jet or laser printer is fine, as is any typewriter ribbon.
- ♦ If you've got such extensive work experience that your résumé goes to two pages, use two separate pages and staple the two pages together (paper clips are too easily lost).
- ♦ For layouts, see Appendix A at the end of this chapter, choose one, and copy it. There's no real reason to step outside of any of the formats I've provided for you there. Remember, it's what's *on* your résumé that will get you noticed, not some avant-garde layout.

H. THE 10 BIGGEST RÉSUMÉ MISTAKES (WITH HILARIOUS EXAMPLES)

Throughout this chapter, I've given you advice about mistakes to avoid on your résumé. What I'm going to do here is to highlight the 10 most common boners law students make when they formulate their résumés. To some extent, this will overlap with things I've already told you — but these mistakes are sufficiently important to avoid that it's worth restating them!

1. DON'T BE TOO GENERAL

Remember, legal employers are only interested in what you've done to the extent that it reflects on what you *can* do for *them*. If all you do on your résumé is list your jobs and your duties, legal employers won't make the leap for you and figure out how those duties generated transferable skills, if any. *You've* got to do that. As Georgetown's Marilyn Tucker says, "You can't just say, 'researched and wrote memoranda on a variety of areas' — you have to be *specific."* Lisa Kellogg points out, "Tell them what *kind* of research you did. What kind of law? Was the research on-line? Also, if you tell them you 'wrote motions,' that's not specific enough! Were they motions you copied from a form book? Or were they summary judgment motions, that require a lot of thought?"

This also means that you should *quantify* your experience to the greatest extent possible. Rob Kaplan gives the example of being president of your fraternity or sorority. "It's one thing to say, 'Oversaw budget, conducted weekly meetings.' You'll have a much bigger impact if you say, 'Served as chief officer for 115 member organization. Administered a $40,000 budget.' The reader gets a different sense of the level of responsibility you had if they know that it's a hundred members instead of 10, and a $40,000 budget versus $5,000."

The bottom line — make sure you include sufficient detail so that you make it plain to a legal employer exactly what you can do. Take pride in your accomplishments, and provide as much detail as is necessary to convey that! But, by the same token, you should remember the flip side of this coin, which is . . .

2. DON'T DRONE ON AND ON AND ON . . .

Unless you've got a really substantial prior career, there's no reason for your résumé to go on longer than one page. None of the résumés I've provided as samples in Appendix A go on any longer than that, and you won't need to, either. If you do, it's probably because you're losing your focus on exactly what a résumé is supposed to *do* for you. As Sophie Sparrow points out, "It's not a statement of who you *are* — it's just supposed to feature what an employer might be interested in!" And Diane Reynolds adds, "Some people are just too wordy. As a rule of thumb, the more words there are on your résumé, the less chance it'll be read!" If need be, have different résumés for different kinds of positions, focusing on different areas of your background. But the fact remains, no one legal employer needs more than one page on you!

On the one hand, you may be tempted to go into meaningless detail as a means of puffing up a scanty résumé. Don't! Smoke-and-mirrors tricks are a real irritant to employers. For instance, one career services director told me about a guy who had a "publications" category on his résumé, and he included six *independent* listings for articles he wrote in the school's student newspaper! As she pointed out, "That just didn't merit a separate publications category. Use what you have for your résumé; if you don't have it, you don't have it. Don't try to be too clever!"

Even if you *aren't* trying to cover up what you consider a scanty résumé, avoiding droning on and on involves knowing when to cut out meaningless details. There's a difference between explaining what transferable skills you took from a job and delving into far more detail than a prospective employer needs. For instance, as Drusilla Bakert points out, "Nobody needs the details of what you did as a bank teller!" This is particularly true for nonlegal jobs, where the *only* things that matter are skills that may be applicable to a legal employer. If you feel that you don't have a good intuitive sense of how much detail is appropriate, *definitely* go to your career services director for advice. Reviewing résumés is one of the things they do extremely well!

3. DON'T LEAVE GAPS IN YOUR CHRONOLOGY

If you went straight from college to law school, this isn't likely to be a problem for you. But if you've taken off some time, either during college, after college, or during law school, it may be that you don't want to mention what you did with that time. You may consider it irrelevant, or you may be embarrassed by it. I *strongly* encourage you to fill in the gaps, regardless of your reason for leaving them. If you think that something you've done is irrelevant, it's probably because it's work experience in another field. Just *mention* what you did; you don't have to go into any detail. And if you're embarrassed about it, or think it may hurt you, it may be because you took the time to travel the world, or just took a sabbatical from life to "find yourself." If that's the case, I've got pleasant news for you — that's not a negative at all! From an employer's perspective, they'd rather that you got that out of your system before you went to work for them. And furthermore, it creates an interesting résumé item to talk about! As Boston University's Betsy Armour suggests, "All you need to do is create a category that says something like 'Life Experience.' Under that, you can put 'traveling in Europe, living on a kibbutz' — whatever you did. It gives the employer a window into who you are!" Benesch Friedlander's Deanna Coe Kursh echoes that: "It's important for an employer to see a complete chronology. It really doesn't matter what you did — *say* it! 'I traveled,' 'I decided my life's path' —

there's nothing wrong with that. Students tend to think they have a lot more negatives than they really have!"

Furthermore, if you leave a gap in your chronology, the employer will think the worst — like you were in the federal penitentiary, or confined to a mental hospital, or something like that. So don't be embarrassed or concerned about your past. Just make sure that everything is present and accounted for!

4. PROOFREAD — AND HAVE *OTHER* PEOPLE PROOFREAD!

Some of the most hilarious boners I heard about were the result of silly proofreading mistakes. Here are two of my favorites:

♦ One young woman spell-checked her résumé, and figured that would take the place of proofreading it. It didn't! She had an "objective" line at the top of her résumé (a mistake in and of itself), which said that her objective was public service experience. Her spell checker overlooked the fact that the "public" in "public service" was missing an "l." To make matters worse, she didn't bother to show this résumé to her career services director until she had sent out *several hundred of them in a mass mailer.* I wonder what kind of responses she got?

♦ A guy sent out a huge mailer, consisting of a résumé and a cover letter. The cover letter said that he was a first year student, and the résumé said he was a third year student. When he discovered the mistake, he sent a letter to all of those hundreds of prospective employers. The letter read, "Upon further review, I find that I'm a Third Year."

As these anecdotes suggest — you need to proofread all of your correspondence, including your résumé! Now it's inherently difficult to proofread your own stuff; you're so familiar with it that you'll tend to gloss over mistakes. So have another set of eyes look at your résumé before you do anything with it — ideally, the eyes of your career services director, who'll be able to give you some substantive tips, as well!

5. DON'T LIE AND DON'T MISLEAD!

I'm not saying this in order to be a Pollyanna, but rather because it's just too easy to get caught when you're dealing with the legal market. For instance, let's say that you're in the 35th percentile in your class, and you're tempted to round that up on your résumé and say "top third." Well, the fact is, you aren't in the top third; you missed it by two percentage points. Big deal? No, not in an objective sense. But if a prospective employer asks for you transcript, they'll see that you lied. And then you've got a credibility problem that will be difficult to explain away.

Those kinds of lies are pretty obvious, and it's unlikely you'll try anything like that — especially now that I've told you not to. But it's just as important not to be misleading, and that's a *much* more tempting trap. Especially in your hobbies and activities section, you may be tempted to suggest that you do things you don't do, or have abilities you don't have. Don't! Since this is such a fertile ground for conversation in an interview, if you lie or mislead, you're likely to get caught. I'll give you a particularly vivid example. A career services director told me about a student who put "golf" under his skills and interests section on his résumé. He got a call from an interviewer who said, "I'm so sick of sitting in an office. Instead of coming to the office for an interview tomorrow, why don't we go and play nine holes." Well, that would have been great, except that the student put "golf" on his résumé, without mentioning that what he liked about golf was *watching* it on TV. He didn't know how to *play* it! With only 12 hours before his interview, the student frantically tried to learn to play golf from his roommate. To make a long story short — it didn't work. He picked up the interviewer and drove him to a golf club the following day, and within a hole or two, it was obvious that he didn't know what the heck he was doing. The interviewer was livid, and said, "Why didn't you just admit it up front?" To make matters even worse, on the way home, the student's car developed a flat tire — *and he didn't know how to change it!* The interviewer, already steaming from the golf fiasco, had to change the tire!

That anecdote drives home for you better than any advice I could give you as to the importance of telling the truth. So overcome the temptation. Don't lie — and don't mislead!

6. DON'T BE CUTE!

Whenever I tell you the importance of being interesting, whether it's in a cover letter, on a résumé, or in an interview, I realize that I run the risk that you'll go overboard and do something off the wall. Don't!

When it comes to humor on résumés, it's OK to include something that makes you smile, but make sure you tread the fine line between being humorous and being cute. For instance, one career services director told me about a guy who worked as a flagger on highway construction projects during the summer. On his résumé, under his flagger experience, he put: "Extensive work with irritated motorists." That's fine; it's funny, and it's memorable. On the other hand, another career services director told me about a student who sent her résumé in a package with a nerf basketball, and attached a note that said, "Please don't toss my résumé in the trash." That's going too far. Remember, you're interviewing with a conservative profession, not standup comics!

As a rule of thumb, if you don't know where to draw the line — I'm not so sure *I* would know where to draw it! — and you're thinking of doing something unusual, check with your career services director first. As Diane Reynolds advises, "You'll usually find that an unusual approach doesn't work. It's a *very* conservative profession!"

7. DON'T LEAVE VALUABLE THINGS OFF YOUR RÉSUMÉ BY FAILING TO APPRECIATE THE TRANSFERABLE SKILLS THEY INFER

It may be that you have things in your background that you just can't relate to law. Maybe you've gone through all of my advice earlier in this chapter, and you haven't been able to pull your transferable skills out of your background, and you've chosen instead to leave certain experiences off of your résumé. *Please* think twice before you do that — you may be ignoring something valuable!

I'll give you an example that a career services director told me about. There was a woman who was in the top quarter of her class. On her résumé, that's all she listed — she didn't say anything about extracurriculars or part-time work — because she didn't see the relevance of what she did outside of school. She didn't get any interviews, and it was because she seemed somewhat one-dimensional. Well, it turns out that she had three children, all under the age of 6, and she was taking care of them at school while her husband operated his family's business some 300 miles away. *That's* why she didn't have time to take part in any extracurriculars! Well, as you might imagine, if she *had* said something about her children, it would have shown any employer that she was extremely good at balancing her responsibilities — she was getting admirable grades while raising a family, and that's not an easy trick.

When it comes to something like family responsibilities, especially if you're a woman, it pays to mention that you have children that account for at least part of your time out of school. As Florida's Ann Skalaski points out, "This is actually a plus for employers. Saying that you already have children and decided to go to law school *with* them means that you won't be having them on the *employer's* time!" And you may want to use some of your mothering experience as work experience. As Diane Reynolds suggests, you can include things like scheduling and volunteer work. The point is this: Don't write off your nonlegal experience because you think it won't be relevant to an employer. If you're on the fence as to the value of your experience, sit down with your career services director and hammer out a way to word your experience so that it shows you off in the most positive light. Just don't ignore something valuable!

8. DON'T INCLUDE PERSONAL INFORMATION THAT HURTS YOU

I've told you that it's important to include a hobbies and interests section on your résumé, and I just spent the last couple of paragraphs telling you that you should be careful about leaving off valuable information from your résumé just because you can't see how it relates to law. But the flip side of all of that is that you should avoid personal information that will hurt you. For some employers, that's going to include the highly-charged résumé items, like politics, religion, and gender issues that I discussed earlier in this chapter. But there are other ones, as well. For instance, perhaps you have a spouse in the military. That might not strike you as a negative, but here's what it says to an employer: they're going to waste their investment in you because you'll have to move within a couple of years.

Age is another personal item that might hurt you. If you're beyond your thirties, there are legal employers who will screen you out just on the basis of your age alone. As a result, you may want to remove the date you graduated from college, and delete from your résumé any work experience you've got that dates back more than 15 years. I know it's not *fair*, and it's ludicrous that anyone reacts this way, but it's the truth — and I want to help you get as many interviews as you can.

So the watchword here is: Don't include personal information on your résumé if it might hurt you. If you're not sure whether a particular item on your résumé will have that effect, check with your career services director before you send out any résumés!

9. DON'T USE AVANT-GARDE VISUALS TO GET ATTENTION!

I've told you how important it is to get an employer's attention, and that's why I encourage you to be as interesting as possible. However, don't translate this into employing avant-garde visuals on your résumé. Stick with white paper, black ink, standard-size type — and let what you've done and how you word it speak for you! After all, if you follow the advice I give you in this book, you'll be getting your job on the basis of contacts you make. Even if you have to resort to mailing résumés to get a job, I *promise* you that using off-the-wall visuals to get attention won't get you the job you want — it'll have just the opposite effect!

A few anecdotes will give you an idea of what you *shouldn't* do. In every case, these are things that students have actually done — and that you should *never* do!

- One student used letters that were 2" high, on pink paper.

- One student had a four-color résumé that ran to three pages. The last page consisted of a checklist, with the headline, "Is there a fit between us?" It then listed a series of requirements, saying things like, "The firm must value autonomy, flexibility, rapid action, it must be communication oriented, the tasks must involve multiple goals, and there must be no interference in the performance of those tasks."

- One student printed her résumé on neon green paper. It got attention, all right — the lawyer who received it passed it around the office for a good laugh.

So if you're tempted to do anything off the wall with your résumé, and you just can't be talked out of it, what you *should* do is reconsider your profession — the kind of creativity you have would be prized in a field like advertising, but it certainly *won't* be appreciated in law!

10. DON'T OBSESS OVER MINUTIAE

As you may have noticed, I zipped through issues like type fonts, and paper quality, and that kind of thing. The fact is, you're never going to lose a job if you send out a résumé that's photocopied instead of printed, on copy paper instead of bond paper, and with a font that's one point size too big or too small. One career services director told me about a student who was losing sleep because no one could answer this question for him: On his two-page résumé, should the staple connecting the pages be horizontal or at an angle? The reason no one could answer that for him is that *no one cares.* If you ever hear stories about employers rejecting people on the basis of minutiae like this, I *promise* you that you're hearing an urban myth; that is, you'll never be able to trace the story to its original source, because that kind of thing just doesn't happen.

So don't waste time with minutiae. You've got enough to do, between making contacts, and setting up interviews, and sending correspondence, to keep you *plenty* busy.

I. BEFORE YOU SEND A SINGLE RÉSUMÉ: GO TO YOUR CAREER SERVICES OFFICE!

Throughout this chapter I've stressed the importance of running your résumé past your career services director before you send it out. I'm giving this piece of advice its own section because I *implore* you to follow it! Everything I've told you in this chapter will help you formulate a perfect résumé, but there are elements of personalization that I can't help you with here. For instance, figuring out which employers are grades-conscious, or whether you've included enough (or too much) detail on your résumé, or how employers in certain areas of the country react to certain items on résumés (for instance, west coast employers equate "surfing" with "lazy"). Your career services director *can* tell you things like that, and they'll be happy to help you out. Take advantage of that before you send out a single résumé!

Great Sample Résumés to Use as Models

The following résumé samples incorporate the advice I've given you in this chapter. They're all concise, yet they highlight the person's accomplishments and transferable skills. I encourage you to flip through these and use the one that you like the most as a model for your own résumé.

Keep in mind that because this book is smaller than the standard 8½" x11" size of a résumé, the type size on these résumés is much smaller than you will use. Stay with a font between 10 and 14 points in size, so that your résumé is easily readable!

By the way, these samples are reprinted with permission from the *Case Western Reserve University School of Law Career Services Handbook*, written by Debra Fink.

RÉSUMÉ #1

A results-oriented résumé with insightful descriptions of activities and experience.

Scarlett O'Hara

1 Peachtree Road	Atlanta, Georgia	(404) 555–1212

EDUCATION   Case Western Reserve University School of Law
Cleveland, Ohio
JD expected 199*

Emory University   Atlanta, Georgia
BA 199* Major: theater, Minor: Mathematics
Financed 50% of undergraduate expenses through summer
and part-time employment.

ACTIVITIES   **Zeta Zeta Zeta:** Theater Fraternity President, 199*. During tenure, increased membership over 200% and average monthly philanthropy hours from 5 to 25 through conception and implementation of traveling play program for local innercity high schools. Previous offices held: Chairperson, costume design group; Cochairperson, publicity and scheduling. Member, 199*–9*.

The Fiddle-Dee-Dee News: Features Editor, 199*, for student-run weekly magazine distributed communitywide. Expanded column and reviews regarding local nightlife to include activities for readers of all ages, helping to increase nonschool community circulation by 20% in 2 years.

Have appeared in principal and supporting roles in numerous school and community plays, including dramas, comedies, and musicals. Received favorable reviews in local newspapers.

EXPERIENCE   **Cuyahoga County Auditor's Office**   Cleveland, Ohio
Clerk, summers and school breaks, 199*–9*. Rotated through every department during first summer; developed ability to substitute with minimal training for most clerical staff during vacations. Received excellent reviews each summer; noted for flexibility, attention to detail in repetitive tasks, organizational skills, reliability on very short notice, and ability to learn quickly.

Undergraduate Admissions Office, Emory University
Atlanta, Georgia
Work Study Student, 199*–9*. Employed 15–20 hours per week during school year. Learned basic office procedures and customer service techniques. Given increasing responsibility in drafting correspondence and speaking directly with prospective students and their parents.

REFERENCES   Professor Rory Schach   Sally E. Fingerhoofen
(professor in several under-   (direct supervisor)
graduate courses)   Office Manager
Theater Department   Cuyahoga County Auditor's
Emory University, Bldg. 3-D   Office
55 Noname Plaza   1 Breathalizer Place
Atlanta, Georgia 12345   Cleveland, Ohio 67890
(404) 555–1234   (216) 555–6666

RÉSUMÉ #2

This résumé saves space by combining all similar positions in a career of substantial length into one description. The unusual name/address arrangement at the top is another way you can save space. You may want to consider this approach if you've got a lot of prelaw school work experience. (Also, note that this student highlights her interest in health law by including her relevant coursework.)

Melanie Hamilton

12345 Carpetbagger Way   Dayton, Ohio 54321   (516) 555–5555

Education

Case Western Reserve University School of Law   Cleveland, Ohio
Anticipated date of graduation: 199*
GPA: 3.21/4
Relevant Courses: Health Care Controversies (interdisciplinary law/medicine seminar); Health Care Advanced Research Seminar; Health Law; Health Law Clinic (one semester involving representation of indigent clients in litigation and transactional matters)
Mock Trial Competition: will participate, 199*–9* Advocacy Program: ranked in top 15% in oral component of moot court competition, 199*–9*
Health Matrix: The Journal of Law-Medicine: Editor on student-run, scholarly journal, 199*–9*; Associate Editor, 199*–9*; Staff Member, 199*–9*

University of Maryland School of Nursing   Baltimore, Maryland
Date of graduation: 19*; BSN, *summa cum laude*
Inducted into six honorary societies

Legal Experience

Larry, Curly, and Moe, LPA   Cleveland, Ohio
Law Clerk for eight-attorney firm specializing in medical malpractice defense. Conduct research into recent trends in malpractice cases involving obstetrical actions in high-risk pregnancies. Receive exposure to court procedures through attendance at pretrials, mediation hearings, and one trial. Regularly discuss cases and other issues and legal points with supervisors. May 199*–present

Professional Nursing Experience

Bay General Hospital, Intensive Care Unit. February 199*–July 9* Baltimore, Maryland
Mideast General Hospital, Pediatric Intensive Care Unit. 198*–9* Milan, Ohio
Cleveland Clinic, Palliative Care Unit. 198*–8* Cleveland, Ohio
Liberty Services Corporation, Coronary Step-down Unit. 198*–8* Liberty, New York

In addition to providing intensive and palliative care to patients, advised doctors of daily changes in status and counseled families under great stress. Acted as patient advocate in many situations; used creativity, resourcefulness and diplomacy in acquiring special services for patients and families, whose resources were limited. Regulary worked 12- to 14-hour shifts, occasionally around the clock, in situations requiring ability to make complex life and death decisions and handle continuing and ever-changing stress. Position required advanced and continually updated knowledge of medical procedures, pharmaceutical applications, and ethics.

Personal Interests

Competitive Masters swimmer, brown belt in karate.

RÉSUMÉ #3

This résumé shows how you can highlight your legal experience by placing it in a separate section above nonlegal experience. Note how a typical temporary clerical position can be treated to maximum effect! Also, notice how first and second year grades are separated to emphasize a strong upward trend in grades.

RHETT BUTLER
120 Cavalry Charge Run
Cleveland, Ohio 44106
(216) 555–5555

EDUCATION

Case Western Reserve University School of Law, Cleveland, Ohio
Expected Graduation: 199*
Second Year GPA: 3.42/4.00; First Year GPA 2.97; Cumulative GPA 3.20
   Appellate Advocacy Program: 12/75 overall rank in moot court competition.
   Academic Scholarship, renewable for 3 years.
   Black Law Students Association, Secretary: directed production of first regional handbook for all members.

Ohio State University, Columbus, Ohio
BA History, *cum laude,* 199*
GPA 3.78/4
   President's Scholarship: four-time honoree for ranking in top 5% of class.
   Student of the Year, History Department: selected by faculty.

LEGAL EXPERIENCE

Winken, Blinken & Nod, Cleveland, Ohio
Law Clerk, Summer 199*. Drafted briefs for all stages of trial and appellate practice. Majority of summer spent researching, conducting interviews, and preparing clients for testimony at depositions and arbitration hearings of one case. Assisted as second chair at one trial, involving client's right to credit information in denied credit case.

Samson & Delilah Co., LPA, Washington, D.C.
Law Clerk, Summer 199*. Coauthored brief in opposition to consolidation of plaintiffs of class action suit. Drafted *amicus curiae* brief submitted to U.S. Court of Appeals, regarding urea-formaldehyde. Received exposure to product liability and medical malpractice issues, as well as estate planning and probate law.

NON-LEGAL EXPERIENCE

Stride for Ohio, Ohio State University, Columbus, Ohio
Program Coordinator, 199*–9*; High School Tutor 199*. Conceived and co-ordinated comprehensive tutoring/mentoring program for local disadvantaged high school juniors and seniors. Trained 55 fellow undergraduates to work with over 150 students. Personally visited five area high school principals; received 100% participation. Received Governor's Recognition Award in only second academic year of operation. Maintained less than 1% dropout rate throughout 2 y ears of stewardship.

Corporate Connection Temporaries, Beachwood, Ohio
Temporary Secretary, Data Processor, Inventory Control Clerk, etc. 199*–9*. Eliminated need for school loans through variety of short-term positions. Developed ability to use a wide range of word and data processing, spreadsheet and database programs with little or no training. Was regularly asked to return to same firms to fill subsequent needs.

RÉSUMÉ #4

In this résumé, the student highlights honors by placing them in a separate section immediately below education. Note how part-time and summer employment is accounted for, without long descriptions — or even employer names, job titles, or dates — at the bottom of the résumé.

12345 Twelve Oaks Place
Cleveland, Ohio 44106
ASHLEY HAMILTON   (216) 555–1212

ACADEMIC SUMMARY

199*   Candidate for JD
         Case Western Reserve University School of Law, Cleveland, Ohio
         GPA 3.02/4

199*   BA Political Science
         Georgetown University, Washington, DC
         GPA 3.56/4
         Relevant courses outside major: accounting, finance, micro and
         macro economics

HONORS

Case Western Reserve Law Review
 • Note for publication, Spring 199*, entitled "A Continental
   Energy Policy: an Examination of Some of the Current Issues."
George R. Wistle International Scholar Award
 • Selected through merit competition to spend junior year at the
   Sorbonne, Paris, France.
 • All courses were conducted at the graduate level and in French;
   courses included European Common Market Economics and
   Politics, American Economics (from a European viewpoint).

EXPERIENCE

Summer   Phyfe & Drumm, Akron, Ohio
199* to   • As sole clerk, perform wide range of tasks for five attorney
Present   general civil practice.
          • Draft pleadings and discovery; working with increasing inde-
            pendence.
          • Permitted extensive client contact, including initial interviews
            and preparation of clients for testimony at depositions, arbitra-
            tion hearings, and trials.
          • Assisted at trial, provided cross-examination points in case
            which was decided in client's favor.
          • Developing manual and computerized research skills.
198*–9* Earned a substantial portion of undergraduate living expenses
         through part-time and summer service and clerical positions.

HOBBIES & PERSONAL INTERESTS

Speak French fluently. Have traveled Europe extensively, and had travel memoirs
published in local newspapers. Hobbies include platform tennis and Level 5
whitewater rafting.

RÉSUMÉ #5

This résumé is an interesting one in that it uses a functional approach *within* each position description, even though the overall approach is the standard reverse chronological format.

INDIA WILKES

123 Musket Hill Drive	Cleveland, Ohio 44106	(216) 555–5555

EDUCATION

CASE WESTERN RESERVE UNIVERSITY, Cleveland, Ohio
School of Law. J.D. expected   May 199*
Associate, *Journal of International Law:* will write note of publishable quality for Spring 199*, in the area of consolidation of patent applications in international research projects.

UNIVERSITY OF VERMONT, Burlington, Vermont
M.S., Systems Engineering   198*
Concentrations: optimization theory, robotics
B.S., Systems Engineering   198*
Concentrations: systems analysis, electronic circuits

EXPERIENCE

Summer Associate, Intellectual Property Department   Summer 199*
JACKSON, COBERG, HOCHMANN & PHIPPS, Los Angeles, California
Writing — drafted responses and amendments to office actions and Appeals board decisions, complaints of patent infringement, trademark applications. Corresponded directly with several clients on specific technical matters. *Research* — employed Lexis, Westlaw, and Dialog to research a wide range of trademark and patent issues.

Systems Engineer, Consumer Credit Division   198*–9*
TRW, INC., Los Angeles, California
Technical Knowledge — completed high pofile project under budget (5.5%) and ahead of schedule (12%), by applying innovative solutions to software needs. Design is now used by company centers worldwide.
Communication — originated and coordinated "Brown Bag Lunch Techie" series, still in practice, for clerical and professional employees who wished to augment their computer skills. Attendance grew from 22 to 145 and led to significantly increased use of computers in all daily operations, with little need for extra training time and no change of manpower.

HOBBIES & PERSONAL INTERESTS

Have performed in community theater musical comedies. Enjoy writing computer games, playing golf and tennis.

RÉSUMÉ #6

This résumé uses the functional approach, which you may want to consider if you've got an extensive career before law school. What it does is stress the transferability of experience, rather than focusing on position titles, dates, and employer names — none of which would be terribly relevant to a legal employer. It captures only the most important achievements of a lengthy past career.

Pittypat Hamilton

<table>
<tr><td>Permanent Address</td><td>Current Address</td></tr>
<tr><td>1234 Omystars Lane</td><td>123 Flame Way</td></tr>
<tr><td>Centreville, Ohio 44449</td><td>Cleveland, Ohio 44106</td></tr>
<tr><td>(614) 555-5555</td><td>(216) 555-5555</td></tr>
</table>

Education

Case Western Reserve University School of Law, Cleveland, Ohio
199* – J.D. expected

American Institute of Banking, Cleveland, Ohio
198* – Certificate of Completion

Kent State University, Kent, Ohio
197* – B.S., Mathematics, Economics

Business Development

Increased branch deposit levels 19% in a $12 million branch office during each of the last 3 years of operation. Managed $5.5 million portfolio, achieving zero loan default during last 24 months. Increased commercial loan outstandings by 45% in same period. Outsold entire district in cash management products during last 3 years. Exceeded first year sales goal by record amount (first of 752 rookie agents nationwide).

Administration & Management

Managed nine person branch office achieving zero employee turnover through two mergers within a 6-year period. Cut hours of part-time staff by 33% through efficient scheduling without reducing banking hours or customer service. Trained staff in cross-selling techniques to market bank products and service.

Budgeting

Exceeded budgeted goals in deposits, commercial, consumer and real estate loans every year, consistently above district's average increases. Kept noninterest income on target while keeping noninterest expense below budget during same period.

Experience

Vice President — Trust Bank of Ohio, Centreville, Ohio (198*-9*)
Assistant Vice President — Trust Bank of Ohio, Outerville, Ohio (197*-8*)
Loan Officer — Homeowners Financial Corporation, Upperville, Ohio (197*-7*)
Insurance Representative — Acme Life & Casualty Company, Centreville, Ohio (197*-7*)

Community Leadership

Director, Centreville Chamber of Commerce (198*-8*)
Trustee, Centreville Community Improvement Council, a United Way agency (197*-present)

RÉSUMÉ #7

This résumé emphasizes an upward trend in grades, and co-
and extracurricular activities. Note the interesting personal information included at the bottom of the résumé.

FRANK KENNEDY

Permanent Address   **Campus Address**
1234 Miniball Road   1234 Main Street
Highland Park, Ohio 44444   Cleveland, Ohio 44106
(614) 555-5555   (216) 555-5555

EDUCATION

199*   J.D. candidate
         Case Western Reserve University School of Law; Cleveland, Ohio
         G.P.A.:   Fourth semester 3.21/4.00   Third semester 2.97
                   Second semester 2.64   First semester 2.39
                            Cumulative 2.82
199*   B.A.   Major: English   Minor: History
         Case Western Reserve University, Cleveland, Ohio
         G.P.A.: Major 3.52/4.00   Overall 3.36

ACADEMIC ACTIVITIES

Spring   **Craven Moot Court Competition,** Team Member. One of four selected
199*   to participate in national competition involving constitutional issue.
199*-9* **Dean Dunmore Moot Court Competition,** Competitor. Ranked 8/75,
         overall score in competition portion of Appellate Advocacy program.
         Advanced to national competition the following year.
199*-9* **National Handicapped Law Students Association,** Treasurer. Helped
         found local chapter in order to raise campus awareness of a group's
         special needs. Helped to lobby successfully for escorts in campus vehicles,
         better equipped public facilities in law school, and electronic system
         for rapid library stacks assistance.

EXPERIENCE

Summer   **Judge Edwin I. Smythe, U.S. District Court, Northern District of Ohio;**
199*   Summer Extern. Drafted bench memoranda for a variety of civil lawsuits.
         Analyzed evidence, ascertained facts and researched applicable law.
         Assisted Judge with status calls, pretrial conferences, settlement
         negotiations, evidentiary and sentencing hearings. Regularly discussed
         issues with Judge and law clerks; gained insight into judicial decision-
         making and court process; improved written and oral communications
         through detailed critiques.
Summer   **Professor Albert E. Jones, Case Western Reserve University School**
199*   **of Law;** Cleveland, Ohio; Research Assistant. Analyzed legislative history
         and recent developments of the Civil Rights Restoration Act of 1987
         and the Americans with Disabilities Act of 1989, for law review article
         on the rights of the disabled. Researched judicial and administrative
         law, as well as congressional action and social policy. Drafted two
         sections of article.

ADDITIONAL INFORMATION

Childhood spent in France and Germany, leading to native fluency in
both national languages. Highly skilled in computer programs and applications, including word processing and spreadsheet software. Gaining
proficiency in Lexis and Westlaw.

RÉSUMÉ #8

This résumé has an unusual, albeit still conservative, visual arrangement. Notice the wording that emphasizes reasons for holding positions, rather than recitations of duties.

Belle Watling

Permanent Address:
1234 Demimondaine Place
Centerville, Ohio 44444
(614) 555–5555

Campus Address:
123 Bustier Avenue
Cleveland, Ohio 44444
(216) 555–5555

EDUCATION

Case Western Reserve University	Cleveland, Ohio
School of Law	Expected Graduation: 199*
GPA	2.86/4.00
Activities	Journal of International Law
	CWRU Jazz Ensemble: tenor saxophone
University of Toronto	Toronto, Ontario, Canada
BA	199*
Major	Political Science, concentration in international relations
GPA	3.3/4.0
Honors	Dean's List, 4 semesters
	Varsity hockey and lacrosse
Activities	UT Jazz Quartet: tenor saxophone

EXPERIENCE

Cuyahoga County Prosecutor's Office	Cleveland, Ohio
Intern	Followed cases through several
Summer 199*	stages, attending trials and hearings, processing documents, observing client meetings and participating in investigations. Gained knowledge of legal process, skill in researching and preparing legal memoranda and interest in prosecution.
Dasher, Dancer, Prancer & Vixen	New York, NY
Docket Clerk	In preparation for law school, volunteered 20 hours per week to gain exposure to lawyers in practice. Concurrently worked as a waitress 35 hours per week.
Summer 199*	
Olive Garden Restaurant	Toronto, Ontario, Canada
Server	Financed undergraduate education
199*–9*	without incurring loans after first year. Employed throughout all 4 years, during term, working 15–30 hours per week.

SPECIAL SKILLS

Computers	Westlaw and Lexis research, word-processing and database applications
Languages	French: proficient in speaking and writing
	German: trained in reading

My Favorite
All-Time Résumé

OK, I couldn't resist including the résumé I've always wanted to send out, but never have. I'm not including it here for any reason other than to give you a couple of yuks. (By the way, if you read through it and don't get it, you'll want to focus a little more closely on the last line of the résumé.)

Kimm Alayne Walton
Post Office Box 1018
Greens Farms, Connecticut 06436

EDUCATION   Harvard University School of Law
             Boston, Massachusetts   JD expected 199*

             Harvard University School of Medicine
             Boston, Massachusetts   MD expected 199*

             Yale University
             New Haven, Connecticut   BA and BS, 199*
             Joint major, Macromolecular Chemistry and Economics

ACTIVITIES   *Harvard Law Review*, Editor-in-Chief.
             Manage 50-person staff and budget of $10 million. Simulta-
             neously authoring law review article on admissibility of DNA
             evidence; U.S. Supreme Court requested prepublication copy,
             and will cite the article in the case *United States vs. Block*.

             Yale Crew, participant.
             Led crew to NCAA championship. Took part in 1992 Olympic
             Games in Barcelona, winning a gold medal for the United
             States.

             Have appeared in local and national theatrical productions,
             earning a Tony for performance in "Hi There, Gorgeous."
             Adopted seven handicapped Asian children. On visit to Mexico,
             deciphered ancient Mayan scripts on tablets at Chichen Itza,
             leading to discovery of ancient cures for cancer. Discovery
             expected to lead to cures for variety of modern cancer-related
             diseases.

EXPERIENCE   **Microsoft Corporation**
             Codeveloped software program as silent partner, which formed
             basis for multibillion dollar software company. Surrendered
             stock to partner in 199*, earning a profit of $745 million.

             Harvard Laboratory for Advanced Medical Research
             Summer intern, 199*. Researched molecular changes caused
             by aging. Discovered link between diet and aging. Patented
             research, which is expected to lead to increasing human life
             expectancy worldwide by 20 years.

HOBBIES &   Founder and President, Pathological Liars Club of the United
INTERESTS   States. Currently has 4.5 billion members and an annual budget
             of a billion dollars. Institutionalization expected imminently.

Chapter 7

Interviewing: The Secrets That Turn Interviews Into Offers

Congratulations! You've done it. You got an interview with an employer you really want to work for. If you play your cards right, you'll turn that interview into a job offer. And guess what? In this chapter, Auntie Kimmbo is going to show you *exactly* how to play your cards right!

Now, maybe you got your interview because you took the initiative and made contacts. Maybe you lucked out and got an on-campus interview. Maybe you responded to a job listing. It doesn't matter. In this chapter, I'll take you soup to nuts through the interviewing process, *regardless* of how you got your interview. I'll show you everything you need to do to prepare for the interview so you'll knock the interviewer's socks off. I'll tell you what to wear. I'll tell you what questions to ask, and what questions you should *never* ask. I'll show you how to answer killer questions with aplomb. I'll tell you the 10 biggest mistakes law students make when they interview for jobs, so *you* can avoid making those same mistakes. And I'll show you how to handle your follow-ups. The bottom line is this: If you do everything I tell you, you *will* turn job interviews into job offers!

With that in mind . . . let's get going!

A. THE SECRET TO SUCCESSFUL INTERVIEWS EVERY TIME — BE PREPARED! (AND THE THREE KEY STEPS TO PERFECT PREPARATION)

The Scout motto applies to interviews, in spades. *Be prepared.* The worst mistake you can make is to show up, cold, at an interview; employers and career services directors told me that time and time again. And I'm not talking about a 5-minute blitzkrieg just before you meet the interviewer, either. As Washington's Teresa DeAndrado says, "Preparation does *not* mean reading the law firm brochure 10 minutes before the interview!" I know it's a pain in the butt to do this prep work, but I promise you it will pay off handsomely. There are three principal steps involved in being prepared. Here's what you've got in front of you:

♦   You've got some *detective* work to do. You have to be a bloodhound and sniff out every clue about the employer and the interviewer that you can possibly dig up!

♦   You've got to come up with an infomercial about yourself, and practice your "Miss Americas" — that is, your likely interview questions and answers. I'll take you step-by-step through formulating your best possible "infomercial," and I'll rehearse you with questions you'll ask and how you'll answer difficult questions the interviewer poses for you.

♦   You've got some *practicing* to do. You've got to practice how you'll present yourself, and how you'll pose and answer questions, so that you're completely relaxed and confident when it's show time.

That may sound like a lot of work to do, but I can cut the burden for you a little bit by pointing something out to you: the thinking and practicing are things you really only have to do once, before your first interview. You'll do a little tuning up for different employers, but the bulk of your work will only have to be done once.

The detective work, I'm afraid, is something you have to do, fresh, for every employer. But depending on how you *got* the interview, you may already have done the bulk of that work.

Remember, when I talked about how to decide what your dream job *is* (Chapter 2), and making contacts (Chapter 4), and writing correspondence (Chapter 5), I stressed the importance of learning everything you can about potential employers. So, there's a strong possibility you already *did* your detective work on the employer before you *got* the interview. So, it may well be that you won't have to spend much time preparing for your interviews, after all!

So we've got some detective work to do, an infomercial to create, some questions and answers to learn, and some practicing to do. Georgetown's Marilyn Tucker summarizes these steps this way: "Know the firm, and let them know you know it. And know yourself, so you can sell yourself." Let's take a closer look at exactly how you should go about doing that!

1. Detective Work. Be a Bloodhound — Sniff Out Every Clue About the Employer and Interviewer That You Can Possibly Dig Up!

You've got to muster every bit of information that you can *before* the interview takes place. I know, I know, you're busy, you don't have time, blah, blah, blah . . . but I'm *begging* you to do it, and I've got several great reasons why you should make the effort.

A. The Benefits of Knowing Everything You Can About the Employer and Interviewer

1. You'll Impress the Heck Out of the Interviewer

Remember, all the way back in Chapter 1, I told you the importance of taking the initiative and showing honest enthusiasm. Nothing proves initiative and enthusiasm more concretely than knowing all that you can about the employer and interviewer, and displaying that in the interview. Think about how flattered *you'd* be if someone came in to interview for a job with you, and they showed through their comments and questions that they'd gone to the trouble of finding out what they could about you. Wouldn't that tell you that they'd be a thorough and dedicated employee? You bet.

In fact, Valparaiso's Gail Peshel told me a story about a student who exemplified this. This student prepared for the firm he wanted as he'd prepare for a final exam. He did full computer searches, talked to alums, and dug up all he could about the firm, especially the people he'd be interviewing with. When he got to the firm, the people he was supposed to talk with weren't there! But he'd re-searched the firm so completely that he knew all about the people he *did* interview with, so he could ask them specifics about projects they were working on . . . *even though he didn't know beforehand that he'd be talking with them!* Were they impressed? As Gail Peshel says, "Who *wouldn't* be?" That kind of research is the kind that vaults you to the stars, regardless of what your credentials are like. *So do it!*

2. YOU'LL COME UP WITH AWESOME QUESTIONS TO ASK

I'm going to give you a detailed list of questions you should ask during your interviews, later on this chapter. But a lot of these questions stem from research you've already done about the firm. In fact, one of the biggest boners you can make during an interview is to ask questions that you could have found the answers to beforehand. Research stops you from making a mistake like that!

3. YOU'LL AVOID MAKING BONEHEADED COMMENTS

One of the biggest mistakes you can make is to lack even the basic knowledge of what the employer's practice areas are. If I've got a little firm that does criminal defense work, and I ask you which specialty you're interested in, *it better be criminal defense work.* If you say "environmental law" — see ya! As Fordham's Kathleen Brady says, "Don't say you don't want to be a tax attorney to someone who's a tax attorney!" San Diego's Susan Benson adds, "Don't ask things like, 'You practice insurance litigation? Really?'" And Florida's Ann Skalaski says, "Don't say you're interested in Houston, Atlanta, and Washington, if the firm doesn't have any offices there!"

Any of these mistakes will immediately delete you from the potential employee pool. But if you've done your homework, you'll easily avoid red flags like these!

4. YOU'LL LEARN MORE ABOUT WHY YOU WANT (OR *DON'T* WANT) TO WORK FOR THIS EMPLOYER

As you research a particular employer, you will sharpen your focus on what you want to do. Inevitably you'll react to things you learn by saying, "Hmm, that sounds good!" or, "I don't think I'd like that. . . . " That kind of self-assessment is *always* useful, because it gives you an idea of what different kinds of employers are like — and it helps you decide exactly which traits you're looking for in an ideal employer.

5. YOU'LL BE A LOT MORE RELAXED AND CONFIDENT DURING YOUR INTERVIEW

Let's face it — the more prepared you are, the more relaxed you'll feel. As Willamette's Diane Reynolds says, "Good research gives you confidence!" That kind of self-assurance is *very* attractive to employers, and it's the happy fallout of research.

"OK, OK, OK, Kimmbo," you're saying. "I believe you! But I don't have any idea how to find out any of this stuff about employers." No sweat — *I* know, and I'm about to tell you. I'm going to divide the information you'll dig up into two categories: hard information, and the inside scoop. Let's see what they are, and where you find them!

B. HARD INFORMATION

What I'm talking about here is *concrete* information about the employer. For instance, for a law firm, it would be information like cities where the firm has offices, the number of partners and associates, the practice areas it specializes in, biographies of lawyers in the firm, and that kind of thing. Here are sources for this kind of information:

1. ON-LINE INFORMATION FROM LEXIS AND/OR WESTLAW

Most schools have computer access to help you with your job search. The two major on-line services are Lexis and Westlaw. These services provide a whole treasure trove of nuts-and-bolts information about many employers, especially the larger ones. Here are the kinds of things you should find out:

♦ Size of firm.

♦ Areas of practice.

- ◆ Biographies of lawyers who work there — including their specialty, when and where they were born, where they went to college and law school, things they've published, awards they've won, and all kinds of things like that.
- ◆ Cases the employer has been involved in.
- ◆ Clients the employer has represented.
- ◆ Any current mention of the employer in the news.

There are bunches of other kinds of information you can get on-line, but that gives you an idea of the *kinds* of things you should research.

What if your school doesn't give you computer access? No big deal. You can use the NALP forms, Martindale-Hubbell, and trade publications (like bar association magazines and newsletters available in your career services office) to find out the same things. Those sources just aren't as convenient as on-line research.

2. THE EMPLOYER'S NALP FORM

The NALP (National Association of Law Placement) form provides all kinds of basic information about the employer — number of lawyers, practice areas (and number of lawyers in each), starting pay, how many lawyers they've hired recently (and expect to hire in the foreseeable future), average billable hours worked, benefits, pro bono policy, and that kind of thing. The forms also include a space for a narrative, where the employer gives a pitch similar to what you'd see in their brochure. Every career services office carries up-to-date NALP forms, so that's where you'd expect to find them.

Keep in mind that small employers don't bother with NALP forms, so don't expect to find one if you're interviewing with smaller employers. But it's always worth checking to see if the employer has filled one out!

3. MARTINDALE-HUBBELL

The grandaddy of research tools, "Mar-Hub," as it's sometimes called, is a huge directory with biographical information on every practicing attorney in the country.

It's available on-line from Lexis, but every law library in the country stocks it. (Westlaw has a similar service, which is called the Directory of Legal Employers.)

You'll want to use Martindale-Hubbell to check the background not just of the person with whom you'll be interviewing, but everybody else in the firm, as well. What are you looking for? As Maine's Tammy Willcox points out, "You want to see what kind of law each person practices. And you want to see who you've got connections with. See if there's anyone from your law school, or your undergrad school. *They'll* mention it, and you'll be tripped up otherwise." And don't just stop with the person or people you're scheduled to meet with. You never know when the interviewer will be called away, and you'll be interviewing with someone *else* in the firm. While you clearly can't memorize the details on every lawyer in a sizable firm, you'll definitely want to do so if the firm is small enough, and you'll want to remember the names of anyone who went to your law school or undergraduate school.

Mar-Hub research gives you the benefit of knowing each lawyer's practice area, which gives you the basis for asking questions about what she or he does. As I'll go into a little bit later, questions relating to what a person practices are among the very best kinds of questions to ask.

4. The Employer's Own Literature, like Brochures, Résumés, and Annual Reports

Almost every law firm and corporation generates literature about itself. If the employer you're interviewing with does on-campus interviews, your career services office will have this kind of literature on file. If not, you should call the employer and ask for this kind of literature to be sent to you in advance of the interview (this, in and of itself, shows initiative).

Reading a firm's literature is a simple way to learn about its specialties, office locations, and basic information like that. But as Boston University's Betsy Armour points out, it's much more valuable than that if you read between the lines. As she says, "Be smart about reading the firm literature, because it can tell you a lot about the atmosphere there." Does the firm use casual, collegial language? Or is it formal and stilted? Are the lawyers presented in such a way as to make them seem friendly and approachable, or are they made to seem more aloof? The literature may also tell you about the firm's summer clerkship program (if that's what you're interviewing for), and that can give you the basis for good questions during the interview. For instance, as Marilyn Tucker points out, if the firm's résumé says that summer interns work in three areas, you can ask whether you get to choose those areas or not.

The literature may also mention clients. Is there a wide client base, or is the firm dependent on one or two large clients? If it relies on a client or two, then you'll want to research those clients, as well, because the fortunes of the firm depends on the fortunes of those clients. For instance, let's say you research the *Wall Street Journal* and find that the single large client of the firm you're interviewing with is on the block, and it's going to be moving to the other coast. That doesn't bode well for your potential employer, does it?

So, be sure to read the employer's own literature and squeeze all of the information from it that you can!

C. INSIDE SCOOP

This is the information that tells you what it's *really* like to work for a certain employer. Let's face it: What would you rather know in making your job decisions? That the firm has practice areas in insurance, securities, and white collar defense work, you rotate through each department for 4 weeks during the summer, and a committee evaluates each of the projects you work on — or that the partners are all insufferable jerks? Aaahh. That's what I thought.

Now, it may well be that in the course of choosing your dream employer, and making contacts, you've already got a lot of the information I'm encouraging you to find out here. In that case, you're a seasoned professional, and you may only need to polish what you need to know. On the other hand, if you haven't done any of this research — for instance, you're doing an on-campus interview that didn't *require* that you make any contacts beforehand — then this will all be new to you. Either way, when you're looking for the inside scoop, this is the kind of information you want: Tidbits about the employer's atmosphere — its working environment; What impresses them; What they really look for in new associates; The kinds of things that really piss them off; Things they like to hear in interviews and things that you shouldn't say; What kinds of demands they put on the people who work there; What their prospects are like, and whether they're confident or fearful about their future. And with regard to the particular interviewer, if you know who it's going to be, get a snapshot of their personality. Are they easygoing? Laid back? Or a ballbuster, who really wants to get in your chops to see if you can take it?

You know the kind of information I'm talking about here. Gossip! To give you a sample, I talked with someone at one of the country's largest, most prestigious law firms, to get a sketch of what it's like to work there. Here's the laundry list of things he said about this particular firm. "It's fairly conservative. Hard work is appreciated and expected. They put a high premium on detail and on people with a sense of humor. They like enthusiasm and the ability to take the lead. You can fall between the cracks if you don't increase your recognition. It's fairly political. You need to be able to take job development into your own hands; nobody spoon feeds you." Now, if you can't see how valuable it is to know information like this, you will, when we get to talking about how to prepare an "infomercial" on yourself before your interview, on page 309. Until then, just keep in mind that this is the kind of information you're looking for when you look for the inside scoop.

The *best* sources for the inside skinny on any employer are *people*. As you speak with them, take detailed notes on what they tell you. Let's go through the people you should seek out before your interview.

1. YOUR CAREER SERVICES DIRECTOR

An *excellent* and frequently overlooked source of gossip! Remember, a large fraction of your career services director's time is spent networking, so they normally hear the most excellent gossipy stuff. Even better, your career services director is one person with whom you can be completely frank, asking them questions that wouldn't be appropriate for anyone else. Things like whether the employer demands long hours. They'll also be able to put you on to other people who can give you inside dirt; namely, alumni who work there or who've worked there in the past, upperclassmen who've clerked there, and any other students who've interviewed there. Let's talk about each of those sources.

2. ALUMNI WHO WORK AT THE FIRM

You can't be quite as frank when you speak with someone who still works at a firm. After all, since they *work* there, they probably won't say anything negative about it — and if they *do* say anything terribly negative, you've got to question how long they're going to be there (and if *you* want to be there!). But, nonetheless, you can certainly tell them that you're researching the firm in preparation for an interview there, and ask what it's like to work there, and if they have any advice for you. Remember, since they work for the employer, they'll be evaluating you as a potential colleague. In that sense, your conversation with them will essentially be a mini-interview, conducted over the phone. And that means that before you speak with them, you'll want to go over the interview questions to ask and avoid that I discuss later in this chapter, on page 344. Nonetheless, alumni who work for an employer are an excellent source of information, and so you should make an effort to contact them before your interview.

3. ALUMNI WHO USED TO WORK AT THE FIRM, AND UPPERCLASSMEN WHO'VE CLERKED THERE

Again, these are people you'll find through your career services director. There are pluses and minuses to these sources as compared with alumni who currently work at the firm. On the plus side, since they no longer work there, they'll probably be a lot franker about the negatives at the employer. But on the negative side, be sure you find out why they left there (or, in the case of upperclassmen, aren't returning). As NYU's Gail Cutter says, "You'll want to take their advice with a grain of salt if they left on bad terms."

4. ANY LOCAL ATTORNEYS YOU KNOW

It may well be that through your extracurriculars, or because of family friends, you know local attorneys well enough to be able to ask them what they know about the employer you're interviewing with. This will tell you a lot about how the employer is viewed in the legal community, and that could impact your professional reputation. And they may also know some local gossip, like the firm's prospects or any scandals associated with it, that will be of interest to you.

5. OTHER STUDENTS WHO HAVE INTERVIEWED AT THE FIRM

Depending on how cutthroat the competition at your school is, and the nature of the student in question, other students who've interviewed with a given employer can provide you with valuable insight. For instance, you can find out about the interview style of a particular interviewer, and perhaps topics they like or comments to avoid.

6. FOR LARGE LAW FIRMS, TRY PUBLISHED SOURCES LIKE *THE AMERICAN LAWYER, THE NATIONAL LAW JOURNAL,* AND *THE INSIDER'S GUIDE TO LAW FIRMS*

Normally you don't find good gossip in published sources; you've got to talk to people. That's especially true if the employer isn't an enormous law firm. But if it *is* a large law firm, you've got some published sources you can use. For instance, *The American Lawyer* publishes a survey of summer clerkship programs at large firms based on written questionnaires they send to clerks at the largest law firms. Those are *very* useful. *The Insider's Guide to Law Firms* is a book published by Mobius Press, which provides gossipy stuff about the largest law firms in large cities around the country. The entries are clearly based on "moles" at various firms. However, since the image of each firm depends on the "mole's" opinion, law school career counselors advise you not to rely *exclusively* on the *Guide.* Use every source you can find!

The bottom line here is — if you're looking at an enormous law firm as a potential employer, you can get gossip from published sources, not just people.

So, now you've got a pretty complete picture of the employer you're going to interview with. You know the basics from your research into hard information, and you know the inside scoop to the extent you can possibly find it out.

2. Make up an "Infomercial" about Yourself, and Streamline Your "Miss Americas" (Interview Questions You'll Ask, and Answers for Questions You'll Get)

OK. Admit it. Once in a while — perhaps more than that, you poor dear — you've found yourself, remote control in hand, channel surfing on Sunday morning. You stop on one channel, you're sucked in, and before you know it . . . you've dropped $89.95 in three easy monthly payments on a toenail recycler.

Welcome to the world of infomercials. You may find them shameless and disgusting, but the fact is, they work. And the reason they work is that they promote their product flawlessly. Well, when you're going on a job interview, you've got to do the same thing. You've got a product — you — and you've got to market yourself effectively to get a job offer.

There are two aspects to that. One is to come up with points about yourself that you definitely want to make, no matter what. That's the content of your infomercial. As Kathleen Brady points out, "Sometimes you're not going to want to wait to be asked about your strong points!" She relates a story about the Dukakis presidential campaign, where he was asked about his mother's health and he responded with something like, "She's much better, and she supports my healthcare proposal, too." (And by the way, if you've already read the chapters on correspondence and résumés, coming up with your strengths will be a breeze for you, because you'll be coming up with the transferable skills and examples of those skills that formed the foundation of your letters and résumés.)

The other aspect of coming up with your sales package involves what I call "Miss Americas" — that is, questions, both the ones you'll ask and the ones you'll be expected to answer. You need to have a handful of questions that you intend to ask during the interview. These will have two sources. One is the list that I'll give you here, and the other are questions tailored to the particular employer on the basis of the research you've done about that particular employer (in fact, the purpose of those questions is to *display* your research, not just to get information!). And you also have to be completely comfortable with questions the employer is likely to ask you, and have your answers formulated in advance.

With that in mind, let's take a look at these in a lot more detail.

A. MAKE UP AN "INFOMERCIAL" ABOUT YOURSELF

The purpose of creating an infomercial about yourself is that you've got to have a pitch about you that you feel comfortable saying. It's got to be short, and it has to say the most crucial things about you — the things you want employers to know about you, whether they ask you questions that elicit those assets or not. As William & Mary's Rob Kaplan says, "You have to remember that the interviewer is not your advocate! Their role isn't to find out what's good about you. You need to have points about yourself that you'll *definitely* make, so that you're not at the interviewer's mercy!" And Albany's Sandy Mans adds, "If you have an outline of your major strengths, it'll cut a broad swath of questions you might be asked."

Coming up with this infomercial has five basic steps:

♦ Go through your background and pick out your accomplishments; the things you're most proud of. They can be the result of jobs, or personal accomplishments. You should come up with a short list of them.

♦ Looking at that list, decide the three to five job-related strengths that those accomplishments show you have. What we're talking about here are transferable skills.

♦ If your skills and accomplishments are all job-related, come up with a personal achievement that you want to mention.

♦ Memorize your infomercial.

♦ Tailor your infomercial to the particular employer, on the basis of your research about them.

Before we go into detail on those five steps, I want you to keep in mind exactly what this infomercial is going to do for you: it's going to convince a legal employer that you'll be a great employee. That involves two things: first, and most importantly, it involves proving that you've got the job skills that'll enable you to do the job just the way they want it done. These are called "transferable skills," and I've discussed them before, particularly in the last chapter when I talked about formulating your résumé. And secondly — and this is the one that students invariably overlook! — *you want to show that you're the kind of person they want to work with; your human dimension, the kinds of things that make you a well-rounded person.* This is the functional equivalent of the "Hobbies and Personal Interests" section on your résumé, remember?

Now — why would I want to emphasize this human dimension? Because most of the job search books I've read — and trust me, I've read a bunch — make it sound as though you ought to make yourself sound like a work-chomping automaton in order to impress an interviewer. Virtually every career services director and employer I spoke with emphasized *just* the opposite. That is, they stressed the importance of coming across as someone the employer will *like* to work with. I'm going to get into this idea in detail when I discuss how you ought to handle the interview itself, but for now, remember that while you're constructing your infomercial, you'll want to give it a human, nonskills-oriented spin, as well.

With that in mind, let's take a look at each of those five steps, in detail.

1. PAT YOURSELF ON THE BACK! MAKE A LIST OF YOUR ACCOMPLISHMENTS

This is a real "feel good" exercise, because what I want you to do is write down things about yourself that you're really proud of. The kind of things your folks would tell people about you; the kinds of things that would make your grandma pinch your cheek and say, "Oh, you're such a good ___ (boy or girl, as the case may be)." How many things should you come up with? As Marilyn Tucker advises, make it at least three or four things. I've provided a worksheet for you on page 314, which leaves you room for five accomplishments.

As to content, St. Louis's Wendy Werner says, "Your list should include things like, 'I started this organization in college,' or 'I raised this money,' or 'I wrote best brief' — things like that." Chicago-Kent's Lisa Abrams calls this list your "claim to fame." Maybe you've written something you're proud of. Or you've acted in the theater. Or you raised kids while you went to college, or worked full-time while you got your degree. Or you made the Dean's List in undergrad every semester. Maybe you've climbed Mount

Kilimanjaro. Maybe you held down a job for 2 years when everyone who'd held the position before you was fired within a month. Maybe you were head counselor at a summer camp and you were the first person who didn't have any kids go home early because they were homesick. There's an endless variety of accomplishments, and you need to come up with yours!

Now my advice with this list is to come up with accomplishments that are as colorful as possible. There are two good reasons for this. One is that you'll be giving the interviewer a break. As tough as it is to *be* interviewed, it's even *tougher* to do the interviewing. You'll be using these accomplishments as examples about yourself in the interview, and if you make those examples interesting, you're doing the interviewer a favor, because *every* interviewer appreciates an interesting interviewee. Another plus is that interesting accomplishments will make you memorable. Inevitably you'll have lots of competition for any job you interview for, and anything you can do (within the realm of professionalism) to make yourself stand out is something worth doing.

So your first step in coming up with your infomercial is to make a short list of accomplishments. In case you're wondering why you're coming up with this list, I've got two reasons for you. One is that you're going to use these accomplishments as a fulcrum from which you'll draw your strongest job-related skills, as I'm about to go over in Step 2, below. But apart from that, they provide a crucial backup in your interviews, when interviewers ask what your strengths are, or why they should hire you. If you just say, 'Oh, I've got great writing skills, I'm an excellent researcher, and I work well with people,' and then just sit there looking like a deer frozen in headlights, you won't be very convincing. You've got to have *experiences* to *prove* that you have those skills. And that's why I've asked you to come up with a list of accomplishments. You'll *definitely* use it in your interviews!

Now it may well be that this list of accomplishments is the same list you used in coming up with your résumé, and that's fine. As soon as you've got it done, it's time to . . .

2. DECIDE ON THE 3 TO 5 JOB-RELATED STRENGTHS THAT YOUR ACCOMPLISHMENTS PROVE YOU HAVE

I've told you before that all an employer cares about is what you can do for them. That means that your accomplishments are only relevant to the extent that you can relate how those accomplishments are examples of assets you have, which you'll also be able to put to work for the employer. For instance, in and of itself, it wouldn't much matter to any potential legal employer that I waitressed 35 hours a week to put myself through college, because as a legal employer, presumably they won't be expecting me to take orders for blueberry pancakes and pour coffee without spilling it in a client's lap. That experience is only relevant to a potential employer if I make the logical connection between that accomplishment — working full-time while I went to college full-time — and what it says about what I can do for an employer. And that would include things like having a strong work ethic, and dealing well with people, and being able to organize my time effectively. So *that's* what I mean when I talk about coming up with job-related skills on the basis of your accomplishments. And again, this is very much what I told you to do in the last chapter, when we talked about résumés.

So take your list of accomplishments, and extract from those accomplishments your three to five most valuable job related skills. Write those skills in on the worksheet where you wrote your accomplishments, on page 314.

What kinds of things should you use? Well, if you need inspiration, you can turn back to Chapter 6 on résumés, and look at the list of job-related skills that I gave you there. Remember, what you're looking for here are skills you've learned somewhere else that you'll be able to transfer and use for your next employer's benefit. For legal employers, you'll normally be talking about things like writing ability, analysis skills, a strong work ethic, being able to work under pressure, having good judgment, being a team player, working well with people, having client development skills, being thorough, resourceful, persistent, a self-starter, you name it. A particularly good one is having thoughtful initiative — that is, the ability to anticipate your employer's needs. As Maureen Provost Ryan of St. John's points out, "This is a quality highly prized by employers, and frequently overlooked by students." So what you're doing here is to think about the things you've done, and pull out the skills they indicate.

As you do this, don't undervalue yourself by overlooking the job-related skills you've gotten from nonlegal jobs. One career services director told me about a law student who worked a summer for the corporate counsel for the Professional Golfers' Association. This student felt stigmatized by the fact that he didn't have law firm experience, but he *did* turn the experience to his advantage in interviews. What he did was to look at that job and realize that his boss was a perfectionist, and that the main thing he learned working for him was how to minimize the burden he placed on his boss's time. That meant he learned how to organize questions, manage himself, and be succinct, so as to bother his boss as little as possible. Well, you can imagine that *not only* is that an excellent law-related skill to have, but it was sufficiently off the beaten track to make for interesting interviews! I heard a bunch of colorful examples like this while I talked with career services directors. One student was able to turn to his advantage his experience as a hot dog salesman at Yankee Stadium for seven summers. Another student had put himself through college as a door-to-door Fuller Brush salesman.

Now it may well be that in doing this, you find you have to rethink your list of accomplishments. For instance, let's say that an accomplishment you're particularly proud of is helping out at a homeless shelter, and that the aspect of *that* that you most appreciate is your ability to relate to people who are down on their luck. Well, if you're interviewing with Wall Street law firms, that's a pretty useless trait. You'd be better off relating to people at the Betty Ford Clinic than you would to homeless people, because people from the Ford Clinic at least have some chance of being wealthy and influential, and thus they've got a shot at being in the client pool at a Wall Street firm. On the other hand, if you're interviewing for a public interest position, your ability to relate to the homeless would be extremely valuable indeed. So, when it comes to job-related skills, be mindful of who your audience is!

INFOMERCIAL WORKSHEET:
ACCOMPLISHMENTS AND THE TRANSFERABLE SKILLS THEY PROVE

Accomplishment:

Transferable skills this accomplishment illustrates about me:

Accomplishment:

Transferable skills this accomplishment illustrates about me:

Accomplishment:

Transferable skills this accomplishment illustrates about me:

Accomplishment:

Transferable skills this accomplishment illustrates about me:

Now, it may well be that you've come up with more than five job-related skills. If so, narrow your list to the five most important skills, taking into account the prized skills I mentioned earlier in this section, as well as the list in Chapter 6. Those five job-related skills will become part of your infomercial.

3. If Your Accomplishments Are All Job-Related, Come Up With a Personal Achievement That You Want to Mention

Remember, I said that it's crucial for the interviewer to look at you as a *person*, a complete, flesh-and-blood being, rather than just as another interviewee. What will help you do that is to mention a personal achievement in your infomercial.

Now this isn't to say that just any old personal achievement will do. As I mentioned in Chapter 6, when we talked about résumés, you'll want to tailor your personal achievement to the type of employer you're talking to. Remember the examples I used then? If you're heavily involved in religious activities, or you're a frequent beauty pageant winner, or you have a strongly political background or any other highly-charged facet to your background and personality, take your audience into account before you highlight it. And that's not because *any* of these activities involve any shame — clearly they don't! But let's face it. Most law firms are pretty conservative, so it might not be a good idea to hit them over the head with the fact that you're heavily involved in Democratic politics. Obviously, the final decision on these kinds of things is yours, but *my* advice is to choose something interesting, albeit neutral, as your personal achievement.

I'll give you an example. Probably the nonprofessional thing I'm most proud of is the fact that even though I was a pretty porky kid growing up, a few years ago I dropped 50 pounds, and I've kept it off. Now I'm not going to toot my own horn here by going into detail about what truly incredible things that accomplishment says about me, but you can see that it's the kind of thing that is both memorable and neutral — and it has the added benefit of illustrating discipline, *yet another* good trait for a lawyer.

So go through your personal life, and look for something that makes you proud. Have you written a children's book? Climbed Ayers Rock? Raised a child while attending law school? Backpacked across Europe? You get the idea — just make it a personal achievement, and make it memorable.

Jot down three possibilities for the personal achievement you'd like to mention:

1.

2.

3.

Once you've thought of three of these, pick the one that sounds most impressive. That's the one you'll include in your infomercial.

4. NOW THAT YOU HAVE YOUR BUILDING BLOCKS TOGETHER, IT'S TIME TO ASSEMBLE YOUR INFOMERCIAL AND MEMORIZE IT

All right. You've got your five (or so) accomplishments. You've got the five (or so) job-related strengths those accomplishments prove you have. And you've got your personal achievement, if your other accomplishments don't include one. What you're going to want to do is to flip around your accomplishments and your job-related skills, and memorize the infomercial that results from that. What I mean is that what you'll do is cite your job-related skills and then use your accomplishments as support for those skills. For instance, for my waitressing experience, I'd say something like, "I'm a hard worker. I put myself through college by working full-time as a waitress while I was taking a full class load."

So you put together your skills, your accomplishments, and your personal achievement, and you've got your infomercial. Now, memorize it. Sit in front of a mirror, and talk about yourself until you can go through it comfortably.

At first, you're either going to want to (1) throw up or (2) laugh. But the kind of calm self-confidence you're looking to project is what you see in a presidential candidate, or a Miss America finalist. They're able to talk about what they bring to the table with a smile and without flinching, and you've got to be able to do the same thing.

Why do you have to memorize this? Remember, these are the points you are going to make in interviews, regardless of whether you're asked about them. So you've got to be able to reel off your job-related skills quickly, tersely, and confidently. Furthermore, they'll help you answer a whole raft of tough interview questions with your infomercial at your fingertips — everything from "What are your strengths?" to "Tell me about yourself" to "Why should we hire you?" Also, keeping your strengths at the front of your mind has the benefit of reminding you how special you are — and why it is that you deserve your dream job, in the first place!

5. TAILOR YOUR INFOMERCIAL TO THE PARTICULAR EMPLOYER YOU'RE INTERVIEWING WITH

I've mentioned before that it's important for your infomercial to be fluid. In fact, you'll find that you probably won't mention more than three job-related skills for any particular interviewer, but with five, you've got some "wiggle" room to make modifications based on the idiosyncracies of any particular employer.

I'll show you exactly what I'm talking about, and by way of example, I'm going to go back to that law firm "snapshot" I gave you when I talked about getting the inside scoop on employers. It was a laundry list of attributes of a prestigious law firm. Remember it? It went like this: "It's fairly conservative. Hard work is appreciated and expected. They put a high premium on detail and on people with a sense of humor. They like enthusiasm and the ability to take the lead. You can fall between the cracks if you don't increase your recognition. It's fairly political. You need to be able to take job development into your own hands; nobody spoon feeds you." Now, what are the job-related skills you'd want to bring up in this interview? An attention to detail. A strong work ethic. Initiative. A sense of humor.

You'll probably have some of those traits on your list already, but I want to focus on sense of humor, because that's a trait that you probably wouldn't mention for most employers, because its connotations aren't entirely positive; an employer might get the impression that you'd be more interested in cutting up than in getting your work done. But if you've done your research and found that a sense of humor is prized by a particular employer, and that happens to be a strong point for you, you'd want to bring it up, being careful to couch it in professional terms. For instance, you might want to say something like, "One of my best traits is my sense of humor. In fact, I was elected Class Clown in my high school class, on the basis of a humor column I wrote for the high school newspaper. I've had a lot of jobs where I've worked in tense situations, and my sense of humor has always given me the ability to ameliorate stressful situations with a little joke."

Another important element to work into your info-mercial comes into play if you're interviewing with an out-of-town employer. Geography is of *paramount importance* to employers; they're terrified that if you're not committed to the city where they're located, you won't stay. And if they think you won't stay, they're unlikely to make you an offer, because they won't make back their investment in training you. So geography has got to be an element of your infomercial if you're interviewing with an employer in a city to which you have no obvious connection (e.g., you go to school there or your family lives there). And your reason has to be *believable*. As Gail Peshel points out, "Geography counts! You can't say that you visited this particular city on vacation and you liked it. That's not enough! Instead, you need something more specific; something like you are interested in a particular specialty, and you know that firms in this particular city are known for this kind of practice."

The bottom line here is: don't look at your infomercial as a fixed speech. Tailor it to different employers!

B. DEVELOP AND POLISH YOUR "MISS AMERICAS" — THAT IS, BE FAMILIAR WITH ALL OF THE QUESTIONS YOU'RE GOING TO ASK, AND ALL OF THE QUESTIONS THE INTERVIEWER MIGHT ASK *YOU*

I know I've been mentioning Miss America a lot, but there's a good reason for it. You *never* see a Miss America candidate (at least, not a *good* one) who stumbles over questions and answers. And you know why? Because they've rehearsed ahead of time everything they're going to ask and everything they're likely to be asked. If you don't like the Miss America analogy, there are a bunch of other ones that fit. You can compare yourself to an expert witness in a trial. Or a presidential candidate in a televised debate. The key in all of these situations is that the player in question is so well-rehearsed that *nothing* comes as a surprise to them — they can handle any situation with aplomb. Well, that's what I want you to do. And you know why? Because if you're a savvy interviewee, you'll come across as a professional. Remember, the person who's interviewing you is checking to see if you'll fit in a professional environment. As Benesch Friedlander's Deanna Coe Kursh says, "The whole interviewing process is designed to weed out people who don't belong." So if you're primed for any questions you might hear, and the questions you ought to ask, you'll interview like a pro — and you'll get job offers that people from better schools, with better paper credentials, *won't* get!

There are three principal elements involved in prepping yourself for questions and answers. They are:

♦ Deciding the questions you want to ask, and the answers you want to give to questions the interviewer is likely to ask you. For these, you should read two sections later in this chapter: "Questions You Should Ask to Make Yourself into the Ideal Candidate," on page 342, and "Killer Answers to the Toughest Interview Questions They'll Ever Ask You," on page 356.

♦ Putting a positive twist on everything in your background, and making yourself feel comfortable talking about it.

♦ Memorizing your résumé, and being very familiar with your writing sample.

Since you'll read the questions and answers later in this chapter, I'll skip those for now. Let's focus on the other two aspects of your "Miss Americas:" getting comfortable with your background, and memorizing your résumé.

1. PUTTING A POSITIVE TWIST ON EVERYTHING IN YOUR BACKGROUND, AND MAKING YOURSELF FEEL COMFORTABLE TALKING ABOUT IT

Everybody, and I do mean everybody, has something in their past they're not particularly proud of, some chink in their armor. So you're not the only one. But if you're not comfortable talking about something in your past, I promise you that you will find yourself in interview after interview feeling as though the interviewer has Superman-like laser vision into your soul, zeroing right in on that weakness.

"Well, gee thanks, Kimmbo," you're saying. "That makes me feel *much* better." I realize the thought of having Achilles' heels is an uncomfortable one, but you *can* overcome it. It all boils down to the wisdom in this saying: *"Nobody can walk all over me unless I lie down first."* In this context, that translates into "nobody can make you feel bad about *anything* in your background unless you let them." And I don't care *what* it is. "Why didn't you get an offer from your last employer?" "Why aren't your grades better?" "If you're so great at what you did before law school, why did you leave that career?" "Why . . . " "Why . . . " "Why . . . " If you've come to terms with everything in your background, nobody can make you feel bad about it! Why didn't you get that offer? Shrug, and with quiet confidence, say, "I was disappointed by that, too. But if you're concerned about whether I can do your work, what's really indicative of my ability is my experience with. . . . " Why aren't your grades better? "Boy, nobody's more disappointed in them than I am! It's true that I don't do well on 3-hour exams. But I know I can perform well for you, because you do Criminal defense work, and in Criminal Law I was in the top 20% of the class, and I took a clinic where I did criminal work, and I consistently succeeded. . . . " I could go on and on and on with this, but you see my point: With everything you consider a flaw, go over and over and over it in your mind until you can answer any question about it with quiet

confidence. *Nobody can walk all over you unless you lie down first!*
What kinds of things should you be on the particular lookout for? This is by necessity only a partial list, but they include . . .

A. GAPS IN YOUR RÉSUMÉ

As I mentioned in Chapter 6 on résumés, you really should avoid having any gaps in your résumé. As one career services director I spoke with said, "If you leave a gap, employers will assume the worst — like you were in jail." If you took off to Europe to find yourself, that's OK. If you needed time to rethink your priorities in life, that's OK — in fact, it's a *positive*, because it shows you've now chosen a course with renewed vigor and enthusiasm. If you took time off to raise kids, fine. If it was just a job you didn't think reflected any transferable skills, no problem. But whatever it is, be sure that you can discuss it comfortably.

B. FLAWS IN GRADES OR PRIOR EMPLOYMENT

These are the toughies — bad grades or poor work experiences. I deal in detail with both of these later in this chapter when I talk about answering tough interview questions, and also in Chapter 10 — "Help! My Grades Stink!" — and in Chapter 9 — "What if You Didn't Get an Offer after Your Summer Clerkship?" If you've got one of these problems, you've probably already taken a look at the appropriate chapter. In a nutshell, what you have to do is look behind the fact and look to what the employer's concern is going to be — namely, "Can you do my work?" If need be, reword any tough questions you anticipate so that you add that as a tag line. "Despite the fact that your grades are bad . . . can you do my work?" "Despite the fact you didn't get an offer from your last employer . . . can you do my work?" To each of which your answer's got to be a resounding "Yes!" with the particular experiences you bring to the table to back that up. As Marilyn Tucker says, "If you've got Achilles' heels, you need *lots* of preparation, otherwise you'll shoot yourself in the foot. You need to be on autopilot for those questions!" And Diane Reynolds adds, "You just need to think of any tricky areas you've got, and have a good attitude about them!"

You may even find employers who really *aren't* concerned that you can't do their work; they just want to see how you bear up under the pressure of tough questions. You've got bad grades? Well, maybe the employer isn't concerned about that, because they had bad grades, too! After all, most employers weren't in the top 10% of *their* class, either! Or you didn't get an offer from your last employer, because that employer was a jerk? Well, maybe the interviewer *knows* that employer, and *knows* they're a jerk — and the interviewer's just asking you about that job to see if you can handle a question about not getting an offer without trashing your former employer. So don't be so quick to assume that what *you* perceive as your flaws are fatal in the eyes of employers!

The bottom line is, if you're comfortable with your background, no interviewer will be able to cow you on it. If you can't get comfortable just thinking things through by yourself — and I'm not saying that you *have* to do that — then talk with your career services director to get ideas on putting your past in a positive light. Remember, no interviewer can make you feel bad about *anything* without your compliance. Once you feel comfortable with everything you've done, you're ready to conquer the world!

2. MEMORIZING YOUR RÉSUMÉ AND BEING VERY FAMILIAR WITH YOUR WRITING SAMPLE

As Case Western's Debra Fink says, "Be congruous! Make sure that everything in your writing sample, your résumé, and everything your references will say about you all match."

She goes on to point out that *anything* on your résumé is fair game for an interviewer to question you about; in fact, some interviewers just look down your résumé and pull out things to ask you. It's not the most imaginative approach to interviewing, but then, most legal interviewers aren't professional interviewers by any *stretch* of the imagination. So, as Kentucky's Drusilla Bakert points out, "Expect to be asked about your résumé! Be prepared to respond in particular to things like chronological gaps, any weird job, personal experiences, grades, foreign experiences, and foreign languages."

Why bother with all of this memorization? Well, if you mess up and stumble over a question about something on your résumé or in your writing sample, you won't look very well prepared. That's a negative. And also, if you say something that *contradicts* what you've got in writing, that's even worse — you leave the interviewer wondering what's true, what you're saying or what you've written. So, if you put on your résumé that you're fluent in French, you better be able to conduct an interview in French (you can always say that you can *read* French if you aren't conversationally fluent). And don't put down any activity that you haven't (or don't) actively participate in.

Just make sure that you're comfortable with everything on your résumé, that you periodically reread your writing sample, and that you have a pretty good idea of what your references will say about you. Remember — *anything* on your résumé, or in your writing sample, is fair game for interviewers!

3. PRACTICE YOUR INTERVIEWING SKILLS

OK. You've done your detective work, and you've made up your infomercial and developed the questions you'll ask and answers to questions you'll get. The third key to perfect interviewing is *practice*. Why? Because interviewing is a lot like sex in that you can read about it all you want, but you don't really know what it's about until you do it. You can read literally hundreds of books on interviewing, but you have to put your skills to the test to become really proficient. As Albany's Sandy Mans points out, "Even students who interview well from the start in law school don't come by it naturally. They have practiced elsewhere, either through public speaking or student leadership positions."

So — how do you *get* interview practice? There are two principal ways: mock interviews and interviews for positions you don't particularly want. Let's take a look at them.

A. SET UP MOCK INTERVIEWS THROUGH YOUR CAREER SERVICES OFFICE

Every career services director I spoke with emphasized the importance of mock interviews, and bemoaned the fact that so few students take advantage of them. As Franklin Pierce's Sophie Sparrow says, "It's important to be aware of how you come across, and you can only get that by doing mock interviews!"

When you do mock interviews, depending on where you go to school, your "interviewer" will either be a professor, or career services person, or, if you're *really* lucky, it'll be a practicing attorney. Why is that so great? Well, as I pointed out in Chapter 4 on making contacts, doing mock interviews with attorneys is a wonderful hidden opportunity. *You wouldn't be the first person who impressed the "mock" interviewer enough to generate a job offer!*

However, no matter who does the mock interviewing, it's an invaluable tool for seeing how you come off in an interview. What you'll want to be on the lookout for is:

♦   Striking the right note between confidence and arrogance.

♦   Establishing a rapport with the interviewer.

♦   Having an open, enthusiastic demeanor.

♦   Avoiding nervous problems like hunched shoulders, a dropped voice, mumbling, fidgeting, and hemming and hawing.

♦   Handling rough spots, like bad grades or lack of experience.

Many career services offices will even videotape your mock interviews for you. If yours does, *definitely* take advantage of this service. It's the best possible gauge of how you'll do during the "real thing"!

B. Consider Interviewing For Positions You Don't Particularly Want

You know the situation. There are on-campus inter-viewers who are known for interviewing just about anybody, like the Armed Forces JAG Corps or certain small firms. You're pretty sure that you can get an inter-view just by dropping off your résumé. The question here is: do you take interviews for jobs you don't particularly want, just as a means of gaining interview-ing practice?

I've got to warn you up front — interviewing for positions you don't particularly want is *very* controver-sial. The only point on which every career services director agrees is that if you just wouldn't take the job under *any* circumstances, don't take the interview. For instance, if it's in a city that you just wouldn't live in even if red-hot bamboo shoots were forced under your toenails, don't interview for the job. That *is* a waste of time and you shouldn't do it.

If you can't rule it out absolutely and completely, that's where things get controversial. There are many arguments both for and against this kind of interview-ing, but on balance, I'm in favor of it, and I'll explain why in just a minute. But first, here are the arguments *against* practising on employers you're not wild about. First is the idea that you can't get enthused about jobs you don't really want, so you generally won't get jobs from these interviewers anyway. Then there's the matter of respect. As Sophie Sparrow argues, "It's disrespectful to interview for jobs that there's little or no chance you'd accept." Cal Western's Lisa Kellogg goes on to say that, "Interviewing for jobs you don't want is unfair to class-mates. It reflects poorly on the school. And employers may *sense* that you're only practicing on them, and they'll resent it." Finally, Wendy Werner points out, "Interviewing for jobs you don't want is a waste of time for everyone. It takes just as much energy to get a job you *don't* want as one you *do.*"

So those are the arguments *against* doing practice interviews with employers who don't really turn you on. But I heard a half dozen great reasons for *doing* these kinds of interviews, and that's why I'm recommending that you do them. (Remember, if you *do* these kinds of interviews, prepare for them with the same kind of fervor you'd bring to an employer you really want, going through all the steps I've outlined in this chapter!) The arguments in favor? First of all, as Jose Bahamonde-Gonzalez of Miami points out, interviewing is such a high-stress, high-anxiety situation, that you need all the practice you can get. He says, "You just never say no to a job interview, until you have an offer!" Second, as Maureen Provost Ryan points out, "It may actually be *easier* for you to establish a rapport with the interviewer if you don't have the anxiety of feeling that you *have* to impress the interviewer!" Third, Vanderbilt's Pam Malone notes, "You don't know when you'll want to change careers, years down the road. If you interview for jobs that don't particularly interest you while you're in law school, at least they give you a realistic frame of reference as to what's out there. When you want to change jobs, you just might remember that interview in a positive light!"

Another reason to interview for jobs you don't particularly want is to meet the interviewers. As George Washington's Amy Thompson points out, "Interviewers can become contacts for you!" Even if you don't want to work for them in particular, you may be able to keep in touch with them, and through them find an employer you really *do* want. Another good reason to do these interviews is to come up with a fall back position if your dream job doesn't come through right away. After all, as Amy Thompson says, "You can't rule everything out while you wait for the perfect job."

Finally — and this is the best reason of all to do these practice interviews — you may stumble into a wonderful opportunity after all! You may find, as many students before you have discovered, that your prior focus was unnecessarily narrow. As Jose Bahamonde-Gonzalez says, "A lot of students think they want international law and nothing else. They don't realize that a lot of times it's just glorified corporate law, and once they're in it, they may not want it at all. And because they didn't interview for anything else, they passed up something they'd really love just because they had a narrow, unrealistic focus!" Many career services directors told me about all kinds of jobs that fall into this "Gee-I-didn't-really-think-I-wanted-it-but-it-turned-out-to-be-great" category. The two most common of these is the Armed Forces JAG Corps and small firms. As Pam Malone points out, "Don't overlook the JAG Corps! People really like it. It's got a lot of hidden assets, like loan repayment benefits, housing, and the fact you can get an L.L.M. for free. Also, the places you live are normally nice. The hours are good. There's not a lot of pressure. It's easy to network for your next move. It's great for women and minorities. And you get a lot of hands-on experience in many different practice areas." All of that for a career that most students reject out of hand! And, she says, "A lot of students are also wary of small law firms because they fear a lack of exposure and low starting pay. But neither one of those is always true. Normally, small firms give you *lots* of hands-on experience. And even if the starting pay is low, you get a lot more money, more quickly." You've probably got a list of your own consisting of jobs you think you wouldn't like, or are somehow "beneath" you. As Maureen Provost Ryan points out, "You just can't assume that any job is beneath you before you check it out. Go on the interview, explore the job, treat it as a 'look-see.' Sometimes fate hands you an opportunity you didn't expect!"

B. SARTORIAL SPLENDOR: HOW TO DRESS FOR YOUR INTERVIEWER

Ah, how I wish you were sitting here with me now. Apart from the fact that I love to meet new people, it would be so much easier to give you advice about what to wear. I'd just lead you to my closet, open the door, and say, "Don't wear any of this!" Why? Because my closet looks like an explosion in a paint factory. I love bright colors, and lots of them. And those are the worst *possible* things to wear on a job interview!

But that doesn't help you decide what you *should* wear. I'll run you through choosing your interview clothes, and I can tell you from the start that it's really pretty simple. There are some basic rules that apply to *any* interview for a professional job, and that's what I'll be giving you here. You probably already know what they are; it's not rocket science, and it certainly doesn't merit wasting *any* time stressing over these rules. As Lisa Abrams says, "The most important thing about the interview is *not* whether you wear a peach or a white blouse, or carry a leather or vinyl portfolio. People just focus on those things because they're *easy.*" So don't waste time worrying about what to wear. *You* know how lawyers look. Dress like they do, and get on with your life!

Now this may seem a little out of character for me, because I'm always telling you to be interesting, and sound interesting, and stand out. It's actually not inconsistent. What you're doing by dressing professionally for interviews is telling the interviewer, "I fit in with you guys." That's *extremely* important, and that's why you want to dress quietly! So, yes, your *personality* should shine. Your suit *shouldn't.*

By the way, follow these rules on dress even if your research turns up the fact that people dress pretty casually when they actually work for a particular employer. Why should you ignore this, and dress more formally for your interview? It's largely a matter of respect. It shows that you care enough about the job to get dressed up and make a good impression. I know this from personal experience. It may be that I sometimes show up for work in a Mets sweatshirt and torn jeans, but if a law student came to interview with me, I'd be a bit put off if they wore their "I'm With Stupid" T-shirt.

So unless that you're absolutely *positive,* on the basis of what people tell you while you're doing your research, that the employer welcomes casual interviewees, then stick with these basic rules:

1. RULES OF THUMB FOR MEN

Go with a good quality navy or gray suit, white shirt, conservative tie, shined shoes, blah blah blah. Surely you already know this! You can get away with a conservative pinstripe, too. The main point here, as Diane Reynolds notes, is to buy a good suit, even if you've got to borrow money to get one. One career services director told me about a student who seemed to be wearing a navy pinstripe suit to an interview, but on closer analysis, she noticed that *some of the pinstripes had started to come off in the wash!* As a rule of thumb, don't buy a machine-washable suit, OK? And don't wear a double-breasted suit; some employers won't mind them, but some will.

When it comes to details, make sure your overall appearance fits with the employer's image. No dirty fingernails, no overpowering cologne. As Jose Bahamonde-Gonzalez points out, "If you're interviewing with a corporate law firm, and you're a man, cut the ponytail and leave the earring at home."

2. RULES OF THUMB FOR WOMEN

If you've got any doubts about your judgment when it comes to wardrobe, Debra Fink suggests renting the Melanie Griffith movie "Working Girl." She says, "If you want to be viewed as a professional, dress like Melanie Griffith *after* her transformation into a professional woman. If you want to be seen as a secretary, dress like her *before*. Wear a short suit, bleached hair, and too much makeup." She goes on to point out that "a leotard is not a blouse, and cleavage is *never* appropriate!"

Northern Illinois' Mary Obrzut advises that, "It's crucial not to look like a cute young thing." However, that doesn't have to mean a navy suit. As Debra Fink points out, "There are a bunch of nice suits with plaid jackets and solid-color skirts. And different colors are OK. As long as it's a good wool suit, you can even get away with a muted purple or red." Diane Reynolds suggests jazzing up a conservative suit with a classy scarf or a nice pin.

So, you've got room for a little bit of flair with your interview wardrobe, with the emphasis on "little bit." Make sure your hair is neat; if it's long and wild, consider wearing it pinned up or back in a ponytail. Wear medium to low heels, and flesh-colored pantyhose. (Carry a spare pair in your purse in case you get a run; that's what Princess Di does, and you never see *her* looking unkempt, except for those zoom-lens Caribbean beach shots.) Tone down the makeup and don't wear strong perfume. Keep the jewelry low-key — pearls and button earrings, that kind of thing.

While we're discussing jewelry, it's worth talking about . . .

3. RULES OF RING FINGER FOR WOMEN

Whooo boy; here's a bit of advice that may really send you ballistic. It's this: A number of career services directors suggested that if you're an engaged woman, you remove your engagement ring for interviews. Why? In some employers' minds, if they see an engagement ring, they'll perhaps subconsciously assume that you'll shortly be getting married and be starting a family, and that means you'll perhaps be diverting some of your attention from your job to your personal life. Ignoring for a moment that it's none of their business, you may want to avoid the issue altogether by removing your engagement ring for the duration of the interview. As one career services director told me, "If you wear your engagement ring, expect to be asked about it. It's a red flag! If you don't feel comfortable discussing your impending marriage don't wear your ring. If you *do* wear it, expect to speak to the employer's underlying concern that you'll start a family and leave, by reassuring them that you have no intention of leaving."

Now remember, all I'm talking about here are appearances. As several career services directors pointed out to me, in reality, law firms work out all kinds of ways to accommodate new mothers. But to avoid having to deal with even the perception that you might leave, consider not wearing your engagement ring to the interview!

4. WHETHER YOU'RE A MAN OR A WOMAN, BE MINDFUL OF THE UNIFORMS IN DIFFERENT KINDS OF PRACTICE

As you know, it's possible to spend a couple of hundred dollars on a suit, and it's possible to spend a couple of thousand. Where you draw the line has as much to do with the kind of employers you're interviewing with as it does to the elasticity of your credit line. As Kathleen Brady points out, "On Wall Street, you need to wear the most expensive suit you can afford. But when you go to the D.A.'s office — drop the $800 Armani." So, be sensitive to the general wealth of the employer *and* the clients you'll be dealing with when you're deciding on what to wear to your interview!

5. NO MATTER WHAT YOU WEAR — BE COMFORTABLE!

No matter what the culture of the employer is or what you think the uniform ought to be, you *have* to wear something you're comfortable in. If you don't, your discomfort will show, and that's far worse than any wardrobe *faux pas* you could make. As Jose Bahamonde-Gonzalez points out, the worst thing to do is to show up for an interview thinking, 'I feel bad in this suit. I look like a grandmother. These flat shoes make my legs look fat." You should focus on how you're going to impress the interviewer with what you say and how you behave — not how you look! So dress within the realm of professionalism, but make *sure* you feel comfortable with what you're wearing!

6. THE "PURPLE SUIT" SYNDROME: IF YOU JUST CAN'T WEAR A PROFESSIONAL UNIFORM, THINK TWICE ABOUT THE IMPACT YOUR CLOTHES WILL HAVE ON THE INTERVIEWER

Maybe you pride yourself too much on your individualism to be able to give up your funky clothes for an interview. Maybe you'd sooner grow a third eye than wear a navy blue suit. Maybe you're so proud of your credentials and your savvy that you believe you can overcome any *outre* impression you create with your clothes. For instance, one career services director told me about a guy who insisted on matching his ties to his socks. If he wore red socks, he wore red ties. He refused to give up this practice for his legal interviews. Another career services director has a name for this; she calls it the "purple suit" syndrome, in honor of a female student who would wear a bright purple suit to interviews.

What the "purple suit" syndrome says is this: If you've got a flamboyant personality that's reflected by a purple suit, you may insist on wearing a purple suit on the grounds that if the employer doesn't like the purple suit, they won't like you. I'm not saying you'd be wrong to think this, or to match your ties to your socks, or, for that matter, your *hair* to your socks. Here's the thing: No matter how much of a world-beating personality you have, no matter how good your credentials are, if you don't wear the uniform there are employers who will reject you just on the basis of your wardrobe. Now I'm not talking about whether or not your suit is the right shade of navy, or whether your blouse is cream instead of white. I'm talking about big, loud *wardrobe statements.* Sexy dresses, fire-engine red fitted suits, spike heels, multicolored fingernails or hair, that kind of thing. If it doesn't bother you that certain employers will reject you out of hand, wear whatever the heck you like. But do me a favor: If you've got to dress this way, reconsider whether you actually want to work for a conservative legal employer in the *first* place. Perhaps you should consider working for a more liberal employer, someone who will appreciate and welcome your individuality!

C. THE NIGHT BEFORE YOUR INTERVIEW: THE FINAL TUNE-UP

The night before your interview, take time to just sit and *think*. That's right. Take a few minutes for yourself, and mentally prepare for the interview. Visualize yourself arriving with a confident, enthusiastic attitude. Review the answers to tough questions you're likely to face. Go over your infomercial. As Laura Rowe at George Washington points out, "Don't worry about sounding canned. You'll sound *comfortable*." And if you're comfortable, you'll interview well!

By the way, for whatever period of time you're interviewing make sure you keep up with current events — read the paper, or catch the news on the radio or TV. Why? Because interviewers inevitably break the ice by talking about what's going on in the real world. You'll sound like you've got tunnel vision, and you'll put the interviewer on edge, if you say something like, "I don't have time to keep up with what's going on." Remember, part of what you're trying to do is project the image that you're well-rounded, and knowing what's going on in the world around you is an excellent way to help prove that!

D. DON'T STUMBLE AT THE STARTING GATE: GET THERE ON TIME, WELL-ARMED, AND DON'T INSULT THE HELP!

It's almost show time. It's the day of your interview. There are really only three issues here: timing, what to bring, and how to handle the receptionist.

1. TIMING

This is both easy and obvious: *be on time*. Whether you're talking about an on-campus interview or an interview at the employer's office, or anywhere else, aim to be 5 minutes early. If the interview is at a place you're not familiar with, build in a cushion of time beforehand in case you run into traffic or get lost. *However*, if you get to the office more than 5 minutes early, wander around outside or walk around the block so that you'll be no more than 5 minutes early.

2. WHAT TO BRING

Again — this is really easy. Bring an extra copy of your résumé, your transcript, a copy of your writing sample, copies of any references you have, and a urine sample. Just kidding about that urine sample; I just wanted to see if you were paying attention. Anyway, bring everything (except the urine sample) even if you've sent a copy of all of these things ahead of time. It's easy for an employer to mislay papers, and you want to help them out of they've done that.

It's worth carrying everything in a slim, leather carry-all. Don't bring a backpack or book bag. Remember, the look you're aiming for here is professional. Don't remind the employer that you're a student!

Also, if you're going to the employer's office or any location other than school, pick up a copy of *The Wall Street Journal* and take it with you. I know this sounds like a petty thing, but look at it this way. If you're an employer and you show up late, what's going to impress you as being more professional — seeing an interviewee reading the *Journal,* or seeing them reading a tabloid with the headline *Boy Locked In Refrigerator Eats Own Foot?* You see my point? Also, if there's a particularly interesting story in the *Journal,* it'll give you something you might want to use to break the ice during the interview itself.

3. DON'T BE LULLED INTO A FALSE SENSE OF SECURITY BY THE RECEPTIONIST OR SECRETARY!

That sweet old blue-haired lady at the reception desk may be a wolf in disguise! I've heard countless stories, from hiring partners and career services directors alike, about students who were careless about how they came across to the interviewer's support staff . . . and paid the ultimate price of rejection *before the interview even began!* Don't you make that mistake! As Mary Obrzut warns, "Be conscious of the receptionist — even friendly questions may be meaningful. You have to assume that any answer to their questions will get back to the attorney you're interviewing with." So for instance, if you're sweetly asked whether you have children or where you live, assume that your answer is going straight to the interviewer. Similarly, as Amy Thompson warns, don't confess *anything* negative to the receptionist, like the fact that you really don't like this city, or you're only interviewing here because you have friends in town.

Also remember your *attitude*. The receptionist's opinion of you may carry great weight with the interviewer. As Tammy Willcox warns, "If you ignore the receptionist, you've shot yourself in the foot and you'll walk out of there bleeding! Attorneys rely on their secretaries *before* their associates!" On more than one occasion a student has lost a job opportunity because the receptionist rang the interviewer to say that the student was arrogant! So when it comes to receptionists and secretaries, follow Mary Obrzut's advice: "Be friendly — but be careful!"

E. SHOW TIME! THE SINGLE FACTOR THAT DETERMINES WHETHER OR NOT YOU'LL GET AN OFFER

There's only one factor that determines whether or not you'll get an offer, or in the case of a first interview, whether you'll be invited back for a second interview. And it's this. *Does the interviewer like you?* That's it. That's the touchstone of successful interviews, and it boils down to one simple rule:

People want to work with people they like.

I hope this doesn't come as a shock to you. You may have thought that you'll get the job if you convince the interviewer that you'll be a great employee. Well, sure; that's part of it. Convincing the interviewer that you can do the work is part of getting them to like the idea of working with you. But that's not really all that tough. Convincing the interviewer that you can do the work is something that most students can do, especially if you follow all of my advice about putting your job-related skills in the best possible light. No, here I'm talking about something much more subtle, much more elusive than that. I'm talking about the importance of personality. You can prove this to yourself with a simple test. Pretend *you're* the interviewer. You've interviewed approximately six kajillion law students, and you're pretty convinced that at least two-thirds of them can do the job. Who are you going to hire? The one you want to work with. And who's that going to be? *The one you like the best.* Pam Malone calls this the "3 a.m." test; that is, if it's 3 a.m. and you're still at the office, who are you going to want to be working with? Mary Obrzut uses a twist on this that she calls "JLM." That stands for "Just Like Me," and, as she says, "People look for someone Just Like Me. They're asking themselves — if we hire you, will you fit in?"

There are many facets to this "Just Like Me" principle. Maureen Provost Ryan points out, "People hire people they like, people in their own image, so they trust your judgment and what you'll do when they're not supervising you." Deanna Coe Kursh notes, "The stress and long hours at work are all minimized if you're working with someone you like."

Phew! Convinced yet? You should be. To add fuel to the fire, you should hear the statistics on how fast interviewers make a decision on you: *studies show that it's between 40 seconds and 4 minutes!* And that's because it's in those first few minutes that a personal rapport is forged, if it's going to be at all.

I know *exactly* what you're thinking right now. You're thinking, "Geez, she's been telling me all of this stuff I have to do to prepare for this stinking interview, and now she's telling me to forget about all that, because all that matters is all this yippy-skippy stuff about personal rapport and making friends. What is this? Mr. Rogers' neighborhood?" Well, you can resent it all you want, but it's true that you have to forge a rapport with the interviewer if you want to get the job. And you've got to do it *fast*. But the good news is — I'm going to tell you how to do just that!

1. HOW TO MAKE THE FIRST FEW MINUTES OF THE INTERVIEW WORK *FOR* YOU, NOT *AGAINST* YOU

Here's how to shoot out of the starting gate on sure footing. For one thing, if you've prepared yourself as I've advised you to, then you should be entering the interview with an air of self-confidence. You don't want to be arrogant, but you want to have the appearance of someone who knows what they're bringing to the table. And after all, you *do!* You've got all of your ducks in a row — you know everything you can about the employer and the interviewer, and you know yourself, what you're going to ask, and how you'll respond to any tough questions. There's no better start than that!

You want to shake the interviewer's hand firmly, greet them by name, make eye contact, smile, and let the interviewer lead the conversation. In the first couple of minutes, the interviewer will usually engage in some small talk to break the ice. *Go along with whatever the interviewer wants!* Whatever you do, don't get caught up in the idea that you've got to hit the ground running because you've only got 20 minutes or so to make your pitch. If you do that, you'll get nervous as every second ticks by, thinking that you're running out of time to explain why you're so qualified for the job. *Don't do it!* Let the interviewer talk themselves into liking you, first! If they bring up sports, or the weather, or something in the news, go along with it. Remember, I told you to keep up with current events for just this purpose!

So the key here is to let the interviewer talk themselves into liking you in the first couple of minutes. Follow their lead. It'll pay off!

2. THROUGHOUT THE INTERVIEW, BE *POSITIVE* IN YOUR WORDS AND YOUR BODY LANGUAGE. ENTHUSIASM COUNTS!

I've hammered you over and over again with the importance of displaying honest enthusiasm. Well, it's so important that I'm hammering you with it again, here. As Lisa Abrams says, "You're *really* ahead of the game if you show enthusiasm." Drusilla Bakert echoes that, saying, "You need to act like you're interested in getting the job. Employers always say they want *eagerness.*"

As Mary Obrzut points out, "Your entire attitude should exude, 'I know who you are and I want to be with you.'" Show an interest in everything the interviewer says. If the interviewer says something negative, don't be put off — *you* stay positive no matter what! If the employer suggests that you're going to have to work hard, smile and say that you're up to the job. As Gail Cutter points out, "You need to act as though you won't be fazed by hard work! You've got to be enthusiastic!" Convey in your tone of voice, the words you use, and your body language that *this* is the job you want. Sit up in your chair. Lean forward slightly. Don't rest your elbows on the table or desk between you and the interviewer, if there is one. Sit up straight, with your shoulders back. Don't cross your arms or hunch. Don't play with your hair, or tug at your clothes, or play with your jewelry, or fidget. (One interviewer even told me about a law student who casually tidied up the interviewer's desk during the interview!) And maintain eye contact in a comfortable way — staring at the interviewer is just as bad as constantly avoiding their gaze. Let everything about you say, "I know myself, I know you, and I want to work with you!"

You may also want to try a psychological tactic known as "mirroring." What happens when you "mirror" someone is that you pick up on the interviewer's body language, and mirror it yourself. Facial expressions, eye movements, speech rate, tone of voice, breathing rate . . . these are all things that are subject to "mirroring." If you think it sounds like too much to think about, you're wrong — mirroring is something that researchers have found that people do all the time in social situations, even though they might not be aware of it. If you *are* aware of mirroring, you can work it to your advantage in an interview situation. What it does is to create the subtle impression in the interviewer's mind that you and they are alike. And remember, that's exactly the kind of bonding that leads to great interviews!

You may be thinking that this sounds just hopelessly Pollyanna-esque and distasteful to you. Maybe the idea of showing your interest turns you off completely. There may be a couple of reasons for that distaste. One is that an aura of unattainability is attractive socially; we all know the allure of someone who's hard to get. Well, this is an interview, not a date. This is *not* the time to make the other person think you're not interested. You may also be put off by the idea of seeming enthusiastic because it puts you in a one-down position. That is, it's implicitly saying, "Interviewer, you have the power to give me something I want, and that makes you better than me." Well, let me share a little secret with you. That's absolutely true. The interviewer *does* have something you want, and you *will* have to show enthusiasm to get it. That's not to say that you shouldn't be confident in what you bring to the table, or that you shouldn't be a discerning interviewee — you should use the interview as an opportunity to decide which employer is right for you, as well. But the fact remains, you *are* at a social disadvantage because the interviewer *does* have something you want. If that bothers you — acknowledge it, get over it, and show that you want the job!

Remember, I started off this book telling you that honest enthusiasm is very hard for an employer to resist. Let it work for you!

3. REMEMBER THAT THIS IS A *SALES* PRESENTATION YOU'RE MAKING

Boy, if your stomach hasn't turned yet, I'll bet it did when you read those words "sales presentation." Well, that's exactly what an interview is. When you are interviewing, you have something to sell — yourself. As Illinois' Cindy Rold points out, "The biggest mistake students make is that they're just too modest." Don't fall into that trap. Sell yourself!

Think about the ramifications selling yourself has as to how you have to present yourself. It's just a spin on the idea of being positive. To make this clear, imagine yourself walking into a car showroom. You've got at least some vague notion that you want to buy a car, otherwise you wouldn't be there. You stroll over to one of the cars and a salesman walks up to you. You say, "Tell me about this car," and the salesman says, "Well, it's pretty good for getting around, but the gas mileage stinks." You'd look at that salesman as though they had lobsters crawling out of their ears, wouldn't you? Of course you would! And that's because *when you're buying something, you're also being sold something — and you'll only be sold on positives.* Instead, what the car salesman is going to tell you is, "This is a great car!" And they'll back that up with a description of its positive features.

Alternatively, you can think about the singles ads that populate all kinds of classified sections in newspaper and magazines. If you ever made a habit of reading these things, you'd probably get the feeling that the entire rest of the world is populated with men and women who are gorgeous, successful, smart, rich, and fun to be with. You know from your own personal experience that that's not true, but what these ads are doing is *selling.* When you're in an interview, you're doing the same thing, with yourself. When the interviewer asks you questions, give positive answers. Volunteer only positive information about yourself. As Marilyn Tucker points out, "Remember that the unspoken question on the floor throughout the interview is this: 'Why should I be interested in you rather than the next person?' Don't wait for them to *ask* that question before you *answer* it for them, by *showing* them why they should be interested in you!" Heck, you've done all of this preparation for your interview. You know everything about the employer that you can possibly know, and you've rehearsed your questions and answers out the wazoo. *None* of that matters unless you show it off to the interviewer. In short: Sell! Sell! Sell!

4. BE TRUE TO YOURSELF SO THAT YOUR PRESENTATION IS BELIEVABLE!

Having hammered home to you the importance of enthusiasm and selling yourself, it's equally important for you to be comfortable with your pitch. It doesn't matter how well you've researched the employer or rehearsed your questions and answers if what comes out sounds artificial and canned. You can't sound forced when you express enthusiasm. As Jose Bahamonde-Gonzalez puts it, "You can't put on a scam." Instead, when I talk to you about selling yourself, and showing enthusiasm, I'm encouraging you to bring the *very best qualities* of yourself out in the interview, to give you the greatest possible chance of getting a job offer. Presumably you're only interviewing in the first place because somewhere inside of you, you want this job. So showing enthusiasm is just a matter of bringing that desire bubbling to the surface so that the employer sees it. Maybe you're naturally a very outgoing, enthusiastic person. Maybe it takes you a little more effort to get psyched up and express enthusiasm. Whatever it takes, make sure that the pitch you're making is the best of what comes naturally to *you*. If you feel like you're being a fake, you won't be comfortable, and you won't interview well. So incorporate your research and your infomercial and your questions and answers into a patter that *you* can handle with ease.

5. REMEMBER THAT THE *INTERVIEWER* ISN'T PERFECT — HELP THEM OUT!

It's easy to get so wrapped up in preparing yourself for an interview that you forget that it's a living, breathing — and *flawed* — person who's doing the interviewing. Because they're in a position to give you something you want, you may cloak interviewers with god-like characteristics that they simply don't have. In fact, quite the opposite is sometimes true; as one career services director told me, "Most interviewers are *terrible!*" Another one said, a little more charitably, "Most interviewers aren't very good at it. They're normally only doing the interviewing because their arm was twisted." Remember, they're under a lot more pressure than you are. If *you* drop the ball and have a bad interview, your disappointment is confined to yourself. But if the *interviewer* drops the ball, makes the mistake, and invites a real clown back to the firm (or, even worse, makes an offer to one), then they have to bear the slings and arrows of all of their colleagues saying, "Where the heck did you find *this* idiot?" As Sandy Mans points out, "Attorneys who do interviewing are under *tremendous* pressure to find the right person!" So the downside risk *they* face in the interview is, in some ways, a lot worse than yours!

I don't expect your heart to bleed for interviewers. I only mention their situation by way of pointing out that you're probably going to have a few bad interviewers simply by dint of the fact that you're not being interviewed by professional interviewers.

What ramifications does that have for you? A few principal ones. For one thing, a bad interviewer will probably ask you some pretty stupid questions. In fact, some of the questions I characterize, later on in this chapter, as tough, really aren't so much tough as they are stupid in that they don't elicit any useful information from you. But it doesn't matter how stupid the questions seem to you; you have to answer them, and you have to do so with a respectful tone, without in any way suggesting that you're put off by the question.

Sometimes a terrible interviewer just won't have any idea of what an interview is supposed to do. They won't be prepared, and they won't have any idea how to conduct it. In that case, you've got to help them out. How? Well, ask them the questions you've prepared, focusing on the interviewer specifically, and asking about their job, what a typical day is like for them, how they chose that particular employer; all the kinds of questions that I recommend on page 342.

Or maybe the interviewer will drop the ball by simply not talking about the firm, or you, at all. One career services director told me about an interview where the interviewer spent the whole time talking about her wedding! What do you do? Well, look for any possible conversational opening, and relate it to your own agenda as best you can. Remember, you've memorized an infomercial, and you've got to look for any opportunity to bring up things you want the interviewer to remember. If you've got the wedding interviewer, and she's talking about how tough it is to find bridesmaids' dresses, you can sympathize, and say, "Gee, I can see where that would be tough. I've never been in that situation myself. I remember I had a problem when I was working for Judge Plotkin, and I had to find a particular case, and I only had a couple of hours to search for it. . . . " I know it's a stretch, but if the interviewer is a real stooge, you've got to do the best you can. Follow their lead to some extent, but remember your purpose, as well: you're trying to make yourself memorable!

Another possibility is that the interviewer, either by design or default, will make the job sound horrible. One career services director told me about an interviewer for the public utilities commission who made a job there sound just horrible — he made it seem mundane, boring, with absolutely nothing interesting to commend it. What do you do in *that* situation? What I've been advocating all the way through here — help him out! When the interviewer makes the job sound terrible, that may not be deliberate. So make the job sound more appetizing than the interviewer does. For instance, you can say that you look forward to the opportunity to see what the attorneys there do, that you'd like to see different writing styles. If you've done your research, you can always bring up *something* positive that you've heard about the employer. As this particular career services director told me, "It leaves a good taste in the interviewer's mouth if you make the position seem better than they do!"

Of course, there are myriad other ways in which an interviewer can be horrible. Toward the end of this chapter, I talk about how to handle stress interviews, where the interviewer is deliberately trying to put you on the spot. And there are countless other ways for interviewers to make your stomach churn. My advice? To the extent you possibly can, roll with the punches. If they're casual, you be casual. If they stray way off the track, bring up the points from your infomercial to the extent you possibly can, and leave it at that. If they're nervous, ask them friendly questions to set them at their ease. Remember, you've got the ultimate power, because you can *always* walk away; there's no employer that you *have* to work for. But before you do that, remember that, in many cases, if an interviewer seems incompetent, it's only because they're not a trained, professional interviewer, not because they really *are* incompetent. To the extent you can do so, give them a break. They'll appreciate it!

6. REMEMBER THAT THE BEST INTERVIEWS ARE GREAT *CONVERSATIONS*

Ideally, the interview will be a give-and-take between you and the employer. After all, if you wound up working together, that's what you'd do — talk back and forth to each other conversationally!

What ramifications does that have for you? Well, one is that you should go with the flow in an interview and not stick strictly to a rehearsed script. Sure, you'll have memorized the questions you intend to ask, and the answers you intend to give, but those *can't* be engraved in stone. If the interviewer says something that sparks your interest, follow up on it! And if the interviewer answers one of your questions while he's describing the employer, then delete that question from your list — otherwise, it'll be obvious that you're not paying attention, and you're too concerned about following a prearranged script!

The idea of a conversation also means that you shouldn't bring in a written list of questions for the interviewer, and you shouldn't take notes during the interview. In a real conversation, you'd pay attention to what the other person was saying, look at them while they talked, and do some of the talking yourself. That's *exactly* what you should do in an interview!

7. WIND-UP THE INTERVIEW ON AN "UP" NOTE!

Remember, the last thing the interviewer will recall about you is your goodbye, so make sure you finish up on an "up" note! Ask for a business card. If the interviewer doesn't have one, ask how their name is spelled, if you don't already know it from your research (you'll need it when you follow up). Ask when you'll be hearing from them. Smile, shake hands, and, as a parting line, you might try a variation on this theme: "I've really enjoyed meeting you, Mr. XYZ. Your practice sounds wonderful and I'd love to be a part of it." So what you've done is thanked the interviewer for the interview; mentioned their name (and use "Mr." or "Ms.," unless they've expressly told you to call them by their first name); and reiterated your interest in the job (assuming that, in fact, you still *are* interested in it!)

Later on in this chapter, I talk about how to follow up *after* an interview. I'll also cover how to deal with "postmortems" on interviews, but in a nutshell: don't do it. You can't always tell how an interview went, and the important thing to remember is, you only need *one* job, and if you follow my advice, then you've given every job opportunity your best shot. You can't do more than that, so put every interview — good *and* bad — behind you, and move on!

F. QUESTIONS YOU SHOULD ASK TO MAKE YOURSELF INTO THE IDEAL CANDIDATE

Aha! I'll bet when you think of questions in interviews, you think of things the interviewer will ask *you*. In fact, the questions you ask the interviewer are just as important — perhaps *more* important to whether you'll get an offer! As Sandy Mans points out, "The questions you ask give you a real opportunity to distinguish yourself."

If you ask questions intelligently — and I'm going to show you *exactly* how to do that — you'll accomplish three important things:

♦ You'll gather information about the firm.
This may seem pretty obvious, but students frequently overlook the role of the interview as an information-gathering opportunity. Debra Fink calls this being a "strategic interviewee."

♦ You'll forge a personal rapport with the interviewer.
Remember, I just told you how important it is to make a personal connection with the interviewer. Well, the questions you ask can help you do just that, if you ask about the interviewer's own personal experiences (which are my *favorite* kinds of questions to ask).

♦ You'll show off your research on the firm.
There's no point to doing a lot of research on your prospective employer unless you show off that knowledge in the interview, and asking questions that relate to your research helps you do just that. Interviewers find these kinds of questions *very* impressive. Why? Well, remember the power of honest enthusiasm. If you ask questions that stem from the research you did on the employer, you're implicitly indicating your desire to work for them. Asking questions based on research also shows that you "value your importance and that you're capable of making the right choice for you," according to Deanna Coe Kursh.

So intelligent question-posing is an *extremely* valuable interviewing skill, and that's what I'll teach you to do in this section. We'll discuss three principal topics: first, timing; second, great questions to ask; and third, awful questions to *avoid* asking.

1. TIMING: *WHEN* TO ASK QUESTIONS

This is an easy one. You should ask questions as often as possible, throughout the interview. As Debra Fink points out, "If it gets to 5 minutes before the end of the interview, and the interviewer asks, 'Do you have any questions for me?' it's too late!"

Now, obviously you're going to have to follow the interviewer's lead in this, and if you get an interviewer who rattles on incessantly without giving you an opportunity to speak, that's a real problem.

Just do your best to squeeze in questions without seeming as though you're trying to take control of the interview.

The other end of the spectrum — where the interviewer is constantly firing questions at you — is easier to handle. All you have to do is follow up your answers to questions with related questions of your own. For instance, if the interviewer asks, "Why do you want to work for us?," you can answer, and then immediately follow up with, "What made *you* choose the firm?" That takes the heat off of you, and gives you valuable insight into the firm *and* the interviewer.

2. QUESTIONS THAT WILL MAKE YOU INTO THE PERFECT INTERVIEWEE

OK, here they are. What I've done is to lump the questions you ought to ask into five categories. They are:

- ♦ Personalized questions designed to evoke an emotional response from the interviewer (the *very best kind* of interview question, by far!).
- ♦ Questions that show off your research into the firm and the interviewer.
- ♦ Carefully-worded questions about what your own job experience at the firm would be like (and I emphasize *carefully worded,* because you should ask very few of this kind of question).
- ♦ Questions that depend on the size of the law firm and the age of the interviewer.
- ♦ Questions involving awkward 600-lb. gorillas — that is, bad news and scandals.

Before we get into these in detail, I want to warn you about a couple of things. One of them is this: I'm going to give you the questions that will impress the *vast majority* of interviewers. It would be *impossible* to include *every* interviewer in that category, because you might run into some real outliers. As Susan Benson points out, "Certain interviewers dislike *any* particular question, even *good* questions!" So if you start asking a certain kind of question and you can see from the interviewer's response and body language that they aren't responding favorably, don't forge ahead; instead, ask a different kind of question. For instance, virtually everybody responds favorably to personalized questions. But let's say you've got a real sourpuss who just doesn't want to talk about what they do (that in and of itself tells you something valuable about what they, or their job, must be like!). In that case, you'd back off and ask questions about the firm that you've developed as a result of your research.

My second warning to you comes courtesy of Diane Reynolds, who says that you should make sure that your questions don't sound canned or rehearsed. Of course, they *are* canned and rehearsed, and to be a confident interviewee, they *have* to be! But they shouldn't *sound* that way. Be sure that you ask questions in an enthusiastic tone of voice, and the look on your face should suggest that you are eagerly awaiting the interviewer's response. You want to create the impression that you've never asked these questions before, even if you've asked them of 20 other interviewers. This shouldn't actually be very difficult in light of the kinds of questions I want you to ask. Because they focus on the interviewer's own personal experiences, you really *are* asking fresh questions every time, because every interviewer's experiences will be unique. But the warning remains: don't let your questions sound rehearsed. Inject them with enthusiasm!

With those warnings in mind, let's take a look at the kinds of questions you ought to ask during your interviews.

A. THE HANDS-DOWN BEST KIND OF INTERVIEW QUESTION TO ASK: PERSONALIZED QUESTIONS DESIGNED TO EVOKE AN EMOTIONAL RESPONSE FROM THE INTERVIEWER

When I say "emotional response," I'm not suggesting that you turn into Barbara Walters and try to get the interviewer to cry. Instead, these are warm, human questions that go to the personal aspects of the job — the kinds of things that contribute heavily to job satisfaction. Why am I such a big fan of these kinds of questions? For one thing, they'll help you forge a rapport with the interviewer. And for another, these are really the kinds of things you *ought* to be focusing on when you're looking at potential employers, namely, what's it really like to work there, day in and day out? The former *Washington Post* editor Ben Bradlee has said that the purpose of biography is to answer one, simple question: *What was he like?* Well, the purpose of the questions I'm giving you here is similar: *What is it like?* Specifically, what's it like to work for this particular employer? That simple, underlying question determines whether or not this job *really is* your dream job!

Now these questions are slanted somewhat in favor of the typical interviewer, who is someone who's not very senior with the organization; for instance, in a firm, it'll typically be a junior or mid-level associate. With that in mind, here are the kinds of questions you should ask:

- You seem to like your job. How did you choose it?
- What kinds of cases are you working on?
- What's a typical day like for you? (Remember, most initial interviewers are young associates, so what they do is probably what you'd get to do if you worked there.)
- Did you clerk here?
- How is your job different than what you expected it to be?
- What do you wish you'd asked when you interviewed here? (Or a variation on that, like "What do you wish you'd known before you got here?")
- What do you like about your job?
- What's the best thing that's happened to you working here?
- If you were to stay for 20 years, why would you stay? (Or, alternatively — and be careful how you put this across, because you don't want to seem negative! – "If there were anything at all that would make you leave, what would it be?")
- If you could change anything about your job, would you? If so, what would it be? (Be careful — you don't want this to come across as a negative question.)
- What's the most interesting case you've worked on?
- What have you learned as a result of working here?
- How long were you at the firm before you had significant client contact?
- Did you start off in your current practice area? If not, why did you switch?
- What do you find most challenging about being a lawyer?

You can imagine how questions like these will warm up even the most cold-hearted interviewer. As Michigan's Nancy Krieger points out, "People love to talk about themselves. It also takes the pressure off of you, as an interviewee!" These questions serve the dual purpose of showing your interest in the interviewer, as well as gaining valuable insights into how the employer operates, and what you can expect if you work there.

A couple of warnings. First, to reiterate what I warned you about earlier, don't make these questions sound memorized (although, of course, they are). Make them sound natural. Smile as you ask them. Also, don't ask them in order; pay attention to what the interviewer says in response, and see where those answers lead you.

B. QUESTIONS THAT SHOW OFF YOUR RESEARCH INTO THE FIRM AND THE INTERVIEWER

Remember all that homework I made you do? Talking to people about the employer, and going on-line on Lexis and Westlaw, and reading Martindale-Hubbell, and any current articles you can dig up on the firm, and all of that? Well, you may find that your research unearths wonderful questions — and remember, a large part of the reason you do that research in the first place is so that you can show it off to the interviewer!

What kinds of questions should you ask? Well, as Sophie Sparrow suggests, "You can ask anything that's thoughtful and shows your research. For instance, 'I see you've done a lot of mergers and acquisitions work. Will that continue?'" Or, as Amy Thompson suggests, "I read that you represented so-and-so. Do you do a lot of that kind of work?" She also points out that you can ask questions that tie the employer's practice to current events. For instance, you can ask how they're prepping clients for a new law, or how they're handling a merger one of their clients is involved in. Diane Reynolds points out that "Good questions show that you know the firm, and can translate that into a personal concern. For example, what if the firm just added an environmental law department? You can ask how they made that decision, and whether there are other specialties they intend to add, and how they see the environmental law department expanding in future."

You can also show through your questions that you spoke with *people* about the firm. As Debra Fink points out, "If you found someone who's worked there before, and asked them what they did, you can use that in the interview! Say to the interviewer, "So-and-so said he did this when he clerked for you. That's exactly the kind of thing I want to do. Will I get a chance to do it? Employers are always impressed if you've sought out someone who's worked for them!"

As you can see, these questions not only indicate you've researched the firm, but they should also elicit interesting responses. They also show that your questions don't have to be profound; just think about what you learn about the firm as you research, and ask the questions that spring to your mind as a result of what you learn.

That doesn't, however, mean that *anything* you discover about a firm is fertile grounds for questions. Questions with a negative tone are dangerous (as I discuss below, in "Questions Involving Awkward 600-lb. Gorillas" and "Questions You Should Avoid like a Pit Viper.") Also, don't ask about topics you don't have the sophistication to discuss. For instance, one career services director told me about a student who asked an interviewer, "So, I see that you were head of the licensing executive council." The student had no idea what that was; he had just dug that tidbit up in his research. As the interviewer told the career services director after the interview, "There was no way to have a meaningful conversation with this student about it, so there was no point in him asking it!" If you *do* want to ask about something like this, find a way to bring it back to your level. For instance, in that particular situation you could ask, "Did you start out in professional associations from the beginning of your practice?" *That* question would tell you something you could use, *and* it shows you researched the interviewer!

C. CAREFULLY-WORDED QUESTIONS ABOUT WHAT YOUR OWN JOB EXPERIENCE AT THE FIRM WOULD BE LIKE

"Carefully-worded" are the key words here, because this kind of question is dangerous. Why? Well, remember that one of my basic tenets of job searches in the first place is that employers hire you based on what you can do for *them*, not what they can do for *you*. So any questions that involve what's in it for you have to be broached carefully so that they don't leave a bad impression on the interviewer.

Having said that, of course there *are* things about what you an expect from the job that you have a *right* to know, and if you skirted this area entirely, the interviewer would probably think that was kind of strange. For instance, it's fine to ask questions like:

+ Who'll assign my work? (If that's not obvious from the firm's literature.)
+ What will a typical day be like for me?
+ Will I get feedback on my work?
+ What kinds of cases will I work on?
+ What kind of work will I do?
+ How does someone become a star — what makes them stand out?

If your résumé preceded you into the interview, you can also ask:

+ What was it about my résumé that got me this interview?

The key here is that although these questions focus on what's in it for you, they suggest that you're sufficiently interested in the job that you *want* to know what the job will be like. If you weren't *at all* curious about it, the interviewer would question your desire!

Having said that, before you consider asking *any* questions about what your experience will be like, *please* read the section below, entitled "Questions You Should Avoid like a Pit Viper." Self-centered questions, unless they're worded carefully, are ones you shouldn't ask!

D. QUESTIONS THAT DEPEND ON THE SIZE OF THE LAW FIRM, AND THE AGE OF THE INTERVIEWER

There are certain questions that are dependent on the size of the firm you're interviewing with, and the age of the interviewer. If you ask inappropriate questions based on either of these factors, it'll seem as though your questions are canned and you really haven't given this particular employer much thought — both of which are pretty bad boo-boos. Here's how to avoid making those kinds of mistakes.

1. QUESTIONS TO ASK DEPENDING ON THE SIZE OF THE EMPLOYER

There are some questions that are size-related. For instance, as Laura Rowe points out, "For a large firm, you'd ask if there are mentors? How often you get evaluated? Who decides your 'to do' list?" and that kind of thing.

For a small employer — and remember, there are many more small employers than large ones — you need to show an entrepreneurial spirit. As Debra Fink points out, "Show that you can *learn,* as well as produce work they can use. Ask things like whether you'll be able to discuss issues with lawyers. Whether you'll be able to sit in on depositions. In other words, show that you want to get more out of the job without taking up their time." Furthermore, it's appropriate to ask about how quickly you'd be expected to take part in client development when you interview with a small firm, whereas with a large firm that might seem a little odd coming from a law student or new graduate. However, with small employers, avoid the institutional questions that would be appropriate for something larger. For instance, questions about rotations through different departments just aren't relevant for smaller employers, who don't have such a formalized structure!

2. QUESTIONS TO ASK DEPENDING ON THE AGE OF THE INTERVIEWER

I've already tipped my hand on this one, by mentioning in the ideal question list that first time interviewers will tend to be close to your peer group. The point is this: If you're interviewing with someone who's been with the employer for less than 4 years or so, the "What's your routine day?" question is more appropriate than it would be for a senior partner at the firm. Also, asking a senior partner why he chose this particular employer will not be terribly intelligent if he founded the partnership! So be mindful of the age of your audience and tailor your questions accordingly.

The flip side of this is that there *are* questions that you should ask of senior partners that wouldn't be appropriate for junior associates. Questions like:

- How has the practice changed over the last 5 years?
- How have your clients' needs changes over the last 5 years?
- Where do you see the partnership heading in the next 5 years?

Senior partners have the perspective to answer these kinds of questions, and asking them reflects well on you! Why? As Maureen Provost Ryan points out, "These kinds of questions show that you are thinking beyond your nose — you're thinking like a partner. You're tapping into the interviewer's own sense of the firm." And that's a real plus!

E. QUESTIONS INVOLVING AWKWARD 600-LB. GORILLAS — THAT IS, BAD NEWS AND SCANDALS

What I'm talking about here are situations where you interview with an employer who's in the news — and not for a *good* reason. For instance, one of the senior partners was involved in a sordid sex, drug-related, or murder scandal. Or some of the senior partners have just broken away and started a rival law firm. The story is splashed all over the newspapers, and the interviewer knows that *you* know about it, because anyone who hasn't been under a rock for the last few months would *have* to know about it. Well, that story is a 600-lb. gorilla, because both you and the interviewer are painfully aware of it. The dilemma I'm dealing with here is this: do you bring it up? And if so, how?

Interestingly enough, the career services directors I spoke with about this all said that when these situations arise, interviewees *don't* ask about them — *and that shocks the interviewers, who are girded and ready to respond!* As Nancy Krieger points out, "If a partner is involved in a scandal, the interviewer will *expect* you to ask about it! You can ask, for instance, how it's effecting clients." Of course you're not going to ask the interviewer to dish the dirty details, but from a professional standpoint, it would be kind of strange if you *didn't* want to know about something that was impacting the firm in such a major way! Diane Reynolds echoes that, recounting a situation where a large local firm was all over the papers because of an acrimonious split in the firm. The firm conducted on-campus interviews, and nobody asked about it. As she points out, "They *should* have asked, 'How has morale been affected by the split?'"

Of course, it's important to be sensitive when you're dealing with 600-lb. gorillas like these. But if you *don't* ask about them, the interviewer's going to call into question both your judgment and desire to work for the firm. After all, with scandals like these, the future of the employer may hang in the balance, and that would have a *significant* impact on your decision to work there!

So be careful in how you ask about scandals — but be sure that you *do* ask!

3. Questions You Should *Avoid* Like a Pit Viper!

The traditional advice on asking questions in interviews is just to "sit and think about what you really want to know, and ask it." That is simply *awful* advice! Just as you can make yourself into the ideal candidate by the questions you ask, you can drum yourself out of an offer by asking the *wrong* questions! I'm going to give you a whole list of questions that you should *never, ever ask on an interview*. Some of these may seem obvious to you; others will not.

The real trap here? *Many of these questions are things you really, really want to know!*

What I've done is to separate the pit viper questions into six categories. We'll talk about:

+ The "What's-in-it-for-me?" questions.
+ Questions with a negative tone.
+ "Imponderables."
+ Any question you could have answered yourself through simple research.
+ Any question that shows you're clueless about what you've already covered in the interview.
+ The worst question boner of all: not having any questions.

Let's take a look at each of these in detail.

A. Any Questions That Have a "What's-in-it-for-me?" Flavor

Don't ask *any* of these questions on an interview:

- What are the hours? (It indicates an unwillingness to work long hours.)
- What's expected of me?
- Tell me about your pro bono program.
- What billable hours do you expect?
- What's the benefits package like?
- How much vacation time will I get?
- What's the salary?
- What kind of secretarial support will I get?
- How many people besides me are you hiring (or interviewing)?
- How long is the partnership track here?
- What's your policy on maternity leave?

Why are these "What's-in-it-for-me?" questions so poisonous? *Because nobody cares about you, that's why.* Remember, the employer only wants to know what's in it for *them*, how you're going to make money for *them*, and that's what you've got to convey in order to get a call back or an offer. I'm not saying that the answers to these questions aren't important; they are. But they won't help get you a job, and that's the point of the interview! Anyway, you can find out all of the hours, salary, and benefits scuttlebutt from your research, by talking with your career services counselor, and looking at published sources. It's also fine to ask about salary, benefits, and the like, *after* you've gotten an offer. But you've got to *get* to that point, first, and that's what *my* concern is!

B. QUESTIONS WITH A NEGATIVE TONE

Remember — the interviewer isn't on trial. If anyone is, *you* are! So, don't ask questions like:

- I've heard rumors about your firm. Are you not doing well?
- What *don't* you like about the firm?
- How many minority (or female) attorneys do you have? (When asked in a belligerent manner. It's possible to ask this benignly, or, better yet, find out in your research so you don't have to ask it at the interview at all.)

♦   How does your firm compare to X firm?

These questions have a challenging, belligerent undertone which will turn off the interviewer. Remember, you succeed in an interview by getting the interviewer to *like* you. Alienating them doesn't help your cause!

C. "IMPONDERABLES"

These are questions that might sound good when you're thinking about them at home, but they're simply unanswerable. The two principal questions of this type are:

♦   What's the culture of the firm?

♦   What's the firm atmosphere?

As Sandy Mans points out, "How does the interviewer explain this? Anyway, it's something you can pick up for yourself if you get called back for an office interview, by looking for things like interaction between attorneys and support staff, and whether anybody's still there after 5 o'clock, or whether they leave as soon as possible."

So be sure that you only ask questions capable of meaningful responses. Otherwise you'll be putting the interviewer on the spot, and that's a no-no!

D. ANY QUESTION YOU COULD HAVE ANSWERED YOURSELF THROUGH SIMPLE RESEARCH

I encourage you to avoid any question whose answer you could have gotten through reading the firm brochure, or Martindale-Hubbell, or the NALP employer form, like:

♦   How many attorneys do you have?

♦   What are your practice areas?

♦   In which cities do you have offices?

Also — and this is a little more controversial – I would avoid questions that are essentially meaningless to whether or not you'd choose to work for the employer. By this I mean things like asking about how many people review you, and asking about how the clerks rotate through departments. Be honest now: are you really going to make a job decision based on the answer to questions like these? They're not interesting, they're not meaningful, and they won't help forge a bond with the interviewer, so they're not likely to result in a call-back interview or an offer. Furthermore, they sound canned and stuffy. So I'd ignore them in favor of the meaty stuff.

E. ANY QUESTION SHOWING YOU'RE CLUELESS ABOUT WHAT YOU'VE ALREADY COVERED IN THE INTERVIEW

Pam Malone sums this up by saying: "Don't be brain dead!" Don't indicate to the interviewer that you've tuned out by asking something they've already covered in the interview. All *that* shows is that you're operating by rote, and you're not really paying attention to anything they're saying. *That's not a good way to make a good impression!*

If this happens to you, it's probably because you were very nervous about the interview, and memorized a list of questions, in order. Remember it's important to keep your questions fluid, just as it's important to tailor your infomercial to the needs of the particular employer. So go in with a list of questions, but make sure you listen — *really* listen — so you can delete any questions the interviewer has already answered.

F. THE WORST POSSIBLE QUESTION BONER: NOT HAVING ANY QUESTIONS AT ALL!

Here's the situation. The interviewer asks, "Do you have any questions for me?" and you respond casually, "Oh, no. I think you've answered everything." As Jose Bahamonde-Gonzalez points out, "Asking questions is a chance to convey how interested you are in the job!" Lisa Abrams adds, "It doesn't matter if you've interviewed with five different lawyers at the same firm. You can ask the same questions of everyone. Whatever you do, don't *ever* say 'All of my questions have been answered.'"

Especially given the kinds of questions I've given you, there's no reason *ever* to run out of questions for an interviewer. If you ask the kinds of personalized questions that I love so much, you'll never get the same answer from any two attorneys, and there's no reason why you can't ask them of *every* interviewer. So don't *ever* fall into the trap of having no questions for the interviewer!

G. KILLER ANSWERS TO THE TOUGHEST INTERVIEW QUESTIONS THEY'LL EVER ASK YOU (AND BONER ANSWERS TO AVOID, AS WELL!)

Don't let the name of this section mislead you! By that I mean that if you do as I advise you in this section, *there really isn't any such thing as a tough interview question!*

That's right. If you're prepared for the curves interviewers might throw you, you can formulate ahead of time the way you'll answer, and you'll defang those questions as a result. You'll come across as confident, self-assured, and self-aware — all very desirable traits indeed!

What I'm going to do in this section is to take you through a list of the most difficult questions you're likely to face. I'll tell you how to go about formulating an answer for them, and I'll tell you answers to avoid. I'm going to give you some humorous responses, as well. Now I'm not suggesting that you answer every tough question with a joke, because you'll probably annoy the interviewer. But being aware of humorous responses helps you relax during the interview, and if you follow up a joke response with a "real" one, you'll be able to defuse what might otherwise be a tense situation.

Before we get into the specific list of questions, there are a few overall pointers I want you to remember.

1. GENERAL STRATEGIES FOR HANDLING TOUGH QUESTIONS

A. REMEMBER THE PURPOSE OF TOUGH QUESTIONS!

When an interviewer puts you on the spot by asking "Tell me about yourself," or "Why weren't your grades better?," or "Why did you go to school in X city if you want to work for my firm in Y city?," they're doing something much more than eliciting information from you. *They're testing you to see how you handle yourself under pressure.* The question that's behind all of these questions is: Can you play the game? Do you have good judgment? Do you have *savoir faire?* When an interviewer asks you a difficult question, your first instinct might be to crumble like cheap luggage. Don't do it! Take a deep breath, take a moment if you need it, respond quickly, and move on. The point is: *the* way *you answer tough questions is far more important than* what you say!

B. FOR ANY TOUGH QUESTIONS, FOLLOW THIS STRATEGY: RESPOND AND REDIRECT

That's courtesy of Debra Fink. She says, "For tough questions, it's important to stop with a short answer, and then turn it around with a related question to get you off the hot seat. For instance, if the interviewer asks you, 'Tell me about yourself?' give a short answer (remember your infomercial!), and then stop. Then ask, 'Is that the kind of background you're looking for?'" You can see that by following this strategy, you won't get mired in what Debra Fink calls the "babble factor," where you waste precious minutes in your 20-minute interview trying to dig yourself out of a hole.

C. ALWAYS END ANSWERS TO TOUGH QUESTIONS ON A POSITIVE NOTE!

You should leave every answer on a positive note. Sandy Mans gives the example of the answer to the "Why didn't you get better grades?" question — she says, "You end an answer to that question with a statement something like, 'I've done particularly well in . . . ' and then pick courses that will be of interest to the employer." If you just don't have any good grades, then you pick some job experience or extracurricular project in which you shined. The point is, "Don't dwell on negatives!" as Laura Rowe says. "Just answer — boom! — and move on!"

D. DON'T BE DEFENSIVE!

I've told you this before, but it's worth reiterating in the context of tough questions, because it's in answer to tough questions that you're most likely to *be* defensive. Remember — the interviewer has the right to ask you anything they want to ask you. Not only *that*, but they may not even realize how bad some of these questions are. The people that law firms send to do interviews are not, after all, professional interviewers; they're typically as lost as you are. They may not be intending to put you on the spot. So keep your cool, answer as best you can, and move on!

E. REMEMBER THE IMPORTANCE OF GEOGRAPHY

Every career services director I spoke with stressed that geography is the "silent killer." That is, most students don't realize its importance, and it torpedoes their chances of getting the job.

When I talk about the importance of geography, here's what I mean: Find every opportunity to stress your commitment to the city where the employer is located, its legal community, and your intention to remain there, permanently. The biggest hidden fear of many employers is that they'll go to the expense of training you, and then you'll take off before they can earn back their investment in you. As a rule of thumb, you have to work for an employer for *3 years* before they've broken even on you. If you're not even committed to being in the city where they're located, you're not exactly an intelligent risk as an employee, are you? So, if you're not either (a) from the city in question, or (b) going to school in the city in question, be *sure* that you lace your interview answers with your commitment to staying there, permanently.

F. BE SURE YOU SOUND AUTHENTIC

Jose Bahamonde-Gonzalez stresses the importance of making everything you say sound as though you mean it.

This means that it's *very* important that you *not* memorize the answers I suggest below for tough questions — all they're meant to be are guidelines for creating your own, original answers. If you parrot answers someone else has created for you, you'll sound fake, and the interviewer will wonder who you really are. Instead, think over these answers, at the very least reword them, and make sure that you believe in them.

OK — let's take a deep breath, and plunge into the questions themselves!

2. TOUGH INTERVIEW QUESTIONS: WONDERFUL ANSWERS (AND HORRIBLE ANSWERS, TOO!)

Here they are: the most difficult, most common interview questions you're likely to come up against. I'll go through the questions with you, and explain the motivation behind asking them in the first place. Then I'll give you all kinds of examples of great answers, as well as answers you should avoid.

A. *"TELL ME ABOUT YOURSELF"*

The Queen Mother of tough questions — but if you're prepared, it's a real softball! As Amy Thompson says, "Interviewers love this question because it's an easy way to separate the people who are prepped from the ones who *aren't.*" And you and I both know which category *you* fall into, right? That's why this question won't faze you at all!

1. THE BEST WAY TO RESPOND

Give 'em your infomercial! Remember when I told you to prepare a brief "pitch" of your best three to five job-related skills, examples that show you have those skills, and a personal accomplishment? This is exactly the way to respond to a "Tell me about yourself" question.

What the interviewer is really asking when they ask this question is, "Tell me things about yourself that will make me want to hire you." If you reword it this way, you can see that there are two things that you have to do: You have to stress the fact that you can do the work, and you have to add a personal element to come across as the kind of person they'll *enjoy* working with. As Deanna Coe Kursh says, "When an interviewer asks you this, they're looking for a full dimension. Give the interviewer a chance to *like* you. Make sure you show you're a *person.*"

And be sure that you tailor your infomercial to the interviewer. Remember, I told you to keep your infomercial flexible for just this reason! So, for instance, as Lisa Kellogg points out, "If the interviewer practices environmental law, mention that you're involved with the environmental law group at school." The key here? Remember your audience, and make yourself attractive to *them.*

Needless to say, this is not the time to be bashful or modest. As soon as the question is asked, smile and plunge into your pitch. "Well, I'm a hard worker. During first year, I worked 30 hours a week as a clerk for the Ignatz Dangle law firm. It was a lot to juggle, but I learned how to manage my time well, and I was exposed to many different kinds of law at the firm. I wouldn't have traded the experience for anything! . . . "

You *can* give some of your history, but remember, the history you give should be related to law. So if you talk about college, talk about what it is that led you to where you are now.

2. BONERS TO AVOID

A. THIS ISN'T YOUR UNCLE FRED — DON'T GET INTO FAMILY HISTORY!

There's a temptation to answer "Tell me about yourself" by starting with where you were born. As Laura Rowe points out, "Don't start at birth!" Mary Obrzut agrees. "The interviewer doesn't care about your family or where you were born. So don't spill your guts! Remember, the interviewer's only concerned with one thing — what's in it for them?"

B. DON'T BE BORING!

One of the reasons I suggest including a personal accomplishment in your "tell me about yourself" info-mercial spiel is that it adds excitement to your answer. Some of the job search books I've seen advise you to come up with a very businesslike monologue about yourself, which you recite in interviews. Many career services directors think that's a *big* mistake. For instance, Pam Malone says that "'Tell me about yourself' is an opportunity to sell yourself as a *person*. Lift yourself *beyond* your paper credentials. Mention what you *do* with your spare time!"

Speak with enthusiasm, smile, and remember: you want to encourage the interviewer to *want* to work with you. And nobody wants to work with a bore!

C. DON'T BE APOLOGETIC ABOUT YOUR CREDENTIALS!

I know, I know, I've mentioned this before. Well, I'm going to go *on* mentioning it because the question "Tell me about yourself" is one that tends to encourage law students to step into the confessional, and start apologizing for their weaknesses. *Don't do it!* Remember, this question is your single biggest selling opportunity in the entire interview. Use the car showroom analogy: When you walk into a car showroom, both you and the salesman know that the cars you're looking at aren't perfect. But they'll sell you with the *positive* points about the car. You have to do the same thing when you answer this question: give them reasons *to* hire you — not reasons why they shouldn't!

D. DON'T STUMBLE OR DRONE ON ... AND ON ... AND ON ...

If you've prepared yourself for this questions, stumbling around really isn't a problem. As Teresa DeAndrado says, "The most common mistake students make is to stumble around and say, 'I'm a second year student, I'm taking these classes. . . . '" Wrong! Make your points about yourself and move on!

E. DON'T EXPOSE A WEAKNESS!

If you're prepared, this won't happen. But if you *aren't,* you could easily goof and confess a negative about yourself! As Amy Thompson says, "Don't let an open-ended question like this lure you into exposing something like, 'I'm moving here because my boy-friend's moving here,' or 'I only want to do this for now; my long term goal is . . . ,' or anything like that."

B. "WHAT ARE YOUR WEAKNESSES?"

This is the question where unwary interviewees go to die.
Of all of the questions that I asked career services directors, this was the most controversial. And it's easy to see why; there are so many elements competing within it. On the one hand, there's the value of honesty. But if your biggest weakness is your writing ability, or that you're lazy, or you think you're not too quick on the uptake, *you'd be a complete idiot to tell the truth!*
Instead, you have to look at this question as the ultimate in interview game-playing. What the interviewer is really asking you is, "Are you savvy enough to come up with an answer that doesn't torpedo you as a candidate for this job — but sounds credible at the same time?" Stated another way – "*How well can*

you play this interviewing game?" "What are your weaknesses?" is a lot easier to deal with if you look at it this way!

By the way — everybody *knows* that this is a rotten question. You can't answer it honestly and expect to look good. So why do they ask it? As Columbia's Ellen Wayne explains, "Because once in a rare while a student will be honest and get tripped up; for instance, saying 'My writing skill isn't the best.' And the interviewer's mind will immediately go to that brief he's got to get out today. So it's a trap for the unwary!"

1. THE BEST WAY TO RESPOND

OK, the all time *best* response to this comes from William & Mary's Rob Kaplan, who found it in a comic strip. The interviewer says, "What's your biggest flaw?" and the interviewee responds, "Lying in interviews." I *love* that, and it wouldn't hurt to lead off with it and then follow up with a more serious answer (if the interviewer isn't happy with the joke!). And for a *real* answer, the best response I heard from career services directors was this:

Highlight a past negative that you've corrected.

Kathleen Brady gives this as an example: "Meeting deadlines. I never used to be able to do it. I did a lot of time management courses, and now I haven't missed any deadlines in law school." Another excellent possibility, courtesy of Maureen Provost Ryan and Sandy Mans, is "Shyness. I'm naturally shy. But I took steps to overcome it. I took on leadership positions while I was in college which forced me to do a lot of public speaking, and I joined the Debate Club, and I think I've licked it." A great advantage to the "shyness" idea, if it fits you, is that your very demeanor in the interview can bolster how well you've overcome it! Deanna Coe Kursh suggests a similar one — public speaking. "I'm not a naturally gifted public speaker, but I recognize it and I get all the practice that I can so that I can kick it." And Amy Thompson volunteers this one: "I used to never be able to say 'no' to any project. In law school, I learned that between classes, and Moot court, and softball, I can't do everything. I can still do a lot, but I've learned to set priorities so that I don't drive myself crazy."

I don't mean to sound as though a past negative that you've corrected is your *only* option, it's just that I think it's your *best* one. Why is that? Well, you're answering the question honestly — they're asking for a weakness, and you're giving them a weakness. . . . It just so happens that you've kicked it, that's all. You've answered it *intelligently*, because a problem that you've overcome certainly isn't going to harm your job chances; if anything, it will give you the added luster of being a strong problem-solver. And finally, it smacks of credibility, and I've already stressed the importance of sounding authentic.

So what are your *other* options for approaches to answering the "weaknesses" question? Well, you *could* use humor, like the "lying in interviews" gag. As Debra Fink says, "My favorite answer to this question is, 'Chocolate. That's my weakness.'" She also says, "Company picnics. I just can't play softball!" If you've got the kind of personality that can pull it off, humor can work for you. But remember, always have a more sober-sided answer to follow up.

You could also use this answer to show your comfort level with your credentials. For instance, if you've got really bad grades, or you're just not happy with them, when you're asked what your weakness is, you can always smile and respond, "My grades!" Then you can explain, quickly, other experiences you've had that undercut your grades as a weakness — that is, job experience that shows you're competent, or specific classes you've excelled in. Or, as Sophie Sparrow points out, you can say, "I haven't done as well as I wanted to, so I've been working with this professor to correct that." Remember, you're not apologizing — but if you can confidently say your grades are your weakness, briefly explain, and then quickly move on, you'll impress the interviewer with your honesty *and* your confidence.

As Lisa Kellogg points out, another weakness you can address is that you don't have as much job experience as you'd like — but clearly by looking for a job you're trying to remedy that. And you can even joke that with the interviewer's help, you can overcome what you perceive as your weakness!

You could also use a weakness the interviewer has already brought up. For instance, if the interviewer has already pointed out your grades or lack of experience or lack of paper classes or your lack of connections with the city where his firm is located, he's dropped the answer to your "greatest weakness" squarely in your lap! You can just say, "As you've already pointed out, a weakness for me is . . . ," reiterate whatever the flaw is, and then explain what you've done (or what you're doing) to ameliorate it. That way, you're not exposing *another* flaw when you've already got one you can use!

By the way, I should tell you that the standard advice on handling this question is to turn a negative into a positive; that is, to state a weakness that's really not a weakness at all. The classic response is, "I'm a workaholic. I just don't know when to stop working." Or "I don't go home until everything gets done." Or "I'm a perfectionist." Even though a lot of people will tell you to use this approach, I think it smells. As Deanna Coe Kursh points out, "It's self-serving and it doesn't sound very honest. It would give you a big credibility problem with the interviewer." And as the Dilbert cartoon on page 365 shows, savvy interviewers won't fall for it.

Anyway, when you've got such great alternatives at your disposal, why risk alienating the interviewer this way?

2. BONERS TO AVOID

Boy, there are a *million* land mines with this question. Let's go through the things you should avoid:

A. *ANY* JOB-RELATED SKILL

Don't be an *idiot* and offer as a weakness anything even remotely like the following:

"I don't like research."
"I'm bored with law school."
"I can't write worth a damn." (At best, as Deanna Coe Kursh points out, you can say that other people think your writing is good enough, but you're not satisfied. But be careful — this is a loaded gun.)

"I'm always late."
"I procrastinate."
"I can't manage my time very well."
"I have trouble setting priorities."
"I can't say no."
"I really like to be home by 5:30 to watch the news."
"I'm a night owl — I don't get rolling until 11 a.m."

These all relate directly to your ability to function as a lawyer. As Diane Reynolds says, "You can't respond with *anything* that will stop you from functioning!" And Wendy Werner adds, tongue-in-cheek, "It's important to 'lie' appropriately! You can't say you're stubborn, or you've got a bad temper!" You may get an "A" for honesty, but with a large pool of prospective employees who *don't* have your skill-related flaw, *you won't get the job, because you didn't play the game well!*

B. "STEALTH" JOB-RELATED FLAWS

These are a little trickier because it won't seem as obvious that they're job-related flaws. That's why I call them "stealth" flaws. For instance, let's say that you really don't like working with numbers, and you come to the conclusion that that's not job-related so it's OK to say it. As Gail Peshel points out, "Be careful! Saying you don't like working with numbers can infer that you don't like detail work, and that's what a lot of lawyers, especially new ones, have to do." Or let's say that your problem is that you're bored with law school, or you hate your classes. Those aren't directly job-related, but the interviewer could easily surmise that if you're bored with your schoolwork, you'll be bored with the employer's work, as well — so you won't do a good job of it.

So the watchword for citing flaws is: be careful! If it could possibly be interpreted as job-related, avoid it!

C. ANYTHING THAT'S AN OBVIOUS LIE

I realize that we've been tiptoeing on the borders of truthfulness here, but don't choose a weakness that's a flagrant lie. For instance, as Ann Skalaski says, "If your writing sample is awful and you say you're a perfectionist, the interviewer will *know* what your *real* flaw is — a lack of candor!" So don't choose as a weakness something that's an obvious fib!

D. SERIOUS PERSONAL FLAWS

As Kathleen Brady says, "This isn't therapy." An interview is not the place to talk about your drinking problem or your psychiatric problem, even though if you *have* one of those it probably *is* your greatest weakness. The problem with serious personal flaws is that they loom so large that the interviewer will be afraid that your personal problems will intrude on your work, and that's a big turn-off.

E. DRAWING A BLANK AND SAYING NOTHING

St. John's' Maureen Provost Ryan says, "The worst thing you can do when someone asks your weaknesses is to stop dead in your tracks, like a deer frozen in headlights." You have to come up with *something*. But this is only a problem if you're not prepared; if you've thought through your alternatives, there's no way for a question like this to catch you off guard. (Or *any* question, for that matter!)

F. BE AWARE OF VARIATIONS ON THE "GREATEST WEAKNESS" THEME!

In an effort to catch you off-guard, some interviewers won't simply ask you "What's your greatest weakness?" Instead, they might ask:

♦ What's your *second* greatest weakness?

or

♦ If I called one of your employers, what would they tell me your weaknesses are?

It's not as likely that you'll encounter one of these variations, but it makes sense to come up with a "fall back" flaw — just in case!

C. "WHAT ARE YOUR STRENGTHS?"

This question also comes under other guises, like "If we called your last employer, what would they say your strengths were?" Actually, this alternative focuses you more clearly on exactly what the interviewer's getting at. The question really is, "What can you do for us, and what have you done that proves that?"

1. THE BEST WAY TO RESPOND

Now what you're going to pull out here are the job-related skills from your infomercial. This isn't a personality question; it's purely an issue of what you're going to bring to the table professionally. As Laura Rowe points out, "Remember, you're selling yourself. Sell your strengths, your transferable skills." And Illinois' Cindy Rold adds, "Make sure the skills you choose are directly job-related, and that you're confident about what you've got." What are the possibilities? Things like being enthusiastic, and hard working, or that you've got analytical skills. Those kinds of things. You could say something like, "I'm energetic. I don't mind working late." But whatever you choose, make sure that you have *specific examples* to show *how* it is you know that you've got these strengths. "I'm hard working. Apart from taking a full load of classes, I work as a research assistant for Professor Phlegmlitz about 20 hours a week."

Being asked about your strengths may also be an opportunity to show the fruit of your research. For instance, let's say that while talking to upperclassmen who worked for a particular employer before, they told you that one thing the partners hate is to be bothered with incessant questions; they like you to work on your own. Well, if that's something you think you're good at, an interview with that firm would be a great place to highlight it! "I pride myself on my ability to work on my own initiative. I can organize my work and handle responsibility without taking up my boss's time." Boy — just think of the impact that would have on an employer who doesn't like to be bothered very much!

And remember to cater your pitch to your *audience*. As Diane Reynolds points out, "If you're interviewing with a litigator, and you won prizes for debate, that's a strength he'll definitely want to hear about!"

The bottom line here is pull out strictly job-related strengths, and have examples to back them up.

2. BONERS TO AVOID

If what you *want* to do is to pull out strengths that are job-related, then logically the thing to *avoid* is strengths that won't do your prospective employer any good. For instance, as Laura Rowe points out, "Don't say that your strength is that you're patient. That doesn't really have anything to do with the law." Or that you're good with children.

D. "WHY SHOULD WE HIRE YOU?"

Remember the role the answer to this question plays: As Ann Skalaski points out, "It gives the interviewer ammo to take back to the hiring committee to make a pitch for you!" It's that important! You can see it's *somewhat* related to the "What are your greatest strengths?" and "Tell me about yourself" questions that we've already discussed. But it's not *quite* the same, because you'll want to bring out slightly different things. As Pam Malone says, "Answering this is a combination of "can do" and "will do" factors. You *can* do this job because of your experience, exposure, and abilities. And you *will* do it because of your willingness to work long hours, your thoroughness, and things like that."

1. THE BEST WAY TO RESPOND

If they've already asked you about your strengths, then you can start your answer by saying, "Well, for one thing, the strengths I told you about before are a definite positive. But apart from that . . . " and then go into the elements I'll mention in a minute. As you'll see, they strongly overlap with the kinds of elements you probably already have in your infomercial. If they *haven't* asked you about your strengths yet, then use the list below (and your infomercial) as the basis for this answer.

Regardless of what you give as your strengths, there are a few things that will really make you shine here, including:

- ◆   You're willing to work hard.
- ◆   You'll be loyal to them because they gave you an opportunity.
- ◆   You're enthusiastic.
- ◆   You'll be committed to your work, because you've done your research and you know that theirs is the kind of practice you want to be associated with. (But, of course, if you say this, be sure that it's true, and that you *have* done that research!)
- ◆   You're interested in building and developing clients (in other words, *rainmaking* — there's nothing more valuable to a law firm than this!).
- ◆   You're easy to work with.
- ◆   You're willing to assume responsibility.
- ◆   You're diligent.
- ◆   Any experience that you have that is a transferable skill, e.g., research that you did for a professor in an area of practice that the firm practices, or in an interview for a Legal Aid position, the fact that you did a clinic helping low-income tenants.

As Tammy Willcox points out, "Toot your horn! Make them into believers!" Debra Fink adds that if you can carry it off, once you're finished with your brief explanation of why they should hire you, smile, and add to your response something like, "I guess that leads naturally to the question, why should I work for you?'"

2. BONERS TO AVOID

This question is a real hornet's nest, because there are several tempting ways to get stung if you get away from the idea of simply accentuating the positives you bring to the firm. Here's an idea of what you *shouldn't* do:

A. DON'T BE ARROGANT!

Boy, this is a real temptation when you're lobbed a question like this, but what you don't want to do is to say, "Because I'm the best there is," or anything like it. I know you're walking a fine line here, but there's a world of difference between saying "Because I'll be loyal and committed to my work," which may *imply* that you're the best person for the job, and coming straight out and *saying* it. As Ann Skalaski advises, "Temper your answer with humility! 'I know I don't know about practicing law, but here are the qualities I have that I hope will make me successful . . . ' is the kind of tone you should aim for."

B. DON'T COMPARE YOURSELF TO OTHER STUDENTS

As Maureen Provost Ryan says, "Don't put down other people in an effort to make yourself look better." It doesn't make you look better — it makes you look insecure. Instead, focus on the specific, positive qualities that you'll bring to the job — and let the employer draw the conclusion that you're the best person for it!

C. DON'T LET THE EMPLOYER FEEL AS THOUGH THEY'RE A NAME ON A LIST

While you'll perform well for an employer who gives you the opportunity to do so, don't make it sound as though you're so desperate for a job that you'll take anything from anyone. Instead, as Jose Bahamonde-Gonzalez says, "Make them feel unique." There's a big difference between saying that you'll be loyal to them because, from what you've gleaned from your research, your skills are the kind of thing they've looked for in the past — and saying, "I'd be loyal to anybody who gives me a job." Remember, to the interviewer, their employer *is* the best place in the world to work. If you bolster that feeling, you're way ahead of the competition.

E. "WHAT WILL YOU BE DOING 5 (OR 10) YEARS FROM NOW?"

I know what you're thinking — "Well, excuse me while I pull out my tarot cards, so I can read my future and tell you." Virtually everybody acknowledges that it's a stupid question. As Tammy Willcox says, "No one admits that what they *really* want is to win the lottery and be sitting in the Caribbean drinking rum punch!" So, you may be wondering: Then why the heck does anybody ask it? Because there's a legitimate concern behind it. What they're really asking you is, "If we make you an offer, are you going to accept it, and are you committed to staying with us into the foreseeable future?" Remember I told you the rule of thumb that it takes an employer 3 years to earn back their investment in training you. So when they ask you what you intend to be doing 5 or 10 years from now, they're checking to see if you have any plans now *not* to be with them, then.

1. THE BEST WAY TO RESPOND

Now the difficulty in answering this question is that you have to perform a delicate straddle. As Sandy Mans advises, "You have to have an open mind about your future, but at the same time, for that particular employer, they'll want to know that you're committed to that practice area." Does this mean you should lie? No, but you may have to stretch the truth. As Nancy Krieger says, "The best answer is not *necessarily* the answer inside your soul." With that in mind, here are the elements you should include in your answer to this question:

- A commitment to the geographic location. "I want to be a member of *this* community." This is *absolutely crucial.*

- Working for an employer like the interviewer. As Diane Reynolds says, "Your answer has to be within the employer's ballpark." It's presumptuous to say, "Working for you," but it's a good idea to say, "Working in a firm (or organization) like yours." Or if you're interviewing with a government agency, say the D.A.'s office, Lisa Kellogg advises you to say something like, "I plan on staying in the public sector."

- Career growth. You want to say things like you want to be building a clientele, gaining more responsibilities, developing your expertise.

- Then — follow up with a question of your own. As Debra Fink says, "As soon as you're done, ask, 'Of those who started out with you 5 (or 10) years ago, what are they doing now?' It's a great way to get off the hot seat, and it tells you a lot about turnover!" Or, as Wendy Werner suggests, you can ask them: "Are you doing what you thought you'd be doing 5 (or 10) years ago?" This is another good comeback, as long as you don't ask it with an "in your face" tone of voice!

Apart from the elements that should definitely be included, it's a good idea to throw in a dose of humility on this one. For instance, as Teresa DeAndrado points out, "There's nothing wrong with saying that 'Life happens and no one can guarantee *what* will happen,'" or, as Jose Bahamonde-Gonzalez says, "It's OK to acknowledge that you don't know for sure, by saying something like, 'It's hard to make that forecast now because I'm just starting out,' as long as you go on to say something more definite, like 'Five years of practice in this specialty, and ideally with a firm like yours.'"

Most importantly, simply by reading this you've started to do the one thing that this question requires: namely, to think about it. The students who run into trouble with forecasting their futures, and blurt out things they don't intend, are the ones who haven't sat down and thought about how they ought to respond, beforehand!

So when you're asked what your future will hold, remember most of all to stress geography — you want to be where the employer is; to acknowledge that you don't know for sure; and to stress your career development at an employer *like* them. And then turn around and ask them about the people who started with them 5 (or 10) years ago.

2. BONERS TO AVOID

I think I've heard more classic boner responses to this question than any other! For instance, one young woman interviewing with a San Francisco law firm, said confidently, "I intend to be living with my husband, in Oregon, raising a family." Another student, in an interview with a high-powered firm, answered, "I'm from Southern California, and we don't think past the weekend." Hard to believe, but true. As a general rule, here are the things to avoid:

A. ANYTHING THAT SUGGESTS YOU'RE IN FOR 2 YEARS AND THEN YOU'LL BAIL OUT

... Although, as Maureen Provost Ryan points out, "Everybody knows most people are out the door in 2 years!" So you don't want to say things like, "I intend to have my own practice." The employer will read this as you saying, "I intend to steal your clients." Or that you intend to be in a city where the employer doesn't have an office. Or that you're using this job as a stepping stone for politics, or that you intend to be floating down the Amazon, or that you want to get training with this employer and then go work for a humanitarian effort. Remember — you don't want to be too specific about where you'll *be,* but you don't want to suggest *at all* that you have definite plans to do something *other* than work for this employer!

B. DON'T BE TOO SPECIFIC

This is one of the few instances when I'll advise you that general is better than specific. Don't say anything like, "Working for you," or even more boldly, "Doing your job." It's too flip and too arrogant. Soften it a bit. Mary Obrzut suggests something like, "Working in a firm like yours, doing what you do, right here." Can you see the difference? This is general enough to be believable, while still indicating a sincere interest in working for the employer.

C. DON'T MENTION QUALITY OF LIFE ISSUES

It may be that you intend to balance work with a family. That's a healthy thing to do, but it's *not* a healthy interview answer! Why? As Lisa Abrams says, "The interviewer is interested in your commitment to the firm, so don't say anything like, 'I want to be working part-time.'" Remember, the only thing the employer is interested in is what you can do for *them.* Talking about your commitment to your personal life doesn't fit that agenda!

F. *"ARE YOUR GRADES INDICATIVE OF YOUR ABILITY?"* — OR — *"WHY AREN'T YOUR GRADES BETTER?"*

As Debra Fink points out, "This is a no-win question. If you're not #1 in the class, then you've got to say that your grades don't indicate your ability. But if you *are* #1 in the class, then you'll be branded a perfectionist — and that's not good either!"

But realistically speaking, an interviewer isn't going to ask you this question if you're toward the top of the class. What will happen, instead, is that they'll put you on the spot if your grades *aren't* up to snuff. Now, you and I both know that law schools are populated by smart people, and that the difference between the top quarter of the class and the top half may have huge ramifications in terms of how much work you have to put into your job search — but that huge gulf between the top quarter and top half may spring from one bad performance on one final exam. That all may be true, but it doesn't do you any good to focus on it. Instead, look at what the interviewer is really asking: "Do you have the brainpower necessary to do my work?" When you put it in that light, you can see how it's fairly easy to turn the situation around to your advantage!

Alternatively, the interviewer himself may not have very good grades, either, and he just wants to see how you react on your feet to criticism. Whether they're really concerned with your ability, or just testing you, you can handle this question with aplomb!

1. THE BEST WAY TO RESPOND

This is, to some extent, circumstance-specific. If you *have* some tangible reason for your grades being below par — like a serious personal tragedy — say so. But let's face it — that's not what's behind most mediocre performances in law school. Instead, what you want to do is to *acknowledge* your grades, *acknowledge* that you wish they were better ("Look, my grades aren't what I wanted them to be, either!" "I didn't do well, and I'm not proud of it," "The grade god definitely didn't smile on me," "Boy, I'm sure glad I didn't have to take *that* report card home to Mom!"), but go on to state that you don't think that your overall GPA is indicative of your abilities because . . . and then pull out any of the positives you can from the following list (notice that what you're doing when you choose from this list is to show your sensitivity to the employer's underlying concern about whether you can do their work):

♦ Classes that you *did* excel in — particularly if they're ones that are relevant to the employer (e.g., Torts for an employer who does personal injury litigation).

♦ Paper versus final exam courses — it helps to do better in paper courses, since writing ability is very important to legal employers.

♦ Clinics or academic-oriented extracurriculars in which you excelled. (As Sandy Mans points out, you can say something like, "I supplemented my class work with journal experience, where I learned. . . . ")

♦ Job experience for which you've gotten great reviews.

♦ Certain tough profs that you did perform well for.

♦ The classic "upward trend in grades." Let's face it; not everybody's grades go up. But if yours did jump significantly after first semester or first year, that's a definite plus.

♦ Show that it's just one or two classes that torpedoed you because you did particularly badly in them. But watch out! That draws attention to those problems, and you'll have to show that you did something about them, too — like talking to the professor, going back and looking at the exam and the material to see what you did wrong and correcting it — things along those lines.

As Maureen Provost Ryan points out, "The key here is to stay positive! Don't make excuses. In fact, you can even say that. 'I don't want to make excuses about my grades. But what *is* indicative of my ability is . . . '" and then move on to your list of positives. What you're doing when you pull out the positives, by the way, is to show that you are not defined by your grades! As Laura Rowe says, "Show that you're a well-rounded package, not a number with a decimal point!"

2. BONERS TO AVOID

A. EXCUSES!

There's a difference between an explanation and an excuse. It's the element of defensiveness. Jose Bahamonde-Gonzalez says, "Whatever you do, don't say, 'Oh, this prof's a jerk!'" Nobody wants to hire someone who puts the blame on someone else — even though it may be perfectly true that you got a rotten grade in Property because your professor was, in fact, a jerk. (*Mine* sure was!) Instead, quickly acknowledge that you're not happy with your grade either, and *immediately* dwell on the positives. Making excuses doesn't encourage an employer to hire you!

B. DON'T FLOUNDER

As Sandy Mans points out, "The worst thing to do is to hem and haw, and choke out, 'Well, I'm a C-range student . . . ' and trail off." Be comfortable with your grades, pull out the positives, and practice speaking with confidence about them. Remember, this is an *interview.* It's not so much what you've done, but your *attitude* about what you've done. You can't go back and change your grade — but you *can* change the way you present them!

C. DON'T HIGHLIGHT A DOWNWARD TREND

If your first semester was your best semester in law school, and you've been in a downward spiral since, then don't mention a trend at all. This is just the flip side of mentioning a strong upward trend. If your grades have taken a tumble, then focus on journal experience, or work experience — anything that shows your abilities and takes the focus off of your grades!

D. DON'T MENTION ONGOING PERSONAL OBLIGATIONS

When the factor that contributed to bad grades was a "one shot" event — like the death of a relative or a divorce — you should mention it. But if it's an ongoing personal obligation that got in the way, like raising a family, be careful! The specter you'll raise in the employer's mind is that if you don't have enough time to do well in school, you won't have enough time to do the employer's work, either. As Diane Reynolds advises, "Be sure to mention how many hours you *can* spend, like 60 hours a week," or say that you have live-in help now, or other arrangements so that you can dedicate yourself to your work as much as necessary.

G. "WHY DO YOU WANT TO WORK FOR US?"

If you've done your homework, as I *begged* you to earlier in this chapter, you're going to hit a question like this right out of the ballpark! Remember, what you've done is to talk with your career services director, contacted upperclassmen and, perhaps, alums who've worked for this employer, you've done hard research either on-line or through publications like Martindale-Hubbell, you've read summer evaluations if you can get your hands on them — in short, you've drawn a bead on exactly what this employer is like. *Here's your chance to show it off!*

1. THE BEST WAY TO RESPOND

As my little introduction to this question indicates, the best answer to this question shows off all the research you've done. Maureen Provost Ryan says, "If you're sincere and you've identified this employer as a potential right spot for you, your enthusiasm will show. Show off your research. Talk about the nature of their practice and how exciting it would be to work for them. Visualize yourself actually working for the firm. Show your research and your response will ring with conviction!" And Lisa Abrams adds, "Firms *love* to feel you think that they're special!" The kinds of things you'll want to weave into your answer will be:

A. LOCATION

Remember the importance of geography! As Jose Bahamonde-Gonzalez advises, "It's especially important to explain why you want to be in the city where the employer is if your résumé doesn't show any connection with that city!"

B. THE REPUTATION OF THE EMPLOYER, IF YOU KNOW IT

As Lisa Abrams suggests, it's great if you can say that in all of your research, "One name keeps coming up — XYZ law firm. I want to be a part of it!"

c. The Type of Practice

As Laura Rowe points out, if it's a firm with a variety of practice areas, you'd express your interest in being exposed to a variety of issues. If, on the other hand, it focuses on one practice area, you'd have to bring out what in your background makes you interested in it.

d. A Reflection of the Size of the Employer

If it's a large firm, Deanna Coe Kursh advises stressing that you're interested in getting good training, in getting some experience in different departments so you can serve clients better, and that you're open to new ideas and new challenges. If it's a small firm that takes any case, Sandy Mans advises to stress the things in your background that show you can take the initiative. "I'd like to work in a firm like yours because I've succeeded in these entrepreneurial environments in the past. . . . "

e. Drop Names if You Have Them

That's Kathleen Brady's advice. So if you heard something good about the firm from a former summer associate, or an alum who works there or is otherwise familiar with the practice, say so. If you feel uncomfortable dropping names, then you can always say you heard it "through the grapevine" at school.

f. Any Sincere Strokes to the Employer's Ego

Remember, at this point you've talked with other people who are familiar with the firm. There's absolutely no shame in saying that you want to work there because of this great comment or that great comment. As Kathleen Brady says, "Every firm wants to think it's the best in the world. It's always good to stroke their ego."

2. Boners to Avoid

a. Anything That Smacks of "What's-in-it-for-me"

Please, please, *please* don't respond with any of the following if you're asked why you want to work for a particular employer:

- ◆ "The money."
- ◆ "I gotta pay the bills."
- ◆ "Because it would be a tremendous opportunity for me."
- ◆ "I'll get great training."

As Sandy Mans points out, "The employer doesn't *care* what's in it for you." Of course, those are all the real reasons you want the job — just as the employer doesn't care what's in it for you, you don't really, in your heart, care what's in it for the employer. You care about yourself, as you should. But this is a sales presentation. They've got something you want — a job. And in order to get it, you've got to keep a lid on responses like "Because I need the money"!

B. ANY COMMENT THAT SHOWS A LACK OF RESEARCH

When I talked about the best way to answer this question, I talked about the importance of showing off your research and making the employer feel unique. This is just the flip side of that. For instance, as Maureen Provost Ryan points out, "You can never say, 'I've always wanted to work for a large firm.'" Firms are *different,* and they like to feel different. Even a cursory visit with your career services director will get you more specific insights into a law firm than that!

3. CLASSIC, TRUE, BAD ANSWERS TO "WHY DO YOU WANT TO WORK FOR US?"

As the old Honda ad used to say, "You can't make this stuff up" . . .

- ◆ . . . *"I have a friend who goes to school here, and he did research, and he said you were a good firm to work for. That's why I sent in my résumé."* (To which the interviewer responded, "Really? What's your friend's name? I hope I get to interview *him*.")
- ◆ . . . *"To get back at my father. He's one of your rivals, and he's insisting that I get into his area of practice, so I'm interviewing with you to get back at him."*

H. *"WHY DID YOU GO TO LAW SCHOOL?"* (ESPECIALLY TOUGH FOR SECOND AND THIRD CAREER PEOPLE)

1. ... IF YOU HAVEN'T HAD ANOTHER CAREER ...

If you haven't had another career before law school, this really isn't all that tough. What you'll want to do is accentuate the positive aspects of a legal education — you wanted the intellectual challenge, you enjoyed the idea of pulling apart issues, your idol is your Uncle Pete and he's a lawyer, whatever. Or you could even respond that you've wanted to be a lawyer for so long that you don't remember the original motivation that made you want to go! (However, if this is the case, be able to come up with reasons why it's *still* your dream. Otherwise, you won't sound thoughtful.)

2. ... IF LAW IS YOUR SECOND OR THIRD CAREER ...

"Why law school?" becomes more of a challenge if you've done something before. The problem is that you don't want to seem as though you're a dilettante who won't stick with the law *either*, or that you couldn't cut it at your last career. The safest route is to characterize law as something that always interested you, but something happened that triggered your desire to make the change. After all, the fact that you've tried other things before is a positive in the sense that you've got the experience and maturity to know exactly what you want to do!

3. BONER ANSWERS TO AVOID

The kinds of things you'll want to avoid are ones that suggest you chose law school as a default option. Not that this is *rare*, mind you; according to some studies, fully one-third of law students aren't committed to a legal education! But the thing you don't want to admit is that you never considered law school until you got out of undergrad, and couldn't find a job, and thought, gee, *now* what? (Between you and me, that's what *I* did. But you can bet I never admitted it to any interviewer!)

As Amy Thompson points out, you also want to avoid answers that suggest a bad motivation, like "My parents wanted me to," (it doesn't show any enthusiasm on your part), or even worse, "I was always good at arguing."

I. THE "BE-TRUE-TO-YOUR-SCHOOL" QUESTIONS

+ "Why did you choose this school?"
+ "What other schools did you get into?"
+ "Why did you go to school in X city if you want to work in Y city?"

If you didn't go to Harvard, you're open to these kinds of questions. Let's look at them separately to see how you ought to respond to them.

1. "WHY DID YOU CHOOSE THIS SCHOOL?"

This is an *especially* difficult question if you go to school in a city like New York, or Boston, or Chicago, or L.A., where there are several schools and you're not going to the best one in the area.

A. THE BEST WAY TO ANSWER

What you have to remember to do is to stress the positives about your school. Maureen Provost Ryan suggests saying that "I've been impressed with everything here. The classes are interesting and I like the profs." Gail Peshel says, "Stress the curriculum, the faculty, the size of the school, the clinical programs, writing programs, computer availability . . . " you get the idea! It's fine to mention things you've learned since you *got* to school — the interviewer won't notice, as long as you're cheerleading for your school. You could even say that you had friends or relatives who chose the school and had nothing but praise for it, if that's true. The point here is to bring up positive points about your school.

If you're stuck, pick up a copy of your law school's brochure and see how it sells itself — and mention *those* selling points! But if you *mention* a special attribute — like the school's clinical program — make sure that it's something that you've done (or intend to do), *and* it's relevant to the employer (for instance, a great clinical program would be very relevant to a litigation firm or a public interest employer).

B. BONER ANSWERS TO AVOID

The kinds of things you want to avoid saying are probably pretty close to the truth. They include:

♦ "It was the best (or only) one I got into."

♦ "Yeah, you're right. It stinks."

♦ "I heard the social life here is great!"

Remember — stress the positives, and move on. You can easily get off of this question by asking the interviewer where they went to school, or even better, showing that you know already from your Martindale-Hubbell search: "I know that you went to Moo State Law School. What was your experience there like?"

2. "WHAT OTHER SCHOOLS DID YOU GET INTO?"

This can be sticky if you didn't go to the school that was the highest ranked of the schools you got into, or, alternatively, you got into the interviewer's alma mater and didn't go. As Maureen Provost Ryan points out, "If you list a better school than the one you're attending, they'll think you have poor judgment."

All you can do in this situation is a variation of the answer to "Why did you choose this school?" Stress the school's positive points. Another serious consideration is scholarships; if you got an attractive financial aid package from your school and not one that was technically higher-ranked, you can stress your desire to get through law school with as little debt as possible, to give you the widest possible career choices when you get out. This question may even give you a chance to shine on the geography issue; if the employer is in the same city as your school and your other choices were in other cities, it shows your commitment to the community.

3. "WHY DID YOU GO TO SCHOOL IN X CITY IF YOU WANT TO WORK FOR US IN Y CITY?"

Gee, there's a reason they call these tough questions, huh? Remember, I stated the importance of geography and stressing your commitment to the city where the employer is located. Well, the fact that you didn't go to school there certainly gives you something to explain. But it's really not that bad. As Teresa DeAndrado says, "Just talk about the things about your school's program that you particularly liked, and say that you wanted to see a different part of the country. 'But I don't want to be in X city forever — now I want to go on to Y city.'" And follow that up with what it is about Y city that attracts you. If you do that, you should quickly remove the stigma from going to school in some other place.

J. "WHY DO YOU WANT TO WORK IN THIS CITY?"

Clearly this isn't much of a problem if you're interviewing with an employer who can spot your connection to the city based on your résumé. And that typically means that you either went to college in the city, your law school is there, or you otherwise indicate that you have spent a significant amount of time there.

But — what if you haven't? Remember how important geography is — you have to convince the employer that you're committed to remaining in the community, permanently. And that's a challenge if there's nothing in your background that suggests a tie to the city where the employer is. So — what should you do?

1. THE BEST WAY TO RESPOND

The kinds of things that will help you out are:

♦ Mentioning the word "permanent" a few times in your answer. As Jose Bahamonde-Gonzalez suggests, you can say that you've researched the city, and you want to be in this environment *permanently;*

♦ Stating a strong reason for being in the city, for instance, that you're following a family member there. Jose Bahamonde-Gonzalez says that if you are a woman, you should be careful about mentioning that you're following your husband, because that creates the impression that if your husband get transferred, you'll be gone.

♦ Showing the research that you've done on the community, and features about it that make you want to move there permanently — for instance, a strong upward trend in growth, or a reputation for a practice area in which you've got a strong interest provable by courses you've taken, papers you've written, and the like. (Clearly you're better off if you do an internship in the city first, to show your commitment to it — if you *haven't,* your research may be all you have to fall back on.)

2. BONER ANSWERS TO AVOID

The kinds of things you *shouldn't* mention are those that suggest a lack of research or commitment to the community. For instance, "I vacationed here and liked it" really isn't enough to indicate an intention to stay permanently!

Also, don't respond to anything negative the interviewer says about the city. For instance, as Susan Benson advises, if the interviewer says, "Why do you want to work in a pit like Los Angeles?" stress the positives I've mentioned above, and ignore the slur on Los Angeles!

K. "WHO ELSE ARE YOU INTERVIEWING WITH?"

I've put this question right after the "Why do you want to work in this city?" question because they are very much the same question. As Debra Fink points out, "When an interviewer asks you this, the real question is, do you have ties here? Will you develop them here?" So it's essentially, again, a question of *geography.* With that in mind, what you should do is to mention only other employers in the same city — don't mention any other cities! And mention them by name. If you don't have any other interviews yet, you can say that you are in the process of setting up interviews other prospective employers. I would strongly avoid saying "nobody," because it makes you seem a less attractive candidate.

As an aside — if you do get an interview with an out-of-town firm, call others in the same city and ask if you can meet with them on the same trip. The fact that you already have an interview with someone else makes you instantly more attractive — and makes the most of the dollars you're spending on your trip!

L. "WHAT KINDS OF POSITIONS ARE YOU LOOKING FOR?"

Actually, this isn't all that tough. What you'll want to do is to pull out the features that reflect the job you're interviewing for. For instance, if it's with a small firm, you'll want to talk about how you're looking for something where you'll be able to take on responsibility quickly, to develop clients, to be challenged by a diversity of projects, and that kind of thing. So tailor your pitch to fit the situation.

The *real* reason I included this question is that I have a great joke answer for it. One student's response to this question was, "Anything where I don't have to wear a hairnet." (I don't know if they got the job.)

M. HYPOTHETICAL QUESTIONS

Questions involving hypothetical legal problems aren't common when you're interviewing for a law firm position, but they are par for the course if you're interviewing for a position with Legal Aid, or as a public defender, or for an externship with a judge. In *those* interviews, you're very likely to be asked hypothetical questions. While an externship is likely to involve legal issues that test your reasoning and philosophy, the legal aid and public defender questions will more likely involve ethics, like, "You know your client is lying. What do you do?" Or, "You see another D.A. with drugs at a party. What do you do?" As Amy Thompson says, "For the public defender and D.A.'s office, they *need* to see how you think and how resourceful you are. That's because they give you two weeks' prep, then you're *out* there!"

Here's some advice about how to answer these kinds of questions:

♦ "Don't feel you need to be perfect," says Jose Bahamonde-Gonzalez. "No one expects you to be familiar with all of the case law. What's much more important is for you to maintain a professional demeanor." In other words — don't let the question fluster you!

♦ "Treat it like moot court," counsels Maureen Provost Ryan. "Take a viewpoint and argue the merits of the case. Expect some criticism, and if you get it, stick to your guns — if you don't, the interviewer will think you're weak. But if they come up with a good point, say so, and ask how they came up with it."

♦   What if you don't know the answer, or can't formulate one? "It's OK to say that because you've only had limited exposure to that area of the law, you're not certain what the answer should be," says Gail Peshel. But if you *don't* have an answer, be sure that you come back with information about where you'd look for the answer, how you'd research it. You may also be able to deflect the question by analogizing it with a case you've handled before, and then explain what you did in *that* case. Or, as Sophie Sparrow advises, you can say, "This is how I'd go about finding the answer. Then I'd talk to my supervisor to find the next step."

♦   "Whatever you do, don't hem and haw!" says Laura Rowe. "Silence is OK. Take a moment to think, and then either come back with an answer, or say, 'I'm not familiar with it, but here's how I'd research it. . . . '"

N. RÉSUMÉ GAPS AND RÉSUMÉ ITEMS

1. HANDLING RÉSUMÉ GAPS

If there are gaps in your résumé, there are probably one or two things that account for them: You left off your GPA, or you've got lots of work experience before school and you left off things that weren't law-related.

Neither one of these will pose a problem for you during your interview, as long as you're prepared for the likelihood that the interviewer will ask you about them during your interview. With the GPA issue, as Drusilla Bakert advises, "Just state what your GPA is — and make it exact — and shut up." Don't offer excuses or stumble over it, just come out and say it as though you were recounting your hat size. Let's face it; you got the interview without them knowing your grades, and the fact that your GPA isn't on your résumé kind of telegraphs that you didn't grade onto Law Review, doesn't it? So don't take up precious interview minutes by stumbling and bumbling over a simple number, or, even worse, by saying that you "don't know exactly" what your GPA is (yes, people actually do that!). Just state it, boom, and move on.

When it comes to chronological gaps on your résumé, if the interviewer asks what you were doing — say it! As you know, I'm not a big fan of leaving gaps in your résumé. Amy Thompson points out, "If you don't say what you were doing, the interviewer will assume you were in a jail . . . or worse!" But the fact is, if you've done a ton of things before law school, you may have pruned your experience for the sake of saving space on your résumé. If you did this, and the interviewer questions you about the gap, state what you did, and add that you didn't think it was particularly relevant to your job search, and that's why you left it off. It may be that it is a source of conversation for the interviewer, which is great!

The key here is to *feel comfortable* with your résumé, and your credentials, and *be prepared* to be questioned about anything that's obviously missing from it.

2. HANDLING QUESTIONS ABOUT ITEMS ON YOUR RÉSUMÉ

When it comes to résumé items as opposed to résumé gaps, the important thing, again, is to be prepared to talk about *anything* on it. As Drusilla Bakert points out, what a lot of interviewers will do is just scan your résumé and ask you questions about anything that interests them, anything that's unusual. That means you have to be ready to discuss *all* of it. And it also means that you shouldn't put things on your résumé in the first place that you're not willing or able to discuss. So if you just joined a club or a publication and you haven't had a meeting yet, don't put it on your résumé until you *have* had one — so you'll have something to talk about!

The best anecdote I've heard about the pitfalls of putting things on your résumé that you can't back up is a guy who listed "Personal Interests," and wrote "golf." Well, he got an interview with a law firm, and the interviewer suggested that they meet at the golf course and play nine holes while they talk. Great opportunity, huh? It *would* have been – except that when the student put "golf" on his résumé, he meant that he liked to *watch* golf — he didn't know how to play it! After hacking up bits of turf for the first couple of holes, it became obvious to the interviewer that the guy just didn't know what he was doing — and the interviewer said, "Why didn't you just come out and tell me the truth?" The moral to the story is: Be able to back up *everything* on your résumé!

O. "WHY DIDN'T YOU GET AN OFFER FROM YOUR LAST EMPLOYER?"

This is not just a *tough* question, it's a *killer*. In fact, it's so tough that I've devoted a whole chapter to dealing with the problem of not getting an offer from your summer clerkship employer. It's Chapter 9. If you're in this predicament, I'd strongly encourage you to read it!

P. "IF YOU GOT AN OFFER FROM YOUR LAST EMPLOYER, WHY DIDN'T YOU ACCEPT IT?"

Let's look at the *real* reasons, and talk about tactful ways you can state them. Maybe your last employer was a jerk and you really don't want to work for them because of that. Maybe you didn't like the work; you might have been under too much pressure. Maybe you're bored with the work, and you want to see what else is out there. Maybe the money's no good, and you want something better. Those are all good reasons not to go back, but you have to be careful how you say them! The real key to dealing with this kind of question is not to bad mouth your last employer under *any* circumstances. For instance, let's say that your last employer just dumped too much responsibility on you for your taste. As Gail Cutter points out, you wouldn't say, "They made me sink or swim," but instead you say something like, "I got a lot of client contact immediately."

So — how *do* you answer? Say something like, "My experience working for Larry, Curly, & Moe was very educational, and I'm grateful for the experience. However, now I'd like to bring what I learned there to a new employer, like you." In other words, handle the transition gracefully, without bad-mouthing your old employer or suggesting you'll flit from job to job.

Q. "WHAT'S THE BIGGEST MISTAKE YOU EVER MADE?"

I'd be tempted to answer, "Not being prepared to answer a question about the biggest mistake I ever made." If the laugh doesn't get you off the hook, you'd want to go on to describe a mistake you made *and the steps you took to correct it.* Try to make it something fairly innocuous, like choosing the wrong major in college and having to take extra classes when you realized your mistake, or something like that. If you have something in your background that's pretty serious — you were a crack addict, or you did time for armed robbery, or something like that — it's very admirable that you overcame it and went on to law school, but its impact on the interviewer would be incalculable!

R. "WHAT KIND OF SALARY ARE YOU LOOKING FOR?"

This really isn't so tough, and it also isn't all that common, either. As part of your research, you'll want to learn what the salary range is for different kinds of jobs. NALP forms provide this for large employers; and even for smaller ones, your career services director will be able to give you a good idea of what the starting pay is. All you need is a range, because what you'll want to say is something like, "I understand the salary range for employers like you is between $35,000 and $45,000. That would be fine with me." That way you're not skirting the issue entirely by saying that you're "flexible," but you're not pinning yourself to an exact figure, either. Furthermore, you're showing that you researched the employer, and that's *always* a good thing!

S. "HOW DO YOU LIKE LAW SCHOOL?"

The key here is not to be *completely* negative, even if you *hate* law school. If you like it, great — let your enthusiasm show! Maybe you like the intellectual challenge, you like stimulating conversations with your colleagues and professors — whatever. If you like *some* of it, stress the things you like and don't mention the things you *don't* like. And if you really intensely *dislike* it, put a positive spin on that. For instance, you can say something like, "Frankly, I can't wait to get out and start my career, and I'm frustrated with law school because it's holding me back from doing that!" At least that way you sound like a real go-getter!

T. BOZO PHILOSOPHY QUESTIONS

I'm being a bit unfair in labeling these as "bozo" questions, but the reason I call them that is that they don't solicit anything relevant to your ability to do the job, and they aren't a very direct or viable way of finding out something personal about you — instead, as Mary Obrzut points out, all they do is test your savoir faire. "What these questions are really getting at is, can you think on your feet? What if you get caught off guard?"

There's no way to give you a complete list of philosophical questions you could be asked. And it doesn't really matter what your precise answer is, as long as you can come up with one. But these give you an idea of the *kind* of question some interviewers will ask you. Take a few minute to think about them, so that when you're faced with such questions, you come up with a ready answer instead of sitting there with your mouth open, staring at the interviewer like a deer frozen in headlights.

- ◆ "Who's your hero?" (Parents, grandparents, and great legal minds always sound good here, but even an off the wall answer would be fine. I'd answer, "Ed McMahon.")

- ◆ "Who in history would you like to talk with?" (Let your imagination run wild!)

- ◆ "What would you do if you won the lottery?" ("I'd still want to work for a firm like yours, because that's what I want to do with my life" would be a great answer if you could say it without busting out laughing. "It depends how much I won. If it was a million, I'd pay off my student loans — part of them, anyway." But don't say you'd quit and retire to a South Seas island, because it betrays that you don't really want to work — even though that might be true!)

- ◆ "Are you a 'forest' person or a 'tree' person?" (I'd answer, "I don't know, but I assure you I'm not a Forrest *Gump* person.")

- ◆ "If you were a tree, what kind of tree would you be?" (A legendary Barbara Walters question.)

- ◆ "What's the last book you read?" (Have a *decent* book ready that you can discuss. I'd probably be tempted to answer with the name of *this* book, actually!)

- ◆ "What's the toughest decision you ever had to make?"

H. HANDLING ILLEGAL QUESTIONS

Sometimes you may be confronted with a question that's illegal. What exactly *is* an illegal question? It's a question that's asked only of a certain group of candidates, defined by race or gender or economic status — and it's a question that has nothing to do with your ability to do the work. Probably the most common types of illegal questions involve asking women whether they're married and whether they have (or intend to have) children. Others include asking your age, or where you're from, or your national origin.

What should you do when you get an illegal question? Well, for a start, don't *assume* an evil motive. Remember, most legal interviewers are not professional interviewers; they're lawyers. As Jose Bahamonde-Gonzalez points out, "They're probably as ill-at-ease as you are, and may ask inappropriate questions as a result, just as a means of breaking the ice. After all, asking someone if they're married or if they have children would under any other circumstances just be friendly." Debra Fink adds, "If someone asks 'Are you married?' they may just be using a clumsy way of asking, 'Will you have to relocate?' Remember, a firm needs you to work for them for about 3 years to earn back their investment in training you, and they'll naturally be concerned if there's some impediment to your being able to remain with them into at least the foreseeable future." That's a valid concern, even though asking you whether you're married as a way to get at that concern is *not* the right way to go about it! The most extreme example I heard in terms of how an obnoxious interviewer can have a perfectly innocent motive, is this one. One California firm sent out an interviewer who was obnoxious and also happened to be Jewish. He would ask Jewish interviewees questions like, "Do you keep a kosher home?" When confronted by the career services director (who'd received dozens of complaints about these questions), the interviewer was flabbergasted, and responded, "What's the big problem? *I'm* Jewish!" He honestly didn't believe he'd offended anybody!

So what you want to do right off the bat is to give the interviewer the benefit of the doubt, and *reword* the question to try and get at their valid concern. For instance, if an interviewer asked you, "Do you have kids?," you could respond, "If you're concerned about how much of a commitment I can make to working for you, the answer is that I can devote as much time as necessary to my job." As Kathleen Brady points out, "It's important to be polite and remember your tone of voice when you reword questions. Remember — what you're looking for is the question *behind* the question. Respond to *that*."

Let's say you ignore all of this wonderful advice and you don't reword the question (or alternatively you can't think of what the innocent concern behind it is, or you just can't think of a good way to reword it). You've got two choices: answer it or refuse to answer it. What should you do? Well, one thing you *can't* do is confront them by saying, "Hey, that's an illegal question, Buster!" Because remember, it's only illegal if they ask it of a certain targeted group as opposed to all candidates. Furthermore, if you attack or confront the interviewer, you're *guaranteed* you've cut off any possibility of working for that interviewer's organization.

Now it may be that you find questions about your marital status or parental status so offensive that you truly wouldn't want to work for anyone who would ask such a thing. But, as Mary Obrzut advises, "Don't be so quick on how you think you should handle illegal questions!" It may be that even though the question is illegal, you really want the job. You may not have a bunch of other opportunities, and you don't find the question all that offensive. My advice, and that of most of the career services directors I talked to, is: swallow your pride and answer the question, unless you find the question truly offensive. So if the interviewer asks you, "How many kids do you have?" Debra Fink suggests assuming that the question is innocent, and responding as you would to anybody else — "Two. How about you?" (That's, of course, if you have two children!)

If you do wind up with an offer and go with the organization, you may indeed find out that they are a bunch of offensive stiffs and you wish you'd never worked there in the first place. But at least at that point you've got a little work experience under your belt and it's a lot easier looking for a second job than a first one.

So that's the game plan. Give the interviewer the benefit of the doubt; reword the question to get at their true concern; and if in doubt, swallow your pride, answer the question, and move on. If you really are offended you can (and should) report the interviewer to your career services director.

I. HANDLE DISASTERS WITH APLOMB

Face it — at some point along the interview trail, you're going to encounter a disaster. I heard plenty of them — from men walking out of interviews only to find that their fly was open and their shirt tail was sticking out through it, to a woman who threw up on the hiring partner on her way into the interview, to the guy who spilled water on the partner during an interview dinner, to a woman who lost her blouse on the way to school and wound up interviewing with her suit buttoned up . . . and nothing underneath it!

My favorite interview disaster story is really more embarrassing than disastrous, but here it is. A firm was doing on-campus interviews at a law school, and the interviewer had been assigned a particular conference room for the interviews. The interviewer was late, and the law student scheduled for the *second* interview showed up, wearing his best suit. He sat down outside the interview room, knowing that he was very early for the interview. Well, the student scheduled for the *first* interview showed up a few minutes later. These two students didn't recognize each other – *and each of them assumed the other was the interviewer!* They shook hands, and walked into the conference room (obviously, the interviewer *still* hadn't shown up.) They chatted back and forth for 10 minutes before they both realized that *neither one of them was the interviewer!*

If something unexpected arises during an interview, you may not appreciate it at the time, but it may well be that having a disaster happen to you is a plus — *because it gives you a chance to show off how well you handle the unexpected!* Crises happen, and it's a great positive if you can keep a cool head when they do. So if something untoward befalls you, handle it, and, if you can, laugh about it! My philosophy is always, if you're going to laugh about it when you look back on it, you might a well start laughing now. To use the "lost blouse" woman as an example, when she got to school and realized she'd lost her suit blouse, she tried to cancel the interview. However, her career services director talked her out of it, convincing her to go through the interview with a discreetly buttoned suit. Well, she walked into the interview, and told the interviewer what happened. He was so impressed with the moxie she showed in going through with the interview that she got a callback interview with the organization — *in fact, she's the only one from her school who got one!*

So don't let the thought of disasters intimidate you. If they come up, handle them with aplomb. Who knows — you may impress the interviewer *more* than if *nothing* had happened!

J. HOW TO INTERVIEW WELL IF YOU'RE SHY

I don't mean to talk about shyness as an affliction here. You're never going to go to your doctor, have them examine you, and say, with a look of grave concern, "We're going to have to do something about that shyness." Some people are just outgoing, and others aren't.

Now, is this a problem when it comes to practicing law? Of course not. There are plenty of shy lawyers. Furthermore, the kind of research and analytical skills that go along with introverted personalities are in many ways more valuable to law firms than the lack of concentration you'd associate with someone very gregarious, especially in the first couple of years of practice in large organizations. As Wendy Werner points out, "Introverts can work for long periods without interruption, focus and concentrate well, and typically enjoy writing and can get more done." Those are all *very* valuable attributes indeed!

But the fact is, when it comes to interviewing, shyness is a detriment. Remember, an interview is a sales presentation, and if you aren't outgoing, you won't naturally sell your assets as well as you need to. As Sandy Mans points out, "People tend to like people who are like themselves. Introverts don't naturally click with extroverts, and most firms send extroverts to do interviews. There probably are lots of introverts who work at the firm itself, but you have to get past the interview to get there and meet them!" That's the bad news. The good news is, if you're shy, you can overcome it and interview successfully. How? You'll want to do everything I've suggested throughout this chapter — all of the preparation, and going over all of the questions you should ask and answers you'll give to tough questions. Be sure you leave no stone unturned when it comes to your research, and make a special point of memorizing the answers you intend to give to tough questions. Why? As Marilyn Tucker says, "Preparation is much more important for shy people. Outgoing, extroverted, never-at-a-loss-for-words people can disguise less-than-thorough preparation with their engaging conversational style. But people who are reserved, who must work at appearing easy and conversational, will only be able to achieve the appearance of confidence by preparing to the fullest extent possible."

One reason preparation is such a boon to you if you're shy is that it helps you feel more confident. If a lack of confidence contributes to your retiring demeanor, then feeling comfortable with your background, with what you're going to say and what you're likely to be asked, with knowing the background of the employer, and with any Achilles' heels you have (like grades or lack of experience) . . . all of these will help you converse confidently and freely.

Be sure that the selling points that you have are backed up with specific examples, and that you memorize and practice saying those examples. Why? The *way* you convey information can make you a much more attractive candidate. For instance, let's say that the interviewer asks what you did while working part time at the Otter & Blutarsky law firm. You might be tempted to say, "I worked closely with a litigation partner." But it lacks a little bit of zip, doesn't it? It doesn't exactly pique one's interest about what you did! Instead, as Marilyn Tucker suggests, describe specific details to make it interesting: "I spent my time doing research for John Blutarsky, a litigation partner. I usually conveyed the results of the research orally to Mr. Blutarsky to ensure a quick turnaround time. Nevertheless, during the year I wrote three major memos. In fact, one involved a very complex issue on the impact of damages. Mr. Blutarsky praised my work and incorporated the memo into a trial brief. I see from your firm résumé that you have several lawyers who do medical malpractice cases. I'd be interested in hearing what they have to say about this topic." You can see what happened here; you've taken a blah kind of response and turned it into one that is likely to make the interviewer take an interest in you.

Apart from preparation and memorization, you should practice interviewing as much as possible. I've mentioned the importance of mock interviews; take advantage of them until you feel fully comfortable with your "pitch." It'll give you a feeling of control that you might otherwise lack!

Don't overlook logistics! If the interview is somewhere other than your school, be sure you leave plenty of time to get there. If you arrive too early, you can always walk around until interview time, but it'll help calm you down if you're confident you won't be late.

Finally, pay close attention to body language. When you get to the interview, walk with head high, shoulders back, and greet the interviewer by extending your hand and smiling while you greet them. Be sure to inject enthusiasm into your voice, and to maintain eye contact with the employer and not let your voice drop off, even when you're dealing with tough questions. As Marilyn Tucker says,

"If you look away and let your voice drop when the interviewer asks you a question, you've as good as said, 'You found my weakness; you got me.'" One hiring partner at a medium-sized midwestern firm told me a horror story about an interviewee who had great credentials, but was uncomfortable talking to the point that she didn't really answer questions with words — she *grunted*. The interviewer asked all the questions he could think of, and then, assuming the half-hour interview was up, looked at his watch. *Only 5 minutes had passed.* He looked at the interviewee, who sat gazing away, a surly look on her face. He slapped his desk, and said, "Well, it looks like you're going to be really early for your next interview!" That's clearly an extreme situation — but the point is, personality counts. Even if you don't like to talk — be pleasant!

If you think at some point that the interview just isn't going well because you're not projecting as well as you should be, I've got a great suggestion for you. *Bring it up!* You may be recoiling in horror at the thought of talking about your shyness, but I'm telling you, it's a lot better to do that than to let a job you really want slip away. I'll give you a great example. One career services director told me about a shy woman who had the worst of all possible interviews for a shy person — it was her and *five* attorneys. Even the most confident law student would view *that* one with trepidation! Anyway, she felt throughout the interview as though she was standing at the beach, and the tide was running out with the sand slipping from beneath her feet. It just got worse and worse. Finally, just before the end, *she brought it up, out of the blue.* She said, "I know the people you're interviewing are extroverted, and I'm not, but here are five reasons to hire me . . . " and she listed them. Needless to say, the interviewers were *very* impressed! Wendy Werner suggests a variation on this theme. She says you may want to *open* the interview by saying up front, "The best things about me you won't see in this interview," and explain that that's because you're introverted. The interviewer may be very impressed by your ability to take the bull by the horns like this!

So what's the plan if you're shy?

♦ Do everything I advise in this chapter, but do it in spades — all the preparation, memorize all the questions you'll ask, all the answers you want to provide.

♦ Practice! Do all the mock interviews you possibly can.

- Don't forget body language — smile, maintain eye contact, maintain enthusiasm in your voice — don't let your sentences tail off to nothing.

- If it comes to the point your shyness is unmistakable — confront it, and tell the interviewer why they should hire you anyway!

K. HANDLING STRESS INTERVIEWS

If you do a lot of interviewing, you'll undoubtedly come across "stress" interviews. What are they? They're interviews where the interviewer puts you on the spot. You'll get the feeling from moment one that you can't do anything right. They won't be friendly. They'll be argumentative and belligerent. They'll belittle your credentials. They'll interrupt you when you talk, or look bored or read while you talk. The result? You'll feel like you've been lashed to a spit and that you're being roasted over an open fire.

Now, *why* would an interviewer be like this? Maybe they've looked at your credentials before you got to the interview, and decided that you just weren't going to get the job no matter what. Maybe they're a hard-charging litigator, and they want to see how you can face up to being put on the spot; they're just testing you to see if you can "take it." Maybe the job is so rigorous and so demanding that putting you under intense pressure is the best way of seeing whether or not you're right for the job (after all, judges frequently put lawyers on the spot!). Or maybe they're just a jerk.

Frankly, it doesn't really matter *why* the interviewer behaves this way. Your strategy is the same: Stay cool! As Tammy Willcox advises, "You can't let them push your buttons. Don't let them see that you're rattled. You have to be the unsinkable Molly Brown!" Regardless of how belligerent or obnoxious they get, maintain your composure. Don't respond by raising your voice or getting into an argument. Take slow, deep breaths, and don't panic. As Ann Skalaski says, "You've got to rise above it." You can't let them see that you're flipping out!

What if the interview continues this way, and it's *really, really, really* bothering you? Say so! As Susan Benson recommends, "If the interview seems like a lost cause — bring it up! Say, 'Gee, this seems awful. What can I do to get things on track?' or 'I don't seem to be giving you the answers you want.'" That may be a sufficient shock to the interviewer that you'll be able to salvage an otherwise untenable situation. If you don't feel comfortable confronting the interviewer this way, you always have another option. As Amy Thompson says, "You can leave! Just say that the job isn't for you, shake hands, and go. After all, if they're that rude in an interview, they'd be that way every day." Now, if you *choose* this option, remember that you're not seeing the entire organization, you're only seeing one person — and it may not be someone you'd be working with. It's dangerous to condemn an entire organization on the basis of this single interviewer; as Jose Bahamonde-Gonzalez points out, "Sometimes law firms send arrogant interviewers. That doesn't mean it's an awful place; law firms generally want to put their best foot forward, but sometimes things come up such that they can't. For instance, there's a sudden emergency at work such that they have to send whoever's available. So don't jump to conclusions about the firm based on the interviewer!" That's good advice — but if the interview is going *that* badly, take comfort in knowing that you've always got the "I'm outta here!" card to play!

L. WHEN THE INTERVIEW IS OVER: DON'T POSTMORTEM!

Phew! It's over. You've shaken hands and said your good-byes. Now what?

You may want to jot down a few notes afterwards, for points that you want to remember about the interviewer and the employer. If there were any questions that surprised you, think about how you'll answer them next time. And review in your mind how your *own* questions were received by the interviewer, so you can fine-tune them next time around. But other than that — don't torture yourself by wondering how it went! As Ann Skalaski says, "Just because it went well, doesn't mean you'll get a call back. Think of everyone you meet, and like, but you don't make plans with them anyway!" And by the same token, you can't say for sure that it went badly, either! As Nancy Krieger points out, "You never know! You may think it was just awful, and you'll get a call back anyway."

And what if it really *did* bomb? Well, live and learn. As Jose Bahamonde-Gonzalez says, "Sometimes you're not going to get along with the interviewer, and there's nothing you can do about it." You won't mesh with every interviewer any more than you'll be friends with everyone you meet socially. Doing what I've told you to do in this chapter ups your odds of getting along with the employer *tremendously*, that's true — but sometimes you just won't be able to find any common ground with the interviewer, no matter what. If that's the case, console yourself with the fact that you wouldn't have been happy working with someone you don't get along with, anyway.

So don't waste time doing a postmortem. You've got other employers, and other interviews to think about!

M. FOLLOWING UP YOUR INTERVIEWS

1. SEND THANK YOUS

Thank you letters are always appropriate after a job interview. But I've already told you how to write them, so there's no point in repeating myself! You'll find advice about writing thank you letters in Chapter 5, on Correspondence, on page 208.

2. SHOULD YOU CALL TO FOLLOW UP?

When it comes to following up, employers are like snowflakes: no two are alike. Some will invite you to a second interview right away. Others might not call you for 6 months.

The best way to deal with this is to do what I suggested in the "Questions" section; namely, at the end of your interview, ask the interviewer when they plan on contacting students for call backs or offers. Ask them whether you can contact them (or someone at their office) if you haven't heard either way by that time. Make a note of that deadline after the meeting. Wait a few days after the deadline, and if you haven't heard, call. You'll just say something like, "I'm calling to follow up on an interview I had with Cornelius Rex at State Law School 3 weeks ago." If you're polite, a call like this will never be considered overreaching.

If you neglect to ask the interviewer when you can expect to hear something, Sandy Mans advises that you follow up with a phone call within 2 weeks to see what's going on.

What if the interviewer lets you know in advance that several months are likely to pass before you hear anything? Well, don't let them forget you — if you want the job, that is! Every month or two, send a card or a letter reminding the interviewer of your continuing interest in the job. Remember, with contact this infrequent you aren't being a pest — rather, you're showing that you're a potential employee with a great deal of interest in the employer, and great follow through!

N. You Got an Offer! Now What?

1. If It's Definitely What You Want — Accept It Right Away!

If this is your dream job, there's no point in pussyfooting around. For one thing, as Debra Fink points out, this is a display of enthusiasm that any employer would appreciate!

2. If You Still Have Questions That Haven't Been Answered, Now's the Time to Ask Them!

Maybe there are a few gray areas that you need covered before you feel you can make a decision. If so, make arrangements with the person who made you the offer to arrange for a personal or phone meeting to discuss any questions you have.

And remember, many of the questions I told you to avoid like a pit viper during an interview are *perfectly appropriate* once you've got an offer. You can ask what your pay will be; what benefits they offer; what their pro bono policy is like; how much latitude you'd have in choosing your own projects; what their billable hours requirements (and averages) are; whether or not attorneys are expected to work late evenings and/or on weekends; whether they're expected to meet clients on weekends; what kinds of community activities lawyers are expected to take part in; and that kind of thing. Some of these issues may be very important to you. If so, don't accept an offer before you have them addressed to your satisfaction!

3. Don't Keep an Employer Dangling for Very Long!

As a rule of thumb, Debra Fink advises that you wait no more than 24 hours or so before responding to an offer. As she says, if you wait longer, you'll seem unenthusiastic. It may be that a particular employer will give you a week or more to decide — but don't count on it!

So the watchword here is: be prompt with your decision!

4. What If the Offer Comes from an Employer Who's Not Your First Choice?

This is a toughie. The first thing you'll want to do is put off a decision to the extent possible; perhaps ask for a week to make up

402 GUERRILLA TACTICS FOR GETTING THE LEGAL JOB OF YOUR DREAMS

your mind (being careful to thank them profusely for the offer, of course!). Then, immediately contact the employer at the top of your wish list, and say something like, "I'm calling to let you know that I have received an offer that I'm seriously considering. However, with what I know about your organization, I'm more interested in working for you." This may speed up the decision-making process. And the *worst* that can happen is that you've got it on record that you have a clear interest in your dream employer, so that you can pursue them some time down the road.

If you have *serious* doubts about an employer who makes you an offer, don't accept the offer at all! Remember, my goal with this book is to get you a job you'll really like, and if you follow my advice, I'm *sure* that will happen. Don't jump at the first job that's offered to you out of fear that you'll never get another offer, if you think you'll be miserable working there. I realize that there's a balance involved, in that you do have to get some legal experience under your belt, even if the job in question is not your first choice. But I don't under *any* circumstances think it makes sense to work somewhere that makes you very unhappy. You'd be better off waitering in a restaurant on weekend nights, and doing a Pro Bono America project during the week to get legal experience. The point here is: Don't *ever* feel as though you're trapped into accepting a job you really don't want!

5. ONCE YOU'VE ACCEPTED AN OFFER — *DON'T SHOP AROUND!*

One of the *absolutely, positively* worst things you can do during your job search is to accept an offer and then renege on it. Don't even *think* about interviewing once you've accepted an offer! As Debra Fink says, "Few stories run through the legal grapevine faster than those about lawyers who renege on an accepted offer. Once you accept, there's *no* graceful way to back out!"

Ann Skalaski says that this most often happens when a student isn't sure they're going to get an offer from their dream employer, so they accept another offer — and then, sure enough, they *do* get an offer from their employer of choice. She says, "I always tell students in this predicament, think about how *you'd* feel if a firm that made you an offer called your career services office and said, 'We've found a better student. Can we interview them?' You wouldn't want them to do that, so you shouldn't do it to them! It's just unethical!"

She advises that if you really want to pursue another job, you can always ask the employer who made you the offer how they'd feel about it. It's possible that they'll tell you to resolve your doubts. But they may not be so magnanimous, and may withdraw the offer instead.

So the fact is, reneging on a job offer is just a big, bad, no-no. As Ann Skalaski says, "The value of your professional reputation begins in law school, with your classmates. If they know that you've done something like this, they'll remember it later on. And remember, your classmates may refer business to you later on. That guy you have a beer with could wind up being a judge!" So don't risk your reputation on a foolish mistake. Don't accept offers for jobs you don't intend to undertake!

O. THE 14 BIGGEST BONERS LAW STUDENTS MAKE ON INTERVIEWS — AND HOW TO AVOID MAKING THOSE MISTAKES YOURSELF!

It's unfortunate, but true, that no matter how good your credentials are, and no matter how wonderful an employee you might make, none of that matters if you don't interview well. Regardless of how terrific you are otherwise, a mistake on the interview trail, and boom! No offer. Fortunately, it's easy for you to avoid interviewing mistakes, if you know what they are. I've littered this chapter with warnings about boo-boos in all kinds of situations. What I'm going to do here is to lump all of these mistakes together. They're the biggest, baddest boners law students make when they're interviewing. Whenever you're preparing for an interview, glance through this list to make sure *you* don't make any of these mistakes!

1. DON'T SHOW UP UNPREPARED!

In the first several pages of this chapter I hammered home the importance of preparation. As Sophie Sparrow says, "You need a clear idea of who the employer *is*, and why you're there." In fact, one out of every two legal interviewers lists "lack of preparation" as their pet peeve! So you need to research the employer, through published sources, your career services office, and anyone who might be familiar with the employer. At the *very* least, check with your career services office, read the employer's NALP form (if they have one, it'll be on file at career services), and read the employer's own materials, like brochures. Beyond researching the employer, you need to have all your ducks in a row in terms of the points you want to make about your strengths, the questions you'll ask, and the answers you'll give to difficult questions. That's really all there is to it.

2. DON'T FAIL TO SHOW ENTHUSIASM!

I've already told you that interviewers make a decision about you quickly — typically in the first few minutes of the interview. As Gail Cutter points out, a factor that weighs heavily in the interviewer's mind is this: "Does he really *want* my firm?" That's all about enthusiasm. You just can't afford to be aloof or standoffish. So be sure that your body language is positive. Look attentive, smile, lean forward. Speak clearly, at a moderate pace, and end your sentences on an "up" note. Ask questions. Show off your research. Let the interviewer know that you really want the job!

3. DON'T LET NEGATIVE BODY LANGUAGE NEGATE WHAT YOU SAY!

It doesn't matter if you're saying all the right things, if your body language is belying your words. Greet the employer with a smile and a firm handshake. During the interview, sit up. Lean forward. Smile. Pay attention. Don't fidget or play with your hair or tug at your clothes or nibble your nails. Be conscious of eye contact. Don't fold your arms in front of you. In other words, don't just *sound* as though you want the job — *look* as though you want the job, as well!

4. DON'T HIDE YOUR LIGHT UNDER A BUSHEL — TALK ABOUT YOUR STRONG POINTS!

I've pointed out to you before that the interviewer is not your advocate. If you don't bring out strong points about yourself, there's no way for the interviewer to find out about them. If need be, imagine that you're a lawyer and the interviewer is the judge and jury. You've got the obligation to present your best possible case, and that means bringing out everything that shows why you'd be such a great employee! If you've gone through all of the exercises I've given you in this chapter, you've got your accomplishments, your transferable skills, and your infomercial all rehearsed and ready to go. Make sure that you *make* those points about yourself to the interviewer, whether in the context of answers to the interviewer's questions, or by making comments about things the interviewer says: "It's interesting hearing about Bubble & Squeak's new environmental law department. I started an environmental law club at school, and we brought in speakers from. . . . " *However* you have to get your pitch across — do it!

5. DON'T MISTAKE ARROGANCE FOR SELF-CONFIDENCE!

Here's a riddle for you. Q: What's the difference between self-confidence and arrogance? A: It's the difference between "We'd like you to work with us," and "Get lost!" Employers welcome self-confidence, and shun arrogance. *Nobody* likes working with someone who's obnoxious!

That may seem pretty obvious, but some people find it difficult to draw the line between being self-confident and being cocky. What you want to strive for is an air that says you know yourself, you know what you have to offer, and you feel comfortable with yourself and talking about yourself — but you recognize that this is an interview situation, so you still have to be deferential to the interviewer. If you think you might have a problem with making this distinction, Kathleen Brady suggests talking with your career services director to see how you come off in interviews. Also, arrogance is something that will quickly surface if you do mock interviews.

Of course with every rule, there's an exception — that is, the arrogant person who gets the job. One career services person told me a wonderful story about a student who had been a journalist before law school, and while he was waiting for an on-campus interview, he took out a pen and edited the law firm's brochure, correcting mistakes and tightening up the language. Fine by itself, I guess — but then he took it into the interview, and handed it to the interviewer! Now the vast majority of interviewers would be floored by this kind of brash behavior and would quickly show the student the door. But as it turns out, this particular law firm was a bunch of young, aggressive litigators, and that kind of ballsiness was just what they wanted. The interviewer made him an offer on the spot. But that's the kind of arrogance that is going to alienate *almost* every interviewer — so, for most people, it's just not worth the risk!

6. DON'T VOLUNTEER YOUR FLAWS. INTERVIEWS AREN'T CONFESSIONALS!

As Sandy Mans points out, "If the interviewer doesn't ask about something that will expose a flaw, don't feel you have to state it yourself!" She goes on to point out that students tend to give negative information because they're uncomfortable with talking about themselves, and so they discuss their weaknesses.

This is a *huge* mistake. Remember, in your average interview, you've got only 20 minutes to convince the interviewer that you're the right person for the job. *Twenty lousy minutes*. If you spend 5 minutes of it stumbling over why it is you didn't AmJur every class First Year, you've only got *15* minutes to convince them why they *should* hire you.

When I discussed killer answers to tough interview questions, I explained to you how to crush any question that exposes any of your flaws. If the interviewer asks you point blank about something that's a flaw, then you've *got* to discuss it. Otherwise — shut up about it!

> **Exception: When you know your credentials are not what the employer typically demands.**

Boy, this is a toughie. I don't want you to go into an interview, *ever*, feeling as though you're not "good enough" for the job — because you are, *regardless* of your grades! But you may occasionally find yourself behind the eight-ball, in an interview with an employer who demands credentials you just don't have. For instance, let's say that you make contacts extremely well — probably by following my advice in Chapter 4, right? — and you get an interview with a very prestigious employer who wouldn't otherwise have interviewed you. Or let's say that your school doesn't allow full prescreening. That means that some on-campus interview slots are reserved for students the employer wouldn't otherwise be willing to interview, but they *have* to interview those students to be allowed to do *any* on-campus interviewing at your school. Normally, what you're talking about are large firm employers, because they're the ones who are credential hounds. If you're one of those students the firm is forced to interview, you indeed do not have the credentials they usually insist upon. But it's important to remember that *these kinds of situations are very unusual — the vast majority of the time, if you've got the interview, the employer views you as a viable candidate for a job.*

So, let's say you're in an interview, and because of everything I just discussed you know you don't have the grades they look for — they only take top 10%, Law Review people, and you're in the middle of your class.

In that situation, my advice to you is to take the bull by the horns and bring up your credentials even if the interviewer doesn't — and immediately explain why you believe you would be a great employee even though your paper credentials don't measure up to their usual criteria.

Don't use this wording exactly, but you want to say something like, "I know from talking with associates at your firm, as well as from my other research, that you typically only take students from the top 10% of the class. I can understand why you do that, and I acknowledge that I'm not in that part of the class, but I'd like to tell you why I'm confident I can do your work . . . " and then go on to explain the other factors that go into making you an ideal candidate — perhaps your client development skills, or other publications, or work experience, or performance in certain classes that are important to that employer, the old standby "a strong upward trend," whatever.

So while I stand by my original advice that you should not bring up your own flaws, in the rare situation where you're talking with an employer who would otherwise dismiss you out of hand because of your paper credentials, I *would* bring up that flaw, and crush it *immediately* with proof that you *are* the one for the job!

7. Don't Assume You Can't Get the Job — or the Flip Side of That: Assume That if You've Got the Interview, You've Got a Shot at the Job

You may occasionally find yourself in an interview for a job you think is beyond your reach. As I just discussed, in #6, you may have networked your way into an interview with a prestigious firm that would never have interviewed you based on your paper credentials. Or maybe you lucked out and got an on-campus interview because the employer had to hold slots open for students who don't meet their traditional criteria. There may be other reasons, as well, but the bottom line is that you think you don't belong.

Get over it!

I promise you, I *guarantee* you, there is *no* job that you can't perform based on your paper credentials, no matter *what* the interviewer thinks going into the interview. If you've researched the hell out of the employer, you've talked with everybody you can get your hands on who ever worked there, and you've done whatever you can by way of extracurriculars to show that you're a star in spite of mediocre grades, then *you can get that job if you believe you can get it.*

I've talked before about the importance of the words that you use when you talk to yourself, the Shad Helmstetter approach. There are really two basic ways to look at interviews like this. One is to say, "They never hire anyone with my grades, and they never will. This is a waste of time." Or you can say, "OK, they don't typically hire people who don't have great grades, but that doesn't mean they won't hire me. I've got my work cut out for me, but I *can* — and *will* — convince them I can do the work!" Same situation — two different approaches. Psyche yourself *into* the job, not *out of* it! As Teresa DeAndrado says, "If you got the interview, you *have* to assume you have a chance at the job — *regardless* of what their usual cut-off for grades is!"

8. DON'T TAKE HONESTY TO THE POINT OF FOOLHARDINESS

Oof! This is a *very* difficult topic to address. It's related in some ways to the idea of not exposing your flaws. But it's more than diverting attention from your weaknesses. All of us — well, most of us — like to think of ourselves as honest people. And career services directors always stress the importance of honesty. But the fact is, an interview is a sales presentation. As Mary Obrzut says bluntly, "An interview is not about honesty. It's about sales." And she's right. I'm not advocating, and no one would, that you lie about your job experience or your grades or any other of your credentials. But when you talk about attitude, or character traits or flaws, or any of the other kinds of things we discussed when we handled tough questions in this chapter, *you'd have to be a complete idiot to be flat-out honest.*

I'll give you an example of a conversation I had several times with different career services directors:

"How do you think students should handle the question, 'What's your greatest flaw?'"
"They should be honest and just come out and say what their greatest flaw is."
"OK. Let's say I'm a student, and my greatest flaw is

that I can't write at all. Should I say that?"

"Oh, of course not!"

So you see, you have to balance honesty with the idea of being a savvy interviewee. Honesty in its purest form has no place in interviews. If you *still* have difficulty swallowing this, look ahead a little bit to what you'll be doing as a lawyer. If someone walks into your office and wants you to handle their case, and they've got a really bad case — I mean a truly hopeless one — you're not going to say that. You're going to pull whatever positives you can from the situation, perhaps acknowledging the unlikelihood of success, but stressing that you'll do your very best for them. Well, that's not quite honest, is it? You think their case is a barking dog with fleas. *But as a lawyer, you can't say that.* And as a student interviewing for a job as a lawyer, you are dress rehearsing for the time when you *will* deal with clients. So it's important for you to exhibit that kind of savvy now!

9. DON'T BE DEFENSIVE OR APOLOGETIC

It's inevitable in interviews that the interviewer will put you on the spot. You'll be asked about less-than-stellar grades, or work experience, or what have you. *Whatever* you do, "don't apologize, and don't be defensive!" says St. John's' Maureen Provost Ryan. It's vital that you always maintain a positive spin on your abilities, your record, your character, everything. By all means, *explain.* "I didn't do well on my first year exams because, frankly, the style of law school exams caught me by surprise. But I've spoken with all of my first year professors, corrected the exam-taking flaws I had, and I'm confident my performance this semester will prove that I've overcome them." You've got to admit, that sounds a lot better than hiding your head between your legs and saying, "I know my grades are awful, and I just don't know what happened, but it's not like I'm stupid or anything."

So acknowledge whatever it is that makes you feel apologetic or defensive, but don't let those nasty reactions bubble to the surface. Smile, respond, and move on!

10. DON'T BE INTIMIDATED BY POWER

Depending on where the interview takes place, you may find the interviewer very intimidating, a Wizard of Oz-ish figure. If you feel that way, it will have a tendency to cow you into coming off

as less than self-confident. Remember, if you're dealing with someone powerful, they are still a *person*. At one time, they were a law
student just like you. The only difference between the two of you
is that they've probably got a bunch more years under their belt,
and different experience, but that's it. There were times in law school
when they drank too much beer and worshipped the porcelain goddess because of it. They've had setbacks and personal embarrass-
ments, too. So while you may respect the trappings of power —
the expensive car, office, position, whatever — don't let the importance of the interviewer intimidate you. Be deferential, certainly,
but that's true no matter *how* powerful you perceive the interviewer
to be. Take a deep breath, remember that you're in the interview
to make a sale, and plunge ahead!

11. Don't Be Overwhelmed by What You Perceive as Your Achilles' Heels

As Maureen Provost Ryan points out, "Students always have
a problem with Achilles' heels — they worry about questions they'll
be asked."

In this chapter, we analyzed all of the tough questions you might
be asked and how you should handle them. And in your preparation
before your interview, you did some self-assessment so that you
are comfortable with yourself, and what you bring to the table for
the employer. Remember, no matter what flaw you must overcome
in your background, it's got no predictive value as to how you will
perform for this particular employer *unless you give that flaw that
kind of power over you.* You're no more condemned to live forever
because of something in your background than *I* was condemned
to a life of being fat because I grew up that way. Talk to yourself
over and over and over again in loving, supportive terms, highlighting what you feel are your best traits. Tell yourself why it is that
you'll do a terrific job. As Maureen Provost Ryan says, "View
yourself as the irresistible candidate." And trust me — you'll start
to believe it, and when you do, you won't *have* any Achilles' heels!

12. Don't Be Late!

This is pretty obvious, but so many career services directors
and employers mentioned it to me that I figured it was worth
mentioning to you. Being late to your interview is a cardinal sin!
If something comes up that's going to delay you, call ahead and

warn the interviewer. Obviously, sometimes crises come up and there's no way to avoid *those*. But if it's at *all* avoidable — don't be late!

13. DON'T LET DOWN YOUR GUARD IN FRONT OF YOUNG ASSOCIATES!

It's entirely possible that the interviewer will be a new associate, and that means they're likely to be close to your age. And if you go on call-back interviews, you'll likely find yourself meeting several new associates, and perhaps even having a meal with them. No matter what the circumstances, remember that when you're with anyone from the employer's office, *you're on stage. Don't let your guard down!* It may be that they make you feel sufficiently comfortable that you start saying things like, "Boy, it must be tough working for that Mr. Y — he seems pretty stiff," or "You wouldn't believe the whopper I got away with on this interview," or any other similarly untoward comment. Remember, no matter how comfortable you feel with any person who works for the employer, they're *still* evaluating you from the employer's perspective. Be friendly, but don't let your guard down and say something inappropriate!

14. DON'T DISS THE HELP!

By this I mean, don't talk down to the employer's receptionist or secretary. As I pointed out to you in this chapter, one bad word from the receptionist or secretary about your attitude, and you can kiss an offer goodbye! So when you speak to the receptionist or secretary, pretend you're speaking to the interviewer directly. Be friendly and deferential. *Never* be arrogant or high-handed, even if the employer treats the receptionist or secretary that way in your presence!

Chapter 8

Making Yourself *Into* the Dream Candidate

On the cover of this book I tell you that I'll help you get your dream job regardless of your school, your grades, or your work experience. So you might look at the title to this chapter, and say, "OK, Kimmbo, what gives? I thought you were going to help me get my dream job even if I'm *not* the dream candidate!"

Well, here's the scoop. I really do believe that you can get almost any job with almost any background. But it's a lot *easier* to do that if you do a few things to make yourself into an attractive candidate, and you can do that no matter where you go to school, and even if your grades aren't up to snuff.

Before we get started, clearly the earlier in law school you are when you read this, the better off you are. If you're reading this the week after graduation, it's going to be impossible to do the school-oriented activities that I prescribe here. Instead, I would take part in Pro Bono America volunteer internships, I'd do some legal temping, and I'd get heavily involved in local bar association activities on a volunteer basis — all of which I describe in detail in Chapter 4. This chapter focuses primarily on things you can do while you're in law school to increase your desirability as a job candidate.

The things I'm going to focus on in this chapter revolve around accomplishing four specific goals:

1. Distinguishing yourself from the competition.

You're probably thinking "grades," but that's not necessarily so. What I'm going to do here is advise you to do things that make you stand out from an otherwise undifferentiated mass of law students in the minds of employers.

2. Demonstrating the ability to do the things lawyers do.

Let's face it. There are really only two things lawyers do: substantive work, and getting and keeping clients. I'll outline for you the things you ought to do to show that you, too, can do these things.

3. Showing a concrete interest in a practice area.

Anybody can go to an interview and feign an interest in a practice area, even if they've never given it a moment's notice before. And employers are aware of that, too. So what I'll do here are show you the things you should do to *prove* to an employer that you truly are interested in what they practice.

4. Making yourself geographically desirable.

Geography is a *huge* concern with legal employers. If you're either from a city where you want to practice, or you go to school there, this is no concern for you. And it's not a concern if you're looking for a job with the government, like the D.A.'s office, which expects you to move around. But *otherwise* — legal employers look at investing 3 years in you before they get a return on their investment, and if they think it's likely you won't stay with them that long, you won't get the job. So it's important to make yourself geographically desirable.

With that little preview in mind — let's get started!

A. FOUR KEYS TO MAKING YOURSELF THE DREAM CANDIDATE

1. DISTINGUISH YOURSELF FROM THE COMPETITION

What I'm talking about here is making yourself *memorable*, as a complete package — not just a law student. Now, one clear way to do that is with stellar grades or work experience, but that's not exactly headline news, is it? If you *can* get good grades, *get* them. But that's not really my focus here. Instead, what I want you to think about is *developing unusual hobbies and interests, if you don't have them already.* Can you play an unusual instrument? Learn an offbeat language? Have you traveled anywhere that's unusual, or do you have the opportunity to do so during a break? Have you got an interesting hobby, like white-water rafting, or saltwater fly fishing? Do you collect something unusual, like antique mechanical banks, or British royal commemorative china, or snow globes from around the world? If you aren't inspired, talk to other people and find out what *they* do that might interest you — and remember, make it something that's off the beaten track. Tennis, golf, things like that are fine hobbies — but they aren't terribly unusual.

You may be wondering why the heck I'm advocating this. Because it will help make your résumé stand out and make you memorable to a prospective employer. Even if you're writing to a potential employer through a mutual contact — the very best way to make contact — it helps if you have something to put forth that makes you stand out. Employers told me over and over again that students do them a favor by including on their résumés personal interests and hobbies. And that makes a lot of sense. If you're an employer and you're interviewing law student after law student, you get sick of talking about the same things over and over again. The student who provides you with something new and interesting to talk about does you a *favor,* and you view that student in a better light as a result.

So, consider developing an unusual hobby or interest, or making a point of mentioning those you already have. It'll help you stand out!

2. DEMONSTRATE THE ABILITY TO DO WHAT LAWYERS DO

As I mentioned a couple of minutes ago, what lawyers do boils down to two essential things: the work itself, and getting and maintaining clients, or what's otherwise called "rainmaking." Let's look at each of these, separately.

A. THE WORK ITSELF

Probably the most obvious, traditional indication of your ability to do lawyers' work is your performance on exams. "Oh, no!" you're thinking. "Back to that evil demon, grades!" Well, grades are a part of it, but if you don't have good grades, re-member, they're not everything. There's a strong argument to be made for the fact that your performance on a one-time, 4-hour, closed-book exam doesn't prove anything about whether you can analyze and research a case with full library access at your disposal.

So, how do you prove you can do the work itself? Either do it — via part-time jobs — or do something like it, by doing research projects for professors, or publishing articles in an area that interests you, or doing volunteer projects that involve research. (For writing ideas, read "Writing Activities" in Chapter 4, on page 120; also, check with your career services office.)

B. GETTING AND RETAINING CLIENTS

This is what's called "rainmaking," and it's so important that I've dedicated an entire chapter to it — Chapter 11. For now, it's important for you to know that a demonstrated ability to deal with people is worth a great deal to employers; in fact, as you move up the food chain in a law firm, it's far more important than your ability to do the substantive work.

How do you show it? In a nutshell, as Cal Western's Lisa Kellogg points out, "You do anything that involves marketing or people-oriented skills. Fundraisers, volunteering, that kind of thing." Kentucky's Drusilla Bakert also advises, "Community involvement is the best way to show rainmaking ability. It's a much better idea to do the local United Way Drive than it is to do the Student Bar Association."

So the watchword here is: Make an effort to show that you can meet and deal with people in the community.

3. SHOW A CONCRETE INTEREST IN A PRACTICE AREA

OK, here's the situation. You're desperate for a job, and you're sitting in an interview with Marvin Phlebitz, who specializes in phlegm reclamation law. And you have no problem saying, "Why, yes, Mr. Phlebitz, I've always been particularly interested in phlegm reclamation."

Well, guess what. It's pretty unlikely that Mr. Phlebitz just fell off the ol' turnip wagon, and so he's going to view your interest in phlegm reclamation with a weary eye — *unless there's stuff in your background that backs up your interest!*

So — how do you *do* that? Well, for a start, you *develop* an interest in a particular practice area, or maybe a couple of them. Remember, we discussed that in detail back in Chapter 2. Then, you take part in activities that revolve around that practice area. You could join an appropriate club at school, solicit speakers for on-campus speeches in that area, and write articles about the topic for either student publications or industry newsletters (your library will have a complete listing of these; trust me, if you want to publish an article, there's *always* an outlet for it!).

The flip side of generating opportunities to show an interest in a practice area is to take advantage of opportunities that are built into your curriculum. For instance, most schools have a writing requirement of some sort. As Georgetown's Marilyn Tucker points out, "Take advantage of that writing requirement to market yourself! So, if you're interested in labor and employment law, don't choose securities as your writing topic!"

What will happen if you go out of your way to show your interest in a practice area? Employers will recognize that — and your sincerity will vault you way over classmates who have better paper credentials than you do. Remember, honest enthusiasm always makes you *shine!*

4. MAKE YOURSELF GEOGRAPHICALLY DESIRABLE

All right, let's switch seats. Let's say you're the interviewer, and you've got your legal offices in Honolulu. And you're interviewing me, at my law school, in Detroit. You see from my résumé that I was born and raised in Cleveland. You know that I'm going to have to work for you for 3 years for you to earn back your investment in training me. Now, I don't care whether I'm just the most charming interviewee on the planet. There's a question that's going to be at the forefront of your mind the whole time you're talking to me, and it's this: *What the heck is she doing interviewing with a Honolulu law firm?*

As I discussed in detail in Chapter 7 on Interviewing, geography is a huge, lurking concern with legal employers. It's important to have some kind of geographical tie to the city where you're interviewing. If you grew up there, or you go to school there, or you have friends or relatives there, that's great. If you *don't*, then part of making yourself the ideal candidate is to spend as much time as possible there before you graduate. As George Washington's

Laura Rowe says, "If you know the city you want when you graduate, then spend your summers there!" In other words, do whatever you can to *prove* that you'll accept a job if offered one there, and you'll stay once you *do* accept it.

Now this isn't true for the kinds of jobs where you're expected to start in a rural area and then work your way to bigger cities. In those cases, *nobody* expects you to show a true geographical tie to Moosebreath Junction in the state of Wahoo. So for employers like the U.S. Attorney's office, or D.A.'s office, geography is not a big thing. But for private employers, it sure is. And to make yourself the ideal candidate, you've got to be able to show the geographical loyalty they're looking for!

B. OK — A FIFTH, RADICAL WAY TO DISTINGUISH YOURSELF FROM THE CROWD

Consider taking a semester off. "WHAT?!?" you're saying. "HAVE YOU LOST YOUR MIND, KIMMBO?" OK, OK, OK, I hear you. But once you've calmed down, I want you to think about a couple of things.

First off, there's a possibility — and remember, it's only a possibility — that you're not entirely gung-ho law school. There's a theory that fully a third of all law students are not committed to law. You may be one of them.

Second, as Maine's Tammy Willcox points out, there's less competition in the job market in December — which is when you'd graduate if you took a semester off. Less competition means better access to jobs, right?

Third, if you're going to school on loans, you can generally get a 6-month deferral. So, you don't have to worry about paying back loans while you're away.

And fourth, it's a lot easier to explain a semester off than you think it is. In Chapter 2, when I first discussed the possibility of taking a semester off, I floated the idea of saying something like this in an interview: "Well, I didn't know exactly what I wanted to do with my law degree. So I took my semester off and (fill in the blank) traveled/interviewed lawyers/saw the world/whatever, and that time away focused my energy and made it obvious to me that I want to do what *you* do." Put yourself in an employer's shoes. Not only would that semester off not seem like a *detriment*, it would be a *huge plus!*

Now, what is it that you do with that time off? All the kinds of things that I've already discussed in terms of making yourself into the ideal student, *except* that you don't have the crush of coursework to distract you. Write articles. Take up interesting and unusual hobbies. Do volunteer or other people-oriented work. You'll come back with renewed energy — and you'll have helped make yourself into the dream candidate!

Chapter 9

What If You Didn't Get an Offer After Your Summer Clerkship

(or any other legal job you've held...)

"Whatever has happened to you, it has already happened.
The important question is, how are you going to handle it?
In other words, "Now what?"

Jon Kabat-Zinn

If there's a law school equivalent of a scarlet letter, it goes to students who get dings from their summer clerkship employers. Not getting invited back is an undeniable stigma, and if it happens to you, I feel for you more than any other kind of law student. And I'll tell you one big reason why — It happened to me.

I won't go into detail except to tell you that I clerked for an enormous prestigious law firm. At the end of the summer, the firm made offers to 20 of its 22 summer clerks. I wasn't one of the 20. No matter what size employer rejects you, your feelings will likely be what mine were. Shock. Devastation. Disbelief. But I did bounce back, and I did get other offers from other firms. I look back now and realize I would have been miserable at that firm, and in rejecting me they ultimately did me a huge favor.

But that's not how I felt at the time, and if you've just been rejected, you probably have a hard time believing you'll *ever* feel as I do. But the fact is, you can, and will, bounce back. In this chapter, I'll show you how to overcome the specific problem of a rejection from your last employer. Once you've done this, you can use all the other techniques in this book to find your dream job, regardless of your rejection!

A. CATCH YOUR BREATH

Don't tell yourself that you have to get right back up on the horse the day after you get a rejection from your last employer. As Vanderbilt's Pam Malone says, "It's devastating not to get an offer after your summer clerkship," and Boston University's Betsy Armour adds, "People who don't get offers are usually heartbroken. They have to go through a grieving process."

So don't deny the enormous emotional impact of a rejection. Give yourself a few days when you don't try to explain the situation to *anyone*. If anybody asks about it, thank them for their concern but tell them you're not ready to talk about it just yet. Take a deep breath, regroup, maybe vent with a close friend or your career services director.

Then, when you've got your emotions under control, it's time for a little detective work . . .

B. FIND OUT WHAT HAPPENED

You may be horrified at this prospect, but it's absolutely necessary if you're going to overcome the stigma of a rejection from your last employer. On a scale of difficulty from 1 to 10, almost everything I tell you to do in this book hovers near 1. This is closer to 10, and there's just nothing I can do to make it easier for you, except to say that you only have to do it once. John F. Kennedy said he could tolerate any pain if he knew for certain it would end, and finding out why you were rejected is a pain that you'll only have to endure once. As William and Mary's Rob Kaplan says, "It's painful, but you *have* to get a clear explanation of why you *didn't* get an offer." Once you *have* that information, then I'll show you in Topic C, below, how to use that information to your advantage for prospective employers.

But I'm getting ahead of myself. Right now, we're just concerned with finding out why you didn't get an offer. Rob Kaplan suggests calling your former employer and saying something like, "While I'm disappointed, it's not to challenge your decision — but I have to get information to move forward. I want to be sure that what prospective employers hear from me is consistent with what they hear from you." You really are just calling for information, and you *have* to keep your emotions out of it. It makes it much easier, by the way, if you call someone you really got along with. Inevitably, there will have been *someone* you liked, and they're the obvious choice as a person to call. But remember, no matter how close you were to them, they still work there. You can't diss your former employer, and you can't be defensive. You're just looking for information, and you shouldn't call until you can keep your emotions in check and do just that.

What kind of information are you looking for? You're looking to see which category your rejection falls into. You're really looking for the *whys* of your lack of an offer to return. I talked with many career services directors about this, and the kinds of rejections they told me about fell into four, general groups:

1. Good Reviews, but Bad Economics

In other words, given more money, the firm would have taken you, but they can't.

Within this "economics" category, there are two possibilities: either:

(a) The firm didn't make an offer to *anyone;* or
(b) They made an offer to very few summer clerks (e.g., two out of seven).

2. Personality Conflict

Let's face it: nobody goes through life getting along with *everyone* they meet, and sometimes there are people we just don't get along no matter how hard we try. If you had a personality conflict with an important partner, it probably didn't matter how good your work was; you didn't get an offer because of that conflict.

3. A WORK PRODUCT-BASED PROBLEM

If there was a problem with your work, it probably fell into one of two categories. Either:

(a) You screwed up one project; or
(b) You had a consistent problem, e.g., late assignments.

4. DID YOU SABOTAGE YOURSELF?

As Columbia's Ellen Wayne points out, "You may find that your summer job wasn't what you wanted, after all." I've told you elsewhere that, statistically, a third of all law students aren't committed to law. And most students who go to large firms are not happy there. Whether your employer was a large firm or not, it may well be that you really *didn't* enjoy the work, and you subconsciously sabotaged yourself by performing poorly.

Coming to this conclusion will take a great deal of hard thinking, but if you don't think that any of the three categories I described above really fit you, I want you to think about the possibility that you didn't give it your all because somewhere, deep down inside, you didn't really *want* to. If you find that that's the case, I urge you to go back to Chapter 2 and go through all the exercises that help you decide what the job of your dreams really is. It could be that for the best possible motives — to please your parents, to gain the esteem of your peers — you wound up with a job you, yourself, really didn't want. If that's so, then your former employer did you a favor by bailing you out of it at the earliest possible opportunity; much better to waste only a few months in a job you truly don't want, than years, or even an entire career!

So give some thought to the possibility that you didn't get an offer because in your heart you didn't want one. And if you find that that's so, take heart! Starting today, you *can* decide what you really want to do — and pursue that!

C. PULL OUT THE POSITIVES FROM YOUR LAST JOB EXPERIENCE

OK. We've decided exactly what it is that went wrong with your last job. And remember, we've got four basic categories: economics, a personality conflict, a work product-based problem, or self-sabotage (I've already told you how to deal with the sabotage problem, so we'll leave that one aside, here). Of the remaining three, we had two different kinds of economics problems — one where the employer didn't hire anybody, and the other where they hired a small minority of clerks. And for work product-based problems, we had a mess-up on one project, versus a consistent pattern of mess-ups. I'm going to tell you how to deal with all of these, but from the start, we can easily discard one of them, and it's the economics problem where the employer didn't hire *any* clerks. The reason that one's so easy to handle is that it's not a comment on you or your work; if the money just wasn't there to hire *anybody*, that's the easiest possible thing to explain to any future employer.

The other four possibilities are more difficult, but you'll handle them all in basically the same way: you want to make any corrections to your own work habits or interpersonal skills as are necessary, and you'll want to get positive reviews from anyone at your last employer who will supply them. Those references can take the form of a willingness to speak with future employers, and/or providing a letter of reference. If you can get both, that's great! (You'll probably find that anyone who liked you at your last employer will feel bad that you didn't get an offer, and providing you with a letter of recommendation and making a few phone calls will be something they'll happily do for you.)

First, let's look at the possibility of making corrections to your job skills. If you really did hand in all of your projects late, or you did sloppy research, then you're going to have to tune-up your skills before you can expect another employer to take a chance on you. (Frankly, if you did this, I think there's a substantial possibility you were sabotaging yourself, but I suppose it's possible you could have made mistakes like this *without* having that motive.) So try volunteering, or doing a research project for a professor, where you clearly overcome whatever flaw there was in your clerkship experience. You will also want to try and get any positive reviews from your last clerkship that you can muster. It's unlikely that you fell down on every project; you probably did have someone you worked with who's got something positive to say about your work. If so, lean on that person to be a reference for you.

Suppose your job skills fell down in the area of interpersonal relationships? That is, you had a personality conflict with someone at your last job? Well, you can see what a prospective employer's problem might be: they might think that you're the one with the personality problem, and you might disrupt their office because of it. Now you and I both know that that's usually not the case. Let's face it, there are a lot of jerks out there. But if the jerk in question is a partner on the hiring committee, in the future it might make sense for you to hold your tongue and not speak quite as frankly as you would socially. If for whatever reason you just couldn't get along with an important person at your last employer, it's worth taking a look at yourself and figuring out how you can avoid such a dangerous conflict in future. Acknowledging that someone else has control over you and has the power to make your life miserable, at least for a little while, can be a humiliating experience. But for future reference, the important thing to remember is to hold your tongue and keep the power that comes from being able to make your *own* decisions about whether you stay or leave. If you get a rejection, you don't *have* that power. (I'm not saying, by the way, that you'd want to accept an offer from an employer where you had a strong personality conflict with someone there; it might make your work so miserable that it wouldn't be worth it. I'm just saying, it's worth keeping the peace long enough to get invited to come back, so that you can show that offer to other, prospective employers.)

On the other hand, it might be that no matter how hard you tried, someone at your last job had it in for you and there's nothing you could do about it. Well, no matter what the source of the personality conflict was, you're going to need to get references from people you *did* get along with. You would not expect them to say anything bad about the colleague you *didn't* get along with, even if they agree that that person is a real clown, but they undoubtedly will be able to come up with good things to say about *you* to cut the stigma.

Well, we've talked about problems with your job skills, and personality conflicts. That only leaves economic problems, where the firm made offers to only a few of its clerks. This might not, off-hand, seem like much of a problem, but you can imagine what a prospective employer is likely to think: "Well, I appreciate that they could only afford to hire 3 out of 10, but how come you weren't one of the three?" What you want to do in this situation is what I've suggested twice before: that is, gather people from your last job who will say good things about your work, and use them as references.

D. GET YOUR EXPLANATION DOWN PAT

Now that you know why you didn't get an offer from your last employer, and you've gotten your ducks in a row when it comes to references from people there who *did* respond favorably to you and your work, you've got to get comfortable with *explaining* what happened to prospective employers. It's got to be something that you can state, smilingly and with confidence. It might be something like, "Of the eight projects I worked on all summer, I had one project involving Estate Tax implications that the partner in question wasn't pleased with. I analyzed where I slipped up, spoke with the Estate Tax professor at school about it, and I'm confident that both my knowledge of the area and my research skills are exactly where they should be. In fact, I can direct you to other partners from the firm where I worked, and they can tell you about the quality of my work. . . . " Or you might say, "My former employer could only afford to hire two of the eight summer clerks, and unfortunately I wasn't one of those two. However, if you have any doubts about my abilities, I have letters of recommendation from all of the attorneys I worked for at the firm, and they'll be able to vouch for the quality of my work." Now obviously you're not going to use these word for word, but you can see what they share:

1. They're not defensive.

2. They're clear and concise.

3. They don't bad mouth the former employer (a *big* no-no).

4. They wind up on an up note; namely, your willingness to offer as references people from your old job who *will* say good things about you.

In a way, handling a rejection from an old employer is a lot like overcoming any pitfall in your job credentials, like poor grades or a lack of work experience. The most important thing about it is the spin that you put on it. If you can speak with confidence about the perceived flaw, you can turn any negative into a positive!

E. DON'T EVEN *THINK* ABOUT LYING ABOUT GETTING AN OFFER!

This is a *really* big no-no — but it may be *very* tempting to just avoid doing all of the work I'm telling you to do, and simply lie and tell future prospective employers that you *did* get an offer from your last employer. Don't do it! As NYU's Gail Cutter says, "The legal community is *very* small, no matter how large it seems!" The odds that you'll be caught in your lie are very much against you, and if you get yourself into that kind of a fix, there's nothing ol' Auntie Kimmbo can do to help you out of it. So don't even *think* about saying you got an offer, if you didn't!

F. FORGE AHEAD!

The most important thing to remember is that even though your rejection may loom large in your mind right now, in the grand spectrum of your life it's a very small setback indeed. If the worst career hurdle you ever face is having to explain away a rejection from a summer employer, you will indeed live a blessed life. I promise you that the hurt you feel right now will fade, and given time, you will be able to put the rejection in perspective. If you have bad feelings toward your former employer, put that energy to use to benefit yourself! Here's how: If you let yourself wallow in misery and don't pursue other jobs, what will your former employer's reaction be? "Geez, I'm glad we didn't keep *that* loser!" Whereas, if you turn around and follow the advice in this book to find a job you truly enjoy, one where you'll shine, that old employer's reaction will be: "Hmmm. Maybe we let a really good one get away." So, regardless of how you feel right now, give yourself a little time to grieve, and then take the steps I've outlined in this chapter. I promise you that no matter how badly your last job turned out, you can *still* get your dream job!

Chapter 10

Help!
My Grades Stink!

Quick! How did you do in the 9th grade? What were your grades like?

You don't remember, do you? I didn't think so. The reason I brought that up from the get-go is to highlight something *very important* about your law school grades. *They won't matter for very long.* You don't remember your 9th grade performance now, and within 5 years of when you graduate from law school, you won't remember how you did in law school, either. Trust me on this one; the importance of law school grades fades very quickly.

None of this, mind you, is to minimize the pain or frustration you may feel now because the god of grades hasn't smiled on you in law school. But it's only because you're still in school — or shortly removed from it — that this casts such a huge pall over your mental landscape.

"Well, gee, Kimmbo," you're saying. "Thanks for the pep talk. But everybody knows that grades mean *everything* when it comes to getting a job." Oh, yeah? Sez who? When it comes to getting your dream job, my response to anyone who says your grades determine your job is this: to hell with your grades. There are few easier obstacles to handle than bad grades, if you go about it the right way. And I'm going to show you how to do exactly that.

429

What I'll be doing in this chapter is telling you specifically how to deal with bad grades, so that you can go after your dream job on the same footing as anyone else. Your job search is going to be largely the same as anybody else's — you'll have to make the same decisions about what you want to do (Chapter 2), you'll make contacts to get that job (Chapter 4), and you'll go through the same interviewing and corresponding functions as everyone else. And if you remember back to Chapter 1, you'll realize that when I gave you the two keys to getting the legal job of your dreams — taking the initiative and displaying honest enthusiasm — I didn't mention anything about having great grades. You know why? Because you don't need them.

If you don't believe that, it's because your mind has been poisoned by the evil atmosphere of law school. It's incredible how, as soon as the very first grade comes out, people are immediately typecast by their grades. People in the top 10% of the class are "smart," and their classmates are branded according to rank all the way down the food chain to the bottom of the class. Few things in law school broke my heart as much as seeing classmates who'd entered law school bursting with enthusiasm, full of hopes and dreams, having their spirit broken by a couple of bad grades in First Year. It was cruel and it was largely unnecessary. And do you know why? Because your ability to be a good lawyer is much more a reflection of the qualities you brought to law school, and the enthusiasm you'll bring to your job, than it is on how you performed on a single 3-hour exam for each class. You just don't feel that way because you're in the thick of law school right now. So, much of my task in this chapter is to work on how you feel about those grades, and how you can come to grips with discussing them without feeling defensive or defeatist. I *promise* you, you *can* get the job of your dreams, *regardless* of how bad your grades are. If you don't believe me now, you will by the time this chapter is over! For a start, get a load of these anecdotes about students with bad grades, gathered from career services director around the country:

◆   A career services director at a school in New England told me about a student who'd had great grades undergrad, but bombed in law school. He took bankruptcy as a Second Year, and loved it. He volunteered for a bankruptcy judge, and in that role met several prominent local bankruptcy attorneys. One of them referred him to another lawyer who had just gotten a huge bankruptcy client, and needed a clerk.

The lawyer hired this guy over the phone, telling him that although he didn't have the credentials the firm normally looked for, they'd hire him for this one project and if he did a good job, they'd give him a good recommendation for his next job.

Well, he worked on the project, and did so well that at the end of the summer they made him a permanent offer. A year later, he was hired away by a prestigious firm who has a policy of only hiring students in the top 5% of their class!

♦ A career services director in the midwest told me about a student in the bottom 5% of the class. Desperate for a job, he took a low-paying position with the state department of insurance. Through that, he made contacts at a small insurance company, and got a job there as in-house counsel. Unbeknownst to him when he took the job, the small company was planning to merge with an enormous, well-known insurance company, and when the merger went through, he became assistant general counsel, with a six-figure salary.

♦ A career services director in the northeast recounted to me the story of a first year student with awful grades. This guy had read "Barbarians at the Gate," and dreamed of doing corporate acquisitions — something that only huge firms, hiring top students from top schools, get to do. He was bereft at the prospect of not pursuing his dream, but the career services director talked him into considering clerking for a small firm that does corporate work. He was sure that he would not enjoy working for *anyone* if he didn't have a chance of being in the *Wall Street Journal*. Lo and behold, he found he loved the work as opposed to the trappings of a huge firm. He was made an offer to be an associate after he graduated, and he gladly jumped on it.

♦ A career services director out west told me about a panel she ran that featured alumni in very important positions in Washington, DC. One of the panel members was a guy who was the head of a governmental agency — an extraordinarily good job! After the panel was over, one of the law professors in the audience pulled the career services director aside, gestured toward the guy from the agency, and whispered to her, "Can you believe it? We didn't think he'd make it through law school!"

I've even got an anecdote of my own about beating bad grades. When I was in law school, I shared a dorm room with the worst student on the face of the planet. I don't remember her ever doing a shred of homework throughout law school. She'd go out drinking every night, wake up at 5 to 9 every morning, run her hands through her hair, and show up, disheveled and hung-over, for her 9 o'clock class. She only got one answer right when she was called on in class for the entire time she was in law school, and that's only because she happened to have her *Gilbert's* outline open to the right page. And at the end of the semester, she used that as a basis for trying to argue her grade up a notch! She went to the professor and said, "Come on. Aren't you going to give me any credit for class participation?" He looked at her in disbelief, and said, "You want half a grade, you got it. D! D-plus! What's the difference?" Well, as it turns out, she married a Libyan immigrant while we were Third Years, and through him, she realized there were a lot of people with immigration problems. So after she passed the Bar, she set up a sole practice focusing on immigration law, and became *very* successful. Everything she lacked in terms of studiousness, she made up for in terms of people skills — but her ultimate success would have been hard even for me to predict when we were law students!

As these anecdotes show, it's *always* possible to overcome bad grades and land a dream job. Let's go step-by-step through how you should go about it.

A. BEAT THE MOST SERIOUS EFFECT OF BAD GRADES: THEIR EFFECT ON YOUR SELF-WORTH

The worst thing about getting bad grades in law school is how they make you feel about yourself. Especially if you were a good student in undergrad, law school may be the first time in your life that you've ever had bad grades. As Franklin Pierce's Sophie Sparrow says, "If you're used to outward forms of validation in the form of good grades, it's hard to feel validated when your grades are awful." Florida's Ann Skalaski echoes that, saying, "It's tough to be in the bottom half of the class when you've never been there before."

The most important thing to do when you've got bad grades is to keep them in perspective. That's very difficult to do, because, as Kentucky's Drusilla Bakert says, "Law school destroys your perspective. It trains you to focus, not to look at the universe." But if your grades are bad, it's *very* important to get your perspective back; to step away and look at that universe. And what does it show you? That sitting in a room taking a 4-hour final exam isn't your best skill. *And that's it.* As St. Louis' Wendy Werner points out, "Great. Let's move on. You'll never have to do *that* again." And, she's right. Once you're out of law school, you never have to do anything resembling a 4-hour closed-book exam (well, outside of the bar exam, anyway). So all bad grades really do is show that you're not very good at doing something that you'll never have to do for the rest of your life. That's not really so bad, is it?

You also have to consider that your grades are not a reflection of what kind of a lawyer you will be. As Ann Skalaski points out, "You have to think about what you thought would make you a good lawyer *before* you had grades. Whatever it is that you thought is *still* true." If you have great people skills, or you're a skillful negotiator, or you research well — all of that is still true, and all of those things will have a far greater impact on your success as a lawyer than any stupid grades you might get. As Drusilla Bakert says, "Students have this big misconception that grades are everything. They aren't! Few students appreciate the importance of personality, of relating to people. It's easy to get disillusioned by grades, but it's important to remember that law is a *people* business."

I'll tell you one big reason that it's hard to look past your grades, and it's the impact of on-campus interviews. Legal employers who do on-campus interviews almost always interview the people in the top 10% of the class. And that may give you the impression that those are the only legal employers there are, and that those are the only students who will get jobs. *It's simply not true.* On-campus interviews get disproportionate attention just because they're so visible. Everybody knows about them. But as I've pointed out several times before, they're just the tip of the iceberg. The vast majority of legal jobs don't come about via on-campus interviews; in fact, most legal jobs aren't advertised anywhere at all, and that's why it's so important for you to make contacts, as I outline in detail in Chapter 4, *regardless* of what your grades are like. OK, so if your grades stink, you won't be spending a lot of time dressing up in a suit for on-campus interviews. You're going to have to be a little bit more creative than that. You should take solace in that, and here's why. For one thing, the vast majority of your classmates are in the same boat, no matter where in the class they are. And for another thing, those jobs available through on-campus interviews may be prestigious and high-paying, but if you skip ahead to Chapter 12 where I talk about getting large firm jobs, you'll quickly find that most people are miserable with those kinds of jobs. Sure, they have the aura of success, but you're an unusual bird if you can remain happy very long working hundred-hour weeks in a highly politicized setting; most people don't, and that's why the turnover in that kind of job is so high.

This is all a roundabout way of saying that it's only a matter of where you're sitting right now that makes grades seem so important. As Drusilla Bakert points out, "Two years out of law school, you're not your grades. You're your last case, or what you're working on now." And she's right. I can't remember the last time anyone asked about my law school grades, and if they did now, 10 years after law school, I'd laugh at them; nothing could be less relevant than a bunch of 10-year-old test results.

So don't let yourself be depressed about your grades. They're a reflection of how you performed in a 4-hour timeframe on an exam, *and that's it*. They don't determine your worth, your potential success, or any other facet of your life — and anyone who tries to make you feel differently is insecure enough not to want to face that truth.

B. ACKNOWLEDGE THAT MOST OF THE PEOPLE YOU INTERVIEW WITH WEREN'T ON LAW REVIEW, EITHER

If you've got bad grades, it's easy to put yourself into a party of one, believing that every potential legal interviewer must have done much better than you did in law school. *Not true!* As Wendy Werner points out, "At least 50% of practicing lawyers were in the bottom half of the class. You have *many* peers out there!" Willamette's Diane Reynolds adds, "Lawyers tend to hire from the part of the class they were in. If you're a nice and articulate person, you'll be fine." And San Diego's Susan Benson says, "Many attorneys embrace the fact that they themselves weren't stellar students — and they embrace students who are like they were."

So as you contact people, make sure you don't look at everyone as being a better student than you are. They may not have been. Instead, you want to derive confidence from other sources. Which leads me conveniently to . . .

C. IGNORE YOUR GRADES AND CONCENTRATE ON YOUR EXTRACURRICULAR EXPERIENCE

You may be horrified to hear this. "Oh my god, Kimmbo!" you're saying. "I've *got* to get my GPA up, or I'll *never* get a job!" Relax, OK? I'm not saying that you should never crack a book for the remainder of law school. What I *am* saying is that you have to *diversify* your experience to shift the focus away from your grades. There are a couple of excellent reasons for this.

One is that if your grades aren't good, I'll bet you dollars to donuts that it's not because you didn't study enough. I've never spoken with a law student who'd done poorly and found that it was because they weren't diligent with their studies. Quite the contrary; some of the students with the worst grades are the ones who put in the most hours. It's just that they didn't use that time as productively as they might have. Telling you how to get better grades and work less is beyond the scope of this book; there are a whole bunch of study aids that will help you do just that. Many study aids are extremely helpful, and I know that for a fact, because I wrote a lot of them. Suffice it to say here that if you didn't get good grades, you shouldn't compound the error by doubling the amount of time you spend on your studies.

Another reason that you have to focus more on extracurriculars is that that's how you're likely to lead yourself to the job of your dreams. As Cal Western's Lisa Kellogg points out, "What you lack in grades, you can make up for with experience." Washington's Teresa DeAndrado adds, "Working part-time makes you feel better about yourself, makes law school make sense, and builds something to offer employers." What you want to do is to find things that *make up* for your lack of grades. As Chicago-Kent's Lisa Abrams puts it, you're looking for a "claim to fame" in law school — work experience, a published article, a clinic — a salable, special thing.

What should you do? Any of the extracurriculars that I outline in Chapter 4, when I discuss networking through activities, would be excellent choices — and you'll notice that when I discuss those activities, I don't mention grades, because grades are *irrelevant*. Now as you choose extracurriculars to get involved in, focus on what you've liked about law school. With bad grades, it's easy to let those grades taint your entire law school experience — but there must be something about it that you've enjoyed (and please don't say "lunch"). As Wendy Werner points out, "People with poor grades typically like the practical aspects of law school — clinical skills more than writing skills, and trial litigation more than tax issues. They're typically interested in solving people's problems and arguing before a judge." If that's true for you, go after extracurriculars that involve people. Go for a part-time job at legal services or the public defender's office. Take moot court and trial advocacy. Take part in the client counseling competition at school. Look for pro bono positions — as Lisa Kellogg points out, "They'll pay attention to what you want — for instance, whether you want trial experience, or you want to do research." (I talk more about jobs to look for in Topic E, later.)

The point is, you should focus on getting experience that is not tied to your classes. You want to be fully-rounded, so that when the issue of grades comes up, you can handle it gracefully and guide your questioner to aspects of your experience that are more positive — and that means choosing extracurriculars wisely. They'll have the added benefit of bolstering your self-esteem. After all, people who aren't good at paper exams are typically very good at practical applications. Give yourself a chance to shine by putting your skills to work!

D. COME UP WITH PATTER ABOUT YOUR GRADES THAT MAKES YOU FEEL COMFORTABLE

Whether you're volunteering, looking for a clerkship or part-time work, or looking for your first full-time job, it's *essential* that you become comfortable with your credentials — and that includes your grades. I'm not saying that you'll ever be thrilled with the idea of poor grades, but that's irrelevant. All you need to do is to *sound* nonchalant about them.

As I discussed in detail in Chapter 7 on Interviewing, it's important to be able to present every facet of yourself with quiet self-confidence. If the facet that you're talking about happens to be grades, and if those grades happen to be poor, then this is going to take a bit of practice — but I promise you, it *can* be done.

One of the first things that you have to do is to come up with *some* explanation for your grades. As Diane Reynolds says, "Make your explanation positive and short. For instance, if you had a first semester disaster, you can say something like, 'I was thrown for a loop. But I've taken tutoring, and I've got it under control. Not only that, I did great in Property. . . . '" Or, if you've had consistently bad grades, you can do as Wendy Werner suggests, and simply say, "My best skills aren't taking law exams." Miami's Jose Bahamonde-Gonzalez adds, "You can't say, 'Oh, this professor's a jerk.' What you have to do is dwell on what you've done to improve. You can say something like, 'Getting used to law school was tough, but I assure you that after that initial shock, I found my weaknesses, and I've addressed them, and I'm better now.'" The important thing here is, don't whine, and don't apologize — and immediately add things that show why you *will* be a good lawyer. As Illinois' Cindy Rold advises, "Think of what else you have to offer! You can say, 'I didn't do well in law school because I don't take law school exams well, but I'll be a great lawyer because . . . ' and have other things to show for it." And *that's* where your extracurriculars come in. Whether it's volunteering for the local bar association, or moot court, or the client counseling competition, or working for a professor or a small firm or a judge, whether on a paying basis or not, it's important to have something else to take the "sting" out of your grades.

And by the way, don't overlook your nonlegal experience as a source of great skills. As Maine's Tammy Willcox points out, "It's important to look for what the attorney is looking for. For instance, a public defender will look for students with poise, confidence, and those who are quick on their feet. So let's say you managed an 800-seat restaurant. You'd want to tell that employer, 'I can think on my feet, and make split-second decisions.'" Or let's say that you have experience as a nanny. Ann Skalaski points out, "You'd want to focus on your strong interpersonal skills. You'd say, 'I establish relationships easily and gain people's confidence quickly, as indicated by these people trusting me with their children.'" There are endless variations on this theme, but you get the point — it's not just legal experiences that give you the kinds of skills that legal employers look for.

So what you do is to acknowledge that your grades aren't good, but immediately turn the focus to something that shows why you are a terrific hire anyway. Remember, the biggest impact bad grades have is on your confidence. And if you can *handle* those grades with confidence, you've gone a very long way toward licking the problem!

E. WHETHER IT'S A CLERKSHIP OR A PERMANENT JOB YOU'RE AFTER — RESEARCH TO SEE WHO FOCUSES ON GRADES, AND AVOID THEM

If your grades are poor, and you've got your heart set on being a Supreme Court clerk or waltzing into a large firm clerkship, then it's time to face the music. Unless you've got really juicy photographs of a Supreme Court justice or similar blackmail materials on an influential partner at a large firm, it's not likely to happen. Given that — why waste your time applying for jobs that are heavily grade-oriented?

I don't mean to imply that the United States Supreme Court and huge law firms are the only employers who are grade-obsessed. There are others, as well. Your career services director will be able to direct you *away* from employers who simply focus on grades and nothing else. But that's all I'm going to say about that. I don't want you to get the impression that anywhere even close to a majority of employers focus on grades, because that's not true. As Ann Skalaski points out, "It's not just about credentials. The hidden message from most legal employers is, Will you stay? Will you bring in clients?" That's got nothing to do with your grades. Diane Reynolds adds, "It's true that good grades get jobs. But good interview skills get jobs, as well. With awful grades, the only jobs out for you are large firms and certain judicial clerkships." And Columbia's Ellen Wayne points out, "Small firm practitioners are only really concerned with two things: How much do I have to pay? and, How much do I have to train them?" Grades are a secondary concern. Also, "When it comes to small firms, it's easier to talk your way into a permanent job if you've worked there part-time. That's because the difference between supporting someone at 20 hours a week and 40 hours a week — which is the difference between part-time and full-time — is a much easier decision for a small firm to make than it is to go from zero to full-time."

So — what types of jobs *should* you consider? You can go after anything you want, but the most fruitful employers to try include:

- Small to mid-sized law firms, especially those with non-corporate law focuses like family law, insurance defense, or personal injury law (although you shouldn't rule any firm out strictly on account of its specialty).
- Public interest employers, like Legal Aid and Public Defenders' offices.
- Government employers, like the D.A.'s office or state's attorney's office.
- State agencies, like insurance or environmental agencies.
- Industry and corporate management.

A real plum of a part-time job that you can get regardless of your grades is a volunteer externship with a judge. As Ellen Wayne explains, "You'll be more savvy. You'll see how lawyers negotiate, you'll see the process — and best of all, judges are great references." As she points out, state court judges frequently have no permanent clerks, so anything you can do for them is great. She goes on to explain how you go about getting one of these volunteer externships. What you do is to go through your career services director to find out about who's who locally, or just contact judges yourself. If you choose to contact them yourself, what you should do is to sit in on open court sessions in the town where you want to practice (which may mean using your school breaks for this purpose). Get a feel for the temperament of the judge. When you find one you like, introduce yourself to the court's bailiff, drop off a résumé, and say you'll follow up with a phone call. And if you're interested in a particular specialty, don't overlook the court for that specialty. For instance, if you like bankruptcy, go to bankruptcy court. If you like family law, go to domestic relations court. If the idea of volunteering bothers you, it shouldn't. Your future legal employer will only care that you got the experience; they won't care whether you got paid for it or not.

There are many more types of jobs you can go after if your grades aren't great, but that's a start. The point is: don't make yourself feel worse about your credentials by banging your head against brick walls in the form of employers who will refuse to look past your grades. There are *many* employers who will welcome the assets you *do* bring to the table. Focus your attention on them!

F. FOCUS ON WHAT YOUR FIRST PERMANENT JOB CAN LEAD TO, RATHER THAN WHAT IT WILL BE

It may well be that you looked at the list I just gave you regarding likely potential employers, and said to yourself, "Ugh." It could be that you've had your heart set on practicing corporate law with a huge firm. Or clerking for a federal judge. Well, I want you to go back to the anecdotes about students' experiences that I opened this chapter with and read those. You'll see a connecting link between them is that, in almost every case, the job the students *started* with didn't sound like any great shakes — instead, their first job *led* to something terrific.

That's very important to remember. As Ann Skalaski puts it, "Look at where jobs can lead. People with great jobs didn't necessarily start there!" Drusilla Bakert adds, "You have to think of your career as a continuum. You won't live or die with your first job. Have limited expectations for your first job, because you'll wind up with what you like within 5 years after graduation."

So if you're resentful that the world isn't your oyster coming right out of law school, put it in perspective. If you use the networking skills I taught you in Chapter 4, you'll parlay *any* job you get into a dream job. You'll keep your eyes open, you'll keep expanding your network of contacts, and if you do a good job at *whatever* you do, you'll be able to turn it into what you've always dreamed of. If you don't — if you're resentful of not starting at the top, and you let that poison your outlook — you've got no one to blame but yourself. So make the most of your grades, and your experience, and accept the best job you can find. Like so many other law school graduates before you, you can turn that first job into your dream job!

G. DON'T SUFFER ALONE — TALK TO YOUR CAREER SERVICES DIRECTOR!

Every career services director I spoke with bemoaned the fact that students with poor grades *avoid* their placement office, believing it's only there to help the top 10% of the class with on-campus interviews. That's a huge mistake. As one career services director I spoke with pointed out, "They don't understand that we identify with them. We weren't on law review either!" Your career services director will be able to help you polish your patter about your grades. They'll have the inside scoop on employers who ignore grades. As Drusilla Bakert says, "I talk with people all the time. I know the employers who want a litigator regardless of their GPA, who'll take people because they have common sense." They'll be able to help you, one-on-one, overcome the blow to your self-esteem that results from poor grades. And they'll help you determine what it is that you really want to do. You may find, after some serious thinking, that the reason you've done poorly in law school is that you've been sabotaging yourself, that you really don't want to be a lawyer, and that by getting poor grades, you've subconsciously tried to destroy that as an alternative. But that's really only something you can determine by taking a good hard look at your own motivations, and your career services director can help you do that.

The bottom line? Don't suffer alone. You can always turn to people whose job is to help you find the job you want!

H. Don't Overlook Everything Else in This Book!

Part of my premise in writing this book was that you can get your dream job regardless of your grades. After speaking with dozens of career services directors from all over the country, I believe that. What I hope you'll take away from this chapter is the feeling that although you've got a little extra touch-up work to do because of your grades, you've got essentially the same job search ahead of you as any other law student. You're only stigmatized by your grades if you let yourself be stigmatized by them. Otherwise, go out and make contacts, send letters, do all the things I outline in this book to pursue the job of your dreams — because it *is* within your grasp!

Chapter 11

Rainmaking: What It Is, and How To Show You Have the Potential to *be* a Rainmaker

OK, I'm going to tell you something that it scares me to think may come as a surprise to you: law firms are businesses. What businesses do is to generate some kind of product and sell it. Regardless of the business you look at, when you break down its functions to their most basic components, that's what you get.

So when you talk about law firms, they're businesses, too, so you've got those two functions — creating a product and selling it. Creating the product means representing clients. And selling the product means getting new clients and keeping current ones. There is not a law firm in the world that diverges from this model, although there are many law firms that would cringe at the thought of being characterized so crassly. But it's true. And that function of getting and keeping clients is what's called "rainmaking." Now clearly, if your dream is to work for the D.A.'s office, or the Public Defender, or Legal Aid, or you're interested in being in-house counsel for a corporation, then rainmaking is not going to be a skill you need to accentuate. But if you're looking at practicing any kind of law in private practice, regardless of the size of the firm, I *promise* you, rainmaking is going to be *very* important to your success, later if not sooner.

In fact, since I'm playing schoolmarm, I'm going to key you in on another fact of life, and it's this: the people who are rainmakers — the ones who bring in the customers, who sell the product, are *always* worth more than the people who generate the product itself. To make a baseball analogy, the people who create the product are the singles hitters, and the people who sell it are the home run hitters. Home run hitters are the ones who get the megacontracts. They're the ones who lure more fans to the ballparks, so they get more scratch.

The bottom line here is this: Rainmaking potential is the most potent, most valuable, most sought-after asset in any potential hire. I would liken it to charm, in the sense that if you have it, you don't need anything else. Your grades don't matter, your school doesn't matter, literally nothing else matters if your potential employer believes you are going to be able to shepherd clients through the door. As Case Western's Debra Fink says, "So much depends on your ability to *get* the work, not *do* the work. You're worth so much more! It's the only sure way to ensure that you won't be laid off."

The good news is, you can create the impression that you can be a rainmaker in the mind of any potential employer, and I'm going to show you exactly how to do that in this chapter. I'm going to take a two-pronged approach, along these lines:

1. If you're like most law students, you probably think you haven't done anything that suggests you can be a rainmaker. I'll bet you're wrong! So one thing I'll be doing in this chapter is to show you what kinds of things suggest rainmaking abilities, and how you can cast those activities in the most beneficial light; and

2. I'll suggest activities for you to take part in that will create the aura of rainmaking ability. (It obviously helps to still be in law school if you're going to do things *prospectively* to develop your image as a rainmaker.)

After that, I'll talk about how you go about broaching the topic of rainmaking to potential employers, because it *can* be touchy. You don't want to come off as cocky! But to start with, I want to spend a little bit of time fleshing out exactly what this rainmaking animal *is.* So . . .

A. RAINMAKING ABILITY: WHAT THE HECK *IS* IT, ANYWAY?

Interestingly enough, rainmaking is one area where there was a wide divergence of opinion among the career services directors I spoke to. Some of them characterized rainmaking in fairly traditional terms: namely, your ability to draw clients based on your being the offspring of an influential local family, with deep roots in the community. I consider that a somewhat depressing view of what rainmaking ability is, because it suggests that it's a product of who your family is, and if you aren't born into the right circumstances, you're stuck.

Fortunately, that's not the prevailing view by any means. Many more of the career services directors believe, in the words of Georgetown's Marilyn Tucker, that rainmaking is a skill you can *learn.* What's this broader view of rainmaking talent? It focuses on your ability to make contacts, to get people to like and trust you, on your ability to deal with people comfortably and with enthusiasm. In short, it's being what's sometimes called a "people" person.

That may give you the idea that it's marketing, glad-handing, selling-type activities that will give you a rainmaking aura. That's accurate. The fact is, people almost always give business to people that they like, and much of marketing, glad-handing, and selling, is getting people to like you. It's about showing enthusiasm and an interest in other people and what they do. If you're a social kind of person, you do that already, even though you may not give it those kinds of names. And by the way, if these kinds of activities sound familiar in the context of this book, they should — because they're the very same kinds of things you do when you network, which is the focus of Chapter 4. If you remember, in that chapter I talked about how it is that when you network, you're using the same kind of people-meeting, contact-expanding skills that lawyers use to get and retain clients. Well — that's rainmaking.

Now that you have a firmer idea of exactly what it is that rainmaking *is*, let's talk about how you show employers that you have the ability to do it!

B. FINDING THE HIDDEN RAINMAKING POTENTIAL IN YOUR BACKGROUND AND MAKING THE MOST OF IT!

As William and Mary's Rob Kaplan says, "If you ask most students about client development skills, their first reaction is, 'I don't have that!'" But the fact is, you may have *many* activities in your background that show you have rainmaking potential, without realizing it. I can identify with that, because that's the situation I was in as a law student! Here's what happened. One of the things I was best at in law school was fundraising. I could squeeze money out of just about anybody. But when it came to putting that on my résumé, I was a little squeamish. I thought, "What law firm is going to care about whether I can do fundraising or not?" Geez-o-Pete, fast forward 10 years, and I can tell you that that fundraising skill is probably *more* important than any of the stuff that *did* make it onto my résumé! And I'll bet you've similarly got things in your background whose importance you don't appreciate.

What are they? I would break rainmaking ability into two parts: the kind of rainmaking that springs from your activities, and the kind that's a result of your family and your roots. Let's look at each of them:

1. RAINMAKING ABILITY IMPLIED BY YOUR ACTIVITIES

OK — it's time to get out paper and pencil, and make a list of everything you've done that suggests you can be a rainmaker. As St. Louis' Wendy Werner says, "What you're looking for with rainmaking potential is anything that suggests you can meet people and generate business." So what you're looking for are any activities that are people-oriented, that suggest that you're amiable, that you make friends and contacts easily. With that in mind — have you done anything like any of the following?

- Started your own business (even if it was a part-time or summer business).
- Ran a business.
- Sold or marketed anything, from publications to cars.

- Had a prior career that connected you to a group of potential clients (e.g., you sold commercial real estate, or you were involved in healthcare management).
- Taken part in volunteer activities.
- Held a leadership role in any job or extracurricular.
- Taken part in any fundraising activities (e.g., school phone-a-thons).
- Taken part in United Way drives.
- Client mediation workshops in law school.
- Moot court and client counseling in law school.
- Taken part in the local bar association.
- Civic activities (like Little League or the PTA or serving on local boards).
- Played social sports like golf.
- Belonged to a country club.
- Taken part in the Peace Corps.
- Been involved in church or temple activities.

As you can see, the common thread running through all of these activities is that they involve *people*. And of course, this list isn't exhaustive — but it *will* get you thinking about the kinds of activities that suggest rainmaking potential!

Once you've made a list of activities, hang on to it, because in Topic D, I'll tell you how to broach rainmaking to potential employers. And what if your list is empty? Take heart! In Topic C, I'll show you the kinds of things you can still do in law school that will create that rainmaking aura!

2. RAINMAKING ABILITY IMPLIED BY YOUR FAMILY AND YOUR ROOTS

If your last name is DuPont or Rockefeller or Kennedy, then chances are you don't need to be reading this section about how to make hay out of your family name. But odds are that your connections are a little bit more subtle than that. Perhaps, for instance:

- Your family is firmly rooted in the community, in that your parent(s) either hold positions of prestige (e.g., president of a bank or superintendent of schools), or they are extremely well-connected through community service, or are otherwise socially prominent.

♦ (P.S. — It doesn't hurt to be rich).

♦ You went to a prestigious local private or Catholic school.

I'll give you a personal example. My father is a very prominent venture capitalist. He's quoted in the *Wall Street Journal* and *Fortune Magazine* all the time, and he's got a list of contacts a mile long. (I'm not particularly interested in using them, but they're there.) I'm not saying that by way of tooting my own horn, or my Dad's horn to be more precise, but rather by way of pointing out that that's the kind of rainmaking potential that I'm talking about here. It's the kind that makes an employer scratch their head and say, "Hmm, it probably wouldn't hurt to have this kid's name on the ol' letterhead."

If you do a bit of thinking and decide you've got this kind of rainmaking ability, it probably makes you a bit queasy to think about using it. It makes *me* queasy thinking about it. After all, *nobody* likes to think of getting ahead on Mommy or Daddy's coattails. But you know something? I'd encourage you to bite the bullet and use whatever influence you can to get the job you want. As San Diego's Susan Benson points out, "It's not name-dropping. It's rainmaking. It shows that you understand *business.*" The fact is, no matter where you get a job, if you're an incompetent loser, you won't last; your success in your career will quickly fall on your own shoulders, no matter who your relatives are or how well-connected you are. They may be able to open doors for you, but they won't be able to sit down and do your work for you. And beyond that, think of it from your parents' perspective. One of the peripheral benefits of success is the impact it has on people you care about, and for your folks, that's you. So if you have this kind of rainmaking potential, thank your lucky stars, and by all means, *don't be too proud to use it!*

As with the other, self-generated kind of rainmaking ability, you've got to be careful about how you broach this to employers. In fact, with *this* kind of rainmaking ability you've got to be particularly careful, because if it backfires you'll come off as a snotty little rich kid whom employers will disdain. (In Topic D, I talk about how to put this kind of rainmaking ability on the table in just the right light.)

C. Law School Activities That Suggest Rainmaking Ability

OK. Let's say you went through the exercises in Topic B, on squeezing rainmaking ability from things you've done and from your family. Maybe you found stuff, maybe you didn't. Regardless — take heart! If you're still in school, you can take part in activities that will create the aura of rainmaking ability *just* as profound — if not more so! — than anything else you've ever done!

You know what you can do? Go back to the list of rainmaking activities I offered in Topic B, above. As you can see, many of them are things you can do while you're in law school. Fundraising, involvement in the local bar association, moot court, local United Way drives, leadership positions in extracurriculars — all of those suggest rainmaking, and they're all open to you.

Now if you've already read Chapter 4, on making contacts, then you'll see a large overlap between networking activities and rainmaking activities. As I mentioned to you there, that makes sense, because a lot of what you have to do to *get* a job is what you'll do to get and keep clients once you *have* the job of your dreams. Debra Fink puts it more succinctly: "Networking skills *are* rainmaking skills!" So, in many cases, you'll find that the kinds of activities you're taking part in to meet potential employers are the very same activities that will prove that you have rainmaking ability. If that doesn't prove the existence of a supreme being — it comes pretty darned close, at least in *this* context.

D. Broaching the Topic of Rainmaking to Potential Employers

OK. I've convinced you how important it is to show that you have rainmaking ability. And trust me: the very fact that you're aware of the business of law firms puts you *way* ahead of the competition; it gives you tons of sophistication points. But having your rainmaking ducks in a row begs the question: *Now* what? Rainmaking isn't one of those things you can list on your résumé as a skill — not overtly, anyway. And you can't put it in a cover letter, either. In point of fact, you can't even use the word when you make contacts. In any of those contexts you'll come off as being arrogant. "Geez, Kimmbo," you're thinking. "If I can't ever *talk* about it, what's the use of *having* it?" Relax, relax. You *can* talk about it, it's just that you've got to be subtle about it, that's all. Let's look at how you go about bringing up rainmaking ability in a variety of contexts: when you make contacts, when you send cover letters and résumés, and when you interview.

Let's start with making contacts, or what we noneuphemistically call networking. Remember, networking *itself* is the kind of contact-generating activity that *is* rainmaking, so the mere fact that you're making contacts in the first place suggests you've got rainmaking ability. The important thing here is to make sure you're giving your contact-generating activities your amiable best efforts. So, for instance, when you take part in bar association activities, make sure that you smile, that you initiate conversations, that you collect business cards. As Marilyn Tucker says, "Rainmaking is all about personality. Be outgoing! You don't need to be Miss Congeniality, but students who show little enthusiasm or energy, and wait to be drawn out, aren't going to be seen as a client draw. Employers look at what their potential clients will see!" Vanderbilt's Pam Malone adds, "It's attitude. It's implying, 'I'll go above and beyond' — a 'can-do' attitude." Michigan's Nancy Krieger chips in, "You need to be personable. That's more important than grades. Employers look for people who are *likable*." Ellen Wayne goes even further: "Promote yourself! Be good with people, be comfortable talking with them. Rainmaking today counts a *lot* more than it used to."

So — keep your finger on the pulse of what's going on in your community. No matter how much you think you're buried by schoolwork, you need to avoid tunnel vision if you're going to be a good networker. Have interesting things to say, and show curiosity about other people and what interests them. Be the kind of person you enjoy being around. And when potential employers see you, they'll look at you through the eyes of their clients — and they'll be impressed with what they see!

So that's how you cover rainmaking when you make contacts. What about in correspondence, like cover letters and résumés? That's a little tougher, because rainmaking is all about personability, and that's inherently something you can only do in person, not through the mail. In fact, there are some career services directors who say you can't get it across in writing *at all*. Others say that you can, and I tend to agree with them — you just have to be careful how you word it.

In your résumé, as Wendy Werner points out, you'll of course want to include any experience you have in starting or running a business, or in fundraising — anything that says you can meet people and generate business. In fact, any of the activities I listed in Topic B is appropriate to put on your résumé, and they all suggest that you have rainmaking potential. Be sure that you include nonlegal activities that suggest you can be a rainmaker. This is a particularly insidious trap, because you may think that such activities have no bearing on your ability to be a good lawyer. Taking part in law school fundraisers and phone-a-thons are one example. Another was provided by a career services director who told me about a student who had sold cars before law school. He very much *didn't* want to include that on his résumé. But the career services director knew he was interviewing with firms that required new associates to do some rainmaking, and convinced him to put his experience selling cars on his résumé — and it made the difference. He got the job he wanted!

Willamette's Diane Reynolds also suggests putting down hobbies on your résumé that suggest rainmaking; certainly golf is the most traditional rainmaker. And if your rainmaking potential is a matter of your family connections, Susan Benson encourages you to find *any* way to mention that in your résumé. For instance, if your last name is Bagelschlauf, and you spent a summer loading cement bags at the $50 million dollar Bagelschlauf Construction Company, she says, "Don't be too proud to mention it!" Or if your last name is Harcourt, and you spent a summer as an intern at Harcourt Brace, the megajillion dollar publishing company who published this book, you'd do the same thing. So you can see the theme here — you never use the word "rainmaking" per se, but you mention everything that goes into indicating that you have rainmaking potential.

In a cover letter, it's similarly important *not* to mention the word "rainmaking" itself. It just sounds too cocky. But finding a way to work it in can be a big plus. The most you could do, according to Diane Reynolds, is to say that you believe you have client development ability, and then back it up with something in your background that shows you've generated business before. (If you don't have anything to back it up, then don't mention it.) So, for instance, maybe you're like me, and you are a great fundraiser. In your cover letter, you could say that you particularly look forward to developing clients, because you've enjoyed people-oriented activities like fund-raising at law school.

Interviews themselves are where your rainmaking potential is most likely to bear fruit. Of course, by the time you interview with a potential employer, you've already researched them — and part of your research will be to determine whether or not rainmaking is something they expect of new associates. You'll probably find that for all but the largest law firms, you'll be expected to do some rainmaking fairly soon, and even if it's not expected of you, it would be a welcome addition. As NYU's Gail Cutter points out, "For very large law firms, they may think it's weird if you bring up rain-making." So for large firms, it's not an issue; but for virtually every other law firm, it probably is.

Remember, as the interviewer is talking with you, there's a question swimming around in their minds: *How will our clients view this person?* As Franklin Pierce's Sophie Sparrow points out, "It's important to be comfortable with yourself. If you're nervous, the interviewer won't be comfortable, and they won't want you seeing their clients." Marilyn Tucker echoes this, saying, "Employers look at what potential clients will see. They want to see students who have personality, who are outgoing, who make the interviewer com-fortable." Over and over again, career services directors used the same kinds of words when they talked about exhibiting rainmaking potential in interviews. Being personable. Likable. People-oriented. Self-confident. How does this come across? By doing all of the things I tell you to do in Chapter 7 on Interviewing. Lean slightly forward in your chair during the interview. Maintain eye contact with the interviewer. Smile (at least when it's appropriate to do so). Make your voice sound "up" and enthusiastic. Show with your words and your demeanor that you're happy to be there and grateful for the opportunity to meet with the interviewer. As Vanderbilt's Pam Malone says, "Rainmaking ability often shows *implicitly* in inter-views!"

An interview also gives you the opportunity to bring up items in your background that suggest rainmaking potential. As Wendy Werner points out, "If your dad owns a local bank, I would find a way to squeeze that into the interview, even if you're not asked about it." Catholic's Amy Thompson similarly encourages students to "play up community ties, civic activities like Little League or PTA, to show you're well-connected. And address it *expressly.*" But be careful to bring these items up in a matter-of-fact tone; if you sound like you're bragging, or that you have the ability to deliver tons of legal business just on the basis of who Mommy and Daddy are, you'll turn the interviewer off. You can always bring up connections in reference to something else; for instance, you could say, "I've always been interested in commercial law, because my father owns a bank and I've taken an interest in what he does," or, "My interest in copyright law came about because my mother is president of a publishing company," or "I worked at Northstar Construction during the summers in college because I was interested in learning more about the family business." That way, you're not hitting the interviewer over the head with your connections, but you *are* making them known. And that's important! Remember, a face-to-face interview is your opportunity to make your mark with the employer. And rainmaking is a skill that's highly prized by legal employers. That means that an interview is *definitely* the right time to show that you've got rainmaking potential!

What about the situation where you're interviewing for a job in a city where you've never lived? It's more difficult to establish your rainmaking ability, but as Rob Kaplan points out, it's not impossible. He suggests that you "Turn your lack of contacts in the city on it's head. You can say something like, 'I've lived in a number of places, and I've always been able to establish contacts and feel comfortable in the community. I want to do that here, too.'" Turning a negative into a positive is a tired cliché, but in a situation where you're the new kid in town, you *can* use it to show that you can develop clients even though you don't have any roots in the community.

THE BOTTOM LINE ON RAINMAKING...

If I've seemed gung-ho on rainmaking in this chapter, there's a good reason for it — it's just about the most important thing you can bring to the table for a law firm. Of course law firms need people who *do* the work, and not everybody is expected to be a rainmaker. But as a rule of thumb, the smaller the law firm, the more you'll be expected to generate clients. As Debra Fink points out, "Law *is* sales! When you practice law, you're going into your own business. And the key to your job security is your clientele — so a lot depends on your ability to *get* work, not *do* work. You can't be a good lawyer without clients!"

Ideally, you'll come away from this chapter with an appreciation of just that — that law is a business, and part of that business is *generating* business. That shouldn't intimidate you, because if you do any of the activities I suggest in Chapter 4 on making contacts, you'll find that rainmaking is a natural outgrowth of making contacts. And beyond that, simply being *conscious* of rainmaking as a reality of practicing law puts you leagues ahead of your competition!

Chapter 12

Getting the Large Law Firm Job You're Dying For... No Matter What Your Credentials Are

I'm going to make a little wager here. I'll bet that this is the first chapter you turned to, right? You flipped to the Table of Contents and came straight here. If I'm right, I'm not surprised. It seems like no matter how different people are when they enter law school, no matter how diverse their dreams and aspirations, by the time they get to the fall of Second Year — bang! Everybody wants to get a clerkship with the largest law firm that'll take them on. So if that includes you — well, as I said, I'm not surprised.

In this chapter I will, indeed, show you how to get the large law firm job you want. But I'm going to do something else, as well. Something that might strike you as a little bit cruel. That is — I'm going to try to talk you out of it. You know why? Because based on the hundreds of people I spoke with about this very topic, my guess is that you only *think* you want to work for a large firm. If you're like most law students, you don't really *know* what it's like to work for a large firm, and your misconceptions about it could wind up making you miserable if you pursue your dream. When I talk about getting you the job of your dreams, I mean the job that really *will* make you happy — not the one that you *think* will make you happy. So I'm going to spend a bit of time explaining to you exactly what working for a large firm is like. And it's not my own perception; it's based on the experiences of many, many people, who, like you, thought it was what they wanted.

"Now, wait just a minute, Kimmbo!" you may be saying. "This chapter is supposed to tell me how to *get* a large firm job, *not* talk me out of it!" Well, if you're absolutely sure down to your bones that you know and understand what it's like to work at a large firm and that's what you really want, then skip ahead to Topic D, on page 475. That's where I'll tell you everything you need to do to get a job at a large firm. But if that's *not* you — and I'm betting it's not — read on. I'm going to make your life a lot happier by opening your eyes to a lifestyle you really might not want, after all.

Here's how this chapter's set up. I'll start out by explaining to you what makes large law firms tick. Then, I'll talk about what it's really like to work for a large firm. Then we'll look at your motives in wanting to work for a large firm in the first place, to see if you want it for the right reasons (if you *don't*, it'll just make you miserable). After that, if you're still sure it's something you want, I'll show you exactly how to get a large firm job, regardless of your credentials. I'll show you how to get involved with activities that'll get you into large law firms through the back door. We'll talk about sneaky ways to get on-campus interviews. And we'll talk about what I call getting in through the *side* door; that is, starting out as something other than a traditional associate in order to make an impression with your dream employer.

By the way, as you'll soon notice, there's something that makes this chapter a little bit different than any other one in this book. Specifically, I don't quote anybody by name. Why? Because a lot of people spoke with me very frankly about large firm practice, and it wouldn't be very helpful to them — or their careers! — if their names appeared attached to some of these quotes. Now, not all the quotes are negative, not by a long shot; but it looked odd to attach names to some quotes, and leave off the others, so I just left them *all* off. But the fact is, for every quote in this chapter, there were many people to back it up — so you can believe every word of it!

A. THE PERCEPTION VERSUS THE REALITY: WHAT MAKES LARGE FIRMS TICK?

When you think of large firms, your perception probably goes to the prestige, the classy offices, the fabulous salaries, the front-page clients. You probably haven't given much thought to what makes them *run*. As a jumping off point, it makes sense to explain to you *exactly* how it is that large firms function.

At its heart, a large law firm is just like any other business. It has a product that it sells in return for money. Like every business, it makes more money by doing one of two things: either by increasing its sales or decreasing its expenses. Now when you're talking about products in the context of law firms, you're talking about *billable hours* — that's a term that we're going to see a lot more in this chapter! Basically, a "billable hour" is time that's directly attributable to a client, so the time you spend researching, or talking with a client, or writing memoranda or briefs or contracts, or appearing in court, that's *billable* time. Time that you spend on administrative matters, or breaks, or lunch, or recruiting new associates, or training, or continuing legal education, or pro bono work, or anything else — that doesn't count. All that counts are billable hours, hours directly attributable to a client. So to get back to my point about a law firm's product, the more of its product that it sells to its clients, the more money that it makes. And that means that the more billable hours a law firm's attorneys spend on a client's work, the more money the firm makes.

It's also important to know who *makes* that extra money. As with any business, the profits go to whoever *owns* the business. In the case of law firms, that means the partners. As you probably already know, law firms have two, basic levels of attorneys: partners and associates. Partners, as I just pointed out, own the firm. So if it's more profitable, they make more money. Associates, on the other hand, are salaried employees. No matter how much the law firm makes, the associates get their salary; they don't partake in the profits of the firm (although in many large firms, they do get bonuses; but there need not be any direct relation between those bonuses and the firm's profits).

Pretty simple so far, eh? Well, I'm telling you all this by way of background, because this fairly simple structure has important ramifications for you, if you're thinking of being an associate at a large law firm. In the next section, where I'll talk about the perception versus the reality of working for large firms, I'll get into those ramifications in a little more detail.

B. THE PERCEPTION VERSUS THE REALITY: WHAT IT'S LIKE TO WORK FOR A LARGE FIRM

If you've ever read anything about working at a large firm, you know that most people don't have anything very glowing to say about it. Many of the career services directors I spoke with about large firms bore this out. One of them said, "Most people are *miserable* at large law firms!" Another chimed in with, "Most people shouldn't be associates at large firms. It's an *awful* fit." Another pointed out that "After a couple of years with a large firm, most people look in the mirror and say, 'I want to be *happy*.'" Another said, "Law students don't know what it's like at a large firm! Their sense is it's like the 1950s, when every girl wanted to be a stewardess. They think it's exciting, sexy, adventurous, prestigious. The truth is that it's *really* hard to succeed." A recruiting director for one large firm told me, "There's this misconception that working for a large firm means glamour, excitement, great deals, interesting clients, travel. The *truth* is that they'll spend 4 years in the library. They get lied to a lot!" Another recruiting director added, "Look at large firm people a few years down the road. They look like they've had the life beaten out of them."

I could go on and on, but those comments are representative of what I heard over and over again. It's crucially important that if you really do go for a large firm job, you proceed with your eyes open, knowing *exactly* what you should expect. So what I'm going to do here is go over the elements that you *have* to take into account if you're planning on being an associate at a large firm. We'll talk about the hours, the politics, the lack of autonomy, the structure, the nature of the work, the client contact, who the clients are, and the issue of luck. And then I'll talk about how you see how the firm you're interested in stacks up against this model; after all, there is some variation between large firms. But I'll start with a snapshot of what it's like to work in a large firm, borne of *many* conversations with people all over the country.

Before we get into this, I want to disabuse you of a misconception you might have. It may be that you already know that working at a large firm means long hours, and office politics, and grunt work, at least for the first few years. But maybe there's a little voice in your head that tells you that you'll be the one to break the mold. I hate to throw cold water on you, but trust me on this one, *you won't*. As one hiring partner told me, "As a law student, you may think you can have it all. You think, *'I'll* be the one who won't have to review documents for weeks on end. *I'll* make partner on account of first quality work, without having to do any rainmaking or client development. *I'll* be the one who'll get all my work done without having to come in on weekends.' That's not true!"

With that in mind, let's talk about what it's really like to work at a large firm.

1. THE HOURS

"Hours" isn't really quite the right way to talk about the time commitment being a new associate at a large law firm takes. Nights, or weekends, or holidays, might come closer. Sometimes, the truly horrendous hours you have to put in go by euphemisms like "dedication" or "hard work." The fact is, *time* is the largest sacrifice you make when you work for a large firm. There is *no way* to avoid it.

Don't believe me? Well, all you have to do is look a little deeper into how law firms make money to see where the enormous time commitment comes from. The enormous salaries that you associate with large firms — and they are enormous, with starting salaries for new associates hovering around $80,000 — don't come from a money tree. You see, since you're on salary, the law firm has to pay you that $80,000 whether you work 40 billable hours a week, or 80. The difference is that the more you work, the more money the law firm makes. Let's say that your time bills at $150 an hour. Well, If you bill 40 hours a week, the law firm makes roughly $232,000 out of you (this isn't including the cost of your benefits, or any of the firm's overhead, which for large firms is *enormous*. These figures are just for illustrative purposes). Now if the firm can bill *60* of your hours every week, it makes another $156,000 out of you. And if it can bill *80* of your hours per week, it makes a whopping $544,000 out of you! What conclusion should that lead you to? *That a large law firm is going to squeeze all of the work out of*

8

GUERRILLA TACTICS FOR GETTING THE LEGAL JOB OF YOUR DREAMS

you that it possibly can, because it will make more money if it does so. One recruiting director at a large firm described this situation to me this way: "It's kind of like Amway. The more hours the law firm bills for its associates, the more money the partners make."

What does that mean? It means that no large firm is going to be truly interested in any quality of life issues that concern you. They're interested in hours. And hours. And more hours on top of that. How *many* hours can you expect to put in? Between 60 and 100 a week.

"But wait a minute," you're saying. "I've read the NALP forms. I've seen articles. Some firms only require 2,000 to 2,500 billable hours a year, and that works out to about 40 or 50 hours a week. I can handle that!" I have a couple things to tell you. As one personnel director at a large firm told me rather bluntly, "Don't believe what you read. If a firm says that it requires 2,900 billable hours and that its associates work 3,000 hours a year to get that, that's just a flat out lie. It's more like 3,500 hours." As that quote implies, apart from the fact that you can't believe what you read, you're making a mistake if you confuse *billable* hours with *working* hours. There's a *huge* difference between the two. Remember, when I defined billable hours for you just a few minutes ago, I said that they were hours that are attributable to a particular client's work. Things like document production, or drafting memos or contracts, or research, or client meetings, or court time. *Working* hours are what you *normally* think of when you think about the number of hours you've got to put in; that is, it's all the time you spend at the office. But the fact is, time that you can't bill doesn't count! So any time you spend getting a drink of water or coffee, or going to the bathroom, or taking any other kind of break, or training, or taking a continuing legal education class, or doing administrative stuff, or doing pro bono work — *none* of that counts toward your billable hours. And even if you're really efficient, you'll find you have to work about 10 hours for every 8 hours you bill. So that means if a firm expects you to log 2,500 billable hours a year, you'll have to *work* about 3,125 hours, which puts you up over 60 hours a week — and that's if you work 52 weeks a year, without a break! Compare that to lawyers who work for the federal government, who *work* a total of about 2,000 hours a year and don't have to worry about billable hours at all!

What makes this concept of billable hours even worse is the record-keeping that goes along with it. Large firms require you to keep very detailed logs of your time, so that it gets billed to clients correctly. For instance, a lot of firms break down your time into tenths of hours, and you have to account for every one. That means you have to account for every 6-minute block of time, throughout the day!

If you don't appreciate how much time you waste, or how much of a pain it is to keep track of your time in 6-minute increments, try this little experiment. For 2 days, keep a log of your time, from the moment you wake up until the moment you go to sleep. Break it into 6-minute chunks. So, if you wash your face and brush your teeth in 6 minutes, that's one 6-minute chunk. Keep track of classes, and commuting, and studying, and work, and chatting with your colleagues, and breaks — everything. It'll show you two things. One, it's amazing how little of your time is *actually* spent productively, even if it seems like you work continuously from morning until night. And two, it'll show you how much of an *incredible* pain in the neck it is to keep track of your time this way!

It may be that the concept of working extremely long hours, and keeping track of them in minute detail, doesn't strike you as particularly onerous. If so, it may be because you're thinking of "hours" in general terms. As one career services director pointed out to me, "When I try to explain the reality of large firms to students, I don't talk about numbers of hours, because "long hours" doesn't really mean anything. I give them examples, like this one: 'You've spent a long time planning a vacation with your spouse, and the day before, a partner calls you and says, 'Too bad. Sorry. You've got to stay.' How will you react?' I find that that brings home *exactly* what the time commitment to a large firm means!" A recruiting director pointed out to me that "A feature of long hours that incoming associates don't appreciate is their unpredictability. If you're working on a case, you don't know *when* you're going to be called on to pull an all-nighter. If it's Friday, Christmas is on Sunday, and you suddenly find out that you've got a brief due in court on Wednesday — goodbye Christmas!" A career services director pointed out that "You *do* have to cancel vacations. It's the nature of the beast. If you want flexibility, don't go to a large firm. Because if you have huge clients like large firms have, they can yank your chain like smaller clients *can't.*"

Another feature of long hours is what you give up to put in those kinds of hours. You will not be viewed favorably unless and until you make tremendous personal sacrifices. One recruiting director told me, "If you like to read, or do sports, forget it!" And your family life will *definitely* suffer. As one career services director said, "People who are family-involved have the most trouble at big firms. An alum in one of the most desirable cities in the country told me that there were no married women partners with children at any large firm in that city."

The bottom line? The time commitment at large firms is huge, it's real, and it has tremendous ramifications on the way you live your life. You have to be tremendously motivated, and have a kind of single-minded tunnel vision if you're really going to give it a shot. Are you willing to sacrifice everything else in your life, for the next few years, to make it at a big firm? Taking into account what I've told you here, you're the only one who can answer that!

2. POLITICS

If you're the kind of person who insists on being judged purely on the quality of your work, think twice about going to a large firm. Sure, you've got to turn in excellent work — but if you expect to make it, you've got to be a savvy office politician, as well. Call it schmoozing, brown-nosing, glad-handing, whatever. . . . If you want to survive and succeed at a large firm, you'd better be good at it.

And that doesn't change if you stay at the firm, either. More than one recruiting director pointed out that when it comes to making partner, that decision isn't based on who the best lawyer is. "If a litigator made it last year, and you're a litigator, they may not take you this year no matter *how* good you are."

So, yes, you do have to do good work, otherwise you're out. But being a good office politician is equally important; you won't stay if you can't play the game. And if you can't live with that, you should reconsider working at a large firm!

3. LACK OF AUTONOMY

As one recruiting director pointed out to me, "Something that comes as a real shock to students is that at large firms, you have no control over your own time." Coming from a school environment, where you essentially set your own hours outside of class, that may be very difficult to handle. When you start out in a big firm, you have supervising attorneys who decide how you spend all of your time. You don't have a choice of assignments. You pretty much do what you're told, when you're told to do it. As one hiring partner told me, "You've got to be willing to work as a team player." That means that the good of the project takes precedence over anything *you* may want to do. Large firms are no place for prima donnas! If you chafe at this kind of control, this may be a factor in your success — and happiness — at a large firm.

4. THE NATURE OF THE WORK

It may be that part of the lure of a large firm for you is the idea of exciting, glamorous work, for big-name clients. For people who survive the first few years at a large firm, there *is* some of that. But for the first few years at a large firm — reality check time!

As one career services director pointed out, "A lot of students go to large firms thinking they'll be on the cutting edge of issues, that there will be no monotony or repetition. But there *is* a lot of repetition. There's nobody there to do the crummy work *for* you." Another one stated that, "For the first couple of years, you do grunt work. After that, there's more intellectual stimulation, but for the first couple of years, there's not." An attorney at a large firm told me that, "With a large firm, you just don't get the quality work right away. It's *very* routine."

What does "routine" work *mean*, exactly? You'll spend a lot of time in the library, researching and writing memoranda. Generally the writing assignments you'll get will be a tiny piece of a large case — and they're usually not very interesting pieces, at that. But if you enjoyed paper courses as opposed to exam courses in school, this might be right up your alley. Another common assignment for junior associates at large firms is something called "document review." That means sifting through thousands of documents, and sometimes hundreds of thousands of documents, to see what's relevant. By way of example, let's say that your client is a car dealership, and the car company is trying to terminate your client's franchise. The car company claims the dealership defrauded customers, and wants to see any relevant files relating to customer complaints. Well, your firm is going to have to go through those files, determine what's relevant, and remove anything that's privileged. That means going through every scrap of paper in those files, and analyzing them. If it sounds tedious — it *is*. Clearly a senior attorney isn't going to want to waste time on that kind of chimp work, and so it falls to junior associates — like you, if you're relatively new at the firm. As one associate at a large firm told me, "Large firms just won't give you interesting work with a lot of responsibility until they see that you're 'dedicated' — that is, you've made enormous personal sacrifices for a few years."

Furthermore, if it's client contact you want, you won't get it right away at a large firm. As an attorney at a large firm told me, "The ones who get the 'face time' with clients are the partners, not the new associates." Another pointed out that, "You need to like the nature of the work, not the name of the client. Working at a large firm isn't about flying on the corporate jet, or having dinner with the CEO. The problem for new associates is that it's hard to see clients *at all!*"

So, plan to spend your first few years at a large firm in the library, or doing routine kinds of work. You won't see cutting edge issues, you won't get to work on the big picture, and you won't get much contact with clients, if at all. If that doesn't faze you, proceed on!

5. THE NATURE OF THE CLIENTS

I heard more sad stories about misconceptions over the nature of large firm clients than over any other aspect of large firm practice. As one attorney at a large firm told me, "It's important to know who the clients *are.*"

Here's the problem. When you hear that a large firm has a banking department, or an environmental law department, or a litigation department, you are going to make assumptions about what those departments *do* based on impressions you already have about different areas of practice. What you *do* at a large firm is basically to spend all of your time rearranging the assets of the wealthy. You aren't a counselor or an advisor. You do mergers, acquisitions, and contracts for wealthy people. As one recruiting director at a large firm said, "If you are a do-gooder or you want to make a difference, it's not for you!" She went on to point out that her firm's banking department basically handled foreclosures — that is, kicking people out of their houses. Another hiring partner told me, succinctly, "If you want to save the environment or march on Washington, don't go to a large firm!"

And if you're interested in litigation because you want to go to court, forget a large firm. As one firm's recruiting director told me, "There aren't any Perry Masons in large firms! The clients that large firms get don't want the expense or risk of going to trial. They all want to *settle.*" Another recruiting director echoed that by saying, "Litigators here prepare cases that get settled. They prepare them hoping they will *never* go to trial." And another said, "If you want to be a litigator and get up in court, don't go to a big firm! It's all about document production."

Perhaps the saddest misconception story I heard involved a student who was in the top 10% of her class. She was passionately interested in environmental law, and took part in every activity with an environmental law bent. She marched into her career services office, and told the director, "I want to work for a large law firm, representing the environment." As the director told me, "It was very sad. I asked this young woman, 'Exactly who is going to hire a large firm to represent the environment? Large firms do environmental work from the *other* side. No family of rabbits is going to hop in and say, 'Please protect our habitat!'"

To be perfectly blunt, if you work at a large firm, a lot of times you're going to find yourself representing the "bad guys," because they're the ones who can afford the services of a large firm in the first place. You may have a difficult time emotionally getting a grip on the stance that your clients will want to take. On the other hand, maybe you won't; maybe you're the kind of person who *can* leave your feelings at the door, and you *can* get behind the positions you'll have to take without a second thought. My point here is: be *aware* of the emotional challenge you're in for *before* you set foot through that mahogany door!

6. THE ELEMENT OF LUCK

Luck plays a significant, and unfortunate, role in your ability to succeed at a large firm. No matter how hard you work, no matter how many hours you put in, you may find yourself tanked for factors beyond your control. As one career services director told me, "When you go to a big firm, you have no clue who you'll be working for. You'll have no chance to meet them up-front, and no options about choosing who they are. But the problem is, they have the biggest impact on your success! *I* wouldn't take that risk." Maybe you *will* get assigned to a supervising attorney who is a nurturing, supportive mentor. But maybe you'll get assigned to the firm's Torquemada, who'll humiliate you and make your life hell before spitting you out like a piece of chewed gum. Then you'll be back at square one when it comes to finding a job, except that *now* you've got a rejection under your belt that you have to explain away!

Or maybe you'll make a mistake during your first year or two at the firm. You're not perfect; no one is. Maybe you'll be on a document review, and having pored through thousands of pieces of paper, you'll miss something relevant. Or maybe there's an unreported case that you couldn't reasonably have been expected to find for that brief you've been working on — but your supervising attorney knows about it, and thinks you really dropped the ball because you didn't dig it up. That's bad luck, but it doesn't matter. In baseball parlance, you're outta there. As one large firm recruiting director pointed out to me, "During your first year, if you make one big mistake, you'll get blown out of the water. It's not a business for the faint-hearted!"

7. TALK WITH PEOPLE FAMILIAR WITH YOUR *PARTICULAR* DREAM FIRM TO SEE HOW IT STACKS UP

The factors I've talked about here are ones that are common to large firms. But *of course* there's variation between firms, and each one is going to be *somewhat* different. As a result, I'd recommend taking a little bit of time to research the large firms you're considering, to draw a bead on *exactly* what it's like to work there. Talk with your career services director, and get his or her insights. Ask for the names of alumni who work there, or alumni who *used* to work there, or upperclassmen who've clerked there. If there are some of these factors that concern you more than others — for instance, the lack of autonomy — ask them pointblank how the firm matches up. And take into account the source you're using; your career services director has no reason to be anything but objective, whereas anyone who works there now will tend to say more positive things about the firm, and people who've left there will tend to slant their comments to the negative. The point is: I've thrown up some red flags for you, some considerations you should take into account if you think you want to work for a big firm. Talk with some people for yourself to see *exactly* what it's like to work at any particular firm!

The bottom line to all of this? There are significant considerations to take into account when it comes to large firm practice, and you *can't* adequately make a decision about what your dream job *is* without knowing about them. Maybe you've read through all of this carefully, and none of these strike you as being factors that you can't handle. If so, congratulations! Perhaps large firm practice really *is* where you belong. To make absolutely sure of that, let's look at *why* you're interested in a large firm job. Let's talk about what your motives are . . .

C. WHY DO YOU WANT TO WORK FOR A LARGE FIRM? ANALYZING YOUR MOTIVES

You may get the impression from the title of this section that I'm going to tell you that there *aren't* any good reasons for working at a large firm. That's not true; there *are* good, strong motives for wanting to go to work for an enormous, prestigious law firm, *in spite of* the drawbacks that I suggested in Topic A. But what I'm going to do here is to talk about what your motives might be, and suggest how, in some cases, they might be satisfied in contexts less stressful than a large firm. So take a look at these common motives, and see which ones fit you!

1. "I WANT A PLATINUM AMERICAN EXPRESS CARD"

Money is a *huge* motivator for seeking a job at a large firm. There's no question that the starting pay that they offer — typically around $80,000 or so, plus fabulous benefits packages — is greater than any other single category of legal employer.

On top of that, if you're like most law students, your life right now is probably far from lavish. One hiring partner from a large firm told me, "Law school is the last time poverty is fashionable." You probably want to end that lifestyle as soon as possible. You're probably sick of instant macaroni and cheese, 50¢ draft beers, and secondhand furniture. On top of that, you may have racked up a whopping great big pile of debt in getting your law degree, and you may be facing substantial student loan payments as a result. As one career services director pointed out, "For some students, their student loan debts mean that with a large firm income, after they've made their loan payments, they're living on just an average salary."

Now, who am I to argue with any of that? Wanting a few luxuries that you've been denying yourself, and paying off your debts, are great reasons to want to make a lot of money. But I want to point out a couple of things to you anyway. One is that large firms are not the sole province of huge earning potential. They have the highest *starting salary*, but you can make *wads* of money in other contexts. For instance, if you go into personal injury work, that's *very* lucrative, and it's traditionally only done by small law firms. Furthermore, in a lot of small firms, you start off with a much lower salary than you would at a large firm, but your salary grows much more quickly — so you can soon catch up with and surpass what you would have made at a large firm, even though, technically, you didn't start off with the big bucks.

Also, it's important to look at what you're making in the context of what you're giving up. After all, to paraphrase Orson Welles in the movie *Citizen Kane*, it's not hard to make a lot of money — if money's all you want. Rather, the question is: What are you willing to sacrifice to get that? It may be that you're working the equivalent of *two* full-time jobs when you go to work for a large law firm — and you're giving up everything you could have done with those extra hours you put in at the office! To illustrate this point, let's say that you're considering either a large firm job starting at $80,000, or a job working for a federal agency, say the Justice Department, at $40,000 a year. Well, as I've mentioned to you before, lawyers for the federal government typically work 40 hours a week, whereas, if you're a junior associate at a large firm, you could quite possibly put in 80 hours a week. That means that on an hourly basis, you're making exactly the same amount at each job! And that means that the large firm salary is *not* the windfall that it seems to be.

These drawbacks, however, don't diminish the fact that an $80,000 starting salary is a very strong, and unimpeachable, motivation for working for a large firm.

2. "I Want the Prestige"

Like money, prestige is a *very* strong motivator, and it can be even stronger depending on your circumstances. Maybe you went to an OK college. And maybe you go to an OK law school. That means that no one's eyes have ever gotten wide when you mentioned where you were going to school. So, working for a huge, prestigious law firm may be the first time in your *life* that the name of an organization you're associated with gives you the instant imprimatur of success, and intelligence, and superiority. Or maybe you've always gone to prestigious schools, and so you can't *imagine* doing anything that doesn't reek of prestige.

The problem with prestige is that if it's the only thing that's keeping you going, it wears thin *very* quickly. After all, prestige is something that really only works for *you* when you tell other people where you work. Your happiness is a function of your life on a day-to-day basis. If you're doing something that you don't like, you'll begin to resent it very quickly, whether it's prestigious or not. As one career services director told me, "I don't want to break anyone's dreams, but if all you want is the right office, the right corner, the right view — then you really don't want to be a lawyer." Think about what it is that you're going to be *doing*, not the sound of the firm's name as it rolls of your tongue. After all, it's your *life* we're talking about!

Furthermore, it's a mistake to believe that large firms are the only place where you can find prestige. *Many* career services directors, as well as practicing attorneys, point out that small firms that are recognized for a particular specialty — the so-called "boutique" firms — carry all of the prestige of a large firm without having the drawbacks of working for a large firm. Your career services director, alums, local attorneys, and upperclassmen can tell you who these firms are in your city, and it's worth doing a little bit of digging to find out about them. You might find that your desire for prestige can be satisfied somewhere *other* than a large firm!

Now, it may be that you're not concerned with prestige so much *yourself*, but you want other people — like your family — to be proud of you. Or maybe they're pressuring you to go after the big bucks and prestige associated with large firms. Well, undertaking *any* career move, especially one as demanding as working for a large firm, is something you shouldn't do in response to what anybody wants except for *you*. As one career services director told me, "If your parents want you to work at a 'name' firm, they're only responding to a media thing. They probably only know the splashy names they see on TV or read about in the paper. You may need to educate your folks about what's prestigious. For instance, explain to them how important it is to clerk for a judge, or work for the U.S. Attorneys' office." So if the prestige card is being played by anyone who's pressuring you, don't give in — set them straight!

And ultimately, *regardless* of whether you're responding to your own need for prestige or that of your relatives, you may want to question the value of working for a law firm whose name is recognized by everyone in the first place. As one career services director told me, "Who really *cares* if no one knows your firm's name?"

3. "LARGE LAW FIRM JOBS ARE MOST OF WHAT'S *OUT* THERE!"

You may think that you have to go for a large law firm job because there's very little else available. Wrong! As one career services director told me, "Law students have this perception that large law firms are a majority of the market, but they're not — not by a long shot." Another added, "Most students don't wind up at large firms, but rather at firms with 2 to 10 lawyers."

So, where does this misconception come from? It's borne of the fact that large law firms dominate the on-campus interviewing program. One career services director commented, "Sometimes large firm interest is there just because large firms are so *visible!*" Nationwide, they comprise 70% of on-campus interviews! That dominance makes sense, when you consider that they're the only ones who can spare the horses to *conduct* an on-campus interview program. *Most* legal jobs are never posted, and small law firms can't afford to give up the personnel to interview on-campus.

So check your motivations, and see if your interest in large law firms stems not from anything you'd do if you worked for them, but rather because you think that they're the only game in town. They're not!

4. "*EVERYBODY* WANTS A LARGE FIRM JOB, SO THERE MUST BE *SOMETHING* TO IT"

Peer pressure is an *enormous* factor in creating a luster for large firm jobs. It's perhaps *the* central factor that does it. One career services director told me about a student who was going to work for Legal Aid, and a classmate said to him, "You can't do that! You'll bring our class median salary down!" Another pointed out that "It's definitely true that the success model in law school means working for a large firm, and that's it — since top students are the only ones who are seen as having access to those jobs."

Well, I guess my response to this is pretty predictable. Doing something because everybody else wants to do it is a *really* wrong-headed way to make a career decision. As one hiring partner I spoke with said, "Have realistic expectations about the pay, the hours, the areas of law. Think about what you want to *do*, not what your parents or the student next to you wants!" *Think* about the factors I talked about in Topic A, when I discussed what it's like to work for a large firm. Go in and talk with your career services director about it. Talk with any alums or upperclassmen or lawyers you know who are familiar with large firm practice, and see what *they* say. And, most importantly, think about what *you want*. If you're not sure what you want, go back to Chapter 2 and read it, so that you're sure you're making a decision about your career based on what *you* really want. Because when it comes to choosing a job, *what you really want to do, the way you want to spend your life day after day, is all that matters!* Don't let what other people want color that decision!

5. "I WANT TO DO SOPHISTICATED WORK"

Quick! Define "sophisticated work." If you're like *I* was in law school, that's one of those terms you heard over and over and over again, but I'll be darned if I *ever* knew what it meant. In the process of interviewing people for this chapter, I asked a lot of people for *their* definitions, and now I understand why I never really understood it in law school: no two people had the same definition! I heard things like "cutting-edge issues," or "intellectually challenging work," or "an established practice with big name clients," or "a variety of issues, not just slip and fall cases" — those kinds of things. As one recruiting director said, "Frankly, I don't know what it is — all I know is that *every* law firm says that's what it does!"

There are a couple of things to keep in mind if doing sophisticated work is motivating you to look for a large-firm job. First of all, it's true that large firms do cutting-edge work, and that ultimately, if you stayed, you'd get to do that, too. But as I pointed out in Topic A, when you're a junior associate, that's *not* what you get to do — you get to do tedious work like document reviews, and research, and writing memos and briefs on tiny aspects of huge cases. As one recruiting director pointed out, "You have to ask yourself, what does it mean to *you* if your firm has a sophisticated practice? How does it impact *you?*" So if you're looking for cutting-edge work at a large firm, you're definitely talking about a situation that involves delayed gratification, for several years.

Another point to keep in mind is that large law firms aren't the *only* ones who deal with cutting-edge issues. As one career services director said, " Some sole practitioners change the face of the law!" Another one pointed out, "Frankly, large law firms are dinosaurs. The best and most challenging work isn't being done there anymore. Why? Because large corporations are taking their representation in-house, and for other clients, the same work can be done for less money by smaller firms." One recruiting director suggested that you can find very sophisticated work being done by smaller law firms that have broken away from large firms. To find these firms, talk with your career services director, alums, or any local attorneys you know, or scan the local bar association newsletter to see who's making the move from large firms. If you want to do work on the leading edge of the law, you may be able to do that without necessarily having to go to a large firm!

But having said all that, wanting a sophisticated practice *can* be a sound motivation for pursuing a job with a large firm. For instance, maybe it's your dream to work with certain heavyweights in a particular department of a large firm, people who are real stars in the field. Well, if you've got someone you idolize and want to work with and they're at a large firm, then you'll want to be at that firm, too. Or let's say that you've done a lot of soul searching, and you're intellectually drawn to particular areas that can only be handled by large firms. For instance, securities issues, cutting-edge corporate deals, complex corporate litigation — those kinds of things really can only be handled by large firms — and if they're the kinds of things you want to do, then you'll want to research the large firms, see who's doing the kinds of things you want to do, and pursue them. As one career services director pointed out, "There's a difference between saying you want a certain kind of practice and saying you want to work at a large firm. If you want a certain type of clientele that goes to large firms, that's a good reason to opt for a large firm. But if you just want to be a litigator, you can do that anywhere."

The point here is: Be careful how you define "sophisticated work." It may be that what you're thinking really *is* something you can do at a large firm, in which case it may be worth it to you to make the sacrifices that you'll have to make in order to do that work. But then again — maybe you can get the same thrill some other way!

6. "I HATE THE IDEA OF HAVING TO SCHMOOZE FOR NEW CLIENTS AND I WON'T HAVE TO DO THAT AT A LARGE FIRM"

What we're talking about here is client development, or what's more commonly called "rainmaking." Rainmaking is such a valuable skill in the eyes of employers that I dedicate a whole chapter to it — Chapter 11. Now, if you're uncomfortable with the idea of rainmaking, it may be because you're introverted, or maybe that you simply don't feel comfortable with selling and marketing and social stuff. If that's you, then you're probably wise to avoid job situations which will call on you to start developing clients pretty early on — and that would include most small- to medium-sized law firms. And it's true that large firms *don't* expect you to bring in any clients as a junior associate; that's the job of partners. So you're not at all thinking in a wrong-headed way if you're thinking of pursuing a large firm because you recoil at the thought of rainmaking. But I want you to think about a couple of things. For one, even if you don't have to do any rainmaking when you start at a big firm, if you're thinking of staying there long-term, you simply won't make partner if you're not perceived as a client draw. So if you plan on staying the course, at some point you'll *have* to do some rainmaking; nobody makes partner simply on the basis of wonderful work product. For another thing, there are *lots* of jobs that don't call for rainmaking, outside of junior associate jobs at large law firms. For instance, most government jobs don't require rainmaking. Anything like the U.S. Attorney's office, or the D.A.'s office, or Legal Aid, or any federal agency position — none of them require rainmaking. Working for a judge doesn't involve rainmaking. So don't think that you've got to go to a large firm to avoid rainmaking!

7. "I WANT TO GO IN FOR A COUPLE OF YEARS JUST TO SET MYSELF UP FOR THE FUTURE"

Frankly, this is a *really good* reason to want to go to a large firm. The only real downside to it is that you have to gird yourself for a couple of really stressful years, for all of the reasons that I talked about in Topic A.

But the fact is, if you intend to get in and get out, you may be doing exactly the right thing. Why? For one thing, you *will* make big bucks for a couple of years, and if you've got a heavy debt load, that will enable you to pay it way down before you look for jobs that might pay a lot less. For another, it *is* a notch in your belt to have worked for a big, prestigious firm; it's kind of like having served on Law Review, or having gone to Harvard. It's the kind of credential that you'll carry with you forever. And for another, if you keep your eyes open, you may get an insight into a lot of different specialties. Although you're unlikely to rotate through many departments once you actually start as a full-time associate, you can talk with people who do many other things, and that can give you insight into what you want to do *next*.

Of course, you'd never want to let any employer *know* that this is what you plan to do, although, as one career services director pointed out to me, everyone *knows* that people only stay in their first job for a couple of years, whether it's a large firm job or not!

So, if you're thinking of a large firm as a short-term prospect that acts as a springboard into other things, then that's a pretty sound motivation!

8. "LARGE LAW FIRMS ONLY TAKE THE BEST STUDENTS, AND I'M THE BEST"

For one thing, if you're reading this, I applaud your honesty in being able to admit it. But other than that . . . does the word "insecure" mean anything to you? I realize that there are people who believe that working at a large law firm is the only way to start, and that going anywhere else is admitting failure, and that biggest is best, and that anybody who's any good at all is at a huge firm. But those are all terrible reasons for a making a career decision! For one thing, it's not true; there are many *extremely* prestigious lawyers who work at boutique firms or as sole practitioners; they aren't "all" at large firms by any stretch of the imagination. And for another, you're abdicating a huge responsibility to yourself if you let your perception of "best" decide where you ought to work. Take a look at the kind of work you'll do at a large firm. Talk to people who've worked at large firms, either through your career services director or any other contacts you have. Take a long look at everything you discover, and ask: "Is this really the *work* I want to do? Is this really the environment I want?" If it's not, you'll quickly decide that being at a large law firm is far from being the "best" thing for you!

D. THE TWO CRUCIAL OPENING STEPS IN YOUR QUEST FOR A LARGE FIRM JOB

All right. I'm going to give you all the ammunition you need to go after a large firm job, even if you don't have the credentials large firms normally demand. Now if you do as I say, you *will* get a large firm job. But I'm warning you: it's not going to be easy, and if you think it *will* be, you're in for a rude surprise. But it *can* be done. If you're up to the task — let's get to work!

First of all, let's talk a little bit about how large firms actually do their hiring. Normally, they'll hire a group of people for summer clerkships after their second year in law school. The firms find these clerks via their on-campus interviewing in the Fall of the preceding year. So, if you want a summer clerkship next summer, you'd interview this Fall for it. And then, the firms choose their permanent associates based on who performs well in the summer clerkship program. The number of clerks they hire from the summer clerkship program may vary, but it's generally taken as a given that if you are up to snuff in the summer program, you'll get a permanent offer. Of course, that's not a perfect model, and firms sometimes find themselves with permanent associate spots tc fill that weren't satisfied from their summer program. And they'll interview Third Year students in the fall of Third Year for *those* jobs. Now, as I say, this is the *normal* way large firms hire. If you do as I tell you, you're probably not going to have to fool around with the on-campus interview program, and even if you *do* bother with it, you're going to do so in sneaky ways, because, let's face it, if you don't have great credentials, you're not going to get a regular on-campus interview *anyway*, and there's no point in depressing yourself by butting your head against a brick wall. At least, not when there are so many fertile alternatives available!

In this section, I'm going to lead you through all those "fertile alternatives." But before you make a single contact or take part in a single activity or make *any* outward step toward your goal, there are two crucial things you must do: (1) accept that you're not the person large firms are looking for, and (2) cast the credentials you *do* have in the best possible light. Let's talk about those in a little bit more detail.

1. ACCEPT THE FACT THAT YOU DON'T HAVE THE CREDENTIALS THAT THEY'RE LOOKING FOR, AND THAT'S THAT. DON'T BE RESENTFUL!

By way of preparing yourself for storming the large firm fortress, you *have* to acknowledge that you have a tremendous obstacle to overcome if you don't have sterling credentials. By sterling credentials, I mean top 10%, and preferably Law Review. If you go to a distinguished school, you have more leeway, but for the majority of law schools, those are the credentials large firms demand — and typically get. I say "typically," because there are people — like you! — who will be able to get in *without* those kinds of credentials. And once you get in, to quote an attorney from a huge firm, "You're as good as your last case — nobody cares about your grades any more!" But you've got to get in the door *first,* and to do that you're going to have to do *other* things to convince the firm that you're the perfect candidate for them *despite* the fact that you don't have the credentials they're looking for. There's no way around that, and you have to be willing to do what I'll tell you to do *without* being resentful of it!

I hear what you're saying. "What a crock!" you're saying. "There are *tons* of great lawyers-to-be who aren't in the top 10% of my class!" Well, of course, you're right. And it's not that large firms don't know that, as well. One hiring partner I spoke with was very up front about it, saying, "It's obviously true that there are people who would be excellent attorneys even though they have mediocre grades. But it's a fact of life that with the number of résumés we get and the number of students to interview, you've got to have great credentials to get in through on-campus interviews." Statistics for every large firm bear that out. Baker & McKenzie, for example, gets over *12,000* résumés a year for 25 summer clerkships. Chicago's McDermott, Will & Emery gets 2,500 résumés for 18 summer clerkships. So when you're talking about large firms, you're talking about employers who demand great credentials, to paraphrase the punch line of an old joke, "Because they can." They don't have the time or the incentive to dip below the top of the class, even though there are undoubtedly some Oliver Wendell Holmeses lurking down there. In fact, one large firm did a study to see if there was a correlation between lawyers who made it to partnership, and what their law school grades were like. The only sound predictor was *undergraduate* grades; law school grades were no predictor at all. But large firms, nonetheless, insist on great grades, and that's it.

So if you're going after a large firm job, you've got to acknowledge this. You've got to accept the fact that you don't have the credentials they're looking for, and, undoubtedly, at many points along your trek they're going to point that out to you. You can't be defensive or huffy; you've got to let the criticism slide off your back, focusing exclusively on the things you do well and why you'd be a great associate (which is what I'll show you how to do in the next section). If you resent the thought of criticism about your grades, I've got some advice for you — get over it, if you really intend to go for a large firm job. You have to muster all of your nerve, all of your talent, all of your chutzpah, all of your savvy, and forge ahead with the strategies I'm going to give you if you want to get that job!

2. CAST THE CREDENTIALS YOU *Do* HAVE IN THE BEST POSSIBLE LIGHT

Before you go for a large firm job, you've *got* to go through your record with a fine-toothed comb, and pull out every highlight you can possibly muster. You've probably already done this, if you've read Chapter 4 on making contacts, or Chapter 5 on Correspondence, or Chapter 7 on Interviewing. But in case you *haven't*, it's particularly crucial to be able to recite your strengths when you're looking for a large firm job, because they're so heavily credential driven.

So, whatever positives you can pull out — pull them out! Let's say that the difference between the top 10% in your class and the top 40% is that rotten C– you got in Contracts. Well, if you had one lousy exam result that pulled down your GPA, be sure you can summon that statistic immediately! Or let's say that you've got that old chestnut, a strong upward trend in your grades, such that it was really only your first semester that torpedoed your overall GPA. Again — highlight that on your résumé and whenever you talk with anyone about your credentials, focusing on where you'd be in your class if it wasn't for that first semester. Or let's say you had a personal tragedy that marred your performance first year. The idea of making hay out of a tragedy is enough to make *anyone's* skin crawl, but if that happened to you, it's something you should mention. (You don't need details; a simple "A serious family tragedy occurred in my first semester. I'm fine now, but it dragged down my performance then.") Or let's say that you've had to work full-time to put yourself through school, and that you've had to balance your study time against your work time as a result. Mention that! Or let's say that you've done better in paper courses than in exam courses. Highlight that, because paper courses are analogous to the research that dominates a new associate's time at a large firm.

You can see what the key to all of this is: what you've got to do is to resolve in your own mind that you really do have the brain power that large firms are looking for, even though your grades don't show it. I'm not going to pretend this is easy, but you *have* to come to grips with your own performance in order to appear self-confident when you approach large firms!

Now, if your grades are just not very good and there really aren't any highlights for you to pull out — like a meteorite came through the ceiling of your dorm room and destroyed your outlines the week before finals — then you're going to have to distinguish yourself some other way. I don't mean to be flip about it, but you're just going to have to acknowledge that your grades aren't good, and draw attention to the *other* things you've done (or are *going* to do after you read this chapter!) as a harbinger of the success you'll be at a large firm. Much too much emphasis is put on grades as it is; after all, 90% of your class is below the top 10%. There are *many* ways to substitute other activities for the grades you don't have, so that in a large firm's eyes you'll vault yourself into that top-10% category.

In fact — why don't we talk about those activities now!

E. GET NOTICED BY LARGE LAW FIRMS IN WAYS THAT *DON'T* FOCUS ON YOUR CREDENTIALS

You may think that on-campus interviews are the only way of getting noticed by a large firm. Not true! Especially if your credentials aren't what they traditionally look for, you're *much* better off avoiding the on-campus interview process entirely.

How? There are two principal ways to do it:

♦ Take part in activities at school and in the community that bring you into contact with attorneys from large firms.

♦ Use contacts to get your foot in the door — either alumni who work at the firm (or know people who do), big clients of firms you're interested in, or anyone else you know with connections to the firm in question (family, friends, professors, and the like).

Let's talk about each one of those.

1. TAKE PART IN ACTIVITIES THAT BRING YOU INTO CONTACT WITH ATTORNEYS FROM LARGE FIRMS

If you've already read Chapter 4, you know what a big fan I am of getting your dream job by making contacts. When you're trying to get a job with an employer who's going to frown at your credentials, that's *doubly* true — because you want to get them to see you in a light *other* than the spotlight that focuses on your résumé!

What kinds of activities should you consider? Any of the ones I talk about in Chapter 4 that involve contact with local lawyers would be fine. And by the way, you should read Chapter 4 *anyway* because it primes you for how you ought to deal with contacts once you've met them! All I'm going to do here is to summarize the activities, from those listed in Chapter 4, focusing particularly on how to use these activities to meet people from large firms, not just any employer. Choose the activities that appeal to you most, and go after them!

A. PUBLISH AN ARTICLE IN AN AREA OF LAW THAT INTERESTS YOU

Now when you think of publishing an article, you may think of Law Review, and that's it. But the fact is, there are tons of legal publications, like bar magazines and specialty newsletters, and they all need articles. Check with your law school library and your career services director to find out what's out there.

What you want to do is to pick a subject area that you want to practice in. Then, find out the names of people at large firms who practice in that area. Contact them, by mail or by phone, express your interest in writing an article in the area, and ask if they can suggest a topic that they think needs to be written about. What does this do? It gets you into contact with lawyers at the firm where you want to practice, in a nonthreatening way. Remember — people are flattered when you ask the for advice! Furthermore, you can be sure that if a lawyer recommends a topic to you, they'll want to read the finished product — and that gives you an excuse to keep in touch. You may also want to ask whether you can call from time to time as you write the article, in case you need to ask any questions. All in all — it's a great way to make contacts!

B. IF YOUR SCHOOL HAS A WRITING REQUIREMENT, APPROACH LAWYERS AT LARGE FIRMS FOR WRITING TOPICS

This is a spin on the idea I just gave you, about publishing an article. However, instead of *publishing* what you write, you'll be fulfilling your writing requirement. Either way, it gives you a great way to contact lawyers at your dream firm. Just call or write and explain that you have a school writing requirement to fulfill, and ask what they'd like to read about. Then proceed as you would with a published article, by keeping in touch with them, and sending them the finished product.

C. APPROACH THE LARGE FIRM OF YOUR DREAMS AND VOLUNTEER TO DO A RESEARCH PROJECT

This is yet another spin on the "writing an article" idea, but this time, you contact the lawyer first. What you do is to go to a partner at a large firm who practices in an area that interests you. Volunteer to do a research project on a topic they'd find useful. You can also say that you'll try to get the project published when it's done. Then, if the partner's contribution merits it, you can always share a byline (that is, writing credit). I spoke with one associate who'd gotten his job just this way; he volunteered for an estate planning lawyer, worked on an article with him, and got an offer from the firm as a result.

D. DO ARTICLES ON PARTNERS AT LARGE FIRMS FOR YOUR LAW SCHOOL NEWSPAPER . . . AND IF YOUR SCHOOL DOESN'T HAVE A NEWSPAPER, START ONE!

Everyone is flattered by the idea that you want to write an article about them. So, find partners who practice in an area that interests you (from your career services office or other contacts), contact them, and tell them you'd like to write a profile of them for your school paper. Have a list of questions for them. You'll want to ask the same kinds of things you'd ask in a job interview — about how they chose their specialty, what they like about their job, what a typical day is like for them, what they wish they'd known before they started the practice, what kinds of traits it takes to be successful in their specialty, where they see their specialty progressing in the years to come, and things like that. You can *also* ask very valuable questions that you *couldn't* ask on an interview. Things like what kinds of advice they'd offer to people who want to break into their field, and what the downsides are.

When the article is published, be sure you follow up with the person you interviewed. At that point, you can always say, "Having interviewed you, I'm really excited about what you do, and I'd like eventually to be able to do it myself. How should I go about it?" If you've sufficiently impressed them up to now, they'll be happy to help you!

What if your school doesn't have a newspaper? Start one! Newsletters are cheap to publish, so it's easy to get support from your Student Bar Association. You'll still be able to interview the people you want to interview, but you'll also have the feather in your cap of starting something — which shows the valuable trait of initiative!

E. VOLUNTEER AT YOUR CAREER SERVICES OFFICE

Who do you think sets up all of those on-campus interviews large firms do, anyway? The interview fairy? Your career services office arranges on-campus interviews, sets up panels and seminars, and finds on-campus speakers. And if you volunteer to work at career services, you'll have the perfect opportunity to meet lawyers at the firms you want to work for, in a nonthreatening environment!

What kinds of things can you do? Things like . . .

♦ Help set up panels and receptions by being a liaison with alumni and local practitioners. You're the one who contacts them to see if they can come and speak, or take part in a panel, or attend a reception. Furthermore, the fact that you're working at career services means you'll have input on exactly who those speakers and reception guests should be — and, of course, you'll choose the lawyers from firms where you'd like to practice!

♦ Offer to be a student escort for on-campus interviewers. You escort interviewers to interview rooms, show them where coffee, restrooms, and phones are, and generally make yourself helpful. What do you get? A few minutes alone with the interviewer, in the best possible light — you look good because you're being helpful. And you're not under pressure because you needn't say anything about wanting to meet with them while you escort them. You have the perfect opportunity to break the ice and chat in a casual way. Then follow up with a phone call or letter, which you'll open by stating where you met them. Assuming you made a good impression, it'll be much easier to say you'd like to meet with them to ask their advice for breaking in and doing what they do; you know, an information interview (which I discuss in detail in Chapter 4).

F. HELP OUT WITH YOUR SCHOOL'S SPEAKER'S BUREAU, AND IF YOUR SCHOOL DOESN'T HAVE ONE, START ONE

Most schools have an organization that brings in off-campus speakers. Consider taking part in it! Why? You'll get the opportunity to contact lawyers at large firms, and get them to come and give a lecture on campus. This involves not just making contact with them to come and give a speech (which is a flattering thing), but also gives you a chance to meet them on campus, and perhaps even have a meal with them (since most speaker's bureaus spring for a meal for the speaker). This is yet another nonthreatening way to meet the people you want to work for!

If your school doesn't have a bureau like this, start one! It doesn't take much of a budget, so it's typically pretty easy to get backing from the Student Bar Association. Apart from making great contacts, you'll help your classmates and have a great résumé item to boot!

When do you bring up the idea of a potential job with their firm? Not before they've spoken; you don't want to be that aggressive. Instead, why not call them afterwards, tell them you were impressed with their speech, you'd like to do what they do, and ask for an information interview? (I give advice on conducting information interviews in Chapter 4). It doesn't put them on the spot, and it gets your foot in the door!

G. TAKE PART IN YOUR SCHOOL'S MENTORING PROGRAM, AND IF IT DOESN'T HAVE ONE ALREADY, START ONE!

A "mentoring" program is one where alumni offer to act as mentors for students, giving them advice about careers. Not every law school has such a program, and if it doesn't, offer to help start one! You'd work with your career services office to contact alumni and determine their interest in becoming a mentor. Needless to say, you'll want to focus particularly on alumni who work at large firms — perhaps you can find *yourself* a mentor this way. You can always say, "You know, having spoken with you, I'd really appreciate it if you'd be *my* mentor." If they're willing to take part in the program at all, they'll be flattered by your interest!

H. JOIN THE LOCAL BAR ASSOCIATION OR VOLUNTEER TO HELP OUT

Almost no law students do this, *and that's a big mistake.* There are all *kinds* of things that you can do for the local bar association that will bring you into contact with the lawyers you want to meet.

In terms of joining the local bar association, you'll find that you can do so at a very nominal fee as a student. If you don't want to join, go to meetings anyway. Local bar associations run seminars on all kinds of topics, and they also hold special events and social gatherings. Go and scope out the lawyers who work for firms you want to work for yourself!

Volunteering is an even better way to make contact with lawyers, because you've got a built-in excuse to talk to them. You can man tables at bar committee functions. Make phone calls. Join a bar association committee, offer to do research on a topic, and then offer to speak about it. Whatever. Check with your career services office to see how to get in touch with the bar association. They'll be happy to have your help!

I. GO TO CLE'S (CONTINUING LEGAL EDUCATION CLASSES) OR VOLUNTEER TO HELP RUN THEM

All lawyers, no matter how successful they are, have to take continuing legal education classes to keep their licenses. These classes are called CLE's. You may not know it, but *you,* as a student, can also take CLE's. They're given on virtually every topic under the sun, and they're typically given at law schools, so they're very convenient! On top of that, they're either free to students or very inexpensive, so they won't stretch your budget. Check with your career services office to see what's offered, when, and where.

Once you know what's offered, what do you do? Go to CLE's for topics that interest you, and search out lawyers who work for firms you want to work for. Try to angle a seat next to them, and even if you don't, there are plenty of opportunities to talk — like coffee breaks and lunch. And you've got a built-in topic of conversation to break the ice — the class you're attending. You can always ask what they thought of the seminar, what others they'd recommend — and, of course, you'll want to point out that you're interested in the area of practice and want to get more practical experience in it.

You may even want to volunteer to help run CLE's. You can do everything from manning the reception desk to contacting people. Then, as a follow up, you can send out personalized letters to the people you contacted, leading off with telling them how you met. Say that you were impressed with what they had to say, and you'd like to meet with them and learn more. As I pointed out in Chapter 4, you wouldn't be the first person to get a job in just this way!

J. DO FUNDRAISING ACTIVITIES FOR YOUR LAW SCHOOL

Especially if you've got a great phone personality, this is a great way to meet alums. What you'll want to do up front is to find out who works at firms you want to pursue, and make sure that you get to contact them. If the idea of begging for money turns you off, relax. For one thing, alums expect it. I get about a million calls a year from *my* law school! And for another, you can always make it more comfortable by using it as an excuse to update them about what's going on at school, so that it's more like a conversation than a simple request for money. Make your voice upbeat, and smile while you talk — people can actually *hear* that, believe it or not! You never know when a phone call you make will lead to a longer conversation. And if the opportunity presents itself, you can always say, "I'd love to hear more about what you're doing. Can we set up a meeting?" And take it from there!

K. READ LOCAL BAR NEWSLETTERS AND JOURNALS AND FOLLOW UP ON THEM!

Here are a couple of ideas for you, that give you a great excuse to contact lawyers you'd like to meet.

One is to look at profiles of attorneys who are written up in local bar newsletters. When you see one for an attorney who works for a firm you'd like to work for, and practices something that interests you, call them or write to them and tell them that you read about them. Tell them you're very interested in what they do, and you'd like to set up a meeting so you can find out more about it. People are almost always flattered by this kind of interest, and you will, undoubtedly, get information interviews this way!

The other is to scan bar journals for your city or state, read any articles about areas of practice that interest you, and see who wrote them. These articles are inevitably written by practitioners, and at least *some* of them are written by practitioners from large firms. When you find an author from a firm you want to work for, just call or write and say you read their article, you loved it, and you'd love to hear more about what they do. As an author myself, I promise you that authors are *suckers* for people who compliment their work. It's a great way to make contacts!

L. TAKE A NONPAYING JOB DOING *WHATEVER* YOUR DREAM JOB IS

Why not contact the firm of your dreams and tell them you'd like to volunteer for them? I realize that's going for the jugular, but what have you got to lose? What you're saying is, "I know I don't have the paper credentials you typically demand, but I'm so confident that I'd be a great associate for you that I'm willing to work for free to prove it to you!" Maybe there aren't many firms who'll go for this, but you only need one to say "yes." Then it's up to you to be true to your word, and dazzle them with your work!

M. IF YOU'RE A DECENT ATHLETE, JOIN LAWYERS' SPORTS TEAMS (LIKE SOFTBALL AND BASKETBALL TEAMS)

There's no better, less threatening way to meet lawyers than to play sports with them. Ask your career services office for advice on tracking down where such teams play, and give them a call — or just show up — and ask to be included. The opportunities to chat before, during, and after games, and perhaps go for a postgame beer, provide excellent ways to make contacts. If you're an athlete you probably already know how easy it is to forge a bond with people if you play a sport with them. Turn this to your advantage by playing with people at firms you want to work for!

2. USE *ANY* CONTACTS YOU HAVE TO GET YOUR FOOT IN THE DOOR

Here's the scoop. It's *difficult* to get your foot in the door at a large firm. Use every weapon in your artillery to get there — and if you have connections, that means *using* them!

Maybe you just don't think you *have* connections. Not true! At the very least you have your career services director, and that's an *excellent* connection to use. Your career services director will have connections at virtually every firm in town, including the large ones, and will be delighted to help you with them. Better yet, your career services director will probably know who got into various large firms *without having stellar credentials, either!* So don't be too proud to go to career services for help in making connections like this! Also, don't overlook your professors. If you have a professor you've done some work for who will call and say something like, "This research assistant was a lifesaver; her grades don't represent her skills" — that can *easily* get you an interview.

So there's your career services director and there are your professors. Beyond that, maybe you don't realize that the people you know actually *have* connections you can use. I've pointed out many times that you don't know *who* the people you know, know. As I pointed out in Chapter 4, sometimes the unlikeliest people are your best conduit for networking. I heard a wonderful story about one student who applied three times to a large firm in New York, and didn't even get an interview. He went home over Christmas, and visited his girlfriend's family. Her great uncle was there, and he mentioned to the uncle that he was looking for a job. It turns out that the great uncle had a patient whose neighbor was a partner at this particular firm. By this circuitous route the student got an interview. He was sure it was a joke, but he showed up, and got a full-day interview — and he came out with an offer! So before you leap to the conclusion that you don't have any connections, ask everyone you know! Fraternity brothers, sorority sisters, upperclassmen who think a lot of you and themselves get offers from large firms — you never know whose good word will get you in the door!

Even if you don't think you know anybody, it's not a big deal. You can do other things to make up for it. You can take part in the kind of activities I just talked about, or use a sneaky way to get an on-campus interview, as I discuss in a few minutes in Topic F.

Finally, let's say that you have connections, and you *know* you have them, but you've shied away from using them because it makes you uncomfortable to think of using people. I strongly encourage you to reprogram your thinking so that you put this "connections" business in a more positive light. When you use contacts to get your foot in the door at a large firm, what you're doing is just that — you're making contact with someone who works at a firm, but all you're looking for is *advice* from the lawyers you contact. You want to learn more about what it's like to work at the firm, what their perspective is. Let a desire to help you spring naturally from the communication between you. Ideally, they'll wind up helping you get an interview with the firm, without you ever having to submit a résumé the traditional way, through the on-campus interview process or by mail. Remember, everybody likes to offer advice, but nobody likes to get hit up for a job!

You may even be able to use a firm's big clients to get your foot in the door at the firm itself. How? It means making connections at the client itself, and then using them to get to the firm. First, you have to figure out who the firm's clients *are*. Do a Lexis or Westlaw search for that; perhaps the firm's own brochures mention the names of clients. Assuming the clients are businesses or organizations, find out who it is at the client who deals with the firm. The client will probably have in-house counsel, and with any luck, your career services office will know someone there (or you may know them some other way). Call or write to the in-house counsel, and ask for an information interview with them (I discuss information interviews in detail in Chapter 4). Tell them that you're looking for advice about the firm, just as you'd ask anyone else for it, and state your intention to try and get a job with the firm. If the client is impressed with you, and is willing to put in a good word for you at the firm, that will definitely distinguish you from the crowd — and will at least get you an interview!

3. CONTACT LAWYERS WHO AREN'T DELUGED WITH RÉSUMÉS

Everybody who sends their résumé to a large firm sends it to the hiring partner (if they're relatively smart) or the recruiting co-ordinator (if they're not so smart). As a result, those people are swamped with résumés, and if all you do is send your résumé to them, you're not doing anything to set yourself apart and to get yourself an interview. Instead — contact the head of the practice area that you want to work for.

How do you find out who that is? Do a Martindale-Hubbell or Lexis or Westlaw search to find out who runs the Estates depart-ment, or Litigation department, or whatever specialty it is that most interests you, and direct your attention to that person. Ideally, you're going to use your career services office to find out if there are contacts in that department, but let's say that you've struck out, and so all you have left is the correspondence route. Well, you'll tailor your letter to address your interest in the specialty, back that up with some concrete evidence that you really are interested in the specialty (e.g., course work, or a CLE class, or extracurricular you've undertaken), and you'll ask for an opportunity to meet with them. This is a particularly useful technique, by the way, if you had a career before law school that would be of particular interest to lawyers in a particular specialty. For instance, if you were involved in hospital administration before you went to law school, and a large firm you're interested in has a substantial practice dedicated to hospital work, write directly to the head of that department, highlighting your background and the transferable skills it gives you! You can see where this would be *very* impressive to a practitioner in that specialty, even though your résumé might not have made it past the recruiting director!

You *may* even want to consider sending a cover letter *without* a résumé. If you do that, make sure that your letter contains sufficient information about you to entice the attorney — things about your course work and CLE classes, or anything else that shows you're a go-getter and very interested in their field would fit the bill. The advantage you have if you *don't* send a résumé is that you don't have to worry about the attorney ignoring your letter, and just forwarding your résumé to the recruiting director — which is what you were trying to avoid in the first place! And by the way, *send your letter by Federal Express, Airborne, UPS Overnight, or some other overnight delivery service, if you can possibly afford to do so.* No attorney will ignore something that comes via overnight mail.

Now, what happens if you contact a department head this way? At the very least, you've upped your chances of getting an interview because you've contacted someone who isn't normally contacted by students, and that does two things: it makes you stand out due to lack of competition, and it shows your initiative in seeking them out. Initiative is a trait highly prized by lawyers, as we've discussed several times before! (Once you actually get the interview, go back and read the section on information interviews, in Chapter 4. If it's plain this is a *job* interview you've set up — for instance, the lawyer contacts you and offers to set up a job interview, or asks if it's a summer clerkship or permanent job you're interested in, so the purpose of the interview is plain — then read the information on interviewing in Chapter 7.)

4. BE WILLING TO GO TO LESS DESIRABLE MARKETS

If you're dead-set on the idea of going to a large firm despite less-than-stellar credentials, you might want to look at going to a large firm that happens to be in a smaller, or less desirable, city. I don't mean to suggest that credentials aren't important to large firms in smaller cities — they *are*. But the fact is, the large firms in less attractive markets aren't going to be able to *lure* the same students as ones in the glamour markets, like New York, and Chicago, and Los Angeles, and Boston, and Seattle, and San Francisco, and any other large, glamorous cities I've insulted by leaving them off this list. With less competition, your lower grades won't matter as much. I'm not saying it's a cakewalk, but it's *comparatively* easier, and if you're flexible when it comes to geography, it's worth a try!

F. SNEAKY WAYS TO GET AN ON-CAMPUS INTERVIEW

"Oh, sure," you're saying. "Thanks for the tip. Like they're going to interview *me* if I put my résumé in the folder. No way!" You're right. If you didn't grade your way onto Law Review, it's unlikely you'll get an on-campus interview with a large firm the traditional way — that is, submitting your résumé through career services.

You're going to be cleverer than that. And here's how.

1. CHECK YOUR SCHOOL'S PRESCREENING POLICY FOR ON-CAMPUS INTERVIEWERS

Here's the scoop. Schools vary in the way that they handle on-campus interviewers in terms of the latitude they give firms in choosing the students they're going to interview. For instance, let's say that Upright & Starch wants to come to your campus to interview students, and they can fit 28 interviews into 2 days. Some schools give firms 100% prescreening; that is, they get to sift through the résumés submitted, and choose every single student they want to interview. In this case, Upright & Starch would get to pick all 28 interviewees. Other schools let firms choose only some of the students they get to interview. For instance, at one school in the northeast, firms get to pick about 60%, so Upright & Starch would get to pick 17 of the 28 interviewees, and the school's career services office would pick the other 11.

You can probably see where I'm going with this. If your career services office chooses *any* of the interviewees, do everything you can to see to it that you get one of those slots. Now, the *policy* on filling those slots also varies from school to school. For some, it's a straight lottery system; your résumé is picked at random. Others have a wish list; that is, if you say that Upright & Starch is your dream firm, you've got a good shot at getting one of those school-chosen interview slots. Regardless of your school's policy on filling those slots, I'd go straight to your career services director and beg for an interview slot, even if they're supposedly filled at random. What's the worst that'll happen? You've still got your random shot at being chosen. At best, your career services director will reward your enthusiasm with an interview, or suggest other ways for you to get your foot in the door at Upright & Starch. The bottom line is, you're no worse off if you make the extra effort, even if there's no written policy that says it'll work.

By the way, if you've got a chance at one of these school-chosen picks, this is no time for your pride to rule your head. I've spoken with career services directors who told me that they have students who actually *turn down* lottery picks. Why? Because their pride is hurt — they don't like to accept charity. Or they think that there's no way they'll actually get an offer if they don't have the credentials, and they probably got that misconception from the student grapevine. The fact is, if you have the great good fortune to get an on-campus interview with the law firm of your dreams, *for goodness sake, take it!* What you are being handed on a silver platter is 20 minutes alone with someone who's in a position to make your dream come true. It just doesn't matter *how* that chance came about, and if you wind up as an associate at that firm, I *promise* you *no one* will ever give any kind of a damn how you got your foot in the door! If you don't take that opportunity and make the most of it, you're torpedoing an excellent chance to impress your dream employer. Don't blow it!

2. FIND OUT WHO THE PRESCREENER AT YOUR DREAM FIRM IS AND CONTACT THEM DIRECTLY

As soon as school starts in the Fall, find out if your dream firm is going to be doing on-campus interviews at your school. Call the firm, and find out who does the prescreening. If they aren't willing to tell you directly, then go through your career services office, find an alum who works there, and find out from the alum who does the prescreening. Then do one of two things: go visit that person face-to-face and ask for an on-campus interview, or contact them by phone with the same request. The personal visit is best, but if it's an out-of-town firm or you just feel too squeamish to go in person, then the phone request will be fine. I'm not recommending that you write to them, because, frankly, if you send a letter and a résumé, your résumé's likely to get thrown in the hopper with all of the other résumés they receive.

In this phone call or visit, you've got to have all of your ducks in a row as to why this is your dream job, and why you're the ideal candidate for it even though you don't have the credentials you know they typically look for. Don't be defensive about your record, but don't be naive about it, either; acknowledge it and move immediately to why they should interview you.

Is this going to work every time? No. But sometimes it will! And it's pretty obvious why. Remember what I said way back in Chapter 1 — honest enthusiasm counts for a lot, and if you show the initiative it takes to contact the prescreener, you're definitely ahead of the pack.

3. GET AN INTERVIEW WITH THE ON-CAMPUS INTERVIEWER WITHOUT GETTING AN ON-CAMPUS INTERVIEW

I'll bet you had to read *that* a couple of times! Here's what it means. It's entirely possible for you to meet with the on-campus interviewer in a completely novel way by taking into account the logistics of the interviewer's schedule. From the outset, I've got to tell you that it takes some major-league *cojones* to pull off this kind of thing, but if you've got 'em, by all means give it a try!

Here's what you do, and you've got a couple of choices. One is to suit up as though you really do have an on-campus interview scheduled. Find out which room the interviewer is in, and post yourself outside of it during the last interview. When it's over, walk the interviewer to their car, in a polite but enthusiastic way explaining that you'd love to work at their firm, and giving your "infomercial" (see Chapter 7) on why you ought to get a shot, and again, politely, asking for any advice or help the interviewer can offer. This has, more than once, resulted in offers for determined students. And you can see why — the nerve, determination, and enthusiasm it represents sets them way apart from the crowd, regardless of their grades!

Another possibility would be to post yourself outside the interview room, and wait for no-shows. How often does that happen? Not often. But if it *does*, you're ready to pounce at a moment's notice. After all, that's a 20-minute slot the interviewer had intended to use for an interview. And it might as well be with you!

Yet another possibility requires a little more legwork beforehand, but, again, if you've got the nerve to do it, the payoff can be big. If the law firm of your dreams is out-of-town, find out how the interviewer is getting in. If they're flying in, put on your interview suit, and go down and meet them at the airport. Everybody who travels has to walk through the airport, and most people who travel have to get their luggage. That leaves you, the enterprising student, with a window of opportunity in which to make your pitch. Sounds outrageous? Maybe. But it's resulted in a job offer in more than one instance — and it could work for you!

What's the thread that links these ideas? Nerve. Imagination. A go-get-'em attitude that's bound to impress *anybody*. So if you think you can carry it off, take a deep breath, and give it a try!

G. BE PERSISTENT! NEEDS CHANGE!

It may be that you try a variety of avenues, and you get through the fall without nailing down a job for the following summer, or for when you graduate. And that may bum you out to the point that you give up. My advice to you? *Don't give up!* Many career services directors, as well as recruiting directors, hammered home the point that *needs change*. It's true that large firms do their hiring for the following summer by December. But many times large firms find themselves with an opening they didn't have during the traditional fall interviewing season. For instance, sometimes people with offers change their minds. Or sometimes the firm will get a huge new project or new client, and suddenly need more bodies. There are a myriad of reasons *why* their needs might change, but if they do, you've got to be ready!

So what should you do? If you feel that you came close on a couple of law firms but just didn't nail down an offer, never take a rejection as a permanent matter; instead, say that you'll be contacting them again to see if their needs change. If they don't expressly tell you *not* to, then stay in touch every month or two, just to see if anything has opened up. Contact the recruiting director at the firm, or, if you've made other contacts with attorneys there, call or write to them, instead. I heard of many instances of students getting jobs at large firms in just this way — they persisted where their classmates gave up!

H. GO IN THROUGH THE SIDE DOOR: GETTING THE LARGE FIRM JOB YOU WANT WITHOUT STARTING AS A TRADITIONAL ASSOCIATE

I won't deny it — the suggestions I'm about to give you are very controversial. What I'm going to tell you about are positions that are a step down from a traditional associate, with the idea in mind that once you're in the door, you can move into a traditional associate position by impressing the firm with your work and your dedication. Why's this so controversial? Well, some career services people feel that once you start in a firm as something other than a traditional associate, you'll be typecast, and you'll never be able to shake off your original image. You'll always be downgraded. Others disagree with that, and I fall into that group. Why? Because I've already acknowledged that all I'm doing here is helping you pursue your dream of working at a large firm. It's up to you to decide if you want it badly enough to start a rung down from traditional associate, and whether you have the talent and stick-to-it-iveness to prove yourself once you're there. So I'll tell you about these opportunities, and you can decide for yourself if you want to pursue them.

By the way — in every case, there are people who've started with the job described and moved into a traditional, partnership-track associate's job. It's been done before — and you can do it, too!

1. STAFF ATTORNEY

A staff attorney is simply a permanent associate; that is, no matter how long you work at the firm, you're never going to be a partner. You're not on a partnership track. What does that mean, exactly? Well, on the plus side, you are, in fact, a lawyer at your dream firm with the prestige that goes along with that. You work with sharp minds. You've got a secure job with a good salary and attractive benefits. And, unlike traditional associates, you get to work normal, humane hours. Furthermore, if you distinguish yourself as someone who really is perfect for large firm practice regardless of what your grades were, you can move into a full associateship, either with the firm you're at or by making a lateral move to *another* large firm. As one hiring partner pointed out, "It's always possible to be a staff attorney and get onto someone else's partnership track. It all depends how you perform and what your references are like." After all, if you can't impress people that you work with every day, well, you probably shouldn't be engaged in large firm practice after all.

At this point, you're probably saying, "Geez, Kimmbo, why doesn't *everybody* go after one of these jobs?" One reason is that they're a relatively new phenomenon — not every firm has them and very few people are familiar with them. But beyond that, they've got their downside, as well. You're not going to get the more glamor-ous assignments, because those will go to associates who are being groomed for partnership. You won't get the decision-making oppor-tunities that regular associates get, although that doesn't mean you'll be collating or tagging documents all day long. Instead, what you'll do is something of a hybrid between the decision-making of a part-nership-track associate and the routine document-handling of a paralegal. So you'd typically be involved in large litigation problems and document review, and you'd do some research.

Also, as a staff attorney, you get less pay than a traditional asso-ciate. You're working fewer hours, remember, but less pay is a downside nonetheless. And unless you make an effort to court the partners and distinguish yourself by doing your job very well and seeking out opportunities to strut your stuff, you do run a serious risk of being typecast as something less than a full-fledged lawyer. And that's why a lot of career services people don't recommend staff attorney positions. As one career services director warns, "Being a staff attorney types you as a 'have not.' A worker bee. It really hurts your self-esteem."

Now, it may be that being a staff attorney at a large firm satisfies all your needs, in terms of prestige, security, good pay, and challenging work without stressful hours. But if it doesn't, make sure that you constantly strive to prove that you're capable of doing more demanding work. Volunteer to do additional work on projects, maintain a positive attitude, and by all means do whatever you can to bring new clients to the firm — rainmaking is the one sure way to make yourself indispensable. Furthermore, if you want to make a move somewhere else in a couple of years, you've got the prestige of the law firm's name on your résumé, and *that* sure doesn't hurt. As several recruiting directors recommended, just put on your résumé that you were an associate. If the issue of your being a staff attorney comes up, you can explain why you weren't ready for full responsibility when you took that job, but you are now; for instance, you were raising your kids, and now they're in school. The fact that you didn't take on more responsibility until you were prepared to handle it can be a real plus! So being a staff attorney can act as a good springboard to a full, partnership-track associateship at another firm.

You may be wondering at this point, "Well, Kimm, if being a staff attorney is a good way to get started, what about being a paralegal?" I wish I could recommend it to you, boys and girls, but that's just not the way the world is anymore. Until about 10 years ago, it might have been possible to start in a large firm as a paralegal and then become an associate. But I didn't talk to many people, in career services, or at any firm, who held out much hope for someone who's a paralegal moving onto a full lawyering job with the firm. I'm not one to cut off possibilities, but if a less-than-associate position is where you want to start, it's not a good idea to start as a paralegal.

2. CONTRACT ASSOCIATE

A contract associate is someone who comes on board at a large law firm for one, big project, with the understanding that as soon as the project is over, the job's gone. The job may last 2 months or

3 years; it all depends on the project, although it's likely to be a large lawsuit.

In some ways, a contract associate position has the benefits of a staff attorney job. On top of that, you can get some pretty exciting work. But more importantly, you've got your foot in the door. There's nothing engraved in stone that says that when the case is over you'll be asked to leave. As one career services director told me, "Some firms use contract associate and staff attorney jobs as a way to test potential. It's an audition, in a way." What the case does is give you a window of opportunity in which to prove your worth to the firm. If you like, you can look at it as an interview that lasts for months and months. If you make the most of it, you can — as many people have! — make it into a full-fledged associateship.

If you'd like to go the contract associate route, it makes sense to take some litigation-oriented courses while you're in school, since it's normally large court cases that create the demand for contract associates. Trial practice, moot court, CLE evidence-related courses, all are excellent background for a contract associate.

3. LEGAL TEMP WORK

When you do legal temping, you're taking part in a relatively new industry – temporary lawyers. What you do is work for a legal temp firm, and you go from law firm to law firm, just as any other kind of temp does. In some cases, you may be doing the same kinds of things as contract associates, although of course some assignments will be tedious, as well — document handling and things of that yawn-inducing ilk.

But you already know what I'm going to say about this — *it gives you a chance to get your foot in the door*. If you do any legal temping, view it as an opportunity to make as many contacts as you can. Talk to as many lawyers as you can, get as many viewpoints as possible, and, in general, utilize all the skills I taught you in Chapter 4 on making contacts. Remember, the *hardest* thing to do is to meet and befriend people. Legal temping gives you a great opportunity to do just that!

4. GO IN AS A LATERAL

A "lateral hire" is someone who's got some legal experience under their belt. "Wa-a-a-it just a minute, Kimmbo," you're saying. "This book of yours is supposed to be for law students and new graduates, not people who've already worked for a few years! You're cheating!" Well, I'm not cheating, technically, because what I'm telling you to do is to get a year or two's worth of experience under your belt that will *ideally position* you for the job of your dreams. Stated another way, I *am* telling you how to get the job of your dreams, it's just not going to be the first one out of the gate, that's all! As one career services director said, "Students have a tendency to think that their first job out of law school is where they'll get their gold watch. It's not! Think of your career as a *progression*. You'll change jobs *a lot*. If you can't get what you want right now, that's OK. In the meantime, enhance your marketability!"

So let's go back to our original premise, which is that you want to get a job as an associate at the large firm of Upright & Starch. And of course as a part of your decision-making in settling on that firm, you've thoroughly researched exactly what they do, and who their clients are, and you probably even know the shoe size of the hiring partner. Well, when you plan to go in as a lateral, what you do is to take that information and figure out what kind of a lawyer Upright & Starch would want a couple of years down the road — *and then you make yourself into that lawyer.*

How? Well, let's say that your research tells you that Upright & Starch does some ERISA work. One thing you could do is go to a small firm which does ERISA work, and make yourself a specialist. Then, a couple of years down the road, you apply to Upright & Starch. Here's a pop quiz for you. What do you think is going to be more important to Upright & Starch at that point — the fact that you've shone as an ERISA specialist? Or the fact that you got a C on your Crim Law exam? Aha! What you've done is something that *proves* what you've known all along — you're the perfect candidate for Upright & Starch because you've proven you can do the work, regardless of your grades. Remember, as soon as you've got your foot in the door, you're as good as your last case!

Going to boutique firms is by no means the only way to lateral into a large firm. There are tons of them! For instance, you can lateral from a judicial clerkship. Consider starting with a state court clerkship (since they're the easiest to get) for a year or so, then go to a federal court clerkship, then to a large firm. Large firms fight over people who've done federal court clerkships! Or go to the state's attorney's office, then to the U.S. Attorney's office, then to a large firm. Or go to the IRS, or the SEC, or the EPA. You get the drift!

Another alternative is to find an alum from your school who was a lateral hire at a large firm, and see how *they* did it. You can find alums like this through your career services office, or by doing a search in Martindale-Hubbell or on Lexis or Westlaw.

Now, what's the downside of this? Well, if you go to a small firm first, you're not exactly being the nicest possible person to that firm, since you went in with the intention of leaving shortly. Remember the statistic about returns on investment in associates — firms don't start to make money on associates until they've been with them for 3 years, so if you leave before that, from a financial perspective you were a losing proposition for the firm. But on the other hand, they've had 2 years to impress you enough to keep you. If 2 years with them hasn't persuaded you to stay, that's really not your fault. I could come up with some more rationalizations for you, but if this is the route you take, I'm sure you'll dream up some of your own. Anyway, perhaps you'll find that you truly love the first job you take, and won't want to make all the sacrifices necessary to succeed at a large firm, after all!

Chapter 13

Nontraditional Careers: Getting the Job of Your Dreams If You Don't Want To Be A Lawyer

So, you don't want to be a lawyer? No sweat. The *only* important thing is for you to find a job that makes you happy, and it may well be that the job that *does* that doesn't mean putting "Esq." after your name, as practicing attorneys do. After all, I'd be the worst person in the *world* to try and convince you that practicing law is what you really should be doing, because *I've* got a law degree, and I've *never* practiced law. You may be similarly unsuited to it!

Now, even though you may be looking for a job that's very different from the kinds of jobs I've talked about all along, this chapter isn't a radical departure from the rest of the book. Why? Because almost everything I've told you to do applies whether you're looking for a job practicing law, or whether you're looking for a job as a butcher, baker, or candlestick maker. You'll still have to do some thinking to decide exactly what you want ("not-law" doesn't cut it!). You'll still want to make contacts as your primary means of learning about jobs you think you want, and getting those jobs. The basic philosophy behind correspondence, and résumés, and interviewing is largely the same. You *will*, however, find that there are certain elements of your search that will be a lot tougher. Deciding on what you want to do, if you don't narrow your universe to practicing law, is a lot tougher, just because there's so much more to choose from. And the further you get away from practicing law, the more difficulty you'll have convincing employers that you're the right candidate for the job, when they're looking at your résumé with a big old "J.D." staring them in the face. But the fact remains, you're not taking the easy way out of you go for a nontraditional job. The things you do will be very similar to what we've been talking about all along.

So — what *exactly* will we be doing in this chapter? To start with, we'll talk about the possible reasons *why* you don't want to practice law. You may find out that maybe, somewhere deep inside, you aren't totally turned off to the idea of practicing law after all. And if that's the case, we'll smoke out your motivations for *thinking* you don't want to practice. I mean, forgive me for being skeptical, but if you really didn't want to practice law in any way, shape, or form, it's unlikely you'd be reading a book titled *Guerrilla Tactics For Getting The Legal Job Of Your Dreams*. So we'll start by looking at what's stuck in your craw when it comes to practicing law, and see if maybe there are ways to find you a job practicing law that you would really like. Then, we'll talk about what factors are important to you, so that we have the tools we need to decide what *would* be the job of your dreams. Then we'll talk about how you go about finding out what kinds of jobs are *out* there. Then we'll talk about the transferable skills you bring to the table for employers outside of the law based on your law school experience. And finally, we'll talk about how you go after that nontraditional job of your dreams.

So let's get going!

A. SMOKING OUT *WHY* YOU DON'T WANT TO PRACTICE LAW — AND DISCUSSING THE RAMIFICATIONS OF THAT

You may think, offhand, that it's kind of silly to rehash why it is that you don't want to practice law. Feelings are facts, you don't want it, and that's that, right? Well, not quite. The reason I want you to bear with me and go through this little exercise is it could be that there *is* some kind of legal practice that suits you to a T; you just don't know what it is, that's all. As St. John's' Maureen Provost Ryan points out, "Most students who think they want out of the law wind up recommitted to it in a whole new way. Only 5% give it up all together!" And the reason it's worth figuring out whether you really don't want to practice is that, believe it or not, you give up a *lot* when you decide not to practice law. You don't have the prestige of being a lawyer, and you probably don't have the money, either. Furthermore, if there's any tiny part of you that thinks you might want to practice law, it's a lot easier to practice for a year or two *and then* jump into something else, than it is to abandon law and *then*, a few years down the road, try and get back *into* it; that transition is much tougher. Considerations like those lead to advice like this, from Illinois' Cindy Rold: "Before you become convinced you don't want to practice law, take some time to think about what it *really* is that you think you don't like!"

So, the point of this section is to find the reason why you don't want to practice law, and talk about whether it really means a law career isn't for you. What I'll do here is to start with the seven most common reasons for not wanting to practice law. Then we'll talk about what you should do if you're not *completely* sure that practice isn't for you. And, finally, we'll talk about the ramifications of turning your back on practicing law, so that you know what you're in for.

1. SO — WHY DON'T YOU WANT TO PRACTICE LAW? THE SEVEN MOST COMMON REASONS

Go through these seven reasons, and see which one fits you best.

A. YOU DON'T THINK YOU CAN GET A JOB PRACTICING LAW, AND NONLAW JOBS ARE EASIER TO GET

From the conversations I had with career services directors around the country, this was the #1 reason why law students wanted to turn their backs on law. If you did a lot of job searching before you picked up this book, it could be that you were so frustrated by the search that your mind transmogrified that frustration into a feeling that you just weren't destined to practice law, after all. "Surely," you may be saying to yourself, "it *must* be easier to get a nonlaw job!"

Now it may take a little bit of soul searching for you to realize that this is the reason you don't want to practice. The career services directors I spoke with said that they don't have to scratch the surface very much to find that this is what's motivating many students who come in saying that they don't want to practice law.

So, at its roots, what we've got here is a fear that you won't be able to get a job practicing law, and a perception that nonlegal jobs are easier to get. Let's talk about each of those in turn.

First, let's take a look at the idea that you won't be able to get a job practicing law. Perhaps you're worried that your grades will hold you back. As Cal Western's Lisa Kellogg points out, "Grades make people think twice about practicing law; they get nervous about every decision." Albany's Sandy Mans adds, "'I'm looking for something law-related' is a euphemism. It normally translates into: 'I'm not doing well in school, and I need to rethink it.'" St. Louis' Wendy Werner is even more blunt: "When students say, 'I want a nontraditional career,' it's usually a lie. They're afraid. They think they need to be open to other options. They're afraid of not getting what they want."

If you've read very much of this book at all, you *know* I believe in your ability to get a job, *regardless* of your grades. Instead, it's much more likely that you've been spending your time on things that aren't terribly productive, like mass mailers or responding to job listings. If you follow my system of making contacts as a means of getting a job, there's no question in my mind that you will be happily employed before long. So don't let your fears concerning your grades convince you that practicing law is not for you!

The other element that figures into this motivation is the idea that it's easier to get jobs *outside* of practicing law. In fact, as Kentucky's Drusilla Bakert warns, exactly the *opposite* is true. Wendy Werner points out, "Employers will ask, 'Why don't you want to use your degree?'" And Miami's Jose Bahamonde-Gonzalez adds, "You have to convince employers outside the law that your desire to do something else is a *positive* — nobody wants to hire a failure!" Before you consider turning your back on law because you think it'll be easier to get a job in something else, remember that whatever you choose will be full of people who *do* have the background tailor-made for it! Now, it's true that there are *some* fields where a law degree has cachet, like real estate development, but even in fields like that, you have to show a *positive* interest in them — it's not enough to simply be dissatisfied with the idea of practicing law.

So the bottom line on this particular motivation is this — it's not valid. You should never give up hope on the basis of your grades; if need be, read Chapter 10, on what to do if you have bad grades, and then follow all of the rest of the advice in this book. You *will* get a job *regardless* of your credentials. And don't be misled by the idea that it's *easier* to get a nonlegal job than it is to get a legal one. That's simply not true!

B. YOU CAN'T IMAGINE WORKING WITH PEOPLE LIKE YOUR CLASSMATES OR YOUR PROFESSORS

As Valparaiso's Gail Peshel points out, a lot of students who think they don't want to practice law are really reacting to a bad law school experience. It may be, as San Diego's Susan Benson says, that you just can't imagine going to work with your classmates! Or maybe you've been grilled by professors, and you figure *they're* jerks, and that if that's what lawyers are like, you want nothing to do with the practice of law.

If you feel this way, it's understandable. I remember my class at law school, and I would rather eat slugs than have to work with some of the people in it. But it's a mistake to generalize your law school experience to practicing law. For one thing, even though there may be some real trolls in your class, there must be *some* classmates you like. When you look for a job with the plan I've outlined in this book, you'll gravitate toward organizations that are peopled with the kinds of personalities you *do* get along with. And when it comes to disliking your professors, it's important to remember that they're playing a role when they're in the classroom. Many professors who pride themselves on being really tough in class are actually pretty nice outside of it, and yes, I'm actually writing this with a straight face. So you have to remember the *context* when you think about professors you can't stand.

Furthermore, you've got no guarantee that any field you choose *outside* of law will be populated with people you like *more* than your classmates. Other than the career services directors I interviewed for this book, I've never met an entire profession about whom I can say, "Gee, I really, really liked every *one* of them."

So if you think you don't want to practice law because you don't like the atmosphere at law school — don't give it up! Read the topic, "What to Do if You're Not Absolutely, Positively Sure That You Don't Want to Practice Law" on page 508, and try the techniques I talk about in Chapter 4 before you give up on the profession *entirely*.

C. YOU'VE HAD (OR ARE HAVING) A BAD WORK EXPERIENCE

As Michigan's Nancy Krieger points out, a rotten summer clerkship is a frequent reason students turn their interests away from practicing law. And Case Western's Debra Fink adds, "You may not hate the law, but just the place you're working — the firm, the politics, the people."

If you *are* having a miserable time with work, it's hard *not* to stereotype the rest of legal practice the same way. I can identify very well with this because it was a bad job experience that originally convinced *me* I didn't want to practice law. I clerked after Second Year with one of the biggest, most prestigious law firms in the country, and I was *miserable*. After that, I told myself something like this: "Working for a big firm is what everybody wants to do. It's the best you can do in law. And if *that* makes me miserable, then I must not want to practice law." If you've been reading this book in sequence, you can see the holes in my reasoning. For one thing, working at a large firm *isn't* the "best you can do in law;" it's a huge mistake to think it's the right working atmosphere for even a substantial minority of law students, let alone *everybody*. And furthermore, there's no single job that represents what "practicing law" is like. Your experience at the U.S. Attorney's office will be very different from your experience at a Wall Street law firm, which will differ from the ACLU, and so on. The only thing those jobs have in common is that they happen to fit under the umbrella term "practicing law." They've got different environments, very different kinds of people, and enormously different responsibilities.

So if a bad work experience is convincing you that you don't want law, don't give it that halo effect! Instead, first consider some of the ideas in Topic 2, on page 508, before you turn your back on the law.

D. You've Got Other Interests, and You Just Don't See How You're Going to Mesh Those with Practicing Law

It may be that you have some strong, driving interest, and you're not sure how you can put that together with practicing law. After all, when most people think about practicing law, they think about litigation. But there are *many, many* other options — jobs that blend *all kinds* of interests with the practice of law! Here are a few of the anecdotes I heard from career services directors around the country:

- One career services director in the south told me about a student who was absolutely positive he didn't want to practice law; he'd gone to acting school, and he didn't see how he could do anything related to that. Today, he's a lawyer with the Screen Actors' Guild.

- One student liked the idea of being a forest ranger; he wanted the outdoor life. He went into construction law, which gave him a lot of fresh air — *and* allowed him to keep the prestige (and the salary) of practicing law.

- A student at a school in the northeast was doing insurance defense litigation and hated it. When he dug further into exactly what it was that turned him off, he found that he liked the technical aspects of the work, but he hated the litigation. He made contacts, and did some information interviews to find out how he could keep what he liked about his job, and yet shed the aspects he *didn't* like. The job he found did just that, allowing him to assess potential liabilities without having anything to do with trial work: he's the risk manager at a zoo!

The point here is, no matter how unrelated to law you think your interests are, there may be a way of blending the two so that you'll have a job you *really* like. Go talk to your career services director, tell them your concerns, and solicit their help. They'll be able to open your eyes to a whole *raft* of practice options that I'll wager you never knew existed!

E. YOU THINK LAW IS BORING

Maybe you find your schoolwork boring and you're worried that if you practice law, that will be boring, too. After all, there *are* jobs that require that you do a lot of what you do in law school — research, write briefs, write memoranda, and that kind of thing. (Ironically *enough*, that takes up much of your time if you're a new associate at a large law firm!) But that's not *all* of law, not by a long shot. As Northern Illinois' Mary Obrzut points out, "If you think law is boring, try a year with the state attorney's office or the public defender. It's exciting and relatively easy to get, and it's great experience. It doesn't pay as much as other types of law, but you may find that you really like it after all!" In fact, there are a *whole lot* of law jobs that you'd find stimulating. The reason they may not be obvious to you is that the jobs everybody talks about — namely, big firm jobs — *are* loaded with drudgery, at least for the first few years. So talk to your career services director, and state your concerns. They'll direct you to alums who do exciting things. Or make contacts of your own, as I outline in Chapter 4. The point here is: Don't condemn the entire practice of law on the basis of what you do in school!

F. YOU DON'T LIKE THE ADVERSARIAL NATURE OF LAW, OR IT OTHERWISE DOESN'T APPEAL TO YOU EMOTIONALLY

If you don't like taking a strong position on one side of an argument, any job where that *is* required of you will make you miserable. There *are* areas of the law that aren't adversarial — for instance, trusts and estates and tax work are two areas that aren't — but they may not appeal to you for other reasons.

Or, as Wendy Werner points out, perhaps you don't like the idea of billing your hours, as lawyers have to do; perhaps it's too intrusive, too "Big Brother"-esque for you. Or maybe you *never* wanted to practice in the first place; you just wanted better writing and analysis skills. A classmate of mine was motivated to go to law school because he was a newspaper reporter; his publisher wanted him to start reporting on legal matters, and suggested that he go to law school for background.

Any of these motivations are valid reasons for not wanting to practice certain kinds of law. But as I've pointed out before in this section, it's impossible to lump all of legal practice into one brief description. It's not all adversarial, and there probably *is* something that would appeal to you emotionally. The problem with any of the motivations here is that knowing what it is that you *don't* like doesn't help you get a job doing something you *like*. What you have to do is go through the exercises in Chapter 2, which help you isolate the elements that *you* need for job satisfaction. And talk with people, lots of different kinds of people, to see what they like about *their* jobs. Talk with your career services director, and state your concerns about law. They'll have other ideas for you on jobs you ought to consider.

The bottom line here is that it may be true that you're not emotionally suited to practice law. As Maine's Tammy Willcox says, "Some people would wither and die with a law job!" But make sure you've researched it and that you really don't want it, before you turn your back on it!

G. THE WHOLE REASON YOU WANTED A LAW DEGREE IN THE *FIRST* PLACE IS THAT YOU THOUGHT YOU COULD DO *ANYTHING* WITH A LAW DEGREE

Boy, were *you* sold a bill of goods if you believe this! As Drusilla Bakert advises, "The idea that 'you can do anything with a law degree' is a myth!" And Susan Benson echoes that, adding, "The 'lawyer-as-surgeon' idea, that you can do anything with a law degree, is *nonsense."*

It's *very* important to distinguish things you *can* do from things you *can't* do with a law degree, because although a law degree is a help in some fields, it's a definite hindrance in others. As George Washington's Laura Rowe says, "What a law degree *does* get you is respect in other things, but even then, only *certain* other things."

You can roughly slot jobs into three categories:

+ Jobs where you need a law degree (or really should have one), like practicing law or being a judge.

+ Jobs where a law degree is helpful, like real estate development, or managing a nonprofit organization, or being a law school administrator.

+ Jobs where a law degree is no help at all, and instead you have to explain it away.

So I'm not saying that a law degree is good for *nothing*, but if you got it because you figured it was the "magic wand" degree, that's a mistake! (In fact, as most career services directors pointed out, people who go from law school straight to a nonlegal field typically have prelaw school experience that's *related* to that field.) No matter what kind of job you want, you *still* have to think about the attributes of the job you want, and how you can market your law degree to the needs of that job. If you're convinced it's not law that you want, then go on to Topic B, on page 512. But if you think that *maybe* there are some things about law that you like, then go on to #2, where I'll talk about ways to test the waters on the off-chance that maybe law *is* for you!

So — do you fit one of those seven categories? If not, and you've got your own reasons for not wanting to practice law, that's fine. But before you turn your back on law entirely, consider doing some of the things I'll discuss next . . .

2. WHAT TO DO IF YOU'RE NOT ABSOLUTELY, POSITIVELY SURE THAT YOU DON'T WANT TO PRACTICE LAW

Good! If you're reading this, it means that you didn't skip this section. I'm proud of you, because I think there's a strong possibility that there's a way to practice law that will make you happy.

Here are some things to consider doing if you think there's *some* possible way you'd be happy with law.

A. TAKE THE BAR ANYWAY

That's probably just about the last thing you wanted to hear, but I heard it from a whole bunch of career services directors, and when you think about it, it makes sense. As I discuss later in this chapter, it's *very* important to convince nonlegal employers that you're not choosing them because you couldn't make it in law. Willamette's Diane Reynolds says, "Taking the bar may sound heretical to some people, but you need it to validate that you're a lawyer and not a failure." Furthermore, if you *do* decide you want to practice law in a year or two's time, then you've taken and passed the bar when it's easiest to do so; that is, when you graduate from school and everything is still relatively fresh in your mind.

So if you think there's *some*, slight possibility you may want to practice law, *at least* take the bar.

B. *CONSIDER* BITING THE BULLET AND PRACTICING FOR A YEAR OR TWO

If you think you want to do something *other* than practicing law, many career services directors suggest that you practice for at least a year anyway — *and then* try something else. There are several reasons to consider this.

- ♦ It will stop you from having regrets later on. As Franklin Pierce's Sophie Sparrow points out, "Practicing in a comfortable setting for a year or two before you try an alternative stops you from looking back and saying, 'I gave up. I should have persisted!'"

- ♦ The easiest time to practice, if you think you'll *ever* want to, is after you graduate from law school. As Florida's Ann Skalaski says, "At least *try* practice first, because it's hard to get back in without having a year or two under your belt."

- ♦ It will make you more marketable to nonlegal employers. As Drusilla Bakert says, "The dirty little secret is that the vast majority of nontraditionals practiced law first!"

If any or all of these reasons have an impact on you, then, of course, it's *still* important to find a job you like; I'm not saying to just grit your teeth and do something you *hate* for a year or two. Which leads me directly to my third suggestion . . .

C. TRY SOMETHING THAT REQUIRES A LITTLE CREATIVITY AND EXCITEMENT

If you think you don't want law, it may be because you're not broadening your horizons enough to cover types of practice that you might really enjoy. Jose Bahamonde-Gonzalez suggests "Getting some hands-on experience, like clerking for a judge, or working as a public defender." Ann Skalaski advises students who think they want out of law to "consider the public sector — in-house counsel with schools, city attorney, county attorney — jobs like that." NYU's Gail Cutter tells her students with qualms about traditional practice to "consider law experiences where there's more creativity — for instance, public interest work."

Another experience that many students love is a Pro Bono Students America project, of the type I describe in Chapter 4, Appendix B. With Pro Bono Students America, you volunteer in public interest positions. The jobs last at least 50 hours. You have the opportunity to meet all kinds of interesting people and do all sorts of interesting things. It's a great way to make contacts — and perhaps even revivify your interest in the law!

The bottom line here is — don't condemn all of law without giving a thought to particular jobs that new graduates tend to enjoy. You may be pleasantly surprised!

D. CONSIDER TAKING TIME OFF!

If you're still in law school, and you really think you don't want to have anything to do with the law, consider taking some time off. As Nancy Krieger states bluntly, "If what you really want is to manage a bookstore, why go to law school?"

You may be horrified at the thought of not finishing law school, but if you're really convinced you don't want to practice law *and* you don't want to do anything related to the law, there's a solid argument to be made for leaving. For one thing, you're spending a lot of *somebody's* money to go to law school, if not your own. For another, even if you are in school because you're putting off getting a job — I spent a large part of law school doing just that! — you can do that getting *any* graduate degree, and you might as well make it one that you *like*. And there's always the fact that taking time off doesn't have the negative impact on employers that you *think* it will. As I've pointed out before, employers would much rather that you got your doubts out of your system *before* you started working for them — not *afterwards!* And finally, as Susan Benson points out, it's not as though you can't come back—the ABA gives you 5 years to finish school.

With that time off, you may well meet people and experience things that make you realize that you really are committed to law, after all. Then you'll be able to tackle law school with renewed vigor!

E. PROCEED THROUGH THE REST OF THIS CHAPTER AS THOUGH YOU ARE SURE THAT YOU *DON'T* WANT TO PRACTICE LAW

Here's the thing: A lot of what I'll advise you to do in this chapter applies whether you think you *maybe kinda sorta* want to practice law, or whether you're running screaming from it. That's because I'll show you how to pick out the attributes that are important to you for *any* job you get, and how to find that job. After all, the Holy Grail here is the job of your dreams, and if it means that you don't want to practice law, that's OK. So there's no real harm to pretending, for the time being, that you absolutely *don't* want to practice law. The decision-making process I'll take you through will help you determine what you really want to do, whether it's practicing law or not!

3. IF YOU'RE CONVINCED YOU DON'T WANT TO PRACTICE LAW, BE AWARE OF THE TRADEOFFS THAT ENTAILS!

Perhaps you're utterly convinced you don't want to be a practicing attorney. That's OK; as I've told you before, I made the same decision. What I want to do here is to warn you of some of the hidden obstacles that you face as you move forward, so that you can gird yourself. They include:

A. NONLEGAL EMPLOYERS MAY *NOT* EMBRACE YOUR LAW DEGREE

Depending on the kind of nontraditional career you choose, you may find that your law degree actually works *against* you. (For some careers, a law degree is a definite plus, but in others, it's irrelevant.) I discuss this in great detail in Topic E, later. But for now, suffice it to say, in Wendy Werner's words, that "Nobody wants to be a default option!" Some employers will feel that they're only a fall-back position because you couldn't hack it in the law, and you've got to be prepared to confront that!

B. Your Family and Friends May Feel You're "Wasting" Your Degree

Don't expect everyone you know to be a thousand percent behind your decision not to practice law. As I've mentioned elsewhere in this book, it's been 10 years since I graduated from law school, and I think my father is *still* crying about the fact that I turned down offers to practice law in favor of being a writer.

And, by the way, you'll get this even if you get into something law-related. I've already told you that I created a line of legal study aids called *Law In A Flash*. I've also written several other books about law. Now, it would be pretty difficult to write legal study aids and books about how to excel in law school *without* having a law degree, but even when I tell people about what I've done, they still sometimes say, "But aren't you sad that you're wasting your degree?" So be prepared for that kind of response!

C. You Will Not Have the "Trappings" of Practicing Law – the Prestige and, Perhaps, the Money

It may not seem like it from where you sit, but for a large segment of the population, being a lawyer carries a certain prestige. It is, after all, considered one of the "professions." When you turn your back on a career practicing law, you turn your back on that; you aren't a member of that exclusive little club. You may be able to replace the prestige and money by doing something else that has those same assets, but just be aware that you're giving them up in terms of practicing law.

B. Determine the Factors That are Important to You Regarding Your Career

Whether you want to practice law or not, it's impossible to get the job of your dreams unless you can articulate the parameters that will make you happy. What this requires is some hard thinking. You really have to decide *exactly* what kinds of things go into creating your job happiness. But you know me better than to think I'm going to leave you on your own to do that! I've got two specific things for you to do.

1. GO BACK TO CHAPTER 2. DO NOT PASS GO. DO NOT COLLECT $200

Topics A through C in Chapter 2 give you all kinds of exercises to help you figure out what the heck your dream job would *be* like.

But before you go back, I should point out that none of the exercises in Chapter 2, and, in fact, *no* set of exercises you do from *any* source, will spit out the job title you ought to have. And do you know why? Because jobs in any given area can be *very* different from one another. For instance, let's take nurses. (That's an easy one for me, because my mom's a nurse.) Your job as a nurse will be very different if you work in an emergency room, or a maternity ward, or as a private-duty nurse for an elderly person. And if you work for a doctor in private practice, a lot of what your job will be like depends on the personality of your boss and the responsibilities you're given. In all of these situations, you'll need different personality traits to thrive, and the environment will provide different kinds of stimuli. So a job title like "nurse" doesn't really tell you whether you'll enjoy being a nurse in any particular situation, because they're so different. Instead, what Chapter 2 does for you is to make you aware of the kinds of things that are important to you, *regardless* of the field you choose.

So — off you go back to Chapter 2. Don't worry about me, I'll entertain myself until you get back. I'll hum a tune to myself, or something . . . hmm . . . hmmmmm . . . hmmmm . . .

2. ONCE YOU'VE GOT AN IDEA OF THE FACTORS THAT ARE IMPORTANT TO YOU, DO A FEW SIMPLE EXERCISES TO SEE WHAT *KINDS* OF JOBS APPEAL TO YOU

Hmm . . . hmmmm . . . Oh! OK. You're back from Chapter 2, with a better understanding of exactly what's important to you, I trust? Now, before we talk about what kinds of jobs are "out there," I want you to do a few little exercises first. It's kind of a preview to choosing a job, because the idea is to uncover the kinds of jobs that *really* attract you. Think about the questions on this list (if some of them look familiar it's because you've seen them before, late in Chapter 2). What you're doing is trying to draw out themes that attract you, to see what might appeal to you as a career.

♦ Go through the Sunday paper. Which articles do you read?

♦ What kinds of magazines do you read?

♦ What kinds of subjects in books draw your attention?

♦ When you talk with your friends about substantive issues, what do you like to talk about?

♦ What kinds of television programs do you watch?

♦ Also take into account — do you have many different interests that change over time? Or do you focus on one field and delve into it at great depth?

♦ Go through the job ads in the back of a large city's Sunday paper. Ignoring your credentials, what draws your interest?

♦ Think about classes you've enjoyed — in law school, college, even high school.

♦ Think back to what you wanted to do *before* you went to law school. If you can't remember, go to your admissions office and get your application, and look at the essays you wrote, to get a handle on what you wanted to be.

♦ If you've got substantial work experience in some other field, think about the skills you bring from *that* career that you might want to use in a *new* one. (For instance, with a substantial background in finance, you may want to be an investment banker. Or if you've got experience as a nurse, you may want to be a hospital administrator.)

♦ Talk to your family and friends, and ask what *they'd* see you doing, based on what they know about you. Their insights into your personality can be *very* valuable.

So now you have an idea of the factors that have to be present in the job of your dreams, and an idea of the kind of field that might attract you. That means it's time to . . .

C. FIND OUT WHAT'S OUT THERE!

Let's pretend for a moment that you're a little kid, and you've never been to the grocery store, and your parents only let you watch public television. (I didn't say you were a very common kind of kid, did I?) Anyway, one day your mom says to you, "What kind of cereal do you want me to buy?" Well, you may know that you like crunchy cereals, and ones that are completely devoid of bran, and ones that say "sugar" first on their list of ingredients, and ones that are fruit-flavored. But it's going to be pretty darned difficult for you to say what you want, because you don't know what's *out* there!

Well, it's just as difficult to make a decision about what you want to do if you don't know what's available. So, what I'm going to do here is to talk about how you determine exactly that.

1. WITH AN IDEA OF WHAT KINDS OF THINGS YOU LIKE (FROM THE LAST TOPIC), GO AND CHAT WITH YOUR CAREER SERVICES DIRECTOR

I know what you're beginning to think: In this book, all roads lead to Rome, with Rome in this case being your career services office. Well, I *do* advise you to rely on them for all kinds of things, but here's why I'm suggesting you seek their help in this particular situation: It may be that you've overlooked ways that you can mesh your interests with a legal career. As the anecdotes I told you earlier in this chapter on page 505 illustrated, there are all *kinds* of ways to mesh other interests with practicing law; many times, it's just a matter of digging up jobs that achieve exactly that!

There are several advantages you'll enjoy if you take my advice and talk with your career services director about what you want to do. For one thing, you're talking to a kindred spirit. Remember, most career services directors have law degrees of their own — so they, too, chose a nontraditional career! For another, they'll know of alumni who both have unusual jobs *and* those who were successful in jumping to another kind of career entirely. In both cases, they can put you in touch with people who do things you might enjoy.

And career services directors can also put you onto other kinds of research aids to help you refine your nontraditional job search even further. So I strongly encourage you to pay them a visit!

2. DO SOME RESEARCH ON WHAT KINDS OF JOBS ARE AVAILABLE – AND DISTINGUISH BETWEEN QUASILEGAL AND NONLEGAL JOBS

As you know, there are about six kajillion different kinds of jobs out there. Heck, there are a ton of different jobs available if you're convinced you *want* to practice law; once you take away the "practicing law" constraint, you're really talking about every job in the universe. And that's because having a law degree doesn't really *stop* you from doing anything at all.

But my guess is that you fall into one of two broad categories. Either you're interested in doing something that I call "quasilegal" — that is, something where a law degree is a definite plus, if not a requisite — or you're interested in doing something completely unrelated to law.

For "quasilegal" jobs, what I've done is to give you a description of 16 popular law-related careers. I've included the names, addresses, and phone numbers of trade associations and publications so that you can get more information from them if any of these areas interests you. You'll find this list in Appendix A.

For nonlegal jobs, you're somewhat on your own; after all, you can be a bartender, or an astronaut, or a lion tamer, or a fireman . . . really, you can be anything, if you're not going to use your law degree. What you *will* want to do is pay special attention to how you characterize the transferable skills you've acquired in law school (in Topic D, the next topic), and how you go after nonlegal jobs (in Topic E, which, hardly surprisingly, comes immediately after Topic D).

Regardless of whether the job you're looking for is quasilegal or nonlegal, I've also included a list of other publications for you to look over. They all go into *great* detail in terms of career options outside of practicing law, and if you want to do more, I'd encourage you to give them a look-see. You'll find that list in Appendix B.

Once you've got a pretty firm grasp of what interests you in theory, it's time to do some information interviewing. But remember, *only* do information interviews when you've narrowed your list of potential careers down to a few serious candidates. You can always scrap your original list and start over again, but there's no point in wasting yours (or your interviewee's) time if you don't have a pretty good idea of careers that interest you!

3. DO SOME INFORMATION INTERVIEWING

For virtually any field you can think of, if you shake your tree of acquaintances, you'll find someone who is in that field, or you'll find someone who *knows* someone in that field, or you'll find someone who knows someone who knows someone in that field . . . you get my drift. If you *don't,* then go back to Chapter 4, and go down the list of contacts starting on page 109. Talk to *everybody* you can think of to see who *they* know. The goal here is this: Once you've got a grip on one or a handful of careers that interest you, you've got to talk to people in that career to see if it's really what you want. You'll use people you already know to find those contacts. And it also helps to make those kinds of contacts to help you get a job in that field, if you decide having spoken with them that it really is what you want!

These "talks" with people in fields that interest you (or people who *know* about those fields) are called "information interviews." And they get that name because you're not contacting people begging for jobs; instead, you're getting *information.* I could tell you in detail about how to conduct information interviews. However, I don't have to do that here, because I did it already in Chapter 4, on page 143. As you know, I'm a big fan of getting information from people rather than written resources — so I heartily encourage you to do exactly that with information interviews!

D. DETERMINE THE TRANSFERABLE SKILLS YOU BRING TO THE TABLE ON THE BASIS OF YOUR LAW DEGREE, YOUR UNDERGRAD DEGREE, AND YOUR WORK EXPERIENCE

I've pointed out more than once that employers really don't care about what you've done, not in any general sense. All they care about is what you *can* do for them. And if all you tell them is that you've got a law degree, you can't expect them to make the jump and divine how that translates into how you can help *them.* For instance, let's say that you want to get into some kind of social work. You've got a problem! As Fordham's Kathleen Brady points out, "Lawyers listen to *facts*. Social workers talk about *feelings*." So your law degree isn't going to be terribly appealing to potential employers, *unless you highlight for them the specific skills that you bring to them!* As an example, let's say that you've taken part in the Client Counseling competition, and you've done very well in it. And let's say that you have taken clinics in law school, and as part of that you have counseled low-income people. And let's say that in your spare time you volunteered at a battered women's clinic. In all of these activities, you have honed your ability to counsel, to listen to people's problems, and to help them solve them. *That's* what you bring to social work — but it's only because you've pulled from what you've *done* the skills that you can offer!

So your background only has relevance to the extent that you can extract from it the transferable skills you bring to your future employers. You've got to highlight these transferable skills as you make contacts, and in your résumé, and in correspondence, and in interviews. But before you can highlight them, you have to know what your transferable skills *are!* I'll show you exactly what they are in this section.

Now, where do these transferable skills come from? You'll have three basic sources:

+ Your undergrad schooling;
+ Your work experience; and
+ Law school.

The one I'll focus on most will be law school. I'll show you the skills you've gotten from law school, depending on the activities you've taken part in. Once you've read that, you'll be able to do the same thing by yourself with your undergrad and work experience.

If you've read Chapter 6 on résumés, you've heard all you need to know about transferable skills. If you *haven't*, you should know that transferable skills are not the things you've *done*, but rather the skills that you have on the *basis* of what you've done; that is, the skills that you bring to the table for a future employer. If you blend your undergrad and work skills with the skills you take from law school, you may be able to come up with the perfect job for you! For instance, as Cal Western's Lisa Kellogg points out, "If you were a landscape architect, you may want to consider something like land use planning. Or if you were an English major in college, legal publishing could be a good match."

With that in mind, let's take a look at the transferable skills you take from law school. (By the way, this list is adapted from the excellent book "The Road Not Taken," by Kathy Grant and Wendy Werner.)

Ability to analyze facts.
Problem-solving is the main skill you get from law school. You get it from reading and briefing cases, Moot Court, any journals that you work on, and exams. This is a particularly useful skill when it comes to identifying business problems and creating solutions.

Ability to work in teams or groups.
If you've worked with other students in Moot Court, or in a trial skills program, or in a study group, then you've got the transferable skill of teamwork; that is, the ability to divide responsibilities and come up with a cohesive outcome. This is useful in any enterprise that is project-oriented.

Ability to be a self-starter.
As a law student, most of what you do is independent study. Any work as a law clerk typically exposes you to working without supervision, as well. Every employer appreciates employees who are self-starters.

Risk awareness.
As a law student you learn to be aware of the potential risk involved in transactions, products, policies, and programs. (As I've pointed out elsewhere, sometimes law students are *too* aware of risks, and it paralyzes them in their job search!) As an employee, risk awareness is useful in alerting your employer to any risks they may be taking, and it is very useful in creating preventive policies, products, or programs.

Counseling (including the ability to establish rapport, to listen, to reflect concerns back to clients, to empathize, and to problem solve).
If you've taken part in client counseling competitions, clinics, or classes that involve counseling clients, then you have these transferable skills. These skills are useful in almost any position involving client or coworker contact.

Familiarity with legal terminology.
Going to law school gives you the ability to read and understand documents that are Greek to lay people — things like

contracts, leases, and statutes. This skill is useful to employers in predicting the long-term impact legal documents may have on their organization. It also gives you the ability to communicate comfortably with people who work with legal matters.

Knowledge of specific topics (like insurance, healthcare, tax, criminal law, corporations).

Depending on your coursework, you've got a broad base of knowledge about a wide variety of areas. Especially if you can combine this knowledge with an undergraduate degree that specializes in a certain area (e.g., patent law with an undergrad technical major, or construction law with an undergrad architecture major), you are a potential employee with a lot of knowledge to offer an employer — and a strong background for learning more.

Strong motivation and the skills associated with it (working under pressure, ability to complete projects, ability to juggle multiple responsibilities).

In law school, you respond to an enormous amount of pressure while balancing a heavy workload. As a law student, you have to meet strict deadlines and juggle multiple responsibilities. Also, as a law student you are perceived as having a history of success as well as the ability to complete projects. These skills are all highly prized by employers.

Ability to think independently.

As a law student, you are encouraged to think independently about issues and problems, coming up with your own solutions to them. You are taught to go beyond looking for answers, and instead identify issues. For potential employers, this translates into creative thinking skills and an ability to see the whole picture.

Ability to negotiate.

If you've taken part in clinics, seminars, or classes that focus on negotiation, or any extracurriculars that require you to negotiate (for instance, as the business editor for a journal), then the ability to negotiate is a skill you bring to the table for potential employers. Your ability to negotiate will enable you to open the doors to new clients and new business, as well as to "close the deal."

Ability to persuade.
Taking part in Moot Court, as well as brief writing in your legal writing program, and writing for a journal, gives you the ability to persuade. This is a useful skill for convincing clients, other managers, staff, or peers.

Ability to prepare effectively.
Law school demands that you be always prepared so that you can respond quickly and accurately. This is a useful skill to businesses which must react and respond to new information and industry changes to stay profitable.

Ability to speak before an audience.
Responding to questions in class, as well as taking part in Moot Court and any extracurriculars that require public speaking, will give you a valuable skill for employers. Ease in front of an audience is an asset in presenting facts, information, or business proposals.

Research skills.
Much of the work you do in law school focuses on research, as do many extracurriculars and law clerking jobs. Research skills are a valuable asset for many employers who must rely on employees to dig up accurate and comprehensive information for them.

Writing ability.
Your exams, legal writing program, Moot Court, and any journal experience give you the ability to write in a clear and precise manner. This skill gives you the edge in business communications. Good writing skills are *always* in high demand.

Depending on your own law school experience, you may have many more transferable skills. For instance, if you've done a lot of fundraising, then you've got interpersonal and business development skills that would be valuable to many employers. And your undergrad and work experiences will give you even *more* skills. So, go through what you've done, and take from your background the skills that you can give to future employers. I think you'll find that you're a very valuable package, indeed!

E. GO AFTER WHAT YOU WANT!

Now that you have an idea of what you want to do, and the skills that you bring to the table, it's time to go after that nontraditional career of your dreams!

From the outset, it's important to know the challenge you face as you look for a nontraditional job. When you're looking for a *legal* job, employers assume that you've got some base-level of skills they can use. After all, you *did* go to law school. But the further your interests get from traditional law practice, the less you have, on the basis of your law degree, to bring to an employer. As Susan Benson says, "Employers acknowledge that, yes, law students have people skills — but they won't take that over people with experience in the field. You have to bring something else to the table as well!"

I'll give you a little example to bring this to life. Let's say that I'm the manager of a busy restaurant, and I have two people applying for waitering jobs. There's you, with your law degree, and there's another guy, who's got 3 years of experience at the best restaurant in town. Well, you may consider yourself far "above" a waiter, but the fact is, I'm going to hire him over you. Why? Because he's got the skills I want, regardless of how theoretically prestigious your degree is.

So you can see that going for a nontraditional career is more than just sending your very same résumé to a bunch of different kinds of employers. You've got to do all the researching, all of the networking, *everything* I suggested you do for a legal job throughout this book, *and on top of that* you've got to rejig your job search so that it focuses on the needs of an entirely different kind of employer. You *can* get many different kinds of jobs with a law degree — but only if you can convince those employers that you have the skills they want!

What I'm going to do in this section is to give you a brief overview of the steps that you have to take to get a nontraditional job. (As I've mentioned before in this chapter, if you need more detail go to Appendix B for other sources that focus *specifically* on nontraditional careers.) We'll start by talking about the kind of reaction you can expect from nontraditional employers, because you've *got* to be prepared for it! Then we'll talk about rethinking your approach to correspondence, and interviewing, and your résumé. And finally, we'll talk about the possibility that a different career may mean more education.

1. ANTICIPATE THE KINDS OF REACTIONS YOU WILL ELICIT FROM EMPLOYERS, AND PREPARE YOURSELF FOR THEM!

Remember, you're not taking the easy way out by looking for a nontraditional career. You've got to sell yourself even more than you would for a *legal* employer! Now it's true that for certain law-related jobs, like being a law professor or a bar administrator, a law degree is virtually a prerequisite. But the further you get away from core law-related jobs, the less your paper credentials will mean to an employer. Don't expect them to welcome you with open arms just because you've got a law degree! As Drusilla Bakert puts it, "This idea that 'they'll love to have me in anything' is *wrong!*"

What I'm going to do here is to give you some of the most common reactions you're likely to get from nontraditional employers, *especially* those outside of traditional law-related jobs. You should anticipate these reactions, and prepare yourself accordingly.

A. EMPLOYERS WHO WILL ASSUME THAT YOU'RE A FAILURE, AND THEY'RE A DEFAULT OPTION FOR YOU

Some employers are likely to think that your first choice was practicing law, and because you couldn't get a job in that, you're "settling" for them. As Sandy Mans points out, "No other employer wants someone who's just an unhappy lawyer!"

If you look at it from their perspective, you can see why they might think this. After all, what *they* see is someone who just spent 3 years and umpteen tens of thousands of dollars getting a degree that they now profess not to want! Wouldn't *you* be suspicious? As Jose Bahamonde-Gonzalez points out, "If you don't want law, it's a problem because it's your strongest suit, if you haven't worked before."

How do you combat this? In a number of ways. One is to persuade them at every opportunity that it was your plan all along not to practice. As Diane Reynolds says, "This takes *repeated* convincing!" You need to stress that your wanting to do this particular job is a *positive* desire for it, not a failure to get something else that you want *more*. The way you do this is to research the field, have your ducks in a row regarding your transferable skills, and make plain to the employer your enthusiasm for this job. Diane Reynolds puts it this way: "Your emphasis should be on the fact that you *do* have control over what job you get!" When employers ask you about why you don't want to practice law, don't be negative; smile, and say something like, "There's nothing wrong with practicing law, but I've read a lot about this, and talked with a lot of people about it, and I think I'm better suited to this. I want this more!" It's just important to *realize* that they'll need reassurance that you're not just running *from* the law — you're running *to* them!

B. EMPLOYERS WHO WILL ASSUME THAT YOU'LL ONLY STAY WITH THEM TEMPORARILY, UNTIL A JOB PRACTICING LAW TURNS UP

I've stressed throughout this book how important it is to *legal* employers to feel comfortable that you're not going to get in and get out. They want to feel that you're committed to staying with them, even though everybody knows people generally bail out of their first job within a couple of years or so! Well, in the situation where you're looking for a nontraditional job, this fear is enhanced.

What should you do? Everything I told you about avoiding the appearance that you're a failure applies equally here. Assure the employer that your desire to work for them is honest, and they're not just a way-station until the job you *really* want shows up. You won't say that in so many words, but rather by showing that you've researched the field, and talked with people, and thought about what kinds of skills you bring to the table. If you make the extra effort, you should easily be able to combat the fear that you'll be out the door in 6 months!

C. EMPLOYERS WHO DISLIKE LAWYERS

Gee, here's a headline for a you: a lot of people don't like lawyers. You may be saying to yourself, "Well, geez, Kimmbo, *I'm* not a lawyer, and I *don't want* to be one!" Ah, but you see, people who hear that you've got a law degree *automatically* consider you a lawyer. I don't know why that is, but it is. I've been a writer for 10 years, and some people still insist on calling me a lawyer, even though I've *never* practiced law. So, you have to be prepared for people to be put off by the idea that you're a "lawyer." How to combat that? Well, make it plain that you went to law school, but you have no intention of practicing law. You got your degree because you wanted to . . . and then fill in the blank. If people go on, and insist, "But you're a lawyer because you went to law school," I say, "I majored in Accounting in college, and I'm no more a lawyer than I am an accountant." What you can do *then* is state what you *did* get from law school, and how it benefits what you want to do now. That takes the focus off of your being a lawyer, and puts it where it belongs — on what you want to do *next*.

2. REFOCUS YOUR APPROACH TO CORRESPONDENCE, REVISE YOUR INTERVIEWING STRATEGY, AND REJIG YOUR RÉSUMÉ

To some extent, everything that I've told you in this book about correspondence, and interviewing, and résumés, applies no matter *what* kind of job you're looking for. The two keys to getting the job of your dreams — taking the initiative and showing honest enthusiasm — they're just as relevant if you're looking for a job as a newspaper reporter as they are if you want to be a junior associate at a large law firm. The main thing you have to remember is that you will shift your focus from the importance of your law school credentials to highlight, instead, the transferable skills that you take to whatever career you want (as we talked about in Topic D, earlier in this chapter).

Let's talk about your correspondence, interviewing, and résumé separately, to focus a little more closely on what you should do to gear them toward a nontraditional career.

A. CORRESPONDENCE

Go back and read Chapter 5 on correspondence. As you do, remember that a lot of it still applies to you. You'll still want to keep the three-paragraph approach. It's *still* best to open a letter with the name of a mutual acquaintance. And you'll still be highlighting your research on this particular employer and what you can do for them based on your experience. It's in that middle paragraph, where you do this persuading, that you'll find the biggest difference between legal and nonlegal jobs. That's because it's where you'll explain the transferable skills you bring to them, *even though* you have a law degree. So for instance, if you want to get a job as director of a nonprofit institution, you'd want to highlight leadership experiences, and fundraising experiences, and those kinds of things. You *wouldn't* highlight your research skills, because those aren't relevant to that kind of job. Imagine that you're an employer, looking at a résumé that shows that an applicant's most recent experience is attending law school. Your question would be, "What the heck are they doing applying for a job with *me?*" And you've *got* to answer that question if you hope to get an interview!

Now, remember, the less related the position is to traditional legal jobs, the *more* work you're going to have to do convince the employer that you've got the skills they want. Imagine that they've got the kinds of concerns that I focused on at the beginning of this section, and implicitly overcome those concerns by showing how you've got the skills they want!

B. INTERVIEWING

Much of what's in the interviewing chapter, Chapter 7, applies to you. You're going to research any employer the way you would a legal employer. When it comes to making up an infomercial about yourself, you'll want to tailor it to the transferable skills you bring to this particular type of employer.

For questions and answers, the questions you ask will be largely the same as ones you'd ask of a legal employer. That's because the questions I favor, the quasipersonal ones, are designed to forge a bond with *any* interviewer, not just a legal interviewer. When it comes to *answering* tough questions, many of the ones you get will be very much like the ones I list in Chapter 7. However, you'll face an additional challenge: You will have much greater difficulty showing that you've got the skills the employer wants. You'll want to marshal everything you can from your law school experience, your extracurriculars, your work experience, and your undergrad schooling to show that you're the right candidate. Your focus on law school will depend on how closely related the job you're interviewing for relates to traditional legal careers. Obviously, to be a law professor, you'd focus heavily on your law school experience, particularly any journal experience you have. Whereas, to be a lion tamer . . . well, other than handling difficult professors, I'm not sure *how* law school would prepare you for a job like that! In addition, you have to expect questions that reflect the concerns I started this section with; that is, issues over whether you're just using a nonlegal employer as a default option and whether you'll jump ship as soon as a legal job opens up. Whether or not the interviewer asks these kinds of questions, you'll want to stress that you truly are interested in this particular field. You'll want to squeeze into the interview *somehow*, whether or not the interviewer asks it, why it is that you went to law school if you had an interest in something else. (For this, by the way, you'd want to say that you went to law school to develop certain skills, or because you thought it would be useful in business, or a similar answer tailored to the particular employer; you would *not* want to suggest that you're a Johnny-come-lately to your interest in a nontraditional field, because that suggests that you *really are* reacting to a bad experience of some sort instead of focusing on the positive aspects of this employer. And you'd want to follow up with, " . . . but my interest in [X field] is shown by my [participation in X . . .] [volunteering with X . . . .] [classes in X . . .]," so that you wind-up with a positive.

C. YOUR RÉSUMÉ(S)

Of all of the tools in your job-search bag, your résumé is the one that will change the most if you're looking for a nontraditional career. Again, if you're looking for a job closely related to practice, like being a law professor, you really won't change it much. But for employers further away from the law school orbit, you may find yourself actually *downplaying* your law degree!

Now, to a large extent, everything I told you in Chapter 6, on résumés, still applies — you still want to focus on accomplishments. But remember, you've got to take into account the needs of the employer as you fashion your résumé, and that could well mean having different résumés for different employers! Drusilla Bakert gives the example of a law student applying for a corporate management position. She says, "If it's a position as assistant benefits director that you want, you'd want to emphasize on your résumé that you've taken Labor Law and Trusts & Estates. That way, you're *showing* why you'll fit!"

I'll give you a negative example, as well, based on my own experience. One of the jobs I considered when I graduated from college was the advertising management track at an enormous advertising agency in New York City. When they said they wanted to see my résumé, I sent them the same résumé I'd used for every legal employer I'd contacted. I was swayed by the common misconception that you have one résumé, and it's engraved in stone! Well, my résumé focused on the fact that I'd been on law review, and things like that that would be *very* interesting to a legal employer. I downplayed my fundraising activities, and the fact that I'd written all kinds of brochures for the school. You've probably already guessed what happened. I got rejected. And why *shouldn't* they have rejected me? I didn't make any effort to show the skills I'd learned in law school that would be applicable to what *they'd* want me to do. How else were they going to find that out, if I didn't *say* it in a résumé or cover letter?

So the bottom line is — it's *very* important to convey *expressly* to the employer, on your résumé as well as every other piece of paper that you send them, that you've got skills they want. You can't expect them to learn it through osmosis!

What you may want to consider doing is taking a functional approach to your law school and legal experience; I talk about that in the résumé chapter on page 250, and it's shown on the sample résumé on page 289. Remember, with a functional résumé, you're not listing positions you've held, but rather skills you have or functions you've performed. You'd have sections like "research," "writing," "fundraising," "public speaking," and "management," and you'd summarize your expertise in these areas. Taking into account that employers will generally spend no more than a minute and a half with your résumé, the functional approach may be an effective way to minimize the impact of your law degree.

3. RECOGNIZE THAT A DIFFERENT CAREER MAY MEAN *YET MORE* EDUCATION FOR YOU

If you've used your law school career as a means of avoiding working, deciding that you want a job completely unrelated to law is a great way of continuing down that same path. I don't mean to sound mean about it, because I originally went to law school largely to avoid looking for a job, too. But if the thought of more schooling is anathema to you, it may be that you want to consider getting a job a little more closely related to the law. In fact, if you scratch the surface of a lot of stories about students who've gotten nontraditional jobs, you'll find that they had prior work experience in the field they went into after law school. As Susan Benson points out, "You *have* to fit the employer's needs. Not all students can do it." And if you're not a person with relevant experience, that may mean getting more education to align yourself more closely with the needs of employers in the field you're interested in.

How do you know if this applies to you? If you've done the research I've suggested in this chapter, it's probably pretty clear to you, without having to read *this,* whether or not you'll need an extra degree. People in the field are the very best resource for determining if you've got what it takes, without going back to school yet again.

16 Popular Law-Related Jobs... And How To Get More Information About Them

If you want to use your law degree, but you really don't want to practice law, you may want to consider one of these law-related jobs. For all of them, a law degree is a definite asset, so they'll be an easier "jump" than jobs that have no connection with law at all.

In every case, I've given you the names of trade associations and/or publications, so that if one of these areas tickles your fancy, you can call (or write) for more information about it, including jobs listings and newsletters.

(This list is adapted from the University of Florida College of Law's "Alternative Careers for Lawyers," by Ann Skalaski.)

1. LAW SCHOOL PROFESSORS

Being a professor requires a strong academic background. In addition, judicial clerkships, publishing, and practice experience are desirable. (Needless to say, the more prestigious the law school, the better credentials you'll need.)

ASSOCIATIONS

Association of American Law Schools
1201 Connecticut Avenue, NW, Suite 800
Washington, DC 20036–2605
(202) 296–8851
   (Conducts an annual recruiting conference for law faculty and administrators. Publishes placement bulletin six times a year.)

2. UNDERGRADUATE PROFESSORS

You might consider teaching legal history, political science, business law, communications law, and similar courses.

PERIODICALS

The Chronicle of Higher Education
1255 23rd Street, NW, Suite 700
Washington, DC 20037
(202) 466–1000
   (Published weekly.)

3. COURT ADMINISTRATORS
(At local, state, and federal levels.)

ASSOCIATIONS

The Federal Judicial Center
1 Columbus Circle, NE, Room 6–190
Washington, DC 20002–8003
(202) 273–4000, Extension 5
   (Maintains FJC job listings; handles certification for U.S. Circuit Court Executives.)

National Center for State Courts
300 Newport Avenue
Williamsburg, VA 23185
(757) 253-2000

(Job announcements published twice each month. Includes openings in state and federal court administration and related fields.)

4. LAW FIRM ADMINISTRATORS
(E.g., Librarian, Personnel Director, Client Services or Marketing Director, Recruitment Administrator, Attorney Development Manager.)

ASSOCIATIONS

American Management Association
135 West 50th Street
New York, NY 10020
(212) 586-8100

American Association of Law Librarians
53 W. Jackson Blvd. Suite 940
Chicago, IL 60604
(312) 939–4764

National Association for Law Placement (NALP)
1666 Connecticut Avenue, Suite 325
Washington, DC 20009
(202) 667–1666
(Publishes monthly bulletin which includes job openings for law firm recruitment administrators and law school career services directors.)

National Association of Law Firm Marketing Administrators (NALFMA)
60 Revere Drive, Suite 500
Northbrook, IL 60062
(847) 480-9641

5. BAR ASSOCIATION ADMINISTRATORS
(With local bar associations, ABA committees or sections. Jobs include Executive Director, Director of Lawyers Assistance Program, special project coordinator, and legal services project director.)

ASSOCIATIONS

American Bar Association
750 North Lake Shore Drive
Chicago, IL 60611
(312) 988-5000
(Publishes a weekly newsletter listing positions with the ABA.)

For state bar associations, call directory assistance for the capital city of the state in question. For local bar associations, call directory assistance for the city in question.

6. LAW SCHOOL ADMINISTRATORS

(Possibilities include Law Librarian, Legal Writing Director or Instructor, Admissions Director, Assistant Dean of Alumni Development or Student Services, Career Services Director.)

ASSOCIATIONS

American Association of Law Librarians
53 W. Jackson Blvd., Suite 940
Chicago, IL 60604
(312) 939–4764

National Association for Law Placement (NALP)
1666 Connecticut Avenue, Suite 325
Washington, DC 20009
(202) 667–1666
(Publishes monthly bulletin including job listings for law firm recruitment administrators and law school career services directors)

Association of American Law Schools
1201 Connecticut Avenue, NW, Suite 800
Washington, DC 20036–2605
(202) 296–8851
(Conducts an annual recruiting conference for law faculty and administrators. Publishes placement bulletin six times a year.)

7. MEDIATORS, ARBITRATORS

(Possible employers include national organizations, labor unions, large corporations, dispute resolution boards.)

ASSOCIATIONS (PARTIAL LISTING)

American Arbitration Association
140 W. 51st St.
New York, NY 10020
(212) 484–4179

American Bar Association
Special Committee on Alternative Means of Dispute Resolution
740 15th St., NW
Washington, DC 20005
(202) 662–1000

Federal Mediation and Conciliation Service
2100 K St., NW
Washington, DC 20427
(202) 606–8100

Judicate
The Bellevue
200 S. Broad St., Suite 800
Philadelphia, PA 19102
(215) 546-6200

National Institute for Dispute Resolution
1726 M St., NW, Suite 500
Washington, DC 20036
(202) 466–4764

8. Law Enforcement
(FBI or CIA agent, hearing officer, human relations specialist, investigator.)

U.S. Department of Justice
Federal Bureau of Investigation
Personnel Resources Unit
J. Edgar Hoover Building
Tenth Street & Pennsylvania Ave., NW
Washington, DC 20535
(202) 324–3000
        (Call local directory assistance to find telephone numbers of
        local field offices.)

National Public Safety Information Bureau
PO Box 365
Stevens Point, WI 54481
(715) 345–2772

9. GOVERNMENT

(Some examples include contracts office for government agency
at the federal, state or local level, international or interstate trade
relations specialist, land use examiner, congressional staff.)

PUBLICATIONS

Federal Career Opportunities
Federal Research Service, Inc.
PO Box 1059
Vienna, VA 22183–1059
(703) 281–0200
    (Publishes bimonthly job listings.)

The National and Federal Legal Employment Report
Federal Reports, Inc.
PO Box 3709
Georgetown Station
Washington, DC 20007–0209
(202) 393–3311
    (Publishes monthly job listings.)

10. BUSINESS

(Opportunities exist in a variety of areas including financial planning, banking, insurance, management — the choices are virtually
endless.)

PUBLICATIONS

National Business Employment Weekly
200 Burnett Road
Chicopee, MA 01020
(800) 562–4868

ASSOCIATIONS

American Bankers Association
1120 Connecticut Ave., NW
Washington, DC 20036
(202) 663–5000

Institute of Certified Financial Planners
7600 E. Eastman Avenue #301
Denver, CO 80231-4397
(303) 759-4900

American Insurance Services Group
85 John Street
New York, NY 10038
(212) 669–0400

11. JOURNALISM/COMMUNICATIONS

(Possibilities include legal correspondent for television or radio network, editor or writer for legal magazine or newspaper, reporter on legal issues for any magazine or newspaper.)

ASSOCIATIONS

National Newspaper Association
1525 Wilson Blvd. #550
Arlington, VA 22209
(703) 907–7900

National Newspaper Publishers Association
3200 13th St., NW
Washington, DC 20010
(202) 588–8764

American Society of Magazine Editors
919 3rd Ave.
New York, NY 10022
(212) 752–0055

Federal Communications Commission
1919 M Street, NW
Washington, DC 20554
(202) 418–0200

National Association of Broadcasters
1771 N Street, NW
Washington, DC 20036
(202) 429-5300

Radio-Television New Directors Association
1000 Connecticut Ave., NW, Suite 615
Washington, DC 20036
(202) 659–6510

Public Relations Society of America, Inc.
33 Irving Place
New York, NY 10003
(212) 995-2230

12. CONSULTANT
(Typically requires extensive background or experience. Some possibilities include computer usage, marketing, personnel, associate development, law firm management, legal writing, jury selection, employee benefits.)

LEGAL CONSULTANTS (SAMPLE)
Hildebrandt, Inc.
50 Division Street
Somerville, NJ 08876-2900
(732) 560-8888

13. LEGAL TRAINER/INSTRUCTOR
(For state and local bar associations and independent continuing legal education (CLE) providers who conduct training programs and seminars for lawyers. Other possibilities include an instructor in a legal assistant or court reporter program, or director of a legal assistant program at a community college. Some background in educational programming is desirable.)

CLE PROVIDERS (PARTIAL LISTING)
ALI-ABA (American Law Institute-American Bar Association)
4025 Chestnut Street
Philadelphia, PA 19104
(215) 243-1630

Institute of Continuing Legal Education
1020 Greene Street
Ann Arbor, MI 48109-1444
(734) 764-0533

National Institute for Trial Advocacy (NITA)
Notre Dame Law School
PO Box 6500
Notre Dame, IN 46556-6500
(800) 225-6482

Practicing Law Institute (PLI)
810 Seventh Avenue
New York, NY 10019
(212) 824–5700

14. LEGAL RESEARCH AND PUBLISHING

(Research associate, legal research trainer/marketer for computer research vendor, editor for legal publishers.)

LAW PUBLISHERS (SELECTED LIST)

Aspen Law & Business
7201 McKinney Circle
Frederick, MD 21701
(301) 698-7100

Commerce Clearing House
4025 W. Peterson Avenue
Chicago, IL 60646
(773) 866-6000

The Lawyers Co-Operative Publishing Company
Aqueduct Building
Rochester, NY 14694
(716) 546-5530

Mead Data Central/LEXIS
PO Box 933
Dayton, OH 45401
(800) 621-0391

Shepard's/McGraw-Hill
555 Middle Creek Parkway
Colorado Springs, CO 80921
(719) 488-3000

West/Westlaw
PO Box 64526
St. Paul, MN 55164-0526
(800) 328-9352

15. LEGAL SEARCH CONSULTANT

(Assistant law firms in locating experienced attorneys and merger candidates.)

DIRECTORIES

The National Law Journal Directory of Legal Search Consultants
(Published annually; check with your career services office for
availability.)

16. HEALTHCARE/RISK MANAGEMENT

(Typically employed by hospitals or other healthcare providers.
Some practice, healthcare, or management experience required.)

ASSOCIATIONS

American Association of Nurse Attorneys, Inc.
720 Light Street
Baltimore, MD 21230–3826
(410) 752–3318

American Hospital Association
1 North Franklin
Chicago, IL 60606
(312) 422–3000

American Medical Association
515 N. State St.
Chicago, IL 60610
(800) 262–3211

Other Books To Consider If You're Looking For A Nontraditional Career

If you're hell-bent on a nontraditional career in law, there are several excellent resources I'd like to refer you to — that is, if you feel you need more than what you've read in this chapter! They are:

The Road Not Taken: A Practical Guide To Exploring Non-Legal Career Options. Kathy Grant & Wendy Werner. Published by the National Association for Law Placement.

Breaking Traditions: Work Alternatives for Lawyers. Published by the American Bar Association.

What Can You Do With A Law Degree? A Lawyer's Guide to Career Alternatives Inside, Outside and Around the Law. By Deborah Arron. Published by Niche Press.

JD Preferred: 400+ Things You Can Do With A Law Degree (Other Than Practice Law). Published by Federal Reports, Inc.

Federal Law-Related Careers Directory: A Guide to Over 150 Law-Related Careers. Published by Federal Reports, Inc.

Chapter 14

The Myths of Legal Job Searches: The Five Biggest Mistakes Law Students Make

In this chapter, I've gathered up the mistakes that make career services directors and recruiting coordinators get hot under the collar, because they see students making these mistakes over . . . and over . . . and over again. Some of these mistakes are sneaky; you won't even realize that you're making them. And any one of these mistakes can torpedo the success of your job search!

If you've read the rest of this book, then this chapter will be very much a rehash of points you've seen already. I've put them together in this single chapter just to remind you of how important it is to *avoid* making these mistakes.

By the way, if you've skimmed ahead, you've probably already noticed that I discuss *nine* mistakes in this chapter, instead of five. Before you waste any time wondering what the heck is going on, here's what happened. I wrote the back cover blurb before I finished the book, so I was only *guessing* that there'd be five common mistakes all the experts would tell me about. As it turns out, there were nine. Think of it as getting four "bonus" mistakes!

So let's talk about those nine, common mistakes — and how you can avoid making them!

1. NOT TAKING AN ACTIVE ROLE IN YOUR JOB SEARCH

There's no doubt about it. You *can* get the job you want, but not without effort! Remember that wonderful quote, from Case Western's Debra Fink, about how people who want milk should not sit in the middle of a field and wait for a cow to back up to them. Career services directors all over the country lamented the lack of initiative they see in law students who expect a job to fall in their laps. It won't! As Northern Illinois' Mary Obrzut says, *"You're* responsible for your own search and your own happiness!"

All through this book I've stressed the importance of initiative. Of taking the time to decide what the job of your dreams really *is*. Of utilizing all of the resources at your career services office. Of shaking the trees for people you know who might be able to put you onto people who can help with your job search. Of researching potential employers. At every juncture, I've shown you, in detail, how to use the effort you *do* make for maximum effect. If you follow the plan I've outlined in this book, you *will* get a job. I've told you exactly what to do, but I can't take action *for* you. You've *got* to take the initiative, yourself, if you want to make your dream job a reality!

2. NOT PREPARING FOR INTERVIEWS

This was a pet peeve at the top of many hiring partners' lists. The fact is, going on job interviews takes a lot more preparation than choosing the right outfit, reading the firm's brochure 10 minutes beforehand, and showing up, on time, without spinach stuck between your front teeth. The *worst* thing you can do in an interview is say something like, "Gee, *I* didn't know your firm did litigation!" There's *no excuse* for that kind of ignorance!

In Chapter 7, I hit you over the head with the idea of preparing for interviews with the same diligence and intensity you'd use to study for an exam. You've got to learn as much as you can about the employer and the interviewer, relying on every source at your disposal — written materials, your career services director, and alums and other students who are familiar with the employer. And you've got to practice the questions you intend to ask, and the answers you intend to give to questions the interviewer fires at you. If this kind of advance homework strikes you as a pain in the butt, so be it. But remember this: Interviews themselves are your single best opportunity to make a great impression on potential employers. And if *you* don't prepare for the interview, it's easy for some other student who *is* willing to make the effort to snatch that job right out from under your nose.

So don't go to any interview without first preparing for it. I promise you, that preparation will pay off with job offers!

3. RELYING ON MASS MAILERS AS THE PRIMARY JOB SEARCH TECHNIQUE

You know what mass mailers are, right? Generic letters that you mail-merge and send to hundreds of names you get from a source like Martindale-Hubbell. It's kind of like the carpet bombing approach to a job search.

To be perfectly blunt, you don't get jobs from letters. You get them from people. From making contacts. Statistics bear out, year after year, that the vast majority of students get their jobs from personal contacts. That's not just friends of Mommy and Daddy, by the way — it includes all kinds of personal contacts. The kinds of contacts you can easily make, if you follow my advice in Chapter 4. If you follow the advice in that chapter, you can't *help* but find a job you'll like!

As I pointed out to you in Chapter 5, when we talked about correspondence, mass mailers are a *horrible* job search technique. For one thing, no employer wants to feel like another name on a list. Every single career services director and every single law firm recruiter emphasized this! As George Washington's Laura Rowe points out, "Employers feel, if you treat us like a garden variety employer, we'll treat *you* like a garden variety applicant." And what makes mass mailers even worse is that they bear the *semblance* of furthering your job search. That's *completely misleading*. Virtually nobody gets a job with mass mailers, so all that time you spend merging names with letters, and stuffing envelopes, and mailing them out — it's a waste! Top that off with the enormous toll all of those rejections will take on your spirit, and what you've got is a real *loser* of a job search technique. As Albany's Sandy Mans points out, "There's simply no safety in numbers!" You're *much* better off using your time to make 10 phone calls to contacts than you are mailing out 500 generic letters!

So, why does the legend of mass mailers continue to thrive? For one thing, they're easy to do. But as Valparaiso's Gail Peshel points out, that's the seed of their ineffectiveness. "The fact that they're easy to do means everyone does them — so they don't get *anyone's* attention!" And for another thing, for a very tiny fraction of law students, they *do* work. As Columbia's Ellen Wayne points out, if you've got great credentials, large law firms *will* look at an unsolicited letter from you (although even then, your "hit" rate will be far from 100%). But if you're not the editor-in-chief of Law Review and you're not in the top 5% of your class, don't waste your time with mass mailers!

4. BELIEVING THAT GETTING A GREAT JOB IS A MATTER OF BEING IN THE RIGHT PLACE AT THE RIGHT TIME

Bunk. Luck plays virtually no role in your ability to get the job of your dreams. As Branch Rickey once said, "Luck is the residue of design." You *create* your own luck by doing spadework on making contacts and researching potential employers, and following through by writing stellar correspondence and interviewing like a pro — all skills that I've taught you in this book. Remember my networking poster boy, J.T. Mann — the subject of Appendix B in Chapter 4? He pointed out that people always think he's lucky to get the opportunities he gets — summer legal jobs in Europe, clerkships with federal judges, offers from large firms. They don't see all the work that goes into those ostensibly "lucky" events.

So don't suppress your willingness to go after what you want by shrugging your shoulders and saying, "What the heck. It's all a matter of luck." It's not! Get out there and make your *own* luck!

5. OVERLOOKING THE IMPORTANCE OF BEING INTERESTING

With all of the pressure on your time — school, perhaps work and a family, topped off with your job search — it may be easy for you to get a kind of law school tunnel vision. Many times I've spoken with law students and mentioned a story at the top of the news as a means of breaking the ice, only to be met with a comment like, "I don't have time to keep up with what's going on. I'm in law school."

Well, here's a headline for you. You don't surrender your obligation to be an interesting human being because you're in law school. When you meet new contacts, when you interview, virtually any time you meet someone who can help you, the thing that will make them want to help you is if they *like* you. When interviewers talk to you about a potential job, they're looking at you, thinking, "Will I want to pop my head into this person's office and ask them to go to lunch? When we're facing a deadline, will I want to be working with this person at 3 a.m.?" The answer to that question goes far beyond whether your paper credentials are up to snuff. It requires you to be a living, breathing, human being — not a law school machine! As Kentucky's Drusilla Bakert says, "Few students appreciate the importance of personality and relating to people. It's a *people* business."

So squeeze a little bit of time into your schedule to keep up with what's going on in the world. Pay attention to interesting tidbits you hear, and remember them so that you can repeat them to people you meet. Make an effort not to be dominated by your law school experience. Highlight on your résumé, and in your interviews, and every time you talk with a potential employer, the things that make you special. As Drusilla Bakert suggests, "Mention the summer you spent in Japan, or traveling with an orchestra. Show an expanded view of the world!" Remember — people hire people they *like*. Make sure you're one of them!

6. BELIEVING GRADES ARE EVERYTHING

Grades are most certainly *not* everything! As I've stressed throughout this book, you're a complete package, not just your grades. In fact, the only relevance you have to potential employers is whether or not you can do their work. That may or may not be reflected by your grades, but if it's *not*, there are plenty of other ways to convince them that you're the perfect person for the job! How? By minimizing the impact of your grades, in a bunch of different ways. For instance, by focusing on classes in which you *did* perform well. Or by drawing their attention to your work experience. Or by first meeting them in situations in which you get a chance to shine; perhaps at a CLE class in their area of specialty, or while you're volunteering at a local bar association event.

Now, is it true that you won't get many on-campus interviews if your grades aren't stellar? Yes, it *is* true. But so what? A small minority of law students get jobs through on-campus interviews. As I've pointed out before, the vast majority of students get their jobs through making personal contacts. And that includes students with credentials like *yours*, no matter how bad you think your grades are!

I spent a whole chapter, Chapter 10, talking about how to overcome poor grades and get the job of your dreams. If you're worried about your credentials, I encourage you to read it. I recount in that chapter some stories about people with truly awful grades, who wound up with fabulous jobs. I heard many more stories I *didn't* include in that chapter. But the point is this: No matter what your grades are like, you *can* get the job of your dreams. Don't give up because you're not happy with your grades!

7. BELIEVING ON-CAMPUS INTERVIEWS ARE THE ONLY GAME IN TOWN

You may believe that most law jobs come about via on-campus interviews. And if your credentials aren't stellar, that may have the effect of making you believe you're unemployable, since on-campus interviewers typically require great grades. Don't fall into that trap, because it's simply not true that most, or even a large percentage, of legal jobs come from on-campus interviews! As Boston University's Betsy Armour says, "Most employers aren't serviced by the on-campus dog-and-pony show!" It's just that on-campus interviewers are the most *visible* employers, and that's what gives you that misimpression. In fact, most employers don't bother with on-campus interviews at all. For one thing, it's only enormous law firms (or similar institutional employers) who can afford the personnel and the time to bother with on-campus interviews. Those huge employers make up a small percentage of total legal employers; the majority of legal employers are law firms with between 2 and 10 lawyers. So most employers are ones you'll never find out about through on-campus interviews!

Instead, you'll have to do what I suggest in Chapter 4, and make contacts to determine what's *really* out there. You'll meet all kinds of people, and you'll have the inside track on jobs that students who never make the effort will *never* uncover. So don't be misled into thinking that your job search has to end with on-campus interviews!

8. BELIEVING THAT YOUR FIRST JOB DETERMINES YOUR WHOLE CAREER

If you think that you're going to be stereotyped on the basis of your first job, that can scare you into paralysis — you'll be afraid to take any job at all!

The fact is, most people are out of their first legal job within a couple of years or so. And statistics reveal that they change careers, not just jobs, several times over the course of their working lives. So it's simply not true that your career is engraved in stone on the basis of the first job you get.

Why do I mention this? Because it's important for you to get out there and actually get a job. As I point out several times in this book, sometimes getting the job of your dreams means stopping at a way-station — that is, a job that will perfectly position you for your dream job. For instance, if you really want to work for a large firm but you just don't have the grades, then it makes sense to go to a small, boutique firm or a government agency so that you can get valuable experience in a specialty that will interest a large firm. Or if your grades are really terrible, your first job may mean getting some work experience under your belt to show that you're much more than a couple of crummy grades. And that work experience needn't be awful, either — there are plenty of exciting jobs you can get even if you're not on Law Review, as I explained in detail in Chapter 10.

The point here is: Don't add pressure on yourself regarding your first permanent job by thinking it brands you for life. It doesn't!

9. BELIEVING THAT THE BEST PERSON GETS THE JOB

If by using the word "best" you mean the person with the best paper credentials, then you're wrong if you think they'll always get a job before you will! As George Washington's Amy Thompson says, "Lots of people are good at almost *any* job. It's the best *prepared* person who gets the job!"

I've told you time and time again in this book, that with the right job search techniques, you can vault yourself over people with far better credentials than yours, with more impressive work experience than you have, from better law schools than the one you go to. If you make the effort to make contacts, and research potential employers, and do all the legwork I've told you to do, you'll get offers that people with better credentials than you won't get. You'll have your classmates shaking their heads, and saying, "How the heck does (s)he do it?"

What you do when you engage in all the activities I've told you about is to convince employers that you understand their needs, and you can do what they need you to do. You'll show them that you're savvy, that you understand that being a lawyer has much more to do with the kind of person you are, than the way you perform on 4-hour closed-book final exams. In that way, you'll actually be showing them that *you're* the best person for the job!

Have You Got A Great Job Search Story Of Your Own?

If you're like me, one of your favorite parts of this book is the anecdotes — the real stories of students' job search experiences. Do you have a story of your own? One that's illuminating, or funny, or triumphant? That happened to you or anybody else you know? If so, I'd love to hear about it, and include it in the next edition of "Guerrilla Tactics." If you want to be famous, I can include your name. But if you'd prefer to be anonymous, I'll change all of the relevant details of your anecdote, and OK it with you, before including it in the next edition.

You can reach me by writing to:

Kimm Alayne Walton
PO Box 1018
Greens Farms, CT 06436

I'd love to hear from you!

551

Additional Recommended Reading

Geez-O-Pete, over 500 pages with Kimmbo and you're *still* not satisfied? OK, if you want to look at some other wonderful sources to help you with your job search, give these puppies a try:

Jobs for Lawyers: Effective Techniques for Getting Hired in Today's Legal Marketplace. Written by Kathleen Brady and Hillary Mantis. Published by Impact Press.

The Road Not Taken: A Practical Guide To Exploring Non-Legal Career Options. Written by Kathy Grant & Wendy Werner. Published by the National Association for Law Placement.

From Law School to Law Practice, The New Associate's Guide. Written by O'Neill and Sparkman. Published by ALI-ABA.

It's Who You Know — Career Strategies for Making Effective Personal Contacts. Written by Chin-Lee.

Turning Points — New Paths and Second Careers for Lawyers. Published by the ABA.

Full Disclosure: Do You Really Want To Be A Lawyer? Published by Peterson's/ABA.

Breaking Traditions: Work Alternatives for Lawyers. Published by the ABA.

What Can You Do With A Law Degree? A Lawyer's Guide to Career Alternatives Inside, Outside and Around the Law. Written by Deborah Arron. Published by Niche Press.

JD Preferred: 400+ Things You Can Do With A Law Degree (Other Than Practice Law). Published by Federal Reports, Inc.

Federal Law-Related Careers Directory: A Guide to Over 150 Law-Related Careers. Published by Federal Reports, Inc.

Money-Back Guarantee

So, you want to get your money back, eh? Well, I won't try to talk you out of it. Just try not to think of me and my poor little puppy, Spike, suffering through cold winters, sharing a dry bone for dinner, in a cramped, cold, fifth-floor walkup apartment with the electricity turned off. Really. Don't feel guilty. Go ahead and get your money back. Don't worry about — sniff, sniff — us.

Seriously — if you want to exercise the money-back guarantee, you can. The plan I've outlined in this book is based on the advice from the country's top law school career counselors, who've helped tens of thousands of law students find jobs with the strategies that are in this book. But if for some ungodly reason it doesn't work for you, you can get your money back. Here's what you have to do.

1. You have to have used this book for at least 1 year, or until 1 year from the date you graduate from law school — whichever comes later.

2. You have to write a letter outlining the specific strategies you undertook to find a job. Remember, the guarantee says that it only kicks in if you use the techniques in the book and don't find a job. You can't just leave the book under your pillow for a year and expect to get your money back! So you have to have

made a diligent effort to follow the entire plan in the book, and you have to describe what you did.

3. You must have bought the book from a bookstore or directly from the publisher or from a mail-order house, or any other organization in the business of selling new books. If you bought the book secondhand, you're out of luck; go back to the person you bought it from and see if they'll give you your money back.

4. You have to have saved your receipt.

If you've done all of this, send your letter, and the book, and your receipt, to:

Harcourt Brace Legal & Professional Publications
111 West Jackson, 7th Floor
Chicago, IL 60604

. . . and you'll get your money back!

OTHER TITLES
AVAILABLE FROM
THE BARBRI GROUP

What Law School Doesn't Teach You. . . But You Really Need To Know

Expert Advice for Making
Your Legal Career a HUGE Success

"Be yourself."
"Avoid gossip."
"There's no such thing as a stupid question."

If you believe statements like these, you could jeopardize your job. Why? Because the new lawyers who stand out follow a much more subtle set of rules. Rules that you can use to transform your job, whether you work for a law firm, government entity, public interest organization, or any other legal employer!

In this book, you'll learn the trade secrets that make top lawyers say, "I wish I'd known that when I started out!" You'll discover hundreds of tips and strategies, including how to:

KIMM ALAYNE WALTON, J.D.

WHAT LAW SCHOOL DOESN'T TEACH YOU...BUT YOU REALLY NEED TO KNOW

EXPERT ADVICE FOR MAKING YOUR LEGAL CAREER A HUGE SUCCESS

Author: Kimm Alayne Walton, J.D.
ISBN: 0-15-900453-5
Price: $24.95
(619 pages, 6" x 9")

- Turn down work when you're swamped without saying the dreaded "no"
- Negotiate for more money
- Use gossip to your advantage
- Make an outstanding first impression
- Take criticism and make it an opportunity to shine
- Avoid what irks clients the most
- Identify the hidden dangers of e-mail
- Ace your research assignment, and what to do if you drop the ball
- Handle social events correctly ("just being yourself" can be dangerous)

Author Kimm Alayne Walton talked to lawyers and law school administrators all over the country, asking them for their best advice for new lawyers. Whether you're going for a summer clerkship, your first permanent job, or you've already started your career you'll find a wealth of invaluable insider tips you can use right now. With *What Law School Doesn't Teach You . . . But You Really Need To Know*, you'll feel as though you have hundreds of top-notch mentors at your fingertips!

America's Greatest Places To Work With A Law Degree

And How To Make The Most Of Any Job, No Matter Where It Is!

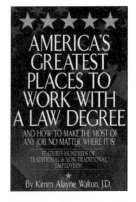

With *America's Greatest Places to Work With A Law Degree* you'll find out what it's really like to work at hundreds of terrific traditional and non-traditional employers—from fantastic law firms, to the Department of Justice, to great public interest employers, to corporate in-house counsel's offices, to dozens of others. You'll learn lots of sure-fire strategies for breaking into all kinds of desirable fields—like Sports, Entertainment, the Internet, and many, many more. You'll discover the non-traditional fields where new law school graduates pull down six figures—and love what they do! And you'll get hundreds of insider tips for making the most of your job, no matter WHERE you decide to work.

Author: Kimm Alayne Walton, J.D.
ISBN: 0-15-900180-3
Price: $24.95
(1170 Pages, 6" x 9")

The bottom line is, no matter what you like, there's a dream job just waiting for you. Discover it in *America's Greatest Places To Work With A Law Degree*.

Behind the Bench

The Guide to Judicial Clerkships

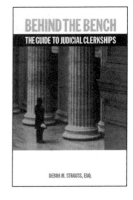

"To clerk or not to clerk?"

Although the answer should be "clerk", the reality is that most students won't apply for a clerkship. The most common reason why students don't apply is a lack of knowledge about what it takes to get a clerkship or how beneficial it will be to their careers.

With *The Guide to Judicial Clerkships* Debra M. Strauss demystifies the clerkship process. Drawing from the experiences of clerks and judges, she explains all aspects of clerkships—what clerkships are, what kind of work clerks do, why you should apply, how to find and apply for the type of clerkship that would be right for you, how to build a successful application and give a strong interview, and why clerkships give you stellar credentials that prospective employers will actively seek out.

Author: Debra M. Strauss, Esq.
ISBN: 0-314-14396-3
Price: $21.95
(345 Pages, 6" x 9")

The Guide to Judicial Clerkships contains everything that you need to make the right choice—clerk!

The Best Of The Job Goddess
Phenomenal Job Search Advice From America's
Most Popular Job Search Columnist

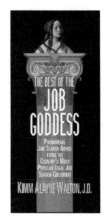

"Should I wear my wedding ring to Interviews? How can
I get a job in another city? I was a Hooters girl before law
school— should I put it on my resume?" In her popular
Dear Job Goddess column, legal job search expert Kimm
Alayne Walton provides answers to these, plus scores of
other, job search dilemmas facing law students and law
school graduates. Her columns are syndicated in more
than 100 publications nationwide.

The Best Of The Job Goddess is a collection of the Job God-
desses favorite columns—wise and witty columns that
solve every kind of legal job search question! If you're con-
templating law school, you're a law student now, or
you're a lawyer considering a career change—you'll enjoy
turning to the Job Goddess for divine guidance!

Author: Kimm Alayne Walton, J.D.
ISBN: 0-15-900393-8
Price: $14.95
(208 Pages, 4¹/₄" x 9")

Proceed With Caution
A Diary Of The First Year At One Of America's
Largest, Most Prestigious Law Firms

Prestige. Famous clients. High-profile cases. Not to mention
a starting salary exceeding six figures.

It's not hard to figure out why so many law students
dream of getting jobs at huge law firms. But when you
strip away the glamour, what is it like to live that
"dream"?

In *Proceed With Caution*, the author takes you behind the
scenes, to show you what it's really like to be a junior
associate at a huge law firm. After graduating from an
Ivy League law school, he took a job as an associate with
one of New York's blue-chip law firms.

Author: William F. Keates
ISBN: 0-15-900181-1
Price: $17.95
(166 Pages, 6" x 9", hardcover)

He also did something not many people do. He kept a
diary, where he spelled out his day-to-day life at the firm
in graphic detail.

Proceed With Caution excerpts the diary, from his first day
at the firm to the day he quit.

The Official Guide To Legal Specialties
An Insider's Guide To Every Major Practice Area

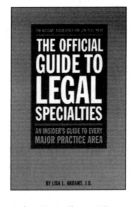

This fast-paced book presents an inside look at what it's like to practice law in major specialty areas, from entertainment to immigration, from tax to telecommunications. From day-to-day activities, to clients, to work environments in all types of settings—blue-chip firms to public interest organizations to government agencies—you'll find that lawyers in every specialty area have fascinating lives.

In this book, you'll find the insights and expertise of top practitioners—the issues they tackle every day, the people and clients they work with, and what they find rewarding about their work. You'll learn about the skills important in different practice specialties, the most helpful law school classes and extracurricular activities, and much more! Over 120 government, public interest, corporate, and private attorneys are featured, from solo practitioners to those in the country's largest firms.

Author: Lisa L. Abrams, J.D.
Price $19.95
ISBN 0-15-900391-1
(516 Pages, 6" x 9")

Specialties included in this book:

Admiralty & Maritime Law	Intellectual Property Law
Antitrust Law	International Law
Appellate Practice	Labor & Employment Law
Banking & Commercial Finance Practice	Legislative Practice
Bankruptcy Law	Military Judge Advocates/ JAG
Civil Litigation	Municipal Finance Practice
Corporate Practice	Public Interest Law
Criminal Law	Real Estate Law
Entertainment & Sports Law	Securities Law
Environmental Law	Solo, Small Firm, & General Practice
Family Law	Tax Law
Government Contracts Practice	Telecommunications Law
Government Practice	Tort Litigation: Personal Injury & Insurance Defense Litigation
Health Care Law	
Immigration Law	Trusts & Estates Law
Insurance Law	

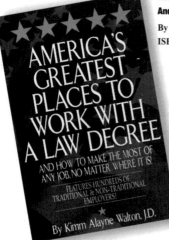